KT-555-206

PRACTICAL PROJECTS

How to make full use of your computer's creative potential

FOR YOUR PC

READER'S DIGEST

PRACTICAL PROJECTS

How to make full use of your computer's creative potential

FOR YOUR PC

PUBLISHED BY THE READER'S DIGEST ASSOCIATION LTD
LONDON • NEW YORK • SYDNEY • MONTREAL

Contents

How to use this book
Find your way quickly around the main sections

This book will bring out the creative talents of your computer, with practical projects of real benefit to you and your family. The main sections are outlined below, colour-coded so you can find them easily.

BASICS covers the things you need to get your PC system up and running and connected to the internet. In PHOTO SMART are projects to enhance and transform your digital photos.

DESIGN WISE makes use of Microsoft's Office programs – Word, Excel and PowerPoint – with practical paper-based results. SOUND AND VISION uses your PC's multimedia features – video, sound and animation. INTERNET ACTIVE has online projects that show you how to get the most out of the web and email. There's an ESSENTIALS section, covering important skills and helping you to master each software area,

as well as serving as a useful reference. At the back of the book, a comprehensive GLOSSARY provides a quick reference to terms and technology referred to throughout the book.

What you'll need

You will need a PC, of course, running Windows XP, and a monitor, mouse and keyboard. A printer is needed for some projects but not all.

At the start of each project are listed the necessary tools – software plus any extra hardware, such as a printer or scanner. Image-editing projects are based on Adobe

BASICS

Get your PC up and running and connect to the internet. Plus buying advice on PCs, hardware and software.

PHOTO SMART

Transform your digital photos and create masterpieces with the help of image-editing software.

DESIGN WISE

Things to make and do with the help of Microsoft Word, Excel and PowerPoint – do it yourself and save money.

SOUND AND VISION

Multimedia projects, from cleaning up and digitising your old vinyl records to making movies and PC karaoke.

INTERNET ACTIVE

Make a website, send fancy emails, talk face to face over the internet and make an online radio broadcast.

ESSENTIALS

Make yourself familiar with the software and learn techniques that you'll need for the projects in this book.

Photoshop Elements. Projects involving page layout, tables, presentations or web-page design use Microsoft's Office applications Word, Excel and Powerpoint. (See page 12 for more details of these programs.) Most other programs are free or come as part of Windows, and you'll find how and where to get them within the projects.

These programs were chosen because they represent the leading products in their fields. If you have alternative programs on your PC – for example, Paint Shop Pro instead of Photoshop Elements – the exact steps may vary, but the broad principles remain the same.

How each project is organised

Following a short description, each project is organised as a series of numbered steps, running

Move the face over

18 Double-click to finish – your selection is outlined with flashing dots. Press V for the Move tool. Click within the selection and drag onto your greetings card. Hold Shift and drag any corner handle to resize the image to fit within the snow globe. Press Return to finish. Press M for the Marquee tool. In the Options bar choose Elliptical Marquee, set Feather to 0 and Mode to Normal.

left to right across the pages. Above each step is shown what appears on-screen as described, with any important details picked out and magnified. Boxes cover any important side issues, ideas or processes associated with the projects.

During each step, on-screen buttons, menus or links that you need to click on are in **bold type**. Text to be typed in, including web-page addresses, is in **red type**. Keyboard shortcuts are also in bold type – for example, **Ctrl+S**, where you should hold down the Ctrl (control) key on

your keyboard while you press the S key (then release both keys).

Ticking the right boxes

The projects in this book make frequent use of menus, toolbars, buttons and dialogue boxes, in Windows and in the programs used. Microsoft programs – Word, Excel, PowerPoint, Movie Maker and Internet Explorer – have menus arranged in a similar way, so it's easy to find your way around. All Windows programs follow similar conventions, so you shouldn't get lost.

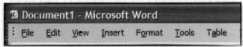

Main menu headings run along the top of the screen – click one of the headings and you'll see a drop-down list of items in that menu. The **File** menu, for example, has associated sub-menus, for saving what you're working on, opening a document you've already saved or creating a new blank page, printing out your work, closing the document or quitting the program.

Most programs have **toolbars** running beneath the main menus, down the sides, at the bottom or 'floating' above the document. These contain the same functions as the main menus, but can be activated by a single click on a graphical button, making them quicker for frequently performed actions.

On the right of the screen, especially in Microsoft programs, is the **Task pane**, where you can select options that relate to whatever you're currently doing. In Word, for example, select **New** from the **File** menu, and the **Task pane** displays a list of document

types you can create, as well as links to download ready-made templates from Microsoft's website. Other Office programs work in the same way.

When your PC needs you to input settings or make a decision, a **dialogue box**

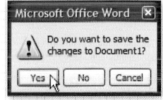

will appear. This could be anything from a simple 'Yes' or 'No' request to the sizes and settings for printing out your document.

Clicking and dragging

Selecting menus, ticking options, drawing and painting, or moving objects are all done with the mouse. The left button is used for most actions, whereas a single click on the right button displays a small pop-up menu of commands relating to what you're currently doing. When you want to paint, cut out, move or resize something – part of a picture, for example – click the left mouse button and drag, then release the button when you're done. A double-click (two clicks in quick succession) usually has the same effect as clicking once and then clicking an **OK** button – for example, when selecting a document to load from within a list of files.

Setting up your PC
Connect up the parts of your system and you're ready for action

You don't need to know how your computer works, but you do need to make sure that everything is connected correctly. These days, add-ons such as printers, external hard disks and scanners connect using a standard plug and socket, called USB (Universal Serial Bus). Other connections are for your mouse and keyboard, audio equipment (speakers and microphone), mains power and network cable (used to link your PC to other computers in your home).

Sockets are usually marked clearly and colour coded, but consult your PC's user manual if you are unsure of where something should go.

Make sure the power is off, then connect your keyboard, mouse, monitor and any other peripheral devices, such as a printer or scanner. Switch on the mains power by pushing the on/off switch. After a short time, Windows loads and you are ready to start using your computer.

CD or DVD drive (**1**) and on/off switch (**2**).

Mains power socket Always disconnect the mains cable completely if you need to open the lid of your PC.

Sockets for keyboard (lilac) and mouse (green). These devices sometimes connect to USB sockets or wirelessly (see page 10).

Serial and parallel (printer) ports. Although present, these are rarely used, as modern devices (including printers) connect via USB.

Monitor socket (also referred to as VGA port). Some digital flat-panel monitors need a different connection, known as DVI (Digital Visual Interface).

Sound inputs and outputs The pink socket is for plugging in a microphone; green and blue are for audio line out and line in. Your PC speakers connect to the green socket. When digitising old records or cassettes (see page 216), connect output from the tape or hi-fi to the blue socket. In the PC shown here, there's also a headphone socket next to the USB ports at the front.

USB ports The more the better, as most PC add-ons connect using USB. Here there are four at the back of the PC and an additional two at the front for easy access.

Network socket (also called RJ-45) for linking your PC to other PCs in your home.

Buying a new PC

Prices of new computers are lower than ever, and it's generally cheaper to replace an aging PC than to upgrade it. When choosing a new system, it's important to know what's inside.

At the heart of the PC is its processor – the part that does the actual computing. The speed at which the processor runs is measured in MHz (megahertz, or millions of actions per second). Generally speaking, the higher the number of MHz the faster the PC will run.

Also important is the main memory (RAM), where data is stored and manipulated during the time the PC is switched on. The more RAM (measured in megabytes or Mb) your PC has the better it will cope with large files and many programs running simultaneously. For the projects in this book, 512Mb or more is recommended.

The hard disk is where Windows, your programs and your documents are stored. Unlike RAM memory, the hard disk doesn't lose its contents when the PC is switched off. Hard disk capacity is measured in gigabytes or Gb (one gigabyte is roughly 1000 megabytes). You should expect a new PC's hard disk to have at least 100Gb. Windows XP should be installed already, together with a range of utility software programs to help you get started.

A monitor is often included in the price. Make sure it's a flat-panel display and not an old-fashioned CRT (cathode ray tube) type.

Laptop computers

An alternative to a desktop PC is a laptop (also called a notebook PC). Prices are slightly higher, but the screen is built in and you can use it away from the mains, running on battery power.

Healthy computing

Usually, a PC finds its place in the home not by design but because of necessity – it goes wherever you can find space for it. But, if you don't create the right environment, you can get all sorts of aches and pains, make yourself tired, strain your eyes, and even cause permanent damage, particularly to wrists and other joints. Here's how you can set up your PC so that it's a pleasure to use, rather than a pain.

Your chair is the most critical component. It needs to be a proper office-style chair that supports your back, especially at the base of your spine, and allows your feet to rest flat on the ground with your thighs supported. Sit right back into the chair rather than leaning forwards, keep your thighs parallel with the floor (use a footrest or a cushion if you can't) and change your position from time to time. When you're seated, the angle between your thighs and your calves should be 90 degrees or greater – don't tuck your feet in under the chair. And remember that if the backs of your knees are tight against the edge of the chair, you'll impede your blood circulation.

The keyboard needs to be parallel with your arms so that your wrists are relaxed and flat. Beneath the keyboard you'll find two small flip-out legs – try these in both the opened and the closed position to find which is most comfortable for you.

If the desk or table top is too high, you can buy a clamp-on 'tray' that slides out from beneath, but make sure it has room for the mouse. If the keyboard and mouse are on top of the table, keep them close enough so that you don't have to stretch to use either.

The best place for your monitor is right in front of you. If you put it to the side, you're more likely to twist your body to use it. You should sit about an arm's length away from a 15in or 17in monitor and a little further if it's 19in or larger. With a 17in or smaller monitor, the top of the display should be at eye level. If it's 19in or larger, the top should be a couple of inches above eye level.

Tilt the screen slightly upward until its surface is perpendicular to your line of sight. To reduce reflections, face the display away from windows or other strong light sources.

1 *Keep arms at the same level as the desk, with elbows open, not tucked into your body.*
2 *Your wrists should be in the neutral position – relaxed and flat.*
3 *With a 15in or 17in monitor, eyes should be level with the top. With a 19in or larger monitor, pick an imaginary line a couple of inches down from the top for your eye line.*
4 *Keep the desktop tidy, and leave plenty of room for your keyboard and mouse.*
5 *Feet should be flat on the floor.*

Choosing a digital camera

Image resolution – the number of pixels in the photos you take – is important. But even budget models today have more than enough megapixels. What really differentiates one camera from another are optics – the quality and range of the lens – and ease of use. Compact cameras (small enough to fit in a shirt pocket) are quick and simple to use. Common features include a zoom lens, a large display screen at the back and movie clip capture.

Further up the size scale are enthusiast cameras. These give you more control over settings for your shots (see 'Understanding camera controls', page 304). Some have extended-reach zoom lenses – up to 12x optical zoom – and most offer image resolutions of 7 million pixels or more.

At the top end, digital SLR (single-lens reflex) cameras work just like 35mm film cameras, offering total picture-taking control and changeable lenses. They are often sold as 'body-only' so you can choose lenses to suit your needs.

To snap up a bargain, look out for models that have been out for a few months as prices fall rapidly after launch.

Buying PC accessories
Hardware essentials and add-ons to get the most out of your PC

There's more to your PC system than just the computer itself. Plug-in devices, or peripherals – usually connected to your PC by cables – expand or enhance its capabilities. The three essential peripherals are your monitor, keyboard and mouse. Other peripherals include anything from a colour printer or scanner to a digital camera or camcorder. Thanks to your PC's USB sockets (see page 8), almost any make or model of PC peripheral can be connected to any PC.

Keyboards and mice

If you are unhappy with your keyboard, replace it with a better-quality model. Choose between a standard keyboard with extra programmable keys and controls, an 'ergonomic' keyboard – curved to fit your fingers – or a wireless keyboard that reduces cable spaghetti over your desk.

If you're replacing your mouse, there's a wide choice of models. It should have at least two main buttons, with a scroll wheel (for navigating web pages and documents quickly) between them. Choose one with a light sensor underneath, rather than the older-style mouse with a rubber ball roller, which tends to clog and require cleaning. Wireless mice are also available and sometimes sold as a set with a wireless keyboard.

Display monitor

A flat-panel display is preferable, as are a large size and high resolution (see 'Size matters', page 311). Screen size is measured diagonally from corner to opposite corner. For general use, choose a 17in or 19in model, with a resolution of at least 1280x1024 (pixels horizontally and vertically). Wide-screen versions are also available, but these are more expensive.

Printers

The two main types of printer are inkjet (fine jets of ink squirted at the paper) and laser (below). Laser printers, like photocopiers, use cartridges of dry toner powder, which is baked onto the paper to form the image. Lasers are clean, easy to use and fast. Although colour lasers are more expensive to buy than inkjets, they cost less to run.

Inkjet printers are slower than laser printers, they don't hold as many sheets of paper, and replacement ink cartridges are expensive. But they are cheap to buy and versatile. They can print in colour on paper, card, plastic film, t-shirt transfer material and almost anything else, and they produce photographic-quality prints when used with glossy paper. Cut down running costs by shopping around for replacement ink as prices vary considerably. Cheap 'non-brand' cartridges and refill kits are available, but printer manufacturers don't recommend using them.

Digital cameras

The simplest way to get photos into your projects is to use a digital camera (see left). The camera records its pictures on memory cards (see 'Digital film', page 306). When one card is full you take it out of the camera and pop in another. The cards never wear out – once you've copied the pictures onto your PC you erase the cards and use them again. The only running cost of a digital camera is recharging its batteries.

Colour scanners

Often, the images you want to use are already printed – old photos, for example. To copy a document or photo you need a scanner (see page 322). Place the original face down on the scanner's glass surface and a light sensor moves beneath it, sending a stream of coloured dots to the PC, which reassembles them into a picture.

Scanners are cheap to buy, cost nothing to run, and the quality of copies can be superb.

Recording video

To capture high-quality video for use on a PC (see page 208), a digital camcorder is best. You can also get a reasonable quality from the video clips that most stills cameras and some mobile phones record. Another alternative is to use a webcam, plugged into your PC's USB socket (see page 8). Webcams are inexpensive, and you'll need one if you want to chat face to face over the internet (see page 296). They also offer a quick and simple way to capture 'live' video for your projects. (See also 'Choosing a webcam', page 16.)

Connecting it all together

USB (Universal Serial Bus) sockets, which you'll find on all modern PCs (see page 8), are used to connect cameras, external hard disks, scanners, modems, keyboards and mice, portable music players, and most other kinds of storage or capture devices. If you run out of USB sockets, a USB 'hub' allows you to split one socket into several (a bit like a mains-power extension lead).

Where to buy

Check internet prices using a price comparison site such as Froogle, http://froogle.google.co.uk, or Kelkoo, www.kelkoo.co.uk. Your keyboard, mouse and monitor are vital to the way you work, so choose them carefully and try before you buy by visiting a computer store.

Pocket PCs and mobile phones

PCs that fit in your pocket, and mobile phones, can record sounds or play music tracks. You can also use them to send emails or surf the web, shop on eBay or search on Google. Most have a built-in camera that can capture photos and video clips – useful for those times when you don't have a standard camera handy. When choosing a new mobile phone, consider one that runs on Microsoft Windows Mobile, which works closely with your desktop PC for almost seamless desktop and mobile computing.

The Apple option

Apple's Macintosh computers ('Macs') offer an alternative to Microsoft Windows that some people consider easier to use and more intuitive. Macs can do all the things Windows can do, and they can share documents with Windows PCs. You need to buy programs specially designed for Apple's operating system (called OSX), although many are included with a new Mac. If you want the best of both worlds, the latest generation of Macs can run Windows as well as OSX. All the projects in this book are based on a Windows PC.

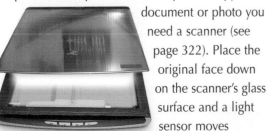

Installing new programs

Most commercial programs you buy come on CD-ROM. Insert the disc in your CD drive and a menu appears with the option to install the software. Click **OK** and follow the instructions. Installing a program you have downloaded from the web is a little different, as no disc is involved. Instead, there's usually a single installer program. Double-click it in Windows Explorer and follow the instructions.

Removing unwanted programs

After you've installed a program, you'll find in the Windows **Start** menu a shortcut to the program itself and, often, a shortcut for removing the program. To remove the program completely, click this shortcut. If there's no **Remove** shortcut, click the **Start** button, then **Control Panel**. Look for the icon labelled **Add or Remove Programs** and double-click it.

Windows then displays a list of installed programs. To the right of each entry, you can see how much hard disk space the program's taking up. Click once on a program in the list for more details, then click the **Change/Remove** button if you want to remove it from your computer.

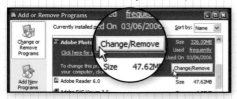

It's important to use one of these methods – don't just delete the files from your hard disk, or you may find that Windows stops working properly.

Software basics

The programs you'll need to get the most out of the projects

Word processor

Word-processing software can do far more than just produce text. Microsoft Word can check your spelling and grammar, index a book and correct errors as you type. It has tools for drawing, and editing photos, and it can turn documents fed in from a scanner back into editable text. Word will even produce web pages (see page 256). As part of Microsoft's Office suite, Word integrates closely with the other Office programs Excel and Powerpoint. You can find out more about Microsoft Office, and download templates and clip art, at **http://office.microsoft.com**. (See also 'Desktop publishing with Word', page 328.)

Image editor

You can enhance and transform photos taken with a digital camera, or create images from scratch, using image-editing software. To carry out many of the projects in this book you'll need Photoshop Elements, **www.adobe.com/products/photoshopelwin**, a budget version of Adobe Photoshop, used by design professionals. Elements retains most of

Photoshop's powerful features as well as its look and feel. Before you buy an image editor, check whether one has been included already with your camera or scanner. (See also 'Introduction to image-editing software', page 308.)

Spreadsheet

You can organise and manipulate numbers, or any type of information that can be laid out in a table format, using spreadsheet software. It will compute totals and statistics for you, create graphs representing the data in your tables, and automatically update its answers if you change any of the figures. The most popular spreadsheet program, and the one used in this book's projects, is Microsoft Excel. (See page 300.)

Presentation graphics

Microsoft's PowerPoint is the most popular presentation-graphics program. It combines images, video clips, text, charts, tables and

graphs, together with music and sound effects, to create a multimedia slideshow presentation. You can watch the results on screen or print hand-outs for your audience to take away. PowerPoint is widely used in business meetings and conferences, but is also ideal for presenting educational or hobby projects. (See 'Creating PowerPoint slideshows', page 302.)

DTP

Books, magazines and periodicals are all designed and laid out using desktop publishing (DTP) software. Professionals use QuarkXPress and Adobe InDesign to bring together text and images from various sources and lay them out for commercial printing. Home DTP can be done with a good word processor, such as Microsoft Word, or an inexpensive program like Serif PagePlus, **www.serif.com**. (See 'Desktop publishing with Word', page 328.)

Video editing

Whether your movies start off as short clips taken with your digital camera or footage transferred from a camcorder, to transform them into a production everyone will want to watch you'll need editing software. Professionals use Adobe Premiere, but a cut-down version – Premiere Elements, **www.adobe.com** – has a huge range

of features at a fraction of the price. Alternatively, Windows includes the free Movie Maker – a capable basic movie editor.

Sound recording

Windows comes with a simple sound recorder that can record short clips. But if you want to record and edit sounds or music for your projects, you'll need something more powerful, such as the free Audacity, **http://audacity.sourceforge.net** (see 'Produce a podcast', page 286). If you want to take things further, commercial composition and recording programs such as Cubasis (see 'Recording and making music', page 332) turns your PC into a virtual music-recording studio.

Anti-virus software

Every PC that's connected to the internet or a network must be protected against damage from viruses. Anti-virus software such as Norton AntiVirus, **www.symantec.com**, is updated frequently to keep up with constantly evolving threats. A variation, Norton Internet Security, is built around Norton AntiVirus, but adds a 'firewall' – a special program that monitors all data going into and out of your PC to prevent unauthorised access – as well as a 'spam' filter to reduce the amount of junk email you receive.

Free software

On the web you'll find free alternatives in just about every software category. Make sure you download from a trustworthy website, such as **www.download.com** or **www.tucows.com**.

Saving and loading documents

To load a document, choose **Open** from the **File** menu, browse to the document you want, click it, then click **Open**.

To save a document (this applies to most programs), choose **Save** from the **File** menu. In the dialogue box, browse to where you want to save the document on your hard disk, type a name for it and, in the drop-down box below, choose one of the file formats shown. Then click **Save**.

By default, Microsoft Word saves its word-processor documents as .DOC files (a full point followed by a three-letter suffix at the end of the file name). Word can also save in many other 'file formats', such as .RTF files (Real Text Format), which can be read by all other word processors, and .TXT (plain text) files – containing no formatting (fonts, bold or italic styles, colours or different type sizes).

Excel saves spreadsheet files in its own special format (with a .XLS extension to the file name), but can save in formats that other spreadsheets (as well as word processors or other types of program) can open. Image editors can save or open many different types of image file. The standard file format for multi-layer images (see 'How layers stack up', page 314) is Photoshop-format files (.PSD). For images to be used on the web, JPEG (.JPG) files are the most common (see 'Size matters', page 311).

The advantages of broadband

The old-fashioned way to connect to the internet is through a dial-up modem (a device that converts digital data from your PC into a form that can be sent down any phone line). Most PCs still have dial-up modems built-in, but they are slow and you can't make phone calls while you are online.

Broadband is a newer type of internet connection that can send and receive data more than ten times as fast, using a special modem. So you can download video clips, listen to CD-quality internet radio, and even watch live TV online. You'll typically pay a fixed fee for broadband access, with no usage charges, though some cheaper deals do have restrictions, largely to stop you hogging the service from other users.

The two main types of broadband are cable, which uses a special modem linked to a cable-TV system, and an Asymmetric Digital Subscriber Line (ADSL). Cable broadband is only available if you can get cable TV and if the TV company offers the service. ADSL uses your existing phone wiring, but doesn't stop you making calls. In the UK, you need a BT phone line for ADSL, but there are many ISPs (internet service providers) that can provide the service over that line.

Once your PC is connected, it stays connected – you don't need to dial up your ISP each time you want to use the internet. So you could listen to internet radio all day, or set your email program to check for new mail every five minutes and download it if there's any there.

Get online
Discover how the internet can bring the world to your desktop

Connect your PC to the internet – through your phone line or cable TV connection – and you can look up information, access your bank account, download programs or music tracks, or send and receive emails anywhere in the world in seconds. You can even use the internet to make free phone calls, or chat face to face with people the other side of the planet (see page 296). Apart from a flat-rate monthly fee, paid to an internet service provider (ISP), your time online costs nothing.

To view a web page, you type its unique address into your web browser (see box, page 15). If you don't know the address, or are looking for any websites with information on a particular topic, a 'search engine' such as Google, www.google.co.uk, will list all pages that match your search criteria.

The internet is made up of millions of computers across the world, all linked together. It's not owned or regulated by any central body. As a result, there's little in the way of censorship, and some content is considered to be offensive, or unsafe for children. To prevent children viewing unsuitable websites, antivirus programs often include a parental-control option, which blocks listed sites. Stand-alone programs, such as Net Nanny, www.netnanny.net, offer similar protection.

The web holds few dangers provided you surf sensibly, though, and the rewards are many. You can contribute, too, by building your own home page on the web using Microsoft Word (see page 256) or dedicated web-design sofware such as Microsoft Front Page. You could even write an online diary with pictures (see page 272), or record your own internet radio show (page 286).

○ Broadband speeds and limits

The rate at which broadband internet can download data to your PC is measured in megabytes (Mb) and ranges from under 1Mbps (megabytes per second) up to 8Mbps or even higher. Most internet providers offer a range of options, or packages, some of which put limits on the total amount of data you can download each month. If you plan to download many videos and music tracks, you could reach your limit, so calculate your expected needs before signing up. A typical budget-priced broadband option may limit monthly usage at 2Gb (gigabytes) each month – this equates roughly to 400 music tracks or two movies. Unlimited options cost more.

○ Going wireless

If you have more than one PC in the home, you can share a single internet connection using a wireless 'modem/router', which connects directly to your phone socket. Each desktop PC requires a plug-in card – usually plugged into a USB socket (see page 8) – while most laptop PCs have wireless features already built in.

This setup is known as a Wi-Fi network, which allows each PC to access the internet as if it were connected directly to its own modem. You can also transfer files between computers, and share peripherals, such as printers and scanners, connected to any of the PCs on the network.

How to explore the web

To view web pages, you need a program called a web browser, such as Microsoft Internet Explorer, www.microsoft.com/windows/ie, or Opera, www.opera.com. Type in an internet address (URL, which stands for Unique Resource Locator), and the words, images and other components that make up the web page are downloaded to your PC for you to read. Many web browsers include features that allow you to read emails, download files and configure security features to filter unsuitable websites or block unwanted advertising pop-ups.

Online project resources

You can find character fonts, clip art or photos, ready-made document templates, sound clips or animations for free or for a small fee simply by using a search engine such as Google, www.google.co.uk. Or you can visit one or more of the following websites.

● Identifont, www.identifont.com, has free character fonts, and a font identifier that can track down those you may have seen elsewhere.

● Yotophoto, http://yotophoto.com, is a search website dedicated to free-to-use photographs,

where you can browse thousands of high-quality images across dozens of categories (see below).

● For free sound clips to download and use in your presentations, visit www.freeaudioclips.com.

● If you're looking for animations to brighten up your home page, you'll find thousands of animated GIFs (see page 264) at www.gifs.net.

● Microsoft's own website has a huge collection of free clip art. Visit http://office.microsoft.com/clipart.

● There are loads of party and other stationery design ideas at www.finestationery.com.

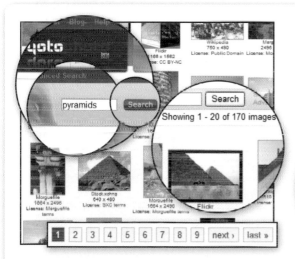

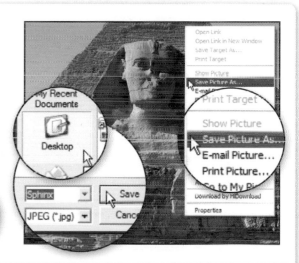

Finding a photo on the web

1 If you need a photo for a project – for example, the pyramids – type http://yotophoto.com into your web browser then press **Return**. When the web page loads, you'll see a search box at the top of the screen, plus category headings towards the bottom. Type pyramids into the search box, then click **Search**. The first page of search results appears on screen as thumbnail images. Links to further results are below.

Choose an appropriate image

2 Beneath each thumbnail is information about the source, the image size and licence terms for use. When you find a photo you like, make sure it's big enough (see 'Size matters', page 311). Then click the **Licence** link – read the conditions carefully when the page loads, then click your browser's **Back** button to return to the thumbnails. Click the thumbnail to load a large version of the image.

Download the image file

3 Right-click on the large image and, from the pop-up menu, choose **Save Picture As**. The **Save Picture** dialogue box appears. Browse through the folders to where you want to save the file, or click the **Desktop** button to save it on your desktop (you can move it later using Windows Explorer). Click **Save**. If you need more photos, click the **Back** button on your browser and repeat the process.

Stay secure on the internet

Installing anti-virus software on your PC (see page 13) is essential. Make sure that you run the program's 'update' feature at least once a fortnight, or your PC won't be protected against the latest viruses.

If you receive an email that looks suspicious or is from someone you don't know, delete it straight away. Even if the email is from a sender you recognise, treat it with caution. Don't open any attached files you weren't expecting to receive – they may contain viruses that will infect your PC, damage files on your hard disk, or allow criminals to gain access to sensitive information stored on your PC.

When downloading files from the web, stick to trustworthy websites. Some 'free' programs contain hidden 'spyware', which tracks what you do on your PC and reports back to junk emailers. Steer clear of anything that looks too good to be true. Illegal sites offering free commercial software or music downloads could infect your PC, even before you download any files.

Window XP includes a 'firewall' feature, which blocks others accessing files on your PC when you're connected to the internet. To turn it on or off, click the **Start** button, then **Control Panel**. Double-click **Windows Firewall**, then tick the **On** or the **Off** button. Unless your antivirus software includes its own firewall built-in, make sure Windows Firewall is turned **On**.

You can find out how well your PC is protected against intrusions, and perform an online virus scan, by visiting Symantec's site at http://security.symantec.com.

Keep in touch with email
Send and receive messages fast and for free

Email is electronic mail. You type a message into your computer, just as you might write a letter with a word processor, but instead of printing it out and putting it in an envelope, you address it with the recipient's email address, click the **Send** button and it's transferred over the internet. When the person you've written to next checks for messages, it will be waiting there to be read. The whole process can take less than a couple of minutes.

You don't pay for each email you send, so they're effectively free, once you're connected to the net. When you sign up for access to the internet, you're usually given an email address. Some websites, such as Yahoo, http://uk.yahoo.com, and MSN Hotmail, www.hotmail.com, offer free addresses, too. Once you know someone's address, it's easy to send a message. You can also add pictures or sounds to emails, so you can send your holiday snaps to relatives in a different country, or attach a personal spoken greeting.

Email software

The most widely used program to access your email accounts is Outlook Express, supplied free with Windows XP. Connect your computer to the internet then tell Outlook Express to send and receive mail, and all the messages you've written will be posted; any new ones waiting for you will be transferred to your computer.

Popular alternatives to Outlook Express are the AOL program, www.aol.com, Eudora, www.eudora.com, Thunderbird, www.mozilla.com, and Outlook (a more advanced relative of Outlook Express supplied with some versions of

○ Choosing a webcam

A webcam is an inexpensive addition to an internet setup that clips to the top of your monitor or laptop screen and allows you to chat face to face (see page 296) with other webcam users. The most basic models capture video at a resolution of 320x240 pixels, which is poor when compared to digital cameras, but adequate for web chat. Spend a bit more to get higher resolution video, better performance in low light and features such as zoom and face tracking – to keep your face centred in the picture.

○ Get a .NET Passport

Many websites require you to sign in with a password before accessing them. Microsoft's free .NET Passport gives you a single secure sign-in ID you can use across hundreds of sites and services, including Microsoft's email service Hotmail, and auction site eBay. To get your own .NET Passport, go to www.passport.net and click **Sign up** on the left side. If you already have an email address, tick **Yes, use my email address**. (Otherwise tick the option to sign up for a free Hotmail address.) Click **Continue** and follow the instructions on screen, choosing a password to use whenever you see the **.NET Passport** sign on a website.

Microsoft Office). All of these programs let you organise your messages. You can, for example, keep work-related emails in one folder and travel-related ones in another, just as you might organise word-processor documents on your PC.

Web-based email

With some internet accounts, you read your email using your web browser, by visiting a web page, giving your email address and password. This is called webmail and it works just like an ordinary email program, even allowing you to organise messages into folders. The advantage of webmail is that, when you're away from home, you can check your email from any cyber café (a café that has computers in it so you can access the internet).

You can use some programs, including Outlook Express, to collect messages from webmail systems, such as Hotmail or Yahoo mail. So you could use webmail when you're on holiday, and Outlook Express when at home.

● Get a junk email address

Sign up for a free email address (see the workshop below) to use just on websites you visit casually and that require you to sign in. Keep your main (permanent) address for emailing close friends and colleagues, signing in to your online bank account and other official online correspondence. That way, if your free email address falls into the hands of unscrupulous marketing firms, or 'spammers', and you start to receive junk email, you can simply stop using it and sign up for a new free address.

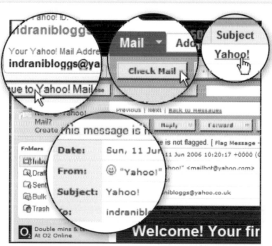

Get a free Yahoo! email account

1 Type http://uk.yahoo.com into your web browser and press **Return**. Click the **Mail** icon to the right of the Yahoo! main heading. On the next page, click **Sign up**. A form appears – fill in your contact details and choose a Yahoo! ID (user name) and password. Near the bottom of the page, enter the code that you see, displayed as distorted letters and numbers. Then click the **I Agree** button below.

Read your first email

2 You'll see a confirmation screen showing your Yahoo! ID and email address. Click **Continue to Yahoo! Mail**. If you see an invitation to try a different version, click **No thanks, maybe later**. The Yahoo! Mail main window appears (you're already signed in). Click **Check Mail** – you have a new message listed. Click the message name to read the welcome email sent from Yahoo!.

Send your first email

3 Click the **Compose** button. A blank email appears. Type an address for your recipient, and a few words in the **Subject** line. In the main area, type your message, then click **Send** – you'll see a confirmation that your email was sent. Now, having signed up, you can check for mail or send emails by visiting http://uk.yahoo.com, clicking **Mail**, entering your ID and password, and clicking **Continue**.

Photo smart

Projects that will help you master your image-editing software and transform your digital photographs into works of art you can share with family and friends

Image building
Revive your old photographs and bring the past to life

Rescuing an album full of photos from the attic and scanning them into your PC is a good way to preserve family memories. But what about the damage they've already suffered? Using image-editing software, you can reverse most of it and restore your snaps to their former glory, as this project illustrates. There's no need to aim for perfection – repair the main parts of the picture and leave a few blemishes for authenticity.

PROJECT TOOLS: Photoshop Elements ● Scanner ● Old photo prints
SEE ALSO: Get creative with your scanner, page 322 ● Image cutouts and photomontage, page 320

SEE ALSO: Get creative with your scanner, page 322 ● Image cutouts and photomontage, page 320

● Quick fix for faded photos

A common problem with old photos is fading, as this family group illustrates (right). Photoshop Elements has several automatic fixes, all found on the **Enhance** menu.

Try **Auto Contrast** first, which attempts to restore an optimum level of brightness and contrast. If the image was scanned in, first crop off any white border (caused by the scanner

Scan your photo

1 Following the instructions supplied with your scanner, and the tips on page 322, scan the photo you want to restore. Choose **600dpi** resolution to capture fine detail and enable the finished picture to be printed out larger than the original if required. Either scan directly into Photoshop Elements using **Import** from the **File** menu or save the scanned image, then run Photoshop Elements and open this file.

lid), or dark shadows or borders (at the edge of the scanned print). These strong tones are not part of the picture, and would affect the accuracy of **Auto Contrast**. Alternatively, use the **Rectangular Marquee** tool to select just the photo or an area within the photo, then apply **Auto Contrast** (near right). To avoid a harsh line between the adjusted area and the edges, increase the **Feather** setting in the **Options** bar to **12** before drawing your marquee.

Auto Levels, also on the **Enhance** menu, rebalances colours in the image as well as boosting contrast. This gives an impression of how a photo might have looked before it faded, or if it had been printed using modern methods (far right). Applying **Auto Levels** will also show up any patchy damage, such as water marks, which you'll need to repair as described in this project.

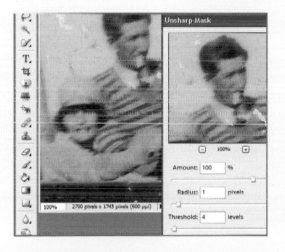

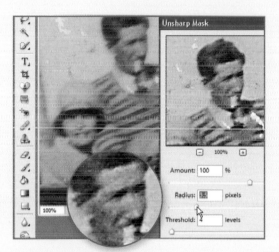

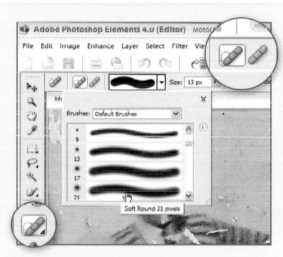

Sharpen the image

2 One of the most obvious problems with any old photo is likely to be that it looks fuzzy or blurred. You can't correct this completely but you can make the picture clearer. Go to the **Filter** menu and choose **Sharpen**, then **Unsharp Mask**. Set **Amount** to **100%**, **Radius** to **1** and **Threshold** to **4**. In the small preview within the box, you'll see little difference except that the photo may look more grainy.

See the detail

3 Move the **Radius** slider to **2** and check the small preview. To see the effect in the main image display, tick **Preview**. Keep increasing the **Radius** until you find a point where the detail of the photo, instead of the grain, becomes noticeably clearer. This will usually be somewhere between **1** and **6**. The blemishes on the photo are also accentuated, which is one reason why it doesn't pay to sharpen too much.

Touch up blemishes

4 Click **OK**. Next, touch up any small light or dark blemishes or 'age spots'. Activate the **Spot Healing Brush** by clicking the sticking plaster icon in the toolbox on the left. Then, in the **Options** bar at the top, make sure that the first of the two icons at the left is highlighted. To the right of this is a preview of the 'brush' you're going to use. Click the triangle next to it to show a list of brushes.

File formats and quality

When saving your scanned photo, choose TIF format for best results. The more common JPEG format sacrifices image quality to make a smaller file (see page 311). If you choose a high-quality setting when saving the JPEG file, the difference isn't visible. But when you edit and adjust a saved image, tiny blemishes introduced by the JPEG process, known as 'artefacts', may emerge. Each time you save the file the image is degraded a little further until problems will become clearly visible. Using TIF instead makes sure your precious photos are perfectly preserved. TIF files include a compression option when saving (called 'LZW compression') that, while less powerful than that used in JPEGs, doesn't degrade the image at all but will result in smaller file sizes than uncompressed TIFs.

Keep aligned when cloning

Always tick the **Aligned** option with the **Clone Stamp** (step 9). After you set a source point and start painting, you can stop for a rest at any time. When you continue, even if you don't click in exactly the same place where you left off, the source area continues to copy seamlessly. Without the **Aligned** option, you'd start again from the original source point, resulting in overlaid copies of the same area. This makes an unsightly blotchy pattern.

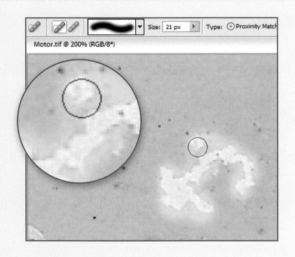

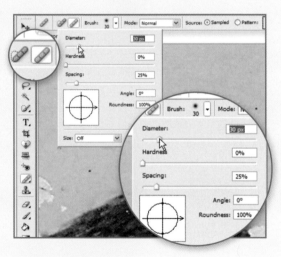

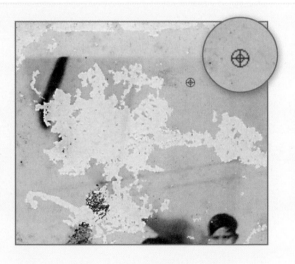

Start painting

5 Select **Default Brushes** in the pop-up menu at the top, then scroll down the list and choose the brush called **Soft Round 21 pixels**. The mouse pointer now shows a circle. With this, click on any isolated blemish on the photo, hold down the mouse button and paint over the blemish. A lightened area shows where you've painted. Make sure you cover the blemish completely, going slightly over the edges.

A little healing

6 Release the mouse button and the blemish disappears. If anything remains, paint it out in the same way. This easy method won't work for larger or more complex areas. Instead, click the second of the two sticking plaster icons in the **Options** bar to activate the **Healing Brush**. The brush settings for this work differently. Make the **Diameter** about **30px** (pixels) and set the other options as shown above.

Find an undamaged area to use

7 Decide on the area of damage you want to cover, then find a place in the photo that's similar to how the damaged area should appear when repaired. If possible, avoid choosing somewhere right next to the damage, to make it less obvious that part of the picture has been copied. To set your 'source point' (see page 321), hold the **Alt** key (the mouse pointer shows a crosshair) and click on this area.

Removing large scratches

Don't attempt to remove large scratches using the **Dust & Scratches** filter (see step 15 of this project). Increasing the **Radius** setting beyond a few pixels will blur the picture too much. Instead, use the **Clone Stamp** (see step 9). Set a source point a little way to the side of the scratch at one end, and you'll usually find you can paint over a substantial proportion of its length in one go. Set a new source point when the copy drifts out of line or the texture changes.

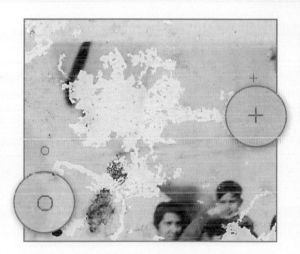

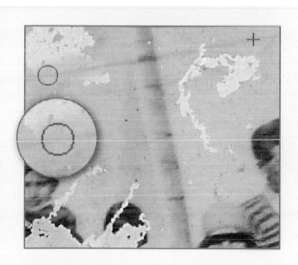

Paint over the damage

8 Release the **Alt** key and click on the equivalent position in the damaged area. For example, if you clicked at the top left of the area you want to copy, click at the top left of the damaged area. Holding down the mouse button, paint over the damage. The area around the source point is copied seamlessly over it. It may look too light or dark, but after you release the mouse button the tone is automatically adjusted.

Choose the Clone Stamp

9 To restore specific details, use the **Clone Stamp** in the toolbox on the left. Click it and make sure the first of the two icons is highlighted at the left of the **Options** bar. Choose a larger **Soft Round** brush. Set **Mode** to **Normal**, **Opacity 100%**, and tick **Aligned**. Holding **Alt**, choose a source point that's an exact match. Here, to restore the telegraph wire on the left, click on the same wire to the right.

Clone a detail

10 Release the mouse button, then click on the exact point where you want to start painting the copied material. The source point was on the telegraph wire; now click on exactly where the wire should go. As before, drag to paint over the required area. The wire continues at the same angle, so the copy fits well. Use this cloning method to replace any details that are repeated elsewhere in the picture.

Make full use of zoom

What you see on screen is only an approximation of the picture that you're working on, unless the zoom level shown in the title bar above the image is **100%**. To fit the whole picture on screen, you may have to zoom out to **50%**, **25%** or even less. But when editing fine detail, always zoom in to **100%** or greater so that you can see exactly what you're doing. Otherwise you could miss small mistakes or blemishes. Useful keyboard shortcuts are **Ctrl+0** to zoom to fit the whole image on screen and **Alt+Ctrl+0** to zoom to **100%**.

Under cover of darkness

Sometimes an area of detail in a photo is lost irretrievably, and there's no matching area to copy. Occasionally there's no clue, even, as to what was there before the damage. A good solution is to clone something dark over it since one object in shadow looks much like another. This trick has been used on the back and front of the car in the photo used in this project.

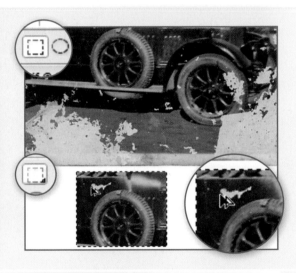

Bring missing faces to light

11 Damage has obliterated two faces of the car's pasengers. But even these can be restored by cloning. The face at the left is at a similar angle to the missing one in the middle, so use this for a source point, painting just enough of the larger face to fill the space (ringed). The face on the right can be cloned from the one at the top. Family resemblance will account for the similarities.

Make spare room on your canvas

12 Sometimes the item you want to clone is repeated within the photo but the wrong way round. Here, the missing part of the front wheel could be cloned from the top part of the spare wheel. To turn your source area around, first make some room to copy it. From the **Image** menu, choose **Resize**, then **Canvas Size**. Increase **Height** by a couple of hundred pixels, and click the top middle **Anchor** position.

Duplicate a section of the photo

13 You now have a blank area. Choose the **Marquee** tool from the toolbar on the left. Drag around the area you plan to clone from. A flashing outline appears when you release the mouse button. Holding down the **Alt** and **Ctrl** keys – the mouse pointer shows a double arrow – drag the selection down. From the **Image** menu, choose **Rotate**, then **Flip Selection Vertical**.

● Black and white in colour

Even if a photograph is black and white, always scan and edit it in colour. First, this preserves the tinted appearance of the photo, keeping your restored version authentic to the original. Secondly, It allows a greater range of tones to be represented. A 'greyscale' image will seem flat and lifeless compared to a colour scan. It's important to choose full colour in your scanning software, because the lost tones in a greyscale scan can't be restored later.

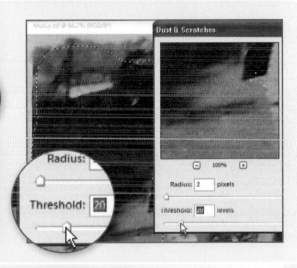

Choose only what you need

14 Press **Ctrl+D** to deselect. Switch back to the **Clone Stamp** (press **S**), then **Alt**+click on the lower right edge of the copied wheel. Using this source point, paint over the bottom right of the car's front wheel. Only clone the parts you need, not the whole wheel. Go back to **Image**, **Resize**, **Canvas Size**, and reset the original **Height**, choosing the same **Anchor** position. Click **OK**, then **Proceed**.

Mark out problem areas

15 Use a combination of the previously shown methods to restore all the larger blemishes and areas of damage. You may still be left with areas that are speckled with dust or minor scratches. Choose the **Lasso** tool from the toolbox on the left (or press **L**) and highlight the first of the three icons at the left of the **Options** bar. Click and drag to draw roughly around the problem area.

Goodbye to dust and scratches

16 In the **Filter** menu, choose **Noise**, **Dust & Scratches**. In the settings box, set **Threshold** to 0, and increase the **Radius** setting until most of the specks disappear. Then, increase the **Threshold** as far as you can without the specks coming back, to preserve as much detail as possible. Click **OK**. Finally, save the restored image as a TIF file (see 'File formats and quality' box, page 22).

Disappearing act
Get rid of unwanted parts of a photo using Photoshop Elements

The camera may never lie, but sometimes you wish it had been a little less truthful. That cathedral looks awe-inspiring – except for the telegraph wires crossing its frontage. Your car would appeal to any buyer – if you'd checked before photographing it and noticed what a pigeon had left on the bonnet. Fortunately, your PC can help make these little annoyances disappear.

PROJECT TOOLS: Photoshop Elements
SEE ALSO: Restore an old photo, page 20 ● Changing places and faces, page 52

○ It's a cover up

The most powerful tool in your retouching toolkit is the **Clone** tool (see page 321). And the key to successful cloning is having – in the same photo or even in a separate photo – background that you can pick up and 'paint' over the problem parts. When there's none available, a useful trick is to paste in an object that will hide the problem while preserving the composition. The same principles apply whether you're cleaning up a cityscape or removing unwanted objects from portraits or group shots.

Decide what needs erasing

1 Run Photoshop Elements and in the **Welcome** box click **Edit and Enhance Photos**. When the **Open** box appears, browse to the image file you want, click to highlight it and click **Open**. Start by identifying the objects you want to remove. In this photo, clutter in the foreground distracts from the main scene, two large lampposts overlap the river and there are also some dark specks in the sky.

● Adding and subtracting

You don't always have to start again if you've selected an area using the **Lasso** or **Marquee** tools and it isn't quite right. Hold down the **Shift** key and draw around an area to add it to the selection, or hold the **Alt** key to subtract an area. The cursor shows a plus or minus symbol to confirm this. Note that you have to hold the appropriate key down before you click.

● Healing spots

An alternative way to remove small specks and blobs in a photo is to use Photoshop Elements' **Healing Brush**. You can find a full explanation of this on page 21, steps 4 to 6. Having activated the tool and chosen a small brush size, click on any isolated blemish to paint it out. The background texture is automatically re-created. This can be quicker than using **Dust & Scratches** from the **Filter** menu when you have only a few specks in your photo to remove.

Set up the Crop tool

2 One way to remove unwelcome elements is to crop the photo to only the part of the scene that you want. Activate the **Crop** tool by clicking C. In the **Options** bar at the top, click the **Aspect Ratio** option to pop up a menu of standard photo sizes, and choose one (see 'Preparing for printing', page 29). Leave the **Resolution** box blank. Click and drag on your photo to draw a crop box.

Careful composition

3 The shape, but not the size, of the box is fixed. If it's wide and you wanted your photo tall, or vice versa, click the double-arrow icon in the **Options** bar to swap the **Width** and **Height**. Drag the box to move it around and drag any of its corner handles to resize it. Try to crop off anything that you don't want in the picture, without spoiling the composition. Here, the grey blocks at the bottom can be removed.

Zoom in to examine blemishes

4 Double-click inside the box (or click the tick symbol) to crop the image. Next, examine your photo carefully for any small items that need removing. Here, there are black blobs in the sky at the top right. Zoom in to see items better by pressing Z for the **Zoom** tool, then click repeatedly on the part you want to examine. To zoom back out, hold the **Alt** key and click.

⚫ Resolution and the Crop tool

When using the **Crop** tool in Photoshop Elements, if you choose a preset **Aspect Ratio** (as in step 2), such as **4 x 6 in**, and set a figure for **Resolution**, such as **300 pixels/inch**, the image will be resized as well as cropped. The resulting cropped image is converted to the new resolution by adding or removing pixels (see 'All about colour and resolution', page 311), and the process can't be reversed later without losing quality. In this project, you crop without setting the **Resolution** (step 2). Within the part of the photo that you keep, the pixels stay unchanged, so quality is unaffected.

A picture cropped to the same aspect ratio as the paper will fill the page when printed (near right). With a different aspect ratio, your print will have to be recropped or will show blank borders (far right).

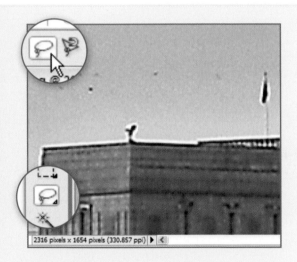

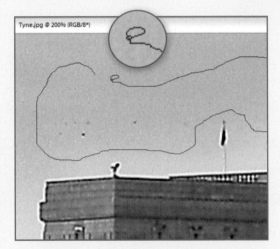

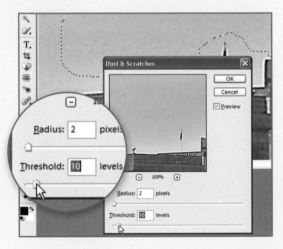

Rubbing out small blemishes

5 One of the specks is a distant flag that is best left. There's also what looks like a security camera. The others appear to be birds and need to be removed to tidy up the scene. Select an area around the specks. Click the **Lasso** icon, sixth down in the toolbox on the left, or press the **L** key. In the **Options** bar at the top, click the first of the group of three icons on the left, choosing the **Normal Lasso** mode.

Draw around the area

6 Click and drag on your photo to draw roughly around the area that needs cleaning up. Include all the specks you wish to remove, but avoid any small items or details that you want to leave in. Go all the way around the area, then release the mouse button. A flashing dotted outline shows that this area is selected. Now go to the **Filter** menu and choose **Noise**, then **Dust & Scratches**.

Make unwanted specks disappear

7 In the **Dust & Scratches** box, drag the **Threshold** slider to **0**. Set **Radius** to **0** as well, then increase it to **1** and look at the preview window above. Keep increasing until the unwanted specks disappear. Now increase the **Threshold**. This brings back the grain of the photo, so the selected area matches the rest. Set the level as high as possible without bringing back the specks.

Hitting the edge

While 'painting' with the **Clone Stamp** tool (see step 11), you may find the cloned material you're applying suddenly stops, leaving a hard edge. This is because the point you've reached in the source area (where the 'paint' is being taken from), has reached the edge of the picture. Undo your painting (press **Ctrl+Z**) and choose a source point further away from the edge of the picture before trying again.

Preparing for printing

You can print any shape of picture on A4 paper and cut it out, but if you want to use pre-cut photo paper, or a digital photo printing service, it's best if your photo is the same shape as the paper used. The processes used by photo bureaux automatically enlarge the image to fill the photo paper, and any excess is cropped. So, when you edit your photos in Photoshop Elements, it makes sense to apply the shape or 'aspect ratio' of a paper size you're likely to use, to avoid losing the edges of your photo when it's printed (see the box on page 28).

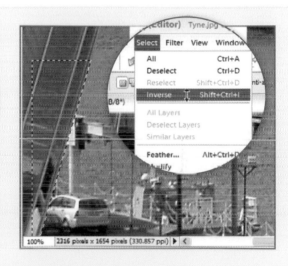

Remove larger objects

8 Click **OK**. Zoom back out. Next, identify any larger objects that need removing from a fairly plain background. This picture would look better without the clutter at the bottom left, where a car and boat are seen below the main building. To remove them, cover them with water. First, protect nearby objects that you don't want to remove, in this case the edge of the building.

Protecting an area

9 Use the **Zoom** tool as before to magnify the relevant area, then switch back to the **Lasso** tool (press L). In the **Options** bar, make sure that **Anti-Aliased** is ticked. Since the building has straight edges, click the last of the three icons at the left of the **Options** bar to switch to the **Polygonal Lasso**. Click at the bottom of the wall, then release the mouse button and move up to make a straight line.

Invert your selection

10 Follow the wall, then click again. Continue beyond the area you want to remove, then take the line across the building and back down to the bottom, to outline a piece of the building. Double-click to finish. You now want to select everything except this area. To do this, choose **Inverse** from the **Select** menu. The flashing dotted border now runs along the edges of the whole picture and around the chosen area.

○ Blank it out by filling

Removing something that seems straightforward may not be possible using cloning because there's nothing comparable in the photo to copy from. In this picture, you may want to remove the lettering from the banners to add your own message. But there are no plain banners to clone.

Instead, use the **Polygonal Lasso** tool (see step 9, page 29) to draw around the banner, between the edge and the lettering. Before you start, go to the **Options** bar and set **Feather** to **3**, giving a soft edge. Having drawn your selection, press **I** for the **Eyedropper** tool. Holding **Alt**, click on the banner to pick up its colour (almost black) as the **Background** colour, shown in the lower square at the foot of the toolbox on the left. Press **Delete** to fill the selected area with this colour. To blend in better with the photo, add **Noise** (see 'Without a trace' box, page 54).

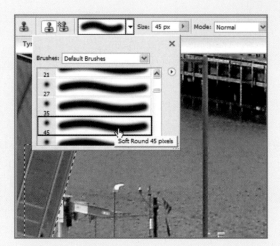

Pick a source point

11 Choose the **Clone Stamp** tool from the toolbox on the left, or press **S**. In the **Options** bar at the top, make sure the first of the two icons on the left is highlighted (**Clone Stamp**, not **Pattern Stamp**). Tick **Aligned**. Holding the **Alt** key, click to select your 'source point'. (For a full explanation see 'Image cutouts and photomontage', page 321.) Here, click on the river to the right.

Choose your brush

12 In the **Options** bar, a squiggle indicates the 'brush' you're going to use. Click the triangle next to this to show a list of brushes. Make sure **Default Brushes** is selected in the pop-up menu at the top, then scroll down the list and choose a plain soft brush (with fuzzy edges) large enough to paint your chosen area comfortably. The mouse pointer turns into a circle showing the brush size.

Clone over the unwanted objects

13 Click and drag to 'paint' over the unwanted objects. See the boxes on pages 29 and 31 for tips on problems when cloning and how to get around them. If necessary, paint over part of the area you want to remove, then choose a new source point and continue. Use **Zoom** frequently – you may want to zoom out to see more of the picture – but always check your work at **100%**.

PHOTO SMART

Running out of source

When choosing your source point (see step 11), try to make sure there's a sufficient area around it that will match the area you're attempting to cover. Sometimes you won't be able to find a single area to clone from that's big enough to cover the whole object you want to remove. In this case, cover a small area first, then choose a new source point to continue. But avoid 'dabbing' numerous tiny bits, as the result won't look realistic.

Gently does it

By choosing a brush **Opacity** of **50%** or less you can gradually blend in cloned background for a more natural look. Don't be afraid to use a large brush – especially where the objects you're erasing are away from the main subject. Here, the source point was set by **Alt**-clicking on a patch of clear shoreline to the right of the objects, before painting over the shoreline to the left.

Removing tricky items

14 You'll need precise cloning where the background is more complicated, as here, where the top of the lamppost crosses the quayside. Press **Ctrl+D** to cancel the selection, then zoom into the relevant area. With the **Clone** tool, go to the **Options** bar, choose a smaller soft brush and untick **Aligned**. Look for an object similar to what would be behind the item you want to remove.

Match your source and target points

15 In this case, the timbers behind the lamppost match those to the right. Holding **Alt**, choose a source point that's clearly identifiable: here, it's where the timbers cross. Release the **Alt** key. Click on the equivalent point where you want to copy the source area (the place behind the lamppost where the timbers would cross) and drag to start painting the source material over the unwanted object.

Paint with one stroke

16 If the clone isn't perfectly positioned, undo (press **Ctrl+Z**) and try again. Because you unticked **Aligned**, the **Clone Stamp** starts painting from the original source point (where you **Alt**-clicked) each time you click. Once it fits in correctly, paint as much as possible in one stroke. Where the underlying background changes, choose a new source point. Remove other objects using the same methods.

Talk in bubbles
Let your photos tell a story with your own comic strip

Blam! Kerpow! Comics provide a fresh and direct way to present words, pictures and ideas, and are popular both with children and adults. It's easy to create your own comic strip, featuring members of your family, or telling the story of a special event. Using image-editing software such as Photoshop Elements, you can turn ordinary photos into comic-style artwork and incorporate them into layouts that look just like the real thing, complete with comic-strip frames, captions and speech bubbles. Your finished layout can be printed out or saved as a graphics file to email to friends and relations. To get started, all you need to do is think of a storyline and take a few pictures to illustrate it. Or maybe you'd like to turn your holiday or family-gathering snaps into cartoon-strip format – the possibilities are endless.

PROJECT TOOLS: Photoshop Elements ● Digital photos
SEE ALSO: Restore an old photo, page 20 ● Font basics explained, page 326

● Metric or imperial?

When entering measurements in Photoshop Elements, use either inches or centimetres as you prefer: type in after the number for inches, or cm for centimetres. All conversions are made automatically. This project is shown on **A4** paper using metric measurements (centimetres). If you have an A3 inkjet printer, it can be adapted to a larger paper size – to frame as a poster, for example – when you come to print out the comic strip.

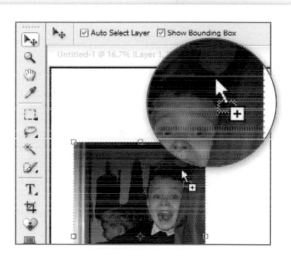

Start with a blank canvas

1 Here we're making a comic strip from four photos. Run Photoshop Elements and choose **Start From Scratch**. In the **New** box, choose A4 from the **Preset** menu. Make sure the **Color Mode** is **RGB Color** and **Background Contents** is **White**. Click **OK** to create a blank canvas. In the **File** menu, choose **Open**, browse to the folder containing the photos, and hold the **Ctrl** key while clicking to highlight all four. Click **Open**.

Crop your first picture

2 Edit your pictures now if you need to. (The fourth image will be altered, as explained in 'Faking a photo', page 39.) Then click on your first photo and press **C** to activate the **Crop** tool. In the **Options** bar at the top, set **Width** to 9cm and **Height** to 13cm. Set **Resolution** to **300 pixels/inch**. Now click near the top left of the photo and drag to draw a crop box around the area you want to use.

Add a picture to your layout

3 Drag the crop box to move it around, or adjust its size using the corner handles. When you're happy with it, double-click within the box. The picture is cut down to this area and automatically resized to the dimensions and resolution you entered. Choose the **Move** tool from the top of the palette on the left (or press **V**). Click on the photo you just cropped and drag it across onto your blank document.

Planning pays

Plan your comic strip before you start. With a pencil and paper, sketch a 'storyboard' showing what will happen in each frame. Then get your actors together and take your photos using a digital camera. Use a good-quality setting with high resolution, and make sure you get your subjects in focus, so that your pictures will look clear even after you crop them down. Small details won't show up in the finished comic, so keep your scenes simple and direct your characters to use their bodies and faces to reflect what's going on in the story.

A coloured background

The comic strip in the project below has a white background, which means you can print it on almost any printer, because the colour doesn't have to go right to the edge. If your printer offers 'borderless' printing, you may prefer a coloured background. After creating your blank canvas (step 1), choose **Fill Layer** from the **Edit** menu. Set the **Blending** options to **Normal**, **100%**. Under **Contents**, choose **Color**, then pick a colour. Click **OK** in each box.

Snap your pictures into place

4 Drag the picture to place it near the top left of the page, leaving a gap at the top. Click on your second photo, and switch back to the **Crop** tool (press **C**). This time, set both **Width** and **Height** to **9cm**. Crop the photo as before and drag it onto your layout using the **Move** tool. Click it and drag it close to the picture you placed previously. Let the photo snap into place, neatly lined up.

Add the remaining pictures

5 Click on your third photo and use the **Crop** tool with the same dimension settings, **9x9cm**, to cut it down. Use the **Move** tool to add it to your layout as before, snapping it to the bottom edge of the first picture. Repeat for the fourth photo, this time setting the dimensions back to **9x13cm**, as for the first picture. When you snap this into place, you should have a neat rectangle of images.

Divide your frames

6 Press **M** for the **Marquee** tool. In the **Options** bar at the top, make sure the **Rectangular** option is highlighted and set **Feather** to **0**. Click the **Mode** option and choose **Fixed Size**. Set **Width** to **0.75cm** and **Height** to **25cm**. Now click anywhere on the layout and drag to draw and position a fixed-size rectangle. Centre it exactly on the vertical line where your pictures meet, overlapping at the top and bottom.

Smooth lines and curves

Photoshop Elements' **Text** and **Shape** tools create special layers in 'vector' format. These can be edited or resized without affecting the quality of their appearance. If you try to apply an adjustment, filter or effect to one of these layers, a box will warn you that it first has to be 'simplified' – converted into a normal image layer. After this you can't edit text, and resizing shapes may make them look fuzzy. So, if you have more editing to do click **Cancel**.

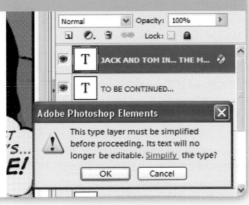

Image editing and memory

Photoshop Elements uses your PC's memory (RAM) and hard disk while it works. If it runs out of space, an error box appears. Try closing any other images in the Window menu, and any other programs shown in the Windows **Task Bar**. To free more memory, go to the **Edit** menu and choose **Clear**, **All** (this disables **Undo**). If this doesn't help, your hard disk may be full. For advice, go to Windows' **Start** menu, choose **Help and Support**, and enter disk too full in the **Search** box.

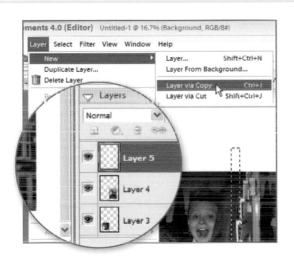

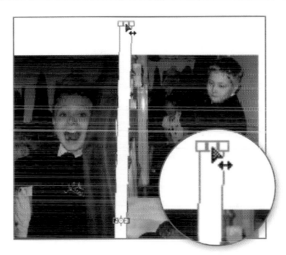

Create a white bar

7 In the **Layers** palette on the right (choose **Layers** from the **Window** menu if you can't see it), you have five layers: four containing the pictures you added, plus the plain **Background**. Click the **Background** layer to highlight it. Go to the **Layer** menu and choose **New**, then **Layer via Copy**. A new layer appears in the **Layers** palette, called **Layer 5**. Click this and drag it to the top of the list, above **Layer 4**.

Angle the bar

8 The new layer contains a copy of the part of the **Background** layer within the selection made in step 6, making a white bar. Go to the **Image** menu and choose **Transform**, then **Skew**. Handles appear around the bar. Place the mouse pointer over the top middle handle, so it shows a grey triangle with arrows pointing to left and right. Click and drag a little way to the right. The white bar skews over.

Duplicate the bar

9 Don't skew it too much, because the shape still needs to cover the edge between the pictures along its full length. To make sure it does so, click within the shape and drag it to the left a little. Finish by clicking the tick button in the **Options** at the top. Holding down the **Alt** key, click the white bar again and drag it to one side. This makes a copy of it in a new layer, called **Layer 5 Copy**.

Comic-book jargon

Comic artists have their own jargon for the elements of a page. The pictures making up your story are 'frames'. The people in them are 'characters'. Text is 'lettering'. Shapes containing words that your characters say or think are 'bubbles', usually 'speech bubbles'; 'thought bubbles' are cloud-shaped. The words they contain are 'dialogue'. Lettering that represents actions – Splat!, Blam!, Kaboom! – is called 'sound fx'. Any other lettering is referred to as a 'caption'.

Organising your layers

Once you build up a number of layers in your Photoshop Elements file, you'll need to know some tricks to keep them properly arranged. To select a piece of text or artwork that's in a layer and move it around the canvas, press **V** to activate the **Move** tool and, in the **Options** bar at the top, make sure **Auto Select Layer** is ticked. Now click on the item you want and drag to move it. To move several items at once, hold **Shift** while clicking on them to select all their layers. To put a new item behind an older one, either press **Ctrl-[** to move it back, or drag its name further down the list in the **Layers** palette.

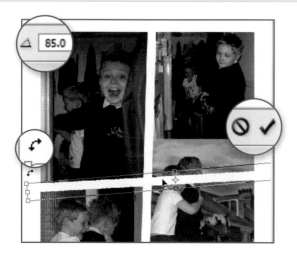

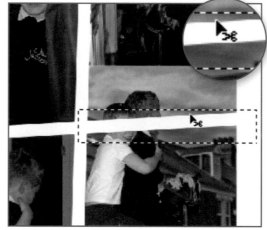

Rotate the copy

10 Place the mouse pointer slightly outside a corner of the new bar, so it shows a turning arrow symbol, then click and drag to rotate the bar. The amount of rotation is shown in the **Options** above: make it about **85** degrees. Drag the bar into place so its left-hand end covers the horizontal edge between the two pictures on the left. Click the tick to finish. Switch back to the **Marquee** tool (press **M**).

Cut the bar in two

11 In the **Options** set the **Mode** back to **Normal**. Click and drag to draw a rectangle around the right-hand end of the bar you created, starting within the gap made by the vertical bar in the middle. Hold down the **Ctrl** key (the mouse pointer shows scissors). Click within the rectangle and drag it upwards until this section of the bar covers the edge between the two right-hand pictures.

Write some text

12 When the bar is in the correct position, press **Ctrl+D**. Now press **T** to activate the **Text** tool. In the **Options**, choose a suitable font (see 'Finding comic-book fonts', page 37). Set the font size to about **18pt**. Press **D** to set the default colours (black on white). Click near the top left corner of your first frame and type a few words to begin the story. Press **Return** where you need to move onto a new line.

● Finding comic book fonts

Despite its name, the Windows font 'Comic Sans' looks nothing like the neat hand-drawn lettering in comics. You can get better fonts, many of them free, from websites such as www.blambot.com, www.pizzadude.dk and www.fontdiner.com. Find a suitable font and choose PC TrueType (TTF) format. When you click to download the font, a warning box appears. Click **Save**, and pick somewhere to put the file, such as **My Documents**. From **My Computer** on the **Desktop**, go to this folder and double-click the file you've downloaded. If it's a 'zip' file, click **Extract All Files** to run the **Extraction Wizard**, then click **Next** and **Finish** to convert it into a folder containing fonts. Install your new fonts as shown in 'Font basics explained', page 326, steps 3 and 4.

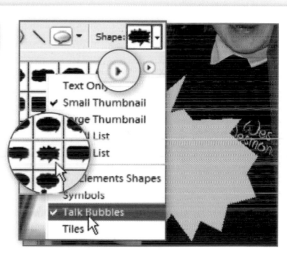

Add a text box

13 Click the tick in the **Options** bar to finish. Press **U** to activate the **Shape** tool. In the **Options** bar, click the **Rectangle** icon. Click the triangle to the right of the **Color** option to pop up a set of colour swatches. Choose **Pastel Yellow**. Click and drag to draw a rectangle slightly larger than your text. Then hold the **Ctrl** key and press **[** (left square bracket). The rectangle moves behind the text.

Arrange your graphics

14 Press **V** for the **Move** tool. In the **Options** bar, tick **Auto Select Layer** and **Show Bounding Box**. Drag the corner handles of the coloured rectangle to adjust its size. Click the tick in the **Options** bar to finish, then click on the text and drag to reposition it if necessary. If you need to resize the text, hold **Shift** while dragging a corner handle. Next, switch back to the **Shape** tool (press **U**).

Create a speech bubble

15 In the **Options** bar, pick the **Custom Shape** tool (the last icon). Click the **Shape** option to pop up the **Shape Picker**. Click the blue triangle at the top and choose **Talk Bubbles**. Pick a shape and choose another pastel colour. Click and drag to draw a bubble over your first picture. Use the **Move** tool (press **V**) to resize and/or rotate it. Reset the default colours (press **D**). Use the **Text** tool to add some words.

Online resources

When you want to take your comic art further, plenty of help is available on the internet. Most of the tutorials available are based on the full version of Photoshop but most techniques will also work in Photoshop Elements. For example, www.polykarbon.com has many expert tips on cartoon design. If you're interested in learning to draw comic strips yourself, rather than working from photos, you'll find several helpful tutorials at http://neondragonart.com/dp/tutorials.

Text tips

When lettering your comic strip, don't forget the basics of typography (see 'Desktop publishing with Word', page 328). Use the buttons in Photoshop Elements' **Options** bar to align the text appropriately, usually to the left for captions and to the centre for bubbles. Next to these buttons is the **Leading** setting. Use this to adjust the vertical space between lines within a block of text. For comics, this should be 'tight' – about the same measure as the font size.

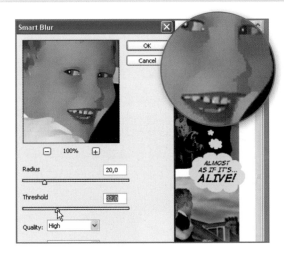

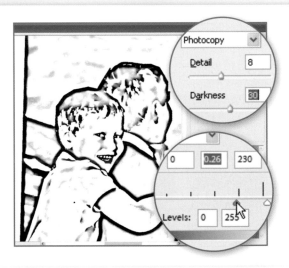

Add more bubbles

16 Repeat steps 12 to 15 to add bubbles and narration to your other pictures. When finished, look at the **Layers** palette. Layers containing text, called 'type' layers, are identified by a letter 'T'. Drag each of these to the top of the list so that all the type layers are at the top. Then click on the highest layer that isn't a type layer. Hold **Shift** and click on the **Background** to select all the layers in between.

Prepare a comic-book art effect

17 In the **Layers** menu, choose **Merge Layers**. Everything except the text is now on the **Background** layer. In the **Filter** menu, choose **Blur**, **Smart Blur**. Set **Radius 20**, **Threshold 32**, **Quality High**, **Mode Normal**. Click **OK**. This smoothes the pictures. Choose **Duplicate Layer** from the **Layers** menu. Type Outlines and click **OK**. In the **Layers** palette, change blending mode from **Normal** to **Multiply**.

Draw black outlines

18 Press **D** for the default colours. From the **Filter** menu, choose **Sketch**, **Photocopy**. Adjust the sliders until a thick black line outlines the main features: try **Detail 8**, **Darkness 30**. Click **OK**, then press **Ctrl+L** to show the **Levels** box. Tick **Preview**. Drag the white slider left until the fainter lines disappear; drag the grey slider halfway up to it. Click **OK**. In the **Layers** palette, click on **Background**.

○ Faking a photo

Anything you can't photograph, you can fake. In this project, to make the boys fly, they're cut out and overlaid on a photo showing rooftops. The comic art effect (steps 17 to 20) will hide any rough edges, so the cutout needn't be perfect.

In Photoshop Elements, press **L** for the **Lasso** tool. In the **Options** bar, pick the **Polygonal lasso**, which draws straight lines. Click at the bottom left of the area you want, and move to draw a straight line. Position this and click again. Continue all the way around, then double-click to finish.

Press **Ctrl+J** to copy this area into a new layer. Open the rooftop photo, then press **V** for the **Move** tool, and drag this photo onto the other. Press **Ctrl-[** to put the rooftops behind the boys. Use the box around the photo to position and resize it. Double-click to finish, then choose **Flatten Image** from the **Layers** menu.

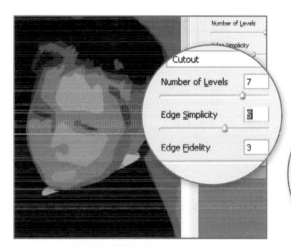

Create blocks of colour

19 From the **Filter** menu, choose **Artistic**, then **Cutout**. Set **Number of Levels** to 7 and **Edge Fidelity** to 3. Adjust **Edge Simplicity** to divide the picture into simple but recognisable blocks of colour: try **5**. Click **OK**. In the **Layers** palette, right-click the **Background** layer and use **Duplicate Layer** as in step 17. This time, in the **Duplicate Layer** box, call the new layer Dots. Click **OK**.

Using halftone effects

20 In the **Filter** menu, choose **Adjustments**, **Equalize** to even out the tones in this copy of the artwork. In the **Layers** palette, change the new layer's blending mode to **Pin Light**. In the **Filter** menu, choose **Sketch, Halftone Pattern**. Set **Size** to 3, **Contrast** to 25 and **Pattern Type** to Dot. Click **OK**. This simulates the halftone dot pattern of cheap printing. Click on the top layer in the **Layers** palette.

Finish with a title

21 Switch to the **Text** tool (press T). Click at the top left of the page and type a title. Adjust the font and size. Choose a dramatic font: here it's **Agency FB**. In the **Styles and Effects** palette, select **Layer Styles**, then choose a suitable effect. Click it to style your text. Save your comic strip (see 'Saving layered files', page 55). Or you can add new pages if you wish, using the same techniques.

Face painting by numbers

Improve the way you look with a virtual makeover

Photos can be unflattering – washed-out skin tones, a shiny nose or pimples do little for anyone's confidence. Thankfully, all these can be easily fixed with the help of photo-editing software. In minutes, you could look as flawless as a model or movie star. And you don't have to stop there. If you're curious about how you'd look with a different hairstyle, eye colour or make-up, just photograph the parts you'd like and try them on for size.

PROJECT TOOLS: Photoshop Elements ● Photos
SEE ALSO: Family card game, page 154

● Taking the ideal photo

You can do a makeover on any photo, but for best results take one specially. Find a place and time when the light is bright but not too harsh, and make sure your face isn't in shadow. If possible, use a white or plain background. Position the camera so that your face fills most of the frame. Use a tripod or place the camera on something firm; using the self-timer is ideal because nobody will wobble the camera during the shot.

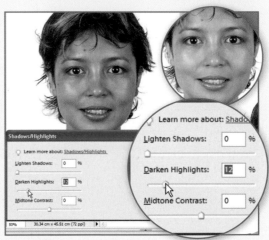

Enhance your skin tone

1 Run Photoshop Elements. From the **Welcome** screen choose **Edit and Enhance Photos**. Press **Ctrl+O** and in the **Open** dialogue box double-click your photo. If you look a bit washed out, go to the **Enhance** menu and choose **Adjust Lighting**, then **Shadows/Highlights**. Set **Lighten Shadows** to **0** and increase **Darken Highlights** a little. For darker skin, try increasing **Lighten Shadows** too. Click **OK**.

A healthy glow

Since the early days of cinema, three tricks have been used to create a 'film star' look: diffuse lighting, soft focus and over-exposure. You can mimic all of these using Photoshop Elements' **Diffuse Glow** function, found under **Distort** on the **Filter** menu. Set **Graininess** to a small amount, such as **2**, then adjust the other sliders – the higher the **Glow Amount** and the lower the **Clear Amount**, the stronger the effect will be.

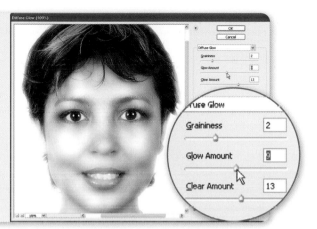

Nobody's perfect

Although this project does a thorough job on its subject, you should be wary of going too far 'improving' a portrait photo. Nobody has a perfect face, and removing a prominent mole or fixing chipped teeth may make someone look odd to those who know that person well. Stick to enhancements such as removing blotches, tidying up hair and whitening eyes, and leave a few flaws intact for the sake of realism.

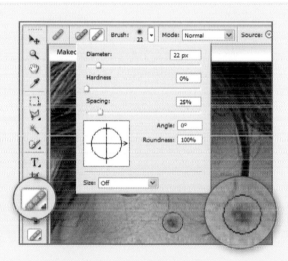

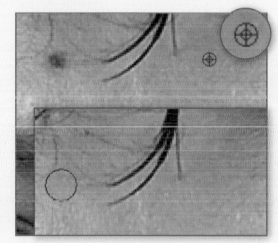

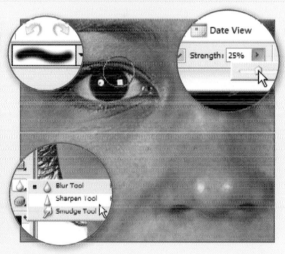

Prepare the Healing Brush

2 Click and hold the **Healing Brush** icon (sticking plaster) in the main toolbox on the left, and choose **Healing Brush Tool** from the pop-out menu. In the **Options** bar at the top, click the icon labelled **Brush**. Set **Hardness** to **0%**, **Spacing** to **25%** and **Roundness** to **100%**. Adjust the **Diameter** so the brush is slightly bigger than the spot you want to remove.

Remove spots and blemishes

3 Also in the **Options** bar, set **Mode** to **Normal** and **Source** to **Sampled**, and tick **Aligned**. Hold **Alt** and click somewhere on the photo where the skin tone is the same as around the spot to be removed. This sets a 'source point' (similar to that used with the **Clone** tool; see page 321). Release the **Alt** key, then click on the spot and drag to cover it. Cover other blemishes, setting a suitable source point each time.

Sharpen your eyes

4 The eyes should be sharp and clear. Click and hold the third icon from the bottom of the toolbox, then choose the **Sharpen** tool. In the **Options** bar, choose a soft brush (plain with fuzzy edges). Set **Size** to about **40px** and **Strength** to **25%**. Click on an eye and, holding down the mouse button, 'paint' over it to sharpen. Sharpen both eyes, but not too much, avoiding the wrinkles around them.

● Put on your virtual wig

Going a bit thin on top? Open your photo in Photoshop Elements and press **M** for the **Marquee** tool. In the **Options** bar, pick **Elliptical** and set **Mode** to **Normal**. Click and drag to draw an oval over the scalp. Press the **Spacebar** while drawing to move the shape. Then hold **Alt** and draw an overlapping oval to subtract the face, leaving a crescent shape selected. Choose **Feather** from the **Select** menu and enter **12**, then click **OK**. Copy this area into a new layer by pressing **Ctrl+J**. Press **D** to set the colours to black and white. Go to the **Filter** menu and choose **Render, Fibers** (**1**). Set **Variance 16, Strength 12**. Click **OK**. You now have hair but it's too straight. From the **Filter** menu, choose **Distort, Wave** (**2**). Set **Generators** to **20**, **Wavelength** to **40 Min** and **80 Max**, **Amplitude** to **1 Min** and **4 Max**, and **Scale** to **100% Horiz** and **Vert**. Click **OK**.

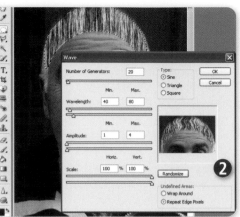

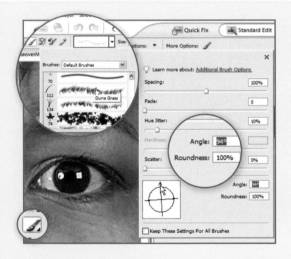
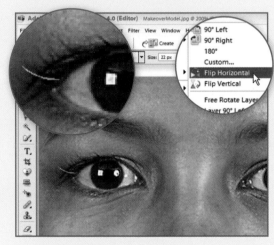
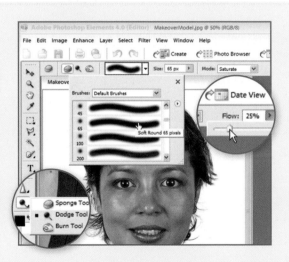

Choose an eyelash brush

5 Pick **Brush** from the toolbox on the left (it shares the icon just above the **Paint Bucket** tool with the **Pencil** and advanced **Brush** tools). In the **Options** bar, click the **Brush** preview, scroll down the list and choose **Dune Grass**. Reduce the **Size** to 22px. Click **More Options**. Set **Spacing 100%, Fade 0, Hue Jitter 10%, Scatter 0%,** and **Angle 94°**. Press **Return**, then press **D** to set the painting colour to black.

Paint thicker, longer eyelashes

6 Click near the outer corner of the eye on the left and, holding down the mouse button, paint on some extra lashes. Adjust the **Size** and **Angle** if needed; the lashes here should be almost horizontal – use the existing lashes as a guide. Click and paint again to add more. Only add lashes near the edge of the eye. To do the other eye, go to the **Image** menu and choose **Rotate**, then **Flip Horizontal**.

Boost hair highlights

7 The photo is flipped over, and you can brush matching lashes onto the other eye. Then use **Flip Horizontal** again. Now turn your attention to the hair, where you can exaggerate any existing highlights. Click the bottom icon in the toolbox and choose the **Sponge Tool**. In the **Options** bar, set **Mode** to **Saturate** and **Flow** to **25%**. Choose a soft brush and a fairly large **Size**.

How to select by colour

When using **Replace Color** (see step 16), pick the **Selection** option. As you hold **Shift** and click on your photo, all areas matching the colour where you click are added to the selection, shown in white. Adjust the **Fuzziness** to select less or more. If you can't avoid other areas getting selected because they're similar in colour, click **Cancel**, then use the **Polygonal Lasso** to draw roughly around the item you want. Go back to **Replace Color** and try again.

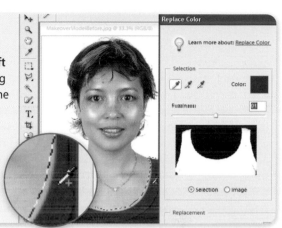

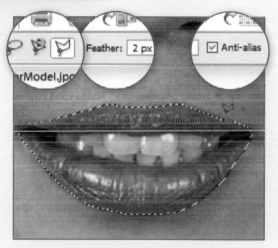

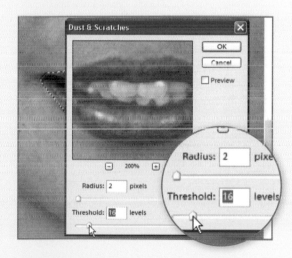

Paint over existing highlights

8 By clicking and dragging, paint over the highlights in the hair to boost their colour. Repaint an area if you want to make it even brighter. Use the **Sponge** tool to enhance colour elsewhere – for example, to make the subtle eye make-up here more obvious and to make the lipstick more vivid. Change the mode to **Desaturate** to remove colour – for example, to conceal red veins in the eyes.

Create fuller lips

9 Click the **Lasso** icon in the toolbox on the left and, in the **Options** bar, choose the **Polygonal Lasso**. Also in the **Options** bar, set **Feather** to 2px and tick **Anti-alias**. Click on the corner of the mouth, then release the mouse button and move to draw a straight line. Position this along the outline of the lip and click again. Continue all the way around and finish where you started.

Iron out wrinkles

10 With the mouth selected (shown by a flashing dotted outline), go to the **Filter** menu and choose **Noise**, then **Dust & Scratches**. In the box, set both sliders to 0, then increase the **Radius** until the wrinkles disappear from the lips – 2 or 3 should do it. Now increase the **Threshold** to around 16, so other details return and the mouth still appears natural. Click **OK**. Press **Ctrl+D** to cancel the selection.

⬤ Borrow a haircut

If you've ever envied someone else's hairdo, all you need is a photo of that person, and one of yourself at a similar angle. Open both in Elements (use **Open** from the **File** menu), then press **V** for the **Move** tool and drag the other person's photo onto yours (**1**). In the **Layers** palette (choose **Layers** from the **Window** menu if you can't see it), change the blending mode from **Normal** to **Soft Light**, so your face shows through (**2**). Drag the corners of the 'bounding box' to resize the new face to match (**3**), lining up the eyes and mouth. It may help to enlarge the window by dragging its bottom right corner down and to the right. Set the blending mode back to **Normal**. Press **E** for the **Eraser**. In the **Options** bar, pick the first of the three icons on the left for the normal **Eraser**. Click the **Brush** preview and choose a medium-sized, plain, soft-edged brush. Carefully paint inside the edges of the hair (**4**) to reveal your own face.

Whitening teeth

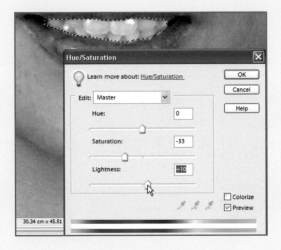

11 Using the **Polygonal Lasso** again (see step 9), draw around the teeth. In the **Enhance** menu choose **Adjust Color**, then **Adjust Hue/Saturation** (or press **Ctrl+U**). In the dialogue box, reduce **Saturation** by about a third to a half (-33 to -50) to remove any yellow, and increase **Lightness** a little for extra sparkle. Be careful not to make the teeth too white or they won't look real. Click **OK**.

Remove lines around the eyes

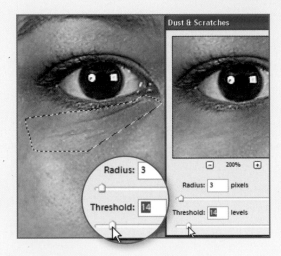

12 Select the **Polygonal Lasso** and draw around any area affected by lines or wrinkles, such as under the eyes or around the mouth. Choose **Dust & Scratches**, as in step 10, from **Noise** on the **Filter** menu. Move both sliders to the far left, then carefully increase the **Radius** to catch the wrinkles, and increase the **Threshold** to keep the skin texture looking natural.

Dealing with shiny skin

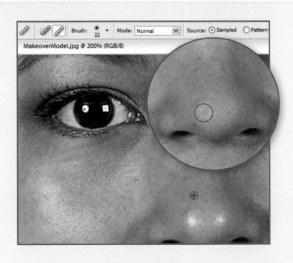

13 Press **Ctrl+D** to deselect. Bright highlights can make skin appear shiny. To reduce the shine, press **J** to switch back to the **Healing Brush** tool, and use it as in step 3 – **Alt**+click to pick up a non-shiny area of skin, then click and drag to paint it over a highlight. If necessary, increase the **Brush Size** in the **Options** bar, but don't try to cover a large area all at once; instead, work inwards from the edges.

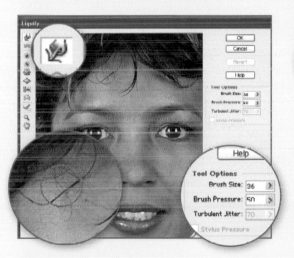

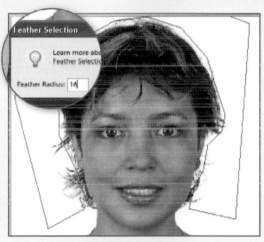

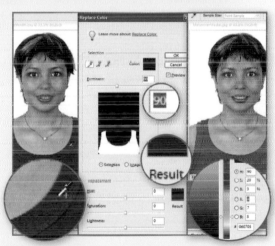

Clean up the forehead

14 There are some hairs lying messily across the forehead. You can push these out of the way. From the **Filter** menu choose **Distort**, then **Liquify** (see step 9, page 157). Click the **Warp** tool at the top of the toolbox on the left of the window. Adjust the **Brush Size** on the right so it's around the diameter of a pupil. Click and drag any wayward locks to tease them into shape. Keep your changes small.

Remove flyaway ends

15 Press **L** to switch back to the **Polygonal Lasso**, then draw around the outside of the face, where you want the hair to finish. Take your outline around and over the top to form a helmet shape. With the selection completed, choose **Feather** from the **Select** menu and enter **16**. Click **OK**. Press the **Delete** key to erase the rest of the hair. This only works if your photo is on a white background.

A change of outfit

16 From the **Enhance** menu, choose **Adjust Color**, then **Replace Color**. Move the mouse pointer over the photo (it shows an eyedropper) and, holding **Shift**, click repeatedly on the item you want to change – here it's the person's top. Adjust the **Fuzziness** slider so this area is shown white, with the rest of the photo black. Click the colour swatch labelled **Result** and choose a colour. Click **OK** to apply it.

All together

Gather your family in a group photo that crosses time and space

It's only on very special occasions that the whole family can get together in one place for a group photograph. And even then, there are fondly remembered relatives who belong in the picture but can't be there. Fortunately, time and space are more flexible in the digital world. Using your PC, you can bring together old and young, newly arrived and long departed, in a single photomontage that will be a fascinating keepsake for future generations.

PROJECT TOOLS: Photoshop Elements ● Photos
SEE ALSO: Restore an old photo, page 20 ● Turn a digital photo into a work of art, page 74

● Fishing for photos

For a comprehensive portrait, ask your family to search their albums for suitable pictures. If relatives have their own PCs with scanners, they can send you scanned images. Those without scanners can post you their prints, but make sure they are sent by special delivery. Scan everything at a high resolution – 600dpi (dots per inch) for a small print if the image looks sharp. (See 'Choose the right resolution', page 323.) Old photographic prints often have far more detail in them than is visible with the naked eye, and you may be surprised what's revealed once they are digitised.

Choose your photos

1 Run Photoshop Elements and from the **Welcome** screen click **Edit and Enhance Photos**. Using **Open** from the **File** menu (or **Ctrl+O**), open all the photos you've managed to obtain. Start by closing any that are too fuzzy or damaged, or where people's heads are chopped off or objects overlap. To see all the remaining photos side by side, go to the **Window** menu and choose **Image**, then **Tile**.

Printing it large

A good size for your own printer is 8x10in. Digital photo printing services offer larger formats, so you may like to create your portrait at, say, 24x32in. Set **Width** and **Height** manually in the **New** dialogue box (see step 3 of this project). Don't set **Resolution** to 300 pixels/inch, or the file will be too large for most PCs to edit; 100 pixels/inch is adequate for a poster-size print, or 150 to 200 pixels/inch for intermediate sizes.

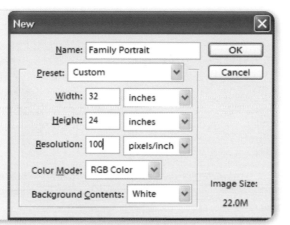

Image quality and resolution

Your photographs may come from many different sources, such as your own digital camera, images emailed from relatives, and family-album prints that have been scanned. Try to work with images at as high a resolution as you can get – 600dpi or higher will give you some leeway to enlarge parts of a photo. It's unavoidable that photos from different periods won't match in tone or colour, but if any are faded or damaged, see 'Restore an old photo', page 20.

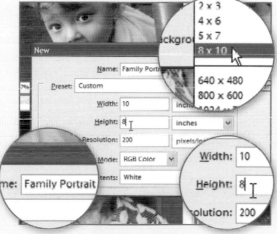

Plan your family portrait

2 Press **Z** for the **Zoom** tool. Click to select a photo, then click to zoom in, or hold **Alt** and click to zoom out. Use the scroll bars to centre on the part you're likely to use in your portrait. Do this for all the photos. Now start to think about how you'll compose your family portrait. The photo at the top right, above, is in a formal setting, and will be used as the background for the family portrait.

Create a blank canvas

3 From the **File** menu, choose **New**, then **Blank File** (or press **Ctrl+N**). In the **New** box, name the file Family Portrait. From the **Preset** menu, choose a size format (8x10in is the standard for a large photo print, and will fit on A4 paper). Depending on your background photo, you may need to swap the **Width** and **Height** settings. To make the picture wide rather than tall, set **Width** 10, **Height** 8. Click **OK**.

Place your background photo

4 Hold **Ctrl** and press **+** to enlarge the window containing your blank canvas. Press **V** for the **Move** tool, then click on your background photo and drag it onto the blank canvas. Click on the photo there and drag it to the top left. Resize it to fit (hold **Shift, to retain the photo's perspective**, and drag the bottom right corner handle). When you've finished, press **Return** to confirm.

● Straighten crooked scans

Scanned photos may be slightly askew, and with older prints that were hand cut the photo may be at a different angle from the edge of the paper. To quickly correct this in Photoshop Elements, press **P** for the **Straighten** tool. Click the **Canvas Options** menu in the **Options** bar and choose **Crop to Remove Background**, then click and drag on the photo along a line that should be horizontal.

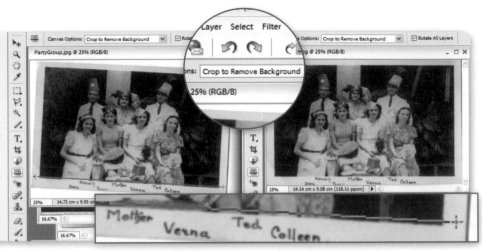

Make a rough cutout

5 Click on one of the other photographs. Press **L** for the **Lasso** tool. In the **Options** bar at the top, click the rightmost of the three icons on the left for **Polygonal Lasso**. Set **Feather** to **0** and tick **Anti-alias**. Click just outside of the part of the photo you're cutting out, then release the mouse button. Move a little way, following your planned cutout route, then click again.

Move the cutout onto the canvas

6 Continue all the way around and finish where you started. Your selection shows a flashing dotted border. Press **V** for the **Move** tool. Click within the selection and drag it onto your new canvas. Don't resize or position it yet. From the **Window** menu, choose another photo. Press **L** to switch back to the **Polygonal Lasso**, and make a cutout from that photo in the same way.

Adjust brightness and contrast

7 Photos taken in different ways and at different times can be faded, too light or too dark. Elements' **Auto Levels** feature can help. You can often improve a cutout after moving it into the canvas by pressing **Ctrl+Alt+L**. If there's no improvement after using **Auto Levels**, press **Ctrl+Z** to **Undo**. Add all your photos to the background photo in the same way, using **Auto Levels** where necessary.

○ Working with layers

Keep an eye on the **Layers** palette. To ensure you're working on the right part of an image, turn layers on and off while you work. To hide a layer, click the eye icon next to its name. To hide all layers except one, click its eye icon while holding the **Alt** key. Right-click any layer to show a menu of options. Remember actions apply to the active (highlighted) layer only, regardless of which ones are visible.

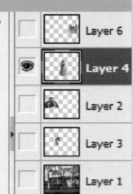

○ Wave your wand

If the background is plain, cut it out with the **Magic Wand**. Press **W** to activate it. In the **Options** bar, tick **Anti-alias** and **Contiguous** – untick **Sample All Layers** and set **Tolerance** to **16**. Click within the area that you wish to remove. If the result is a mess of flashing dots, double the **Tolerance** setting and try again. If some of the background is successfully selected, hold **Shift** and click on the next bit to add it to your selection. Finally, press **Delete** to erase the area you've selected.

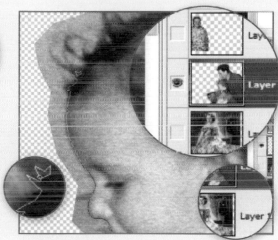

Sort out your cutouts

8 With your **Family Portrait** window active, all your cutouts are shown in the **Layers** palette (if you can't see it, choose **Layers** from the **Window** menu). Press **V** for the **Move** tool, and make sure both options are ticked at the top. To bring a cutout in front of another or send it behind, drag its name up or down in the **Layers** palette, or hold **Ctrl** and press] for up, or [for down.

Compose your family portrait

9 Arrange the photos so that the scene looks natural. Make the ones in front larger than those behind to give a realistic but possibly exaggerated sense of perspective. Resize a cutout by holding **Shift** and dragging a corner handle. When you're happy with the size, press **Return** to confirm. Don't enlarge a picture too much or resize the same cutout several times as this will degrade the image.

Make a more accurate cut

10 When you're happy with the composition, take each layer in turn and isolate it by Alt+clicking the eye icon beside its layer name. Then make a precise cutout by using the **Polygonal Lasso** more carefully. Select the **Lasso** tool as in step 5 but, in the **Options** bar, set **Feather** to **1** and tick **Anti-alias**. Draw neatly, using the same method as before but use shorter lines for accuracy.

● Tackling complex cutouts

Wispy hair is hard to cut out, even for professionals. Here's a trick that may help. Use the **Magic Wand**, as in steps 14 to 15 of this project, but first untick **Contiguous**. Now, clicking will select everything of a similar colour, everywhere in the layer. By adjusting the **Tolerance**, try to capture all or most of the background around the hair. You'll inevitably catch other parts that you don't want – with a light background, the eyes and teeth. Use the **Lasso** with **Alt** to draw roughly around these to remove them. Finish as in step 15, but set **Feather** to **3** instead of **1**. Press **Delete** two or three times to remove the 'halo' around the hair. You may also like to try Photoshop Elements' **Magic Selection Brush**, from the toolbox, or **Magic Extractor**, from the **Image** menu. They are explained on screen and work well for simple cutouts.

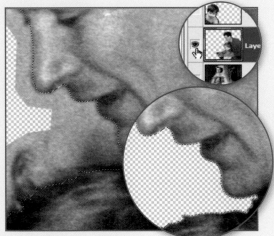

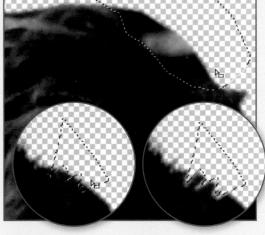

Trim off the rough edges

11 Stay right on the edge of the outline of each subject you're cutting out. Finish back where you started to complete the selection, then press **Shift+Ctrl+I** to select **Inverse** – now everything outside the area you want to keep is selected. Press the **Delete** key to erase this, then press **Ctrl+D** to deselect. In the **Layers** palette **Alt**+click the layer's eye icon to show all the layers.

Add detail to your cutout

12 Repeat the process for all of the cutouts in your picture. Each time, check the outline for any remaining bits of background that show as black or white borders. You can remove these by drawing a shape using the **Polygonal Lasso** (press **L**) that overlaps the edge of the cutout, then deleting it. Make hair more realistic by cutting out small V shapes for tufts.

Make last-minute checks

13 When you've tidied each cutout to your satisfaction, use the **Move** tool (press **V**) to make fine adjustments to sizes and positions. Check for anything that looks odd. Here, the woman at the top left is intended to be in the background, but her dress is visible in front of the baby's toy. Click her layer in the **Layers** palette, then use the **Eraser** (press **E**) to remove any dress showing in the foreground.

Soft shadows lift and separate

By adding a subtle shadow behind each cutout, you can create an impression of greater depth between the foreground and background and help the elements of your composition to stand out. In the **Layers** palette, select the layer you want to cast a shadow. In the **Styles and Effects** palette above, choose **Layer Styles** then **Drop Shadows**. Click the **Soft Edge** button. The shadow appears on the main image and, next to the layer name in the **Layers** palette, you'll see a small icon indicating that a style has been applied to that layer. Double-click the icon. In the **Style Settings** box, adjust the **Lighting Angle** and **Shadow Distance** until you get the best shadow effect.

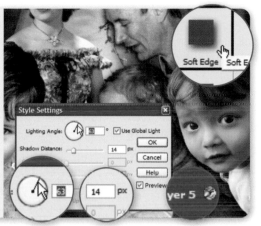

Share your family portrait

Choose **Save** from the **File** menu and save your work as a **Photoshop** (.PSD) file, so that you can edit it in the future. To email your portrait to relatives, use **Save As** from the **File** menu and choose **JPEG** format. After clicking **Save**, adjust the quality setting – lower will make a smaller file to suit slow internet connections. You can also print your portrait, or send it away to a printing service – see the boxes on page 79 for ideas.

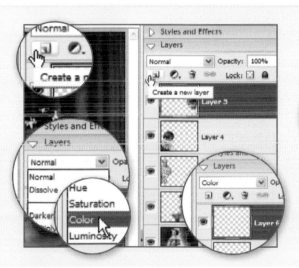

Add a hint of colour

14 All the photos here, apart from one, are from old black and white prints. That's perfectly fine, but adding subtle flesh tones helps to even out differences in image quality and brightens up the whole composition. Start by creating a new layer for the tints. Click the top layer in the **Layers** palette, then click the **Create a new layer** button. In the **Blending mode** box above, choose **Color**.

Pick a colour from nature

15 You'll apply a subtle colour wash, so there's no need to be too precise. Press **B** for the **Brush** tool. In the **Brush presets** drop-down menu at the top, choose a soft brush big enough to cover an eye in one of the foreground cutouts. Set **Opacity** to **40%**, and click the **Airbrush** option. Here a flesh colour for the faces is selected by holding **Alt** and clicking on the face in the colour photo cutout.

Paint faces and hands

16 Colour any exposed flesh. Colouring the eyes can add impact too. Click the **Foreground colour** swatch in the bottom left corner, then pick a bright, strong colour from the palette. Click **OK**. Select a brush size similar to the size of the iris or smaller, and paint over the eye. Colour clothes and other items if you like. Finally, save your composition (see 'Share your family portrait', above).

Faking it

Use some image-editing magic to send granny to the moon

By merging parts from different photos you can create scenarios that would be impossible in real life. All you need are some photos and a bit of imagination. Thanks to image-editing layers, you can adjust, resize, fade or colour each element of your composition independently, then fit them all together seamlessly. The resulting photomontage – whether it's gran on the moon or dad winning Wimbledon – makes an ideal personalised birthday card or framed photo gift. Or just do it for fun.

PROJECT TOOLS: Photoshop Elements ● Photo of an astronaut (see 'Space shots' box, page 53)
SEE ALSO: Image cutouts and photomontage, page 320 ● Make the most of layers and styles, page 314

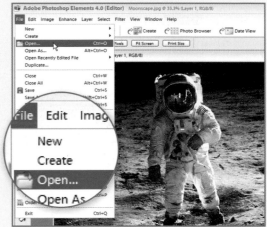

Picture quality

The quality of your finished picture will depend on the photos you use, and particularly on their resolution. For the face, avoid using a photo where the person is very small within the picture because the face won't be clear. But the two photos needn't be the same size or resolution. When downloading photos from the web, choose the highest resolution offered.

Open both photos

1 Run Photoshop Elements and click **Edit and Enhance Photos**. In the **Open** box, choose the downloaded image file of the NASA astronaut photo (see 'Space shots' opposite), then click **Open**. You also need the picture from which you're going to borrow a face. Go to **Open** on the **File** menu (or press **Ctrl+O**) to show the **Open** box again; this time choose your portrait photo and open it in the same way.

○ Space shots

NASA, the US space agency, has a public collection of photos dating from the early days of the space programme up to the present day. Most are downloadable free of charge without any copyright restrictions. Go to www.nasa.gov/multimedia/imagegallery and use the listings and search options to find what you want. The photo used in this workshop is available at http://grin.hq.nasa.gov/IMAGES/SMALL/GPN-2001-000013.jpg.

○ Perfect lighting

Choose your photos carefully when you decide to do a project like the one on these pages. When downloading your space photo, it's important to pick a shot where the astronaut's face is in darkness, so you don't need to remove it before adding your own. Make sure your victim is seen from roughly the same angle as the astronaut. If they're facing in opposite directions, flip one of them over: go to the **Image** menu and choose **Rotate**, then **Flip Horizontal**.

Arrange the images side by side

2 Like other Windows programs, Photoshop Elements lets you see several pieces of work at once in overlapping windows, or choose **Maximise** mode to see only the one you're working on. You can turn **Maximise** mode on and off in the **Images** section of the **Window** menu. Make sure it's off and arrange your windows so the portrait photo is in front with some of the space photo visible behind.

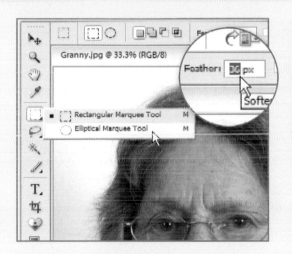

Choose a feathered selection tool

3 Click the **Marquee** icon, fifth from the top in the toolbox on the left, and hold down the mouse button to pop up a menu of alternative modes. From this, choose **Elliptical Marquee**, the oval icon. This is the tool that you'll use to cut out the face. To make the cutout fade off around the edges, increase the **Feather** setting in the **Options** bar at the top to 36.

Create your selection

4 Click at the top left of the face in the photo, hold down the mouse button and drag to draw an oval. Make it fit around the face. During this process you can shift the oval's position if needed by pressing the **Space Bar**, then resume resizing by releasing the **Space Bar**. When it's correctly sized and positioned, release the mouse button. The oval becomes a selection, shown by a flashing outline.

● Without a trace

To combine photos seamlessly, you need to match their grain as well as colours and lighting. Having transferred a face from your own photo into an archive picture, as in this project, zoom in to **200%** magnification. Do this by holding the **Ctrl** key and pressing the plus (+) key until the title bar above the image shows **200%**. Compare the copied face to the area around it and you'll probably see that your own photo has a smooth texture while the other picture is grainy. With the face layer selected in the **Layers** palette, go to **Filter, Noise, Add Noise**. In the **Add Noise** box, set **Amount** to **3%**, **Distribution** to **Gaussian**, and tick **Monochromatic**. Click **OK**. The face becomes grainy, but the grain itself is too sharp. Go to the **Filter** menu and choose **Blur, Blur**. If necessary, you can undo (press **Ctrl+Z**) and change the amount of grain.

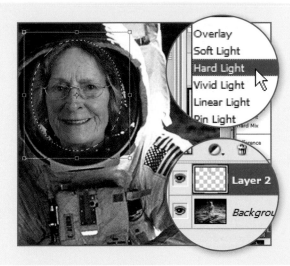

Move the face over

5 Activate the **Move** tool by clicking the first icon in the toolbox on the left. A 'bounding box' appears around your selection. If you don't see one, tick **Show Bounding Box** in the **Options** bar at the top. Click within the box, hold down the mouse button and drag over to the space photo. The face will stop at the edge of the window, but carry on and drop it onto the space photo by releasing the mouse button.

Resize the face to fit

6 The face will probably appear too big. Click any of the handles on the corners of the bounding box and drag it to make the face larger or smaller. Hold the **Shift** key down while you do this to prevent the face changing shape. To move the face around, click and drag within the bounding box. Position the face inside the helmet. Look at the arms to help you judge exactly where it should be.

Change the blending mode

7 In the **Layers** palette at the bottom right, you'll see that the face is in **Layer 2**, while the **Background** layer contains the space photo. If you don't see the **Layers** palette, open it by choosing **Layers** from the **Window** menu. Layer 2's **Blending mode**, shown at the top left, is **Normal**. Click this to pop up a menu and change it to **Hard Light**. Now the space photo partially shows through the face.

○ Shadows help trickery

Cutting out a face and putting it into a space helmet is fairly easy because you don't need the edges of the cutout to be exact – they can just fade off into the darkness. It's more complicated to cut out a face and place it on someone else's body in an everyday scene. When planning your image-editing projects be aware that anything on a plain background or in shadow is easier to fake.

○ Finishing tweaks

If you're not quite convinced by the results of your photo fakery, try a few tweaks. In the **Layers** palette, the layer containing your copied face has an **Opacity** setting as well as a **Blending** mode. Reduce **Opacity** to about **70%** to make the face recede more realistically within the space helmet. If the colour of the face doesn't look quite right, go to **Hue/Saturation**, as in step 8, and move the **Hue** slider slightly.

○ Saving layered files

When you add layers to an image, choose **Save** from the **File** menu, then you'll be invited to save in Photoshop format. Do this to create a file that you can edit later. To save a picture to send to other people or use in other programs, use **File**, **Save As**. Choose **JPEG** from the **Format** menu. This saves a copy of your work as an ordinary image file, which looks the same but lacks editable layers.

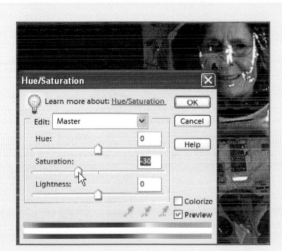

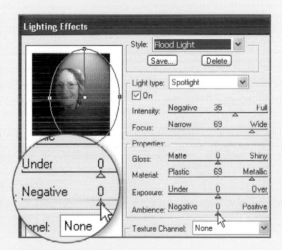

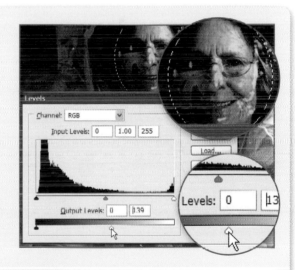

Adjust the appearance of the face

8 The face looks as if it's inside the helmet because the highlights and shadows on the glass appear in front of the face. But the face's colour is intensified, which doesn't match the rest of the photo. To correct this, go to the **Enhance** menu, choose **Adjust Color**, then **Adjust Hue/Saturation** (or press **Ctrl+U**). In the **Hue/Saturation** box, drag the **Saturation** slider to **-30**. Click **OK**.

Match the lighting

9 The face should have the same stark lighting as the suit. From the **Filter** menu, choose **Render**, then **Lighting Effects**. At the top of the **Lighting Effects** box, click the **Style** menu and choose **Flood Light**. Looking at the preview on the left, move the light if necessary by dragging the centre point of the oval. At the bottom, reduce the **Ambience** to **0**, which stops the face getting too bright. Click **OK**.

Reduce excessive highlights

10 Finally, reduce the distracting highlights on the face. These are part of the space photo, so click **Background** in the **Layers** palette to edit it. Using the **Elliptical Marquee** as in step 3, draw around the face. From the **Enhance** menu, choose **Adjust Lighting**, then **Levels** (or press **Ctrl+L**). In the **Levels** box, drag the white slider under **Output Levels** towards the left, darkening the lightest areas. Click **OK**.

Far and wide

Blend a series of snaps into a seamless panoramic landscape

A panorama is a photo with a very wide angle of view. Camera lenses typically have a field of view of around 50 degrees. Panoramic pictures can have a field of view up to 180 or even 360 degrees, so they can include the entire landscape both in front of and behind you. But you don't need a special camera or dedicated software. With the help of Photoshop Elements you can connect several images taken side by side to create a stunning panorama that you can print out and frame.

PROJECT TOOLS: Photoshop Elements ● Digital camera
SEE ALSO: How to shoot great photos, page 304 ● Erase objects from photos, page 26

● Manual exposure is best

Most point-and-shoot cameras calculate exposure (aperture and shutter speed) automatically for each shot (see 'Understanding camera controls', page 304). In a wide panorama, lighting conditions will vary depending on what part of it you're shooting, which could result in noticeable differences between shots. Photoshop Elements can compensate but, if your camera has a 'manual' mode, set identical shutter speed and apperture for all the shots, which will ensure the same exposure throughout the panorama.

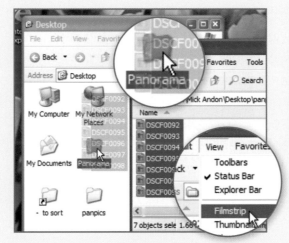

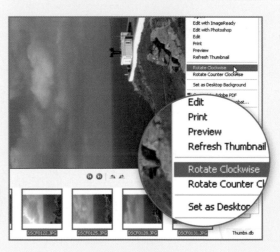

Take photos and transfer to your PC

1 Take a series of photos, overlapping each by around one-third of an image. A tripod isn't necessary, but try to keep the camera level as you turn your body smoothly through 360 degrees. Make several complete rotations to allow for errors or unwanted people or objects coming into view. Transfer the photos to your PC (see the camera's user manual for details of how to do this).

Make a folder for your images

2 In Windows Explorer, create a new folder, name it Panorama, and copy into it your panorama photos. Open the folder, and from the **View** menu select **Filmstrip**, to display your photos as thumbnails. If **Filmstrip** isn't listed, select **View, Customize This Folder**. In the properties dialogue box click the **Customise** tab, choose **Pictures** from the drop-down menu and click **OK**. Then **View, Filmstrip**.

Turn photos the right way up

3 If you took any photos in portrait (with the camera on its side), they will need to be rotated. Click on the first portrait thumbnail, scroll to the right and **Ctrl**-click any others. Right-click the final portrait thumbnail and select **Rotate Clockwise** or **Rotate Counter Clockwise**, depending on which way they need to go. Windows will take a short while to rotate them.

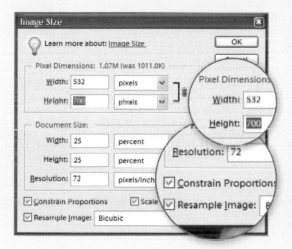

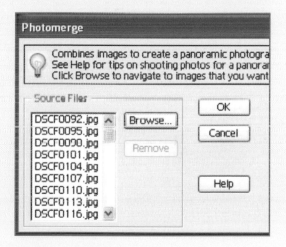

Resize the first photo

4 Run Photoshop Elements. From the **Welcome** screen choose **Edit and Enhance Photos**. In the File menu, choose **Open**. Navigate to and select the first image and click **Open**. In the **Image** menu select **Resize, Image Size**. Make sure the **Resample Image** and **Constrain Proportions** boxes are ticked and, in the **Height** box, type a value of **700 pixels**. The width will adjust accordingly. Click **OK** and save the picture.

Resize the rest

5 In the same way, resize the remaining pictures. Assuming you have six pictures to stitch and that they all overlap by about a third you'll end up with an image that is around 2000x700 pixels. You could make a top-quality 200dpi inkjet print of this measuring 10x3.5in on an A4 sheet of paper (see 'Size matters', page 311). If you have fewer images you can work at a higher resolution.

Start stitching

6 From the **File** menu, select **New, Photomerge Panorama**. The pictures you resized in steps 4 and 5 appear in the **Source Files** list – if there's anything in this list that shouldn't be there, click to highlight it and press the **Remove** button. When you're satisfied with the list click **OK**. Elements will now combine the images and merge them automatically into a panoramic photograph.

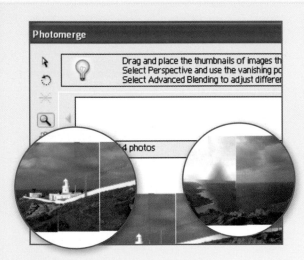

Viewing the merged photos

7 The Photomerge window displays the automatically merged photos, overlaying them as accurately as it can. If any of the photos have been placed badly, you can adjust them manually later. Any images that Photomerge was unable to automatically include in the panorama will be displayed as thumbnails in the **Lightbox** area at the top of the screen.

Check the composition order

8 To add any omitted images to your composition, drag and drop them from the **Lightbox** area at the top into the work area below. You can also drag a photo from the work area back to the **Lightbox**, and substitute with another similar photo to see if it blends better. Use the **Navigator** to the right of the Photomerge window to zoom in and out or pan around the work area.

Stitching by hand

9 To stitch two images together, drag one over the other and look for matching detail in the overlapping area. Photomerge makes the picture you are dragging semi-transparent, so you can see the corresponding detail in the underlying image. Tick the **Snap to Image** box on the right. You don't need to get the positioning exact – if it's in roughly the right position, Photomerge will find the best fit.

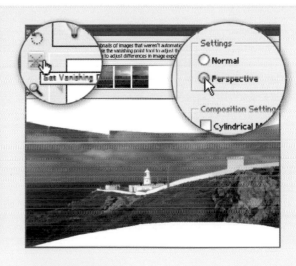

Correct the angle

10 If you didn't manage to keep the camera level when you were shooting some of the photos, and you can't get the detail to match at both the top and bottom of an image, select the **Rotate** tool from the toolbox at the top left. The mouse pointer changes to a two-headed arrow. Position it on the edge of the picture and drag to rotate it in the appropriate direction, then click **OK**.

Match up all the joins

11 Work your way from the centre to each end of the panorama, stitching images as you go until you're satisfied everything is in the right place and you've got the best possible match between adjacent images. Sometimes the software will snap an image into place slightly out of register with its neighbour. If this happens, untick the **Snap to Image** box and position the image manually.

Add perspective

12 To distort the panorama to give a more natural-looking perspective, click the **Perspective** button under **Settings**. The software calculates and applies the perspective distortion. The vanishing point is calculated from the central image in the panorama – to set an alternative vanishing point click elsewhere in the panorama using the **Set Vanishing Point** tool from the toolbox, top left.

● Correcting perspective

The **Perspective** feature (see step 12) is best used on panoramas with a field of view of less than 120 degrees. On wider panoramas the program will display a message saying **Photomerge Was Not Able To Correct The Perspective For All Of The Images**. If this happens, press **Ctrl+Z** to undo, remove an image from either end of the panorama by dragging it to the **Lightbox** and try again. Keep taking images away until **Photomerge** successfully manages to distort the panorama perspective.

Even out exposure variation

13 Brightness differences between adjacent images can be reduced using **Advanced Blending**. In **Composition Settings**, on the right, tick the **Advanced Blending** box then click **Preview**, to view the result. When finished, click **Exit Preview** to go back to the Photomerge dialogue box. Don't press the **Cancel** button or you will return to Photoshop Elements, losing your panorama.

Reduce extreme distortion

14 Applying perspective gives the panorama a bow-tie shape – narrow in the middle and wider at the edges, making the image difficult to crop later. To reduce this effect, tick the **Cylindrical Mapping** box on the right, then preview the image again. **Cylindrical Mapping** can also distort your image – here the sea runs uphill at the left edge. Tick the **Normal** button to turn **Perspective** off.

Apply the changes

15 Make a final check to ensure everything looks how you want it and click the **OK** button, top right. Elements now applies your Photomerge settings to the images and creates a new panorama image file. The photos that you used to create the panorama remain unaffected, so you can go back later and use them to create more panoramas with different settings.

PHOTO SMART

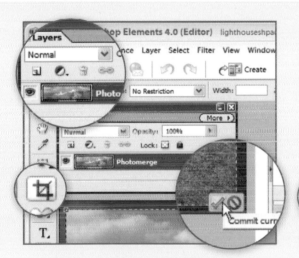

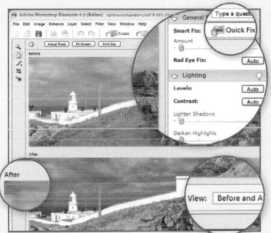

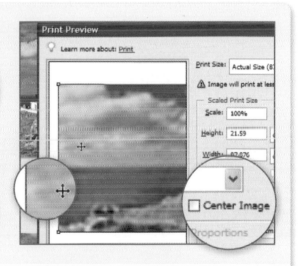

Save and crop the panorama

16 Elements creates your new panorama in a single layer called **Photomerge**. Select **Save** from the **File** menu and save the picture as a Photoshop (.PSD) file. Then select the **Crop** tool from the toolbox on the left. Click and drag across the panorama to create a rectangle outside of which the ragged edges are trimmed off. Click the tick icon, bottom right, to confirm the crop.

Make final adjustments

17 Click the **Quick Fix** button at the top right. In the **View** box, choose **Before and After** (Landscape). In the panel, right, make adjustments by clicking the **Auto** buttons under **Lighting**, **Color** and **Sharpen**, or by moving the individual sliders. See how the adjustments affect your image in the lower, After, panel. (See also 'All about colour and resolution', page 310.) Press **Ctrl+S** to save the adjusted image.

Print your panorama in sections

18 From the **File** menu, choose **Print**. In the **Print Preview** box, untick **Center Image**. Click and drag the preview so that the left end of the panorama is in view. Click **Print** (ignore the warning that clipping will occur). Repeat the process, dragging the next section of panorama into view, then print that section. Repeat for all the parts, then join the prints to form the complete panorama.

All around the world

Create a lasting visual record of your holiday travels

If you've been on the holiday of a lifetime, it's fun to illustrate your trip with a pictorial map poster. Showing the route of your epic journey together with the stunning photos you snapped along the way will show everyone where you've travelled and what you did while you were there. This project shows you how to find the map, add the route and superimpose your photos to produce a spectacular poster to put on your wall.

PROJECT TOOLS: Photoshop Elements ● Holiday photos
SEE ALSO: Produce a poster, page 84

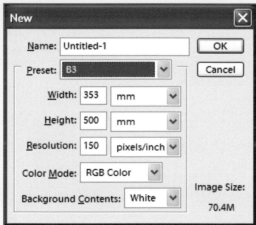

Copyright on maps

Most maps, including those printed in atlases and ones that you find on the web, are covered by copyright, which means it is illegal to reproduce them without the permission of the copyright owner. Even if you have bought a map, you're not entitled to scan it in and print it out. The copyright owner may agree to you copying the map for personal use, but there could be a fee. Otherwise, use maps that are in the public domain (see the box 'Where to get maps', right).

Size your poster

1 Launch Photoshop Elements and click the **Start From Scratch** button on the **Welcome** screen. In the **New** dialogue box, select the **B3** preset. It's a good size for a poster and can be printed across four tiled sheets of A4 paper, which are then glued together at the edges. Set **Background Contents** to White, reduce the resolution to **150 pixels/inch** and click OK.

● Where to get maps

The map of the USA used in this project is available free from the University of Texas Libraries website at www.lib.utexas.edu/maps. The site also has maps of other parts of the world, mostly as JPEG or PDF files that are easily opened in Photoshop Elements and other image-editing programs. Another source for free US maps is www.nationalatlas.gov. World maps can be found at http://cia.gov/cia/publications/factbook/docs/refmaps.html. For UK maps, visit the Ordnance Survey's Get-a-map website, at www.ordnancesurvey.co.uk/oswebsite/getamap.

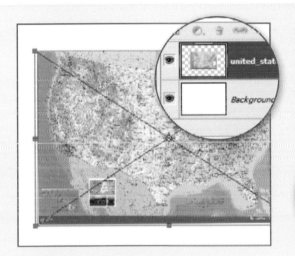

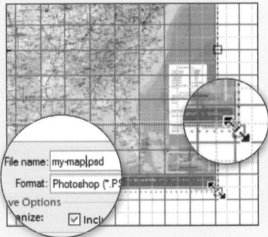

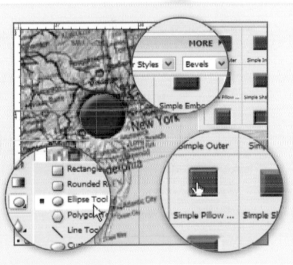

Find and place the map

2 The poster will be landscape format, so select **Rotate** from the **Image** menu, then choose either **90° Left** or **90° Right** from the sub-menu. Download a map to use (see 'Where to get maps', above). Now select **Place** from the **File** menu to add the map background. In the **Place** dialogue box, locate the downloaded map file and click the **Place** button. In the **Place PDF** dialogue box click **OK**.

Size the map

3 You may have to resize the map to fill the page. Holding down the **Shift** key, drag a corner handle to resize the map proportionally until it fills the central area, leaving a wide border all around, then press **Return** to apply the new size. Turn on the rulers and grid from the **View** menu and use them to centre the map. In the **File** menu, choose **Save**, then save your work as a Photoshop .PSD file.

Mark the spot

4 Create location markers to make the places you've visited stand out on the map. Select the **Ellipse** tool from the toolbar on the left, choose a colour from the **Tool Options** bar and click and drag, holding down the **Shift** key to draw a circle at your first travel destination. To give the marker a 3D appearance, in the **Styles and Effects** drop-down menu select **Bevels**, then **Simple Pillow Emboss**.

● Historic journeys

For smaller-scale expeditions – a country walk, for example – consider using historical maps. Those at www.old-maps.co.uk are a hundred years old or more and, unlike modern maps, you are allowed to use them for non-commercial purposes – to publicise your outing or to record the trip. As well as adding character to your project, old maps offer an insight into how the towns and countryside have changed. Type in a place name, address or map co-ordinates, then click the **Search** button to display a map of the area you're interested in. Click **Enlarged View** for a full-screen map. To save the map, right-click on it and select **Save image** from the pop-up menu.

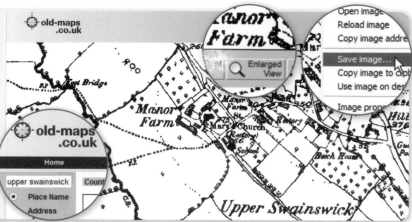

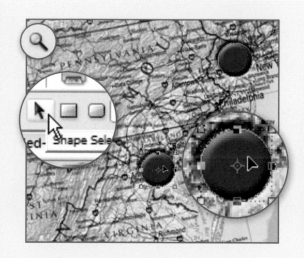

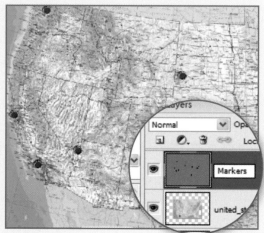

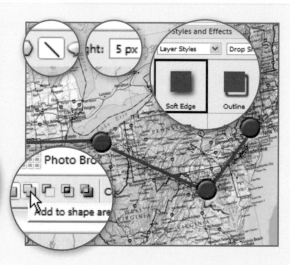

Copying the marker

5 Using the **Zoom** tool, zoom out to see the marker you just made and the next destination on your itinerary. Re-select the **Ellipse** tool, then choose the **Shape Selection** tool (arrow) from the **Tool Options** bar. Hold down the **Alt** key to drag and drop the marker from its original position to the new destination. Pressing the **Alt** key automatically copies the marker, to avoid cutting and pasting it.

Mark all the stops

6 Continue Alt+dragging to create new markers positioned on all your itinerary stops. Using the **Shape Selection** tool to Alt+drag the markers keeps them all on one shape layer. If you used the **Move** tool, a new shape layer would be created for each marker, which would be complicated and unwieldy. Double-click on the name **Shape 1** in the **Layers** palette and rename it Markers.

Join the journey dots

7 Select the **Line** tool on the **Tool Options** bar. Set **Weight** to **5px** (pixels). Click and drag to draw a line between your first two markers. In the **Styles and Effects** palette, select **Layer styles**, **Drop Shadows**, then **Soft Edge**. In the **Tool Options** bar, click the **Add to shape area** button and connect all the markers. Rename the layer Lines and drag it below the **Markers** layer in the **Layers** palette.

Mapping the route

Budget-priced route-planning programs, such as Autoroute, www.microsoft.com/uk/homepc/autoroute, include printable street-level maps for much of Europe and the USA. As well as helping plan your trip, Autoroute's 'map' view displays the route over a map just like the route markers in this project; while a 'list' view lists towns and cities, roads, directions and distances along the way – a useful accompaniment to your pictorial holiday map.

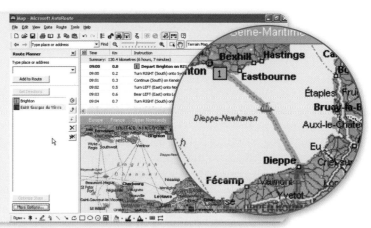

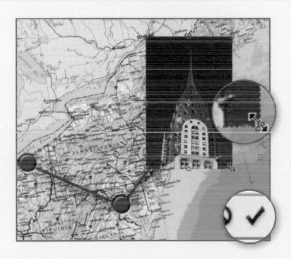

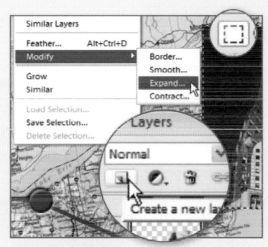

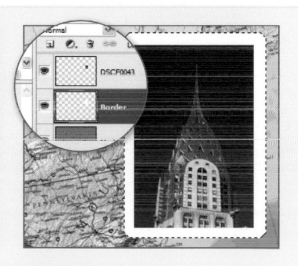

Place your pictures

8 Now it's time to start adding your photos. Select **Place** from the **File** menu, locate the first of your photos in the **Place** dialogue box and click the **Place** button to add it on a new layer. You will probably need to resize each photo you place. Hold down the **Shift** key while dragging a corner handle to maintain its original proportions. Press **Return** or click on the **Tick** button to confirm.

Create a border

9 To add a white border to the picture, select the **Rectangular Marquee** tool and set **Mode** to **Normal**. Click and drag around the photo to make a rectangular selection. In the **Select** menu, choose **Modify**, **Expand**, then enter a value of **15** (pixels) and click **OK**. Next, to create a new layer for the border, click the **New Layer** button in the **Layers** palette. Rename the layer Border and press **Return**.

Finish off the border

10 Fill the selection with white by first pressing **D** (to set the default foreground and background colours of black and white), then press **Ctrl+Delete** to fill the selection with the background colour. Don't worry if your photo looks as if it's been replaced with a white rectangle; the photo is simply underneath it. Drag the border layer below the photo layer in the **Layers** palette.

● World maps and satellite images

Google Earth is a free program that displays maps and high-resolution aerial and satellite photos of just about any place on Earth. You'll need a broadband connection, as images are 'streamed' to the program in real time over the internet. Map layers you can switch on or off include roads, geographical features, tourist information and even city skylines.

   Because Google Earth is 3D and animated, moving from place to place on the planet surface is like taking a personal plane trip. You can experience spectacular aerial flythroughs of the world's wonders or even zoom over your home town or city. Some locations – for example, the Grand Canyon and the Himalayas – include 3D views with accurate perspective. Google Earth can be downloaded from http://earth.google.com.

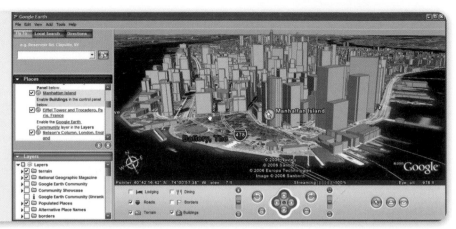

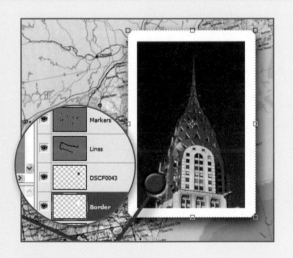

Add a drop shadow

11 Press **Ctrl+D** to turn off the selection. To add a drop shadow to the border, select the border layer, then from the **Styles and Effects** palette choose **Drop Shadows** then **Soft Edge**. This makes the photo look as if it's raised up off the surface of the map. To position the route marker and line layers above the photos drag them both to the top of the **Layers** stack.

Think of a caption

12 To add a photo caption, select the **Horizontal Type** tool (or press **T**) and drag to create a text box, then type the location. Chose a clean sans serif typeface such as **Kabel** that will be legible over the map detail and position it under the photo. **Shift**+click to select the photo, border and type layers in the **Layers** palette and choose **Link Layers** from the **Layers** palette menu.

Give it a tilt

13 Now you can resize, rotate, reposition or transform the photo, border and caption layers as if they were one layer. For an informal look, rotate the photo at a slight angle. Select the photo with the **Move** tool and position the mouse pointer just outside a corner handle – it changes to a curved double-headed arrow. Click and drag to rotate the photo by a few degrees, then click the tick button.

Scan your souvenirs

When you get home, don't throw away all the bits and pieces that have accumulated during your trip. Train or bus tickets, airline boarding passes, hotel bills, passport stamps, museum tickets or even local currency can all be scanned in using a flatbed scanner and added to your map. See also 'Get creative with your scanner', page 322.

Printing issues

It's unlikely your printer is big enough to produce the whole poster in this project on a single sheet, so you'll need to print it out in sections and stick them together (see 'Printing a multi-sheet poster' page 88). Alternatively, take your file on a CD to a copy shop or print specialist, who will print it for you, poster-size, and may offer additional services such as laminating or printing on canvas. See 'Sending out for print', page 79.

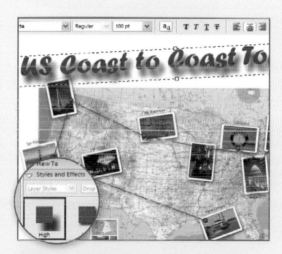

Copying a photo

14 Still using the **Move** tool, Alt+drag the photo/border/caption group to copy it to all of the other locations. Then, for each copied group, right-click its photo layer in the **Layers** palette and choose **Delete Layer** from the pop-up menu. Place a new photo (as in step 8), resizing and rotating to fit the frame (as steps 8 and 14). Click the caption layer in the **Layers** palette and type the new location.

Add a main title

15 Use the **Type** tool to create a large text box above the map. The text will need to be quite big – around **100pt** – to make an impact. Use the same colour as the route line or a strong bright colour from the map for the title text. For even greater impact, rotate the text using the **Move** tool and add a drop shadow style from the **Styles and Effects** palette (see step 11).

Organise your photos

16 To avoid your map becoming cluttered, use only one photo per destination, adding a selection of other photos in the border area. Place, resize and position them as you did previously, adding a drop shadow if you want. Finally, to add a background colour, select **Background** in the **Layers** palette, **Fill Layer** from the **Edit** menu. In the **Color Picker** dialogue box select a colour. Click **OK**.

Bits and pieces

Create a virtual jigsaw puzzle from a favourite photo

Using Photoshop Elements and some free software you can chop up a favourite photo, then transform it with a few mouse clicks into an on-screen jigsaw puzzle – the more pieces you make, the harder the puzzle will be. Drag the jigsaw pieces into place using your mouse to solve the puzzle. The finished files are small enough to send by email so that friends and family can share in your jigsaw-puzzle creations.

PROJECT TOOLS: Photoshop Elements ● Kisekae Set System (KiSS – see box, page 69)

> ● **Choosing your pictures**
>
> Images with lots of different shapes and textures work best. Avoid large areas of similar texture, which can make it hard to see where pieces belong. Strong and varied colours help if you are making a jigsaw puzzle for children to solve. And you don't have to stick to photos – children's paintings and drawings, and scanned-in works of art can make colourful and challenging puzzles.

Start with a photo

1 Run Photoshop Elements. From the **Welcome** screen choose **Edit and Enhance Photos**. In the **File** menu choose **Open**, browse to your image file and click **Open**. Press **C** for the **Crop** tool. In the **Options** bar at the top, set **Width** to **700px** (pixels), **Height 700px** and **Resolution 72 pixels/inch**. This will make a square jigsaw puzzle that's a manageable size on any screen, but you can try different **Width** and **Height** settings.

○ Downloading the free software

Kisekae Set System (KiSS) projects are interactive versions of a traditional Japanese children's game. You'll need two programs, a viewer and a converter. In your web browser, go to www.otakuworld.com/kiss. Click on **KiSS Viewers**, then **PC Windows**. Scroll down and click the icon labelled **Self-Installing**. In the dialogue box, click **Save**. Choose where to save the installer, such as **My Documents**, click **Save** and then click **Close**. Download then double-click the **DirectKiSS Installer** file, click **Run** and follow the steps.

For a converter, go to www.otakuworlkd.com/kiss and click **KiSS-Making Tools**. Scroll down and click **Tail's TLCK Utilities**. In the list of files, click the link under **tlckv.exe** to download a Zip file. In the **File download** dialogue box, click **Save** and choose where to save the file. Open this folder in **My Computer** and right-click the **TLCK** Zip file. Choose **Extract All**, and follow the instructions to unpack the program files into the same folder.

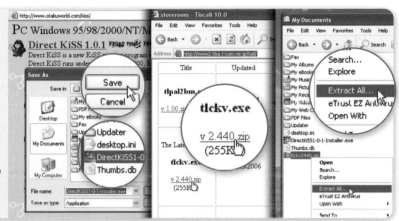

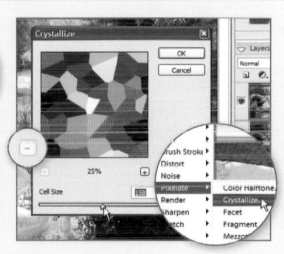

Crop and resize the photo

2 Click near the top left of your photo and drag to draw a crop box. Adjust this so it contains the part of the picture you wish to use for your jigsaw. Because you've preset the size you want, you can't change the shape of the box, but you can reposition it and make it larger or smaller. When you're happy with it, double-click to crop the photo. It will get smaller; hold **Ctrl** and press + to zoom back in.

Copy the photo onto a new layer

3 In the **Layers** palette (choose **Layers** from the **Window** menu if you can't see it), your image has a single layer called **Background**. Right-click its name and choose **Duplicate Layer**. Click **OK**. This identical layer is called **Background copy** and is highlighted to show it's the layer you're editing. Press Ctrl+U for the **Hue/Saturation settings**, then move the **Saturation** slider all the way to the right. Click **OK**.

Generate the pieces

4 In the **Filter** menu choose **Pixelate**, then **Crystallize**. Click the minus button to zoom out until the whole canvas is shown in the preview. The photo is divided into irregularly shaped segments. Adjust the **Cell Size** to change the number of pieces – the larger the cell size, the fewer the pieces. Click **OK**. The shapes are generated randomly, so you won't get exactly the pattern you saw in the preview.

● Solving blurry edges

The **Crystallize** filter (see step 4) normally creates hard edges, but occasionally an edge will come out blurred. The blurred area won't get selected by the **Magic Wand**, and your jigsaw will have a missing sliver. If you spot a blurred edge that the **Magic Wand** has missed, draw around the affected area of the segments using the **Polygonal Lasso** tool (see page 29, steps 9 and 10) while holding down **Shift** to add to the existing selection.

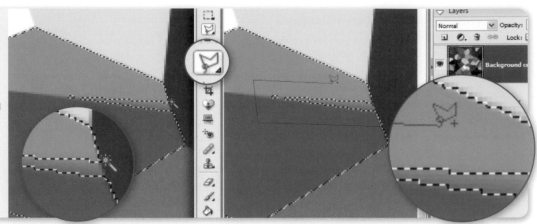

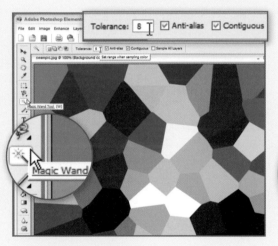

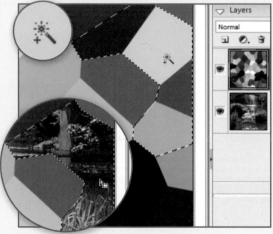

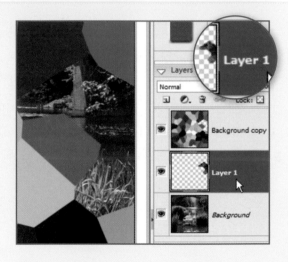

Check your results

5 Sometimes all the segments will come out roughly the same size, other times you'll get some huge and others tiny. If you want to try again, press **Ctrl+Z** to undo, then **Ctrl+F** to repeat the **Crystallize** filter, giving a new random result. Press **W** for the **Magic Wand** tool. In the **Options** bar, set **Tolerance** to 8, tick **Anti-alias** and **Contiguous**, and untick **Sample All Layers**.

Select the first jigsaw piece

6 Click within any one of the coloured segments to select it, shown by a flashing dotted border. Then hold down **Shift** and click an adjacent segment – it's added to the selection. Add three or four segments in this way to make up the shape of your jigsaw piece. Press **Delete** to erase the shape. Then, in the **Layers** palette, click on the **Background** layer, which contains the original photo. This layer is now highlighted.

Create a jigsaw piece

7 Although you're looking at the top layer, containing your segments, you're working on the bottom layer, containing the photo. Press **Ctrl+J** to make a new layer from the selection. This duplicates the part of the photo that's within the segment you selected (now showing through where you erased the shape in the layer above). You now have a new layer containing only this piece of the photo.

Jigsaw-making online

For traditional jigsaw pieces, several websites can help. At www.jigzone.com you can turn a picture into an on-screen puzzle. Click **Sign In** to register (free of charge) to upload your own pictures. At www.jigsawpuzzleplayer.com you can make similar puzzles with a selection of images, or pay for a downloadable program to create your own; while Jigsaw Maker, www.greyolltwit.com, is downloadable for a small membership fee.

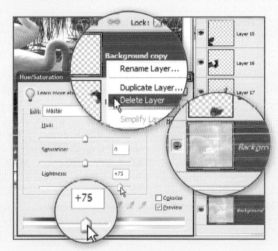

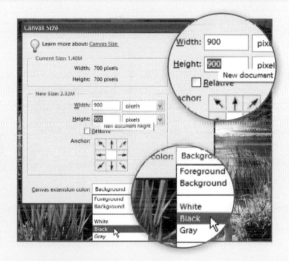

Add the rest of the pieces

8 Repeat the process in steps 6 and 7 to make all the other pieces. Here's a quick recap. In the **Layers** palette, click the layer containing the segments. Hold down **Shift** and click on several adjacent segments with the **Magic Wand**. Press **Delete**. In the **Layers** palette, click on the **Background** layer. Press **Ctrl+J**. You will end up with a layer for each piece, all listed in the **Layers** palette.

Fade out the original image

9 Right-click on the layer that contained the segments, at the top of the **Layers** palette, and choose **Delete Layer**. Click **OK**. Click the **Background** layer. Press **Ctrl+U** and, in the **Hue/Saturation** settings, tick **Colorize**. Increase **Lightness** to around +70 and click **OK**. The final step is to add space around the jigsaw for unplaced pieces. Go to the **Image** menu and choose **Resize**, then **Canvas Size**.

Finish and save

10 Set the units for **Width** and **Height** to pixels, and add **200** to each, so **700x700** becomes 900x900. Choose a background colour from the menu at the bottom; black looks good. Click **OK**. From the **File** menu, choose **Save As**. Choose a folder for the jigsaw, such as **My Pictures** (inside **My Documents**). Enter a new file name and leave **Format** set to **Photoshop (*.PSD)**. Click **Save**.

◯ Send a secret message

If you want to add another layer of interest and fun to your jigsaw, use it to send a hidden message. In Photoshop Elements, either start with a cropped photo (see step 1 of this project) or use **Start From Scratch** and choose **640x480** from the **Preset** menu. Using the **Text tool** (see page 182, steps 4 and 5), add your message. Choose **Flatten Image** from the **Layer** menu, then continue from step 3. The recipient will have to complete the puzzle to read the message.

Roses are red, Violets are blue, At www.janeswebsite.com There's something for you!

◯ Sharing your jigsaw

Once you've saved your jigsaw as an .LZH file (see step 16 of this project), you can email it to others to try out. You don't need to send the .CNF or .CEL files – just the single .LZH file. The recipients will need a KiSS viewer, so pass on the instructions for downloading Direct KiSS. Note that you can't double-click the .LZH file to load it: run Direct KiSS first, then press **Ctrl+O** (**Open**) and choose the .LZH file in the program's file browser.

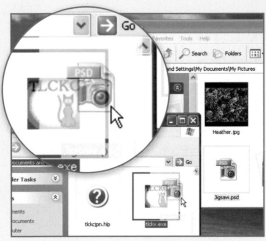

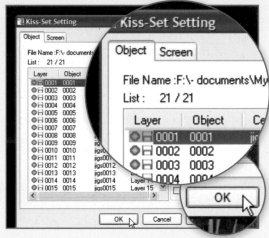

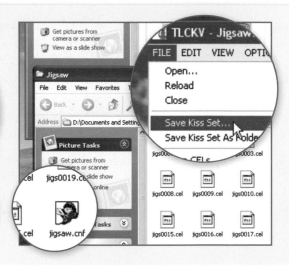

Open the conversion program

11 Right-click the **Windows Taskbar**. Choose **Show the Desktop**. Double-click **My Computer** and browse to the folder where you saved your jigsaw .PSD file. Double-click **My Computer** again, and browse to where you unzipped the **TLCK** Zip file (see 'Downloading the free software', page 69). In the **TLCK** folder, look for the program file with the **TLCK** icon. Drag your .PSD file onto the **TLCK** program icon.

See your finished picture

12 If a security warning appears, click **Run**. Your jigsaw opens in **TLCK**. You'll see the finished picture, made up of all the pieces you created. The **Kiss-Set Setting** window lists all the layers, which will now be converted into KiSS 'cels'. You needn't do anything here except click **OK**. The **Screen** tab can be used to change the size of the image, but you'll want to keep this as it is.

Save the puzzle set

13 In the **File** menu, choose **Save Kiss Set** or press **Ctrl+S**. The conversion is completed automatically. Next, in the **Windows Taskbar**, switch back to the folder containing your jigsaw .PSD file. There's now a new folder with the same name. Open it and you'll see all your jigsaw pieces stored as .CEL files. There's also a .CNF file that contains information about how the pieces fit together.

● Printed jigsaw puzzles

It's easy to create a jigsaw puzzle that you can assemble on your coffee table instead of your PC screen. Start from step 1 of this project but crop to full-page size: set **Width** and **Height** to **27cm x 18cm** for A4 paper, and set **Resolution** to **300 pixels/inch**. After step 8, go to the **Layers** palette and select all the layers containing your pieces: click the last, then hold **Shift** and click the first (scroll up the list). In the **Styles and Effects** palette, choose **Layer Styles** in the first menu and **Bevels** in the second. Choose the **Simple Pillow** style to give your pieces an outline. Use **Print** from the **File** menu to print your jigsaw, then cut out the pieces.

Alternatively, get someone else to do the hard work. Send your photo to an online service such as www.arty-zan.co.uk, www.custompuzzlecraft.com or www.jigsaw2order.com, and they'll manufacture a jigsaw puzzle with however many pieces you choose.

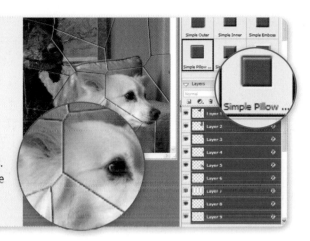

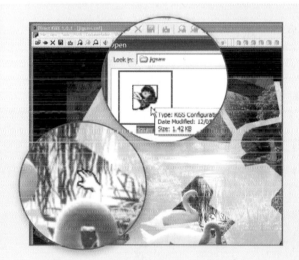

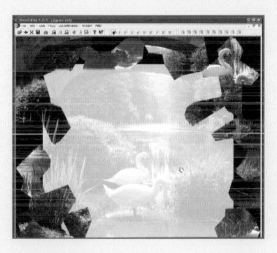

Open the viewer program

14 Run the viewer program you downloaded: click the Windows **Start** button and, from the menu, choose **All Programs**, **Direct KiSS**, then **Direct KiSS**. When the program opens, click **OK** to cancel the **Tip of the Day**, then choose **Open** from the **File** menu. Browse to the .CNF file inside your jigsaw folder. Double-click it to open – your jigsaw appears. Click on it and you'll find you can move the pieces around.

Rearrange the pieces

15 Of course, the jigsaw won't be a challenge if all the pieces start off in the right place. Drag them onto the borders and ensure they're thoroughly mixed up, with each piece well away from its correct position. The only clue to the solution is the faded image on the background. This is the one thing that can't be moved, simply because it fills the whole canvas.

Save your puzzle

16 From the **Edit** menu, choose **Build LZH Archive**. Click **Yes** to save your .CNF file. Enter a new file name, such as JigsawToDo.cnf. Tick **Save current positions**. Click **Save**. In the **Additional Files** box, click **OK**. Again, enter a new file name, such as JigsawToDo (.LZH will be added to the end). Click **Save**. The resulting file, **JigsawToDo.lzh**, contains your jigsaw with all the pieces arranged as you left them.

Paint yourself a masterpiece
Learn how to transform a photo into a work of art

Photography is an art in itself, but there's something attractive and intriguing about a painting that's missing from the average family snap. With the help of your PC and image-editing software, you can turn one into the other in minutes. You can start with a photo from your digital camera, or digitise an existing print using a flatbed scanner (see pages 322 to 323 for more on scanning). This project presents an effective method of turning any photo into a painting, which you can then print out and frame as a gift. As with real painting, correct preparation is vital. You'll find out how to prepare your digital canvas and choose the brushes that will give the most convincing results. And just as an artist in oils would apply a final glaze, you'll use some filter effects to put the finishing touches to your work.

PROJECT TOOLS: Adobe Photoshop Elements ● Digital or scanned photo ● Frame
SEE ALSO: Make your own greetings cards, page 104 ● Restore an old photo, page 20

○ Too dark? Too light?

Some effects work best on light images, others on dark ones, and the general tone of your original picture will dictate the results. If an effect comes out looking wrong no matter what settings you make, you may need to adjust the picture's tonal qualities before you apply that effect. An easy method that often works wonders is to use the **Equalize** command, which is under **Adjustments** on the **Image** menu in Elements. This automatically evens out the progression from dark to light within the image.

Choose your photo

1 Because you're going to manipulate the photo quite heavily, qualities such as lighting and focus don't have to be perfect. Find a good pose, and make sure the faces are clearly shown. Run Photoshop Elements and click the option to **Edit and Enhance Photos**. When the program's main screen appears, choose **Open** from the **File** menu or press **Ctrl+O**, and select the image you want to use.

Set a size suitable for printing

2 You should create your painting at the size you want to print it. Press **C** for the **Crop** tool, or click its icon in the toolbox. In the **Options** bar at the top, enter the **Width** and **Height** you want, followed by in (for inches) or cm. Set the **Resolution** units to **pixels/inch** and enter **300**. You could drop this to 200 to keep file size reasonable, or 100 for large posters (see page 311 for more on resolution).

Crop and scale the image

3 Click at the top left of your photo and drag to draw a crop box. The shape of the box will always match the width to height ratio that you've specified, but you can adjust the overall size to include the portion of the photo you want to base your painting on. When you're happy with the area within the crop box, double-click it or click the tick icon. The photo is cropped and resized.

● Still-life photos make ideal paintings

When working from a photo, a still life of an artistic arrangement of objects presents a similar challenge to a portrait, balancing a painterly look against the preservation of detail. Lighting is all important, so make it dramatic when you take your photo. For an Old Master look, with muted colours, try the **Watercolor** filter, from **Artistic** on the **Filter** menu. Set all the sliders high. Then tint everything brown using the **Sepia** option in **Filter**, **Adjustments**, **Photo Filter**.

Duplicate your photo

4 After you start painting over your photograph, there'll be no easy way to change an area if the picture becomes unrecognisable. So keep an unaltered copy of the photo in a separate layer behind your artwork. In the **Layers** palette in the **Palette Bin** on the right (choose **Layers** from the **Window** menu if it isn't already visible) you'll see that your image has a single layer called **Background**.

Arrange your layers

5 Right-click this layer name and choose **Duplicate Layer** from the menu that appears. In the dialogue box, name the new layer Painting and click **OK**. The **Painting** layer is now listed above the **Background**, and it's this layer that you'll be working on in the main document window. You won't see any change because it's identical. That's all you need do for now; you'll see the benefit later.

Zoom in

6 Before starting to paint, zoom in to a key area of the picture, such as the face. In Elements, you can press **Z**, or click the magnifying glass icon in the toolbox, to activate the **Zoom** tool. Then click anywhere within the canvas to zoom in, or hold **Alt** while clicking to zoom out. Alternatively, hold **Ctrl** and press the **plus** or **minus** key: this resizes the window while zooming. Aim to work at **50%** or **100%**.

Make an impression with landscapes

A good landscape photo lets you take more risks with paint effects because you only need a general impression of the scene. The detail can be compromised without making the picture unrecognisable. For example, try the **Pointillize** filter, found under **Pixelate** on the **Filter** menu. This mimics the pointillist technique developed by the French Post-Impressionist painter Georges Seurat, breaking up the image into loosely placed dots. Use the largest dot or cell size you can.

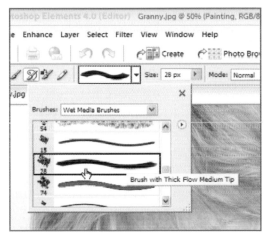

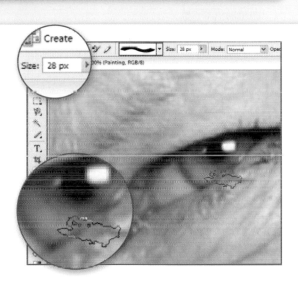

Select the Impressionist Brush

7 The Impressionist Brush interacts with the colours in your photo. Click and hold the Brush icon in the toolbox and choose **Impressionist** from the pop-out options. Or, press **B** repeatedly until the **Impressionist** icon (spiral) is highlighted in the **Options** bar. Here you can choose the brush style and size, as well as blending mode and opacity, which govern its effect on the image (see page 314).

Choose a brush tip

8 Click the arrow next to the brush sample in the **Options** bar to pop up a menu of brush tips. (You can hover the pointer over a brush tip to pop up its name.) Use the drop-down list at the top of this to switch from **Default Brushes** to the various sets available. For paint effects, try **Wet Media Brushes**. From about two-thirds of the way down this list, pick **Brush with Thick Flow Medium Tip**.

Adjust the brush size

9 This is a hard-edged brush, which is good for oil painting with distinct brushstrokes. Softer, more blurry tips suit watercolour effects. When you choose a brush tip, the mouse pointer shows its outline, giving you an idea of size. Check this on your photo: it should be roughly as wide as the smallest feature you need to paint, such as the pupil of an eye. Adjust the brush **Size** setting if necessary.

○ **Digital art materials**

Programs that mimic real art materials are known as natural media software. Two examples are Corel Painter IX, www.corel.com/painter, a professional-standard application that offers realistic tools, including wet painting, and a more basic version called Painter Essentials. If you prefer instant results, try Photo ArtMaster, by visiting www.gsp.cc. Digital painting is even easier with a graphics tablet, available in various sizes, which gives you a pen rather than a mouse (see page 319).

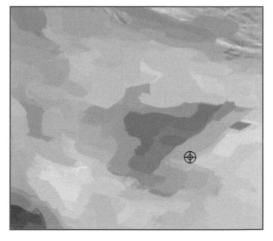

Set more options

10 The brush is also controlled by the **More Options** menu, the last button in the **Options** bar. **Style** governs the way brush strokes are applied, from **Short** to **Long** and from **Tight** (staying close to your cursor) to **Loose** (spreading out). Try **Loose Medium** first. The **Area** setting can be increased if you want to paint more strokes at once. Leave **Tolerance** at zero.

Start painting

11 Click on the face and hold down the mouse button while you drag to paint. The **Impressionist Brush** picks up colour from the photo and paints with it. Notice how the area around the cursor continues to change rapidly as you hold the button down. Begin with brief dabs, moving a short distance before releasing the button to stop. When you're confident, continue over larger areas.

Assess your work

12 If the face still looks too detailed, undo by pressing **Ctrl+Z** and try a larger brush **Size**. If it's unrecognisable, try smaller. Don't try to preserve details such as the eyes, as the overall effect will be too subtle. Instead, paint boldly then restore details using your duplicate layer. To do this, click **Background** in the **Layers** palette, then press **S** to activate the **Clone Stamp** tool.

Printing your painting yourself

The easiest way to get your painting onto paper is to use your own colour inkjet printer. **Colour Photo** output mode is usually best, but you can experiment also with modes for colour business documents. Glossy photo paper will give the best print quality, but to mimic a real painting you may prefer to use ordinary matt paper or even try special art papers from craft shops. Inkjets can cope with a wide variety, but watch out for jams.

Sending out for print

Using a print shop or digital photo service will give you more printing options. Most photo processors offer enlargements up to around 20x30in (50x75cm). For bigger posters, large-format inkjet printing gives excellent quality. Many **services** will also print your picture onto canvas, which you can then have framed. Alternatively, some print shops use a deeper than usual stretcher – the unseen supporting frame – to make the canvas more three-dimensional, with the image wrapping around the sides. This is hung unframed for a more modern look.

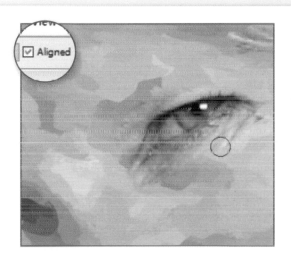

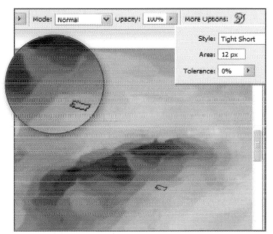

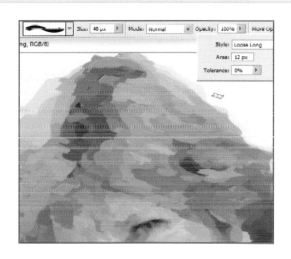

Recover lost detail

13 In the **Options** bar, tick **Aligned**. Untick **Sample All Layers**. Set brush **Size** similar to before, **Mode Normal**, and **Opacity 100%**. Holding the **Alt** key, click on the canvas to set the source for cloning. Leaving the cursor exactly where it is, switch to the **Painting** layer using the key shortcut **Alt+]**. Release the **Alt** key, then click and drag to paint. The original photo reappears where you brush.

Paint detail finely

14 Having restored an area of detail, go back to the **Impressionist Brush** by pressing B. Reduce the **Size** setting in the **Options** bar and, in the **More Options** menu, set the **Style** to **Tight Short**. Now repaint the area. Note that whenever you need to restore another area, you can switch to the **Clone** tool and paint straight away. Thanks to the **Aligned** setting, you only have to set the source point once.

Paint the background broadly

15 Moving away from the face, you can paint other areas with larger, looser strokes, as detail isn't so important. For the hair, increase the **Size** setting by at least half and change the **Style** to **Loose Long**. Areas such as clothing can be painted with an even larger brush. If patterns, such as stripes, appear broken up, try setting **Mode** to **Color** to preserve light and shade, or **Luminance** to preserve colour.

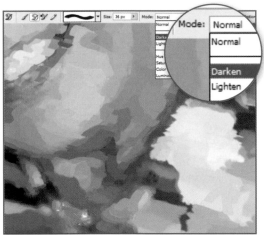

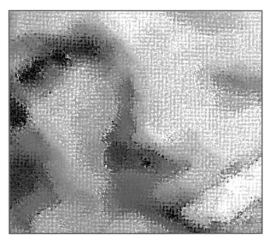

Finish off the brushwork

16 Continue through the rest of the picture. Make sure every part of the photo is covered with brush strokes, not forgetting empty background areas, which still need to have a matching texture. Where necessary, try changing the **Mode** to **Darken** or **Lighten** to paint in shadows or highlights that have been evened out by the brushwork. The same trick can be used to repair overly jagged edges.

Enhance the paint effect

17 For a final touch of realism, use one of Elements' **Artistic** effects, found on the **Filters** menu. Though it may seem inappropriate for an oil painting, choose **Rough Pastels**. Reduce the **Stroke Length** and **Detail** to about **3**, set **Texture** to **Canvas**, and increase the **Scaling** so the texture is clearly visible in the preview image at **100%**. Set **Relief** to 20 and **Light** to **Top Right**. Click **OK**.

Complete the painting

18 From the **Image** menu, choose **Rotate**, **90° Right**. With the picture now turned sideways, reapply the same **Rough Pastels** filter by pressing **Ctrl+F** to repeat the last filter used. This exaggerates the effect and corrects the impression that all the brush strokes are biased in one direction. Then use **Image, Rotate, 90° Left** to turn the picture back the right way up.

Pop Art effects

How about doing what Andy Warhol did with his prints of Marilyn Monroe and Elvis Presley and breaking down your photos into vibrant fields of colour? A useful filter for this kind of effect is **Posterize** (**Filter** menu, **Adjustments**), or you can push up brightness and contrast (**Enhance** menu, **Adjust Lighting**, **Brightness/Contrast**). Even better is Photoshop Elements' **Shadows/Highlights** filter, under **Adjust Lighting** on the **Enhance** menu. Set **Midtone Contrast** to maximum, with the other sliders at zero and then repeat.

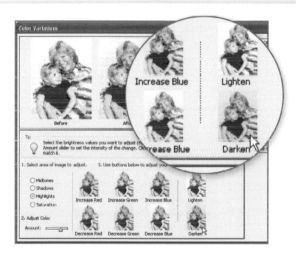

Add a glaze

19 The finishing touch is to alter the picture's colour to more closely resemble a real oil painting. To do this, go to **Adjust Color** on the **Enhance** menu and choose **Color Variations**. In the dialogue box, set the **Amount** slider just above halfway. Select **Highlights**, then click **Increase Green**, **Increase Red**, and **Darken**. Check the preview and click **OK**. Your painting is ready to save, print and frame.

Try sketching

20 Photoshop Elements' **Sketch** filters can turn a photo into a pencil drawing or similar with just a few clicks. Starting with the original photo, crop and scale it as in steps 1 to 3. Prepare it by choosing **Equalize** from **Adjustments** on the **Filter** menu. Go to **Filter**, **Sketch**, and choose an effect: here it's **Charcoal**. Adjust the sliders to give high contrast with shading just visible in the lightest areas.

Create a vignette

21 A vignette is where the picture fades out to form a shape such as an oval. To create this, press **M** twice for the **Elliptical Marquee** tool and set **Feather** in the **Options** bar to about **50**. You can vary this depending on the size of your image. Now click and drag around an area. Choose **Inverse** from the **Select** menu, then press **Delete**. Use the **Crop** tool to crop off the blanked area.

Design wise

Use your computer to design and produce gifts and cards, games and learning aids, party props, t-shirts, stationery, story books, posters and more

Say it big

Grab attention by creating your own posters

It's simple to design a poster using Photoshop Elements, and the end result will get plenty of attention, whether it's advertising a club or school event, promoting a business or just showing off your digital photos. Although your printer will normally be limited to letter-size paper, you can split your artwork onto several sheets and stick them together to make a full-size poster.

PROJECT TOOLS: Photoshop Elements ● High-resolution digital photos
SEE ALSO: Changing places and faces, page 52

● Fill the space

Pictures don't have to start off big to fill a poster. In this project, a picture is mirrored to make it fill more space (see below). Or you could use several images and position them next to each other. Also try filling one-third or two-thirds of the poster with a picture or several pictures arranged to fill a rectangle, then placing your text neatly within the remaining white space.

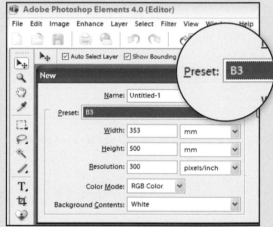

Choose a size for the poster

1 Run Photoshop Elements and click **Start From Scratch**. The program opens and the **New** dialogue box appears. This is where you set the size and resolution of your poster. Click the **Preset** menu to pop up a list of predefined sizes. A good one to pick is **B3**. This is 50cm (20in) high, large enough to grab attention, and you can print it yourself using four sheets of A4 paper.

Text and typography

A poster isn't a book, so you don't necessarily have to follow the usual rules of typography and grammar. In this project, all the poster text is in 'lower-case' or small letters, with no initial capitals for names or the first word of a sentence. It looks less formal and works well with the friendly Cooper Black font (see step 13). But keep things consistent – if you omit capitals then do so throughout.

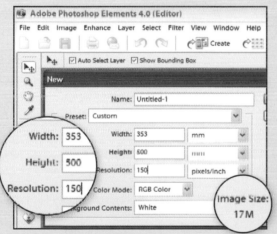

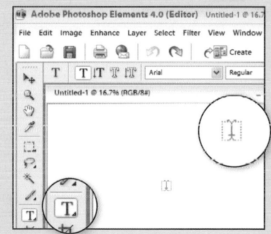

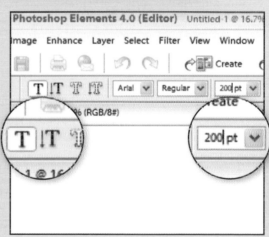

Fine detail is unimportant

2 When you choose B3, the correct width and height appear below. The resolution is set to **300 pixels/inch**, the standard for high-quality printing. As displayed at the bottom right of the box, this makes a very large file – more than 70Mb. But you don't need so much detail because posters are usually viewed from a distance. Change the resolution to **150 pixels/inch** to make a smaller, 17Mb file.

Get writing

3 Make sure the last two options under **New** are set to **RGB Color** and **White**, then click OK. Your blank poster appears. Start by writing the main text for your poster. Activate the **Text** tool by clicking the T icon halfway down the main toolbox on the left or by pressing **T** on your keyboard. The mouse pointer changes to a text cursor similar to that used in other Windows programs.

Set the text size

4 In the **Options** bar at the top, make sure the first of the four text tool buttons, the plain **T**, is highlighted in white. Don't worry about which font is selected – you can change this later – but do set the size. This is measured in points (pt). For a large headline, try **200pt**. The pop-up menu only shows smaller sizes, so double-click on the number shown and type 200 in its place.

Keep it smooth

When using the **Text** tool, make sure the **Anti-alias** button ('aa') in the **Options** bar is highlighted so it smoothes the edges of letters. If they still look rough, check the zoom level shown in the title bar of your image. If it isn't 100% multiplied or divided by a multiple of two – for example, 25%, 50%, 100% or 200% – the display is imperfect. To zoom in or out, hold **Ctrl** and press plus or minus.

Perfect curves every time

Avoid resizing an image more than once or making it too large since this will degrade its appearance. The software has to re-create the image's pixels each time you resize, and that process isn't exact. Text is different. It's stored as 'vectors', which are geometric descriptions of lines and curves. Photoshop Elements converts these to pixels at whatever size the text appears on your canvas. No matter how you resize the text, it always looks perfect.

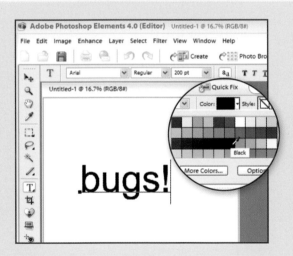

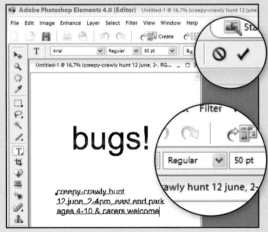

Try a trick

5 At the far right of the **Options** bar, the **Color** box should show black. If not, click the triangle to show a menu of colours, and pick **Black**. Click somewhere on the left of your blank canvas to start typing. Enter a concise headline for your poster, ideally a single word that will grab attention. Adding an exclamation mark is an easy trick to make a headline more exciting.

Add more text

6 Click the tick button at the right of the **Options** bar to finish entering text. Then click lower down the canvas to start a new piece of text. Before entering it, change the text size at the top to a lower setting, say **50pt**, and type in the main text of your poster. Press **Return** whenever you need to move on to a new line – this won't happen automatically as it would in a word-processing program.

Time for a picture

7 Click the tick again to finish. Now go to the **File** menu and choose **Open**. In the **Open** dialogue box, select an image file and click **Open**. Make sure you can see both your poster and the picture (see page 53, step 2), then activate the **Move** tool – click its icon at the top of the toolbox on the left, or press **V**. Click on the picture and, holding the mouse button down, drag onto the poster, then let go.

● Fine-tune special effects

Photoshop Elements includes many preset **Layer Style** effects, like the one used in step 14 to create a shadow. These can all be customised. After applying a layer effect (see step 14), go to the **Layer** menu and choose **Layer Style**, then **Style Settings**. The options available will depend on the **Layer Style** chosen. For example, you can change the direction of a shadow by altering the **Lighting Angle** or how far away it falls using **Shadow Distance** (see right).

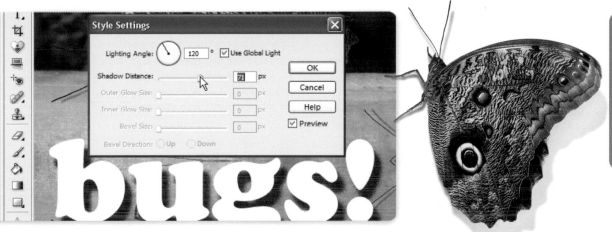

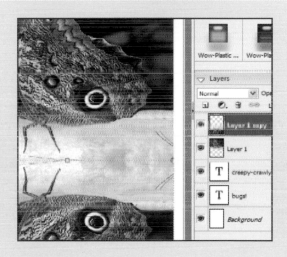

Size is important

8 Because your poster is big, the picture may appear small. To make it larger, drag any of its corner handles (hold **Shift** to preserve the picture's shape). Doing so reduces the picture's quality on the finished poster, so avoid increasing its size by more than about half. This butterfly picture would look poor if resized to fill the whole poster. But don't just leave a small picture in the middle, as it will look lost.

A careful arrangement

9 Instead, arrange one or more pictures creatively. Here's a good solution for this example. First, resize the butterfly picture so that it fills the width of the poster, remembering to hold **Shift**. Go to the **Image** menu and choose **Rotate**, then **Layer 90° Left**. Again, go to **Image**, **Rotate**, and this time choose **Flip Layer Horizontal**. **Double-click** on the picture to confirm your changes (or click the tick in the **Options** bar).

Mirror the picture

10 Holding the **Alt** key, click near the top of the picture and drag down the canvas to make a copy of the picture, which will snap into place directly below it. Go to **Image**, **Rotate** and **Flip Layer Vertical** to mirror the picture. In the **Layers** palette on the right, you now have several layers: the blank white **Background**, two text layers, the original picture ('Layer 1') and the upside-down copy ('Layer 1 copy').

● Printing a multi-sheet poster

By printing your poster across multiple sheets of A4 paper you can produce posters of any size. From the **File** menu, choose **Print**. In the **Print Preview** box, set **Print Size** to **Actual Size**. Click **Page Setup**. Make sure **Paper Size** is **A4**, then click **Printer**. Select your printer, then click **Properties** to see your printer's options. Look for 'poster' or 'tiling'. In the example right, you click the **Page Setup** tab, set **Printing Type** to **Poster Printing**, then set **Page Size** to **B3**. Click **OK** in each box, then **Print**.

If your printer lacks this facility, go back to the **Print Preview** box and untick **Centre Image**. Click the preview of your poster and drag it so the top left corner is about 1.5cm (0.6in) from the top left of the box, indicated by the **Position** setting. Print this, then go back to **File**, **Print**. Now drag the poster so the top right is visible with a similar margin. Repeat for the bottom right and bottom left quarters. After printing, arrange your four sheets to make up the poster, then glue the overlaps together. Use scissors or a craft knife to trim the edges.

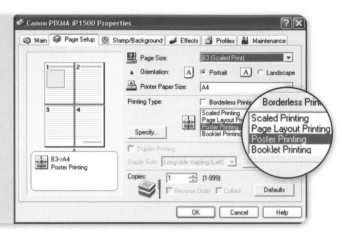

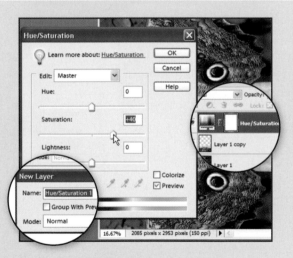

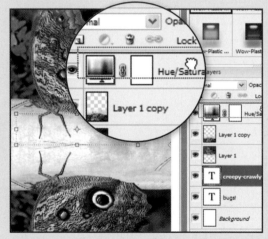

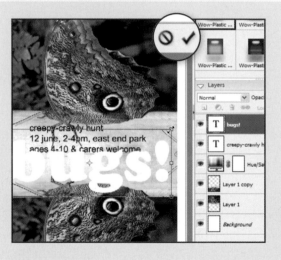

A splash of colour

11 The butterfly looks a bit drab. Go to the **Layer** menu and choose **New Adjustment Layer**, then **Hue/Saturation**. In the **New Layer** box, leave all the settings as they are and click **OK**. In the **Hue/Saturation** box, tick the **Preview** option. Move the **Saturation** slider to the right until the colours in the image look brighter. Don't overdo it, or the colours will become unnatural – about **+40** is enough. Click **OK**.

Get in order

12 An adjustment layer (see 'How layers stack up', page 314) affects all layers below it. In the **Layers** palette, the **Hue/Saturation** adjustment layer is at the top, so it applies to both copies of the butterfly. Your text layers are at the bottom, so they're currently invisible on the canvas. Click each text layer in turn and drag it to the top of the list. Now the text is visible and unaffected by the saturation change.

Style your text

13 Click your headline layer, then press **T** for the **Text** tool. Change the font and size in the **Options** bar. Choose **Cooper Black**, or any bold, clear font. From the **Color** pop-up, choose **White**. Switch to the **Move** tool (press **V**). Use the bounding box to size and position your text. As with pictures, hold **Shift** while dragging a corner to resize without distortion. Click the tick on the **Options** bar to finish.

Saving your poster

Using **File**, **Save**, save your work as a **Photoshop** file, which includes all your layers. This file will probably be larger than the 17Mb quoted in step 2. If you want to send your poster to someone else, or keep a backup copy of the finished result (without layers), go to **File**, **Save As** and choose **JPEG** format. Click **Save**. The **JPEG Options** box appears. Under **Image Options**, set **Quality** to **10**. Click **OK** to save the file.

Add shadowing

14 To make the text stand out, add a 'drop shadow'. Select the text layer. Then, in the **Styles and Effects** palette (above the **Layers** palette), choose **Layer Styles** in the first pop-up menu and **Drop Shadows** in the second. Click the example labelled **Noisy** to add a fuzzy shadow. Click on your other text layer in the **Layers** palette and repeat from step 13 to style and position it and add a shadow.

Make the text stand out

15 At the bottom of the poster, the picture still makes the text hard to read. To fix this, click the upper butterfly layer (**Layer 1 copy**) in the **Layers** palette, then go to the **Layer** menu and choose **New Fill Layer**, then **Gradient**. Click **OK** in the **New Layer** box. In the **Gradient Fill** box, click the triangle to the left of the **OK** button to pop up a menu. Pick the third example, called **Black, White**.

Darken your picture

16 Click **OK** to create a 'gradient fill' layer. To make this darken the butterfly picture instead of hiding it, click on **Normal** at the top of the **Layers** palette to change the fill layer's blending mode. Choose **Linear Burn**. The effect is still too strong, so click the blue arrow to the right of **Opacity** and reduce the level to **30%** by dragging the slider that pops up. Finally, save your poster (see box above).

Letter perfect

Create an exclusive look for letterheads and business cards

Businesses, charities, clubs and societies all need a distinctive and professional identity to present to the public. With Microsoft Word, you can design an expressive logo and use it as the basis for a letterhead, business cards and compliments slips. You'll find plenty to get you started in Word's preset shapes and clip art. Here's an example of how to customise a simple graphic; use the same methods to create your own symbol.

PROJECT TOOLS: Microsoft Word
SEE ALSO: Award certificates, page 98 ● Font basics explained, page 326

Choose the right fonts

The font you choose for your logo says a lot about the nature of your organisation. A chunky, hard-edged typeface implies a businesslike, no-nonsense approach. An elegant typeface with serifs (see 'Font basics explained', page 326) can hint at quality and discretion. Rounded edges and curvy lines may suggest a friendly, caring attitude. Above all, make sure your logo is neat, clear and legible.

For other text, use a font with similar qualities rather than exactly the same one.

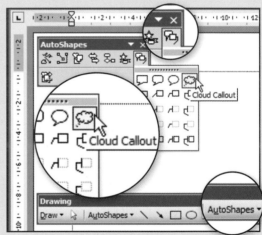

Letterheads – Select a shape

1 Run Word, or if it's already open press **Ctrl+N** for a new document. Set up the page as in steps 1 and 2 on pages 98 and 99, but in **Page Setup** set **Orientation** to **Portrait**. In the **Insert** menu, choose **Picture**, then **AutoShapes**. The **AutoShapes** toolbar appears, with a selection of shapes and connectors. Click **Callouts** and choose **Cloud Callout**, a thought bubble shape. The mouse pointer shows a cross.

● Customising clip art

You're not limited to Word's AutoShapes (see step 1) as the basis of your logo. Click the last button in the **AutoShapes** toolbar to find more shapes among the clip art that you installed with Word or Office. Alternatively, search for any suitable graphics in WMF format in Word's clip art collections on your PC and online, as explained in 'Award certificates', steps 3 and 4 on page 99. Convert the picture for editing as in step 4 of this project, below.

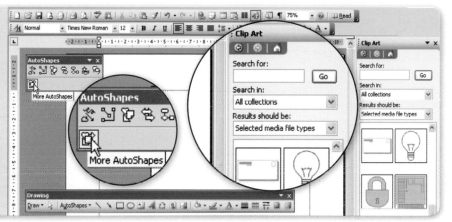

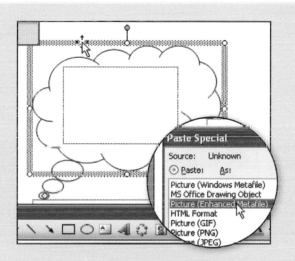

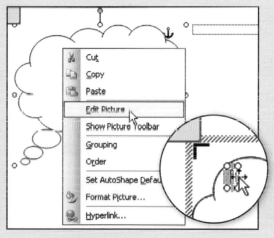

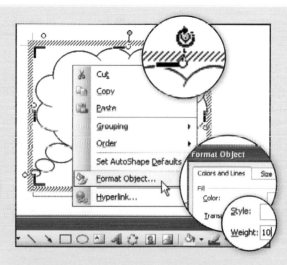

Draw and convert the shape

2 Click at the top left of your page and drag to draw the shape, holding **Shift** to prevent it squashing. To edit it, convert the **AutoShape** into an ordinary drawing. Click on its shaded border, then press Ctrl+X (Cut). From the **Edit** menu, choose **Paste Special**. Under **As**, choose **Picture (Enhanced Metafile)**. This is a standard format for 'vector' drawings, stored as geometric shapes. Click **OK**.

Edit the drawing

3 Now right-click on the cloud and choose **Edit Picture**. You're asked if you want to convert the picture to a drawing object. Click **Yes**. The picture gains a shaded border. Click a blank part of the page to deselect everything, then click on the cloud. The box you see near the top left is the callout text box, which you don't need. Click it to show a shaded border, then click on the border and press **Delete**.

Change the drawing's appearance

4 Click on the cloud to show white 'handles' around it. Then click the green handle at the top and drag to rotate the cloud, straightening it up. Right-click the cloud and choose **Format Object**. Click the **Colors and Lines** tab and set **Line**, **Weight** to **10**. Click **OK**. This gives the cloud a stronger outline. Right-click it again and choose **Grouping**, **Ungroup**. You can now edit the cloud's individual segments.

● The right tool at the right time

Word has so many tools that it wouldn't make sense to display them all at once. The program will generally try to show whichever extra tools you're likely to need. For example, when you insert an AutoShape it will display the **AutoShape** toolbar to pick a shape and the **Drawing** toolbar to edit it. If you don't see the toolbar you need at any time, choose **Toolbars** from the **View** menu and select its name.

● Formatting business letters

Include 'dummy' text in your template (step 17) to format your correspondence. Type the date first and centre it, using the buttons in the **Formatting** toolbar. Press **Return** twice, then type some text for the name and address of the person you're writing to. Change the alignment to **Left**. Continue with Dear…, then the text of your letter, then Yours…. Press **Return** four times to make space for your signature, then finish with your name.

Delete duplicate shapes

5 Click outside the shape to deselect everything, then click on the first bubble and drag it closer into the cloud. A copy remains, as separate objects have been used for the fill (the solid white inside of each shape) and the stroke (outline). Each shape consists of a see-through version and a white filled copy, both with the same thick outline you just applied. Select the unfilled copy and press **Delete**.

Adjust the shapes

6 Drag the remaining filled bubble into place, overlapping the cloud. Drag the white handle on one of its corners to enlarge it, holding **Shift** to preserve its shape. If you wish, hold **Alt** at the same time to adjust in smaller steps. Click the next bubble, and repeat the process from step 5. Again, enlarge it slightly. Delete the last bubble to keep your logo simple.

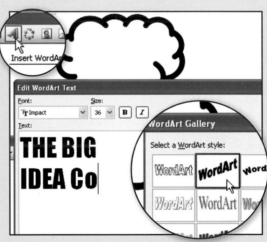

Add text using WordArt

7 To add some text, click the **Insert WordArt** button on the **Draw** toolbar. Choose the second style, slanted but plain. Click **OK**. In the **Edit WordArt Text** box, overtype the default text with the name of your organisation, then choose a font from the drop-down list – here it's **Impact**. Consider how the text will fit into the logo and, if necessary, press **Return** to split it onto two lines. Click **OK**.

Print your own stationery

Creating your own letterhead template in Word means there's no need to pay for preprinted stationery. Use your template to start each letter (see 'Working with templates', right), then print it on your inkjet or laser printer. Choose **Print** from the **File** menu, then click **Options**. Make sure the options for **Draft output**, **Field codes** and **XML tags** are unticked, while **Drawing objects** and **Background colors and images** are ticked.

Working with templates

Saving your letterhead as a template (step 17) makes it easy to reuse. To write a letter, choose **New** from the **File** menu. In the **New Document** task pane on the right, go to the **Templates** section and click **On my computer** to open the **Templates** box. Click the **General** tab and choose your letterhead template. Click **OK**. For special theme templates use the **Search online** box in the task pane.

Adjust the text

8 In the **WordArt** toolbar, click the **WordArt Shape** button. Choose the first shape, **Plain Text**. The text is now straight, but squashed. Click and drag it into position on the cloud, then drag a corner handle to resize it, making it wider so it doesn't look squashed. The text will look stronger if it's closely spaced. Click the last button in the **WordArt** toolbar, **WordArt Character Spacing**. Choose **Tight**.

Convert the text to shapes

9 To make further adjustments, you'll need to edit the letter shapes directly. Press **Ctrl+X** (Cut), then use **Paste Special** as in step 2 to paste it as an **Enhanced Metafile**. Right-click it, choose **Edit Picture**, and click **Yes** to convert to a drawing. The text looks smudgy, with narrow gaps filled in – because it has an outline. In the **Drawing** toolbar, click the **Line Color** button (paintbrush). Choose **No Line**.

Fine-tune the text spacing

10 Right click the text again and choose **Grouping**, **Ungroup**. Each letter is now selected individually. Click somewhere blank to deselect them all. Adjust the **Zoom** setting in the toolbar to at least **200%**. Now, carefully move letters to the left or right to neaten the spacing between them – click a letter, then press the left or right arrow key, holding the **Ctrl** key to move in smaller steps.

Choosing the best paper

The weight (thickness) of paper used for printing good-quality business stationery usually ranges from 90gsm (60lb) to 120gsm (80lb) – see box, page 110. To make an even better impression, choose a 'laid' (textured) paper that's compatible with your printer. Cream or another pale colour can look more eye-catching than white, but bear in mind that any white areas in your logo or watermark may come out coloured.

Designing wedding stationery

Usually, wedding stationery is more flambouyant than business stationery, but you can use the same tools to produce it. Design a wedding day motif in a similar way to a corporate logo – search for something suitable in Word's clip art collection (see 'Customising clip art', page 91). Wedding stationery can include invitations, an order of service, menus for the reception, a wedding gift list and thank-you notes. Find templates for these by searching online (see in 'Award certificates', page 99, steps 3 and 4). If you're using a print shop, check what software it works with. For effects such as embossing or printing in metallic foil, ask the print shop about any special requirements for the artwork you will supply.

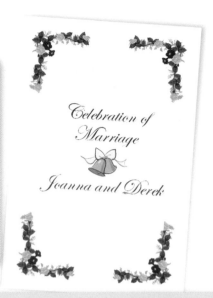

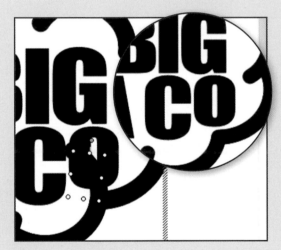

Adjust line spacing

11 Next, tighten the line spacing. Click the first letter, then click the other letters on the top line while holding **Shift**. Use the down arrow key to nudge these letters closer to the second line, holding **Ctrl** for fine adjustment. Finally, **Shift**+click all the letters, then right-click and choose **Grouping**, **Group**. Click and drag the whole of the text to position it on the cloud, and resize it if necessary.

Remove any unwanted shapes

12 If any parts of the graphic interfere with the text, the solution may be to remove them. Here, the curve on the lower right of the cloud obscures the letter 'o'. The curve is a separate shape from the main cloud outline, so click to select it and press **Delete**. When the logo seems finished, zoom out to check how it looks. It's a good time to save your work, so press **Ctrl+S** and name your file.

Regroup and colour the logo

13 Right-click on the cloud outline. Select **Grouping**, **Regroup**. With the complete cloud selected, click the **Line Color** button (paintbrush) in the **Drawing** toolbar and choose a colour for the outline, then use **Fill Color** (bucket) to colour the inside. Click on the text to select it, and set its **Fill Color**. Finally, click the shaded border of the drawing to select the whole logo.

● Design a compliments slip in Word

A compliments slip is usually one-third of a sheet of A4. Create a blank document. Click the **Paper** tab in **Page Setup** from the **File** menu. Set **Width 21cm, Height 9.9cm**. In the **Margins** tab, set each margin to **1.3cm (0.5in)** and click **OK**. Copy and paste the logo and details from your letterhead, and adjust the text where necessary. Create another text box using the **Text Box** icon from the **Drawing** toolbar (see step 16) and type With compliments. Set the size to **24pt**. Go to **Page Setup**, change **Paper** to a full page **(1)** and, in **Margins**, choose **Portrait**. **Shift+click** to select all your items. Hold **Ctrl** and drag to copy them to the foot of the page **(2)**. **Ctrl+drag** to make a third copy in the middle. Print and cut into three.

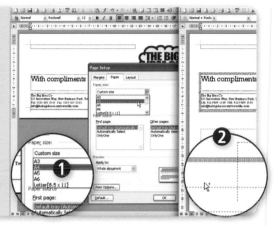

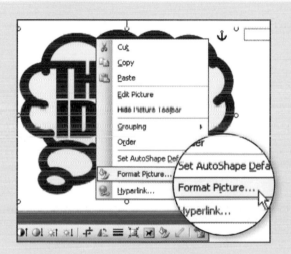
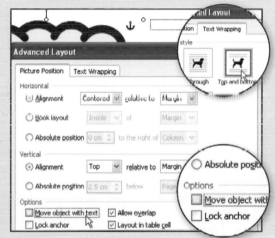

Convert the logo to a picture

14 Your logo needs to be scalable to different sizes. At present, if you resized it the lines would stay the same width, ruining the design. To avoid this, press **Ctrl+X** to cut the drawing, then choose **Paste Special** from the **Edit** menu and set the format to **Picture (Enhanced Metafile)**. Click **OK**. Now right-click the logo and choose **Format Picture**. In the **Layout** tab, click **Advanced**.

Arrange your letterhead

15 Click the **Text Wrapping** tab and select **Top and bottom** – this will make the text on your page start below the logo. Click the **Picture Position** tab. Under **Horizontal**, pick **Alignment** and set it to **Centered relative to Margin**. Under **Vertical**, pick **Alignment** and set it to **Top relative to Margin**. Untick **Move object with text**. Click **OK** in each box. Shrink the logo by dragging a corner; it stays centred.

Add a text box

16 Scroll to the bottom of the page. In the **Drawing** toolbar, click the **Text Box** button. Click at the bottom left margin (marked by lines at a right angle) and drag up and right to make a shallow box across the page. Choose a font in the **Formatting** toolbar, either the same as your logo or something that complements it. Set the size to **10pt** and choose **Center** alignment. Type the details of your organisation.

● Creating a watermark

A background image can enliven your letterhead or indeed any stationery. From the **Format** menu, choose **Background**, then **Printed Watermark**. Choose **Picture watermark** and click **Select Picture**. Browse to the image file you want to use and double-click it. Click **Apply** to see how your background looks. Adjust the **Scale** setting to fill the page; try the preset percentages, and if necessary type a different number into the box. Tick the **Washout** option to lighten the image so that text will be more legible. Bear in mind that Word always shows the image lighter than it really is, so it may look correct without **Washout**, but when printed it could be too dark. Click **Close** to finish.

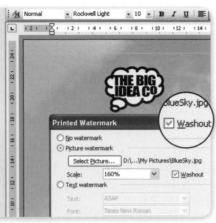

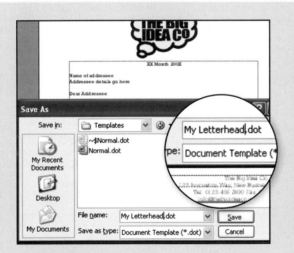

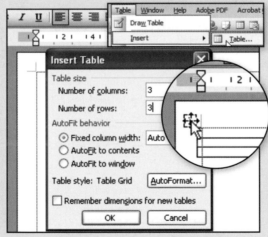

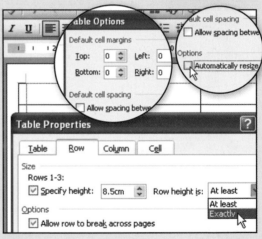

Save your letterhead template

17 In the **Drawing** toolbar, set **Line Color** and **Fill Color** to **None**. Scroll back to the top of the page and click in the main text area below the logo. Choose a font (see step 16) and set size to **12pt**. Type some dummy text (see 'Formatting business letters', page 92). Choose **Save As** from the **File** menu and set **Save as type** to **Document Template** (*.dot). Enter a name and click **Save**.

Business cards – Start your design

1 Press **Ctrl+N** for a new document. Choose **Page Setup** from the **File** menu. In the **Margins** tab, set all margins to **1.3cm (0.5in)** and **Orientation** to **Portrait**. Click **OK**. Nine standard cards will fit on a page. In the **Table** menu, choose **Insert**, **Table**. Set **3** columns and **3** rows. Click **OK**. Move the mouse pointer over the table (a cross symbol appears at the top left). Click to highlight the whole table.

Set the table to business-card size

2 Choose **Table Properties** from the **Table** menu. In the **Table** tab, click **Options**. Set all margins to **0** and untick **Automatically resize**. Click **OK**. In the **Row** tab, tick **Specify height** and enter **8.5cm (3.3in)**. Set **Row height is** to **Exactly**. In the **Column** tab, tick **Preferred width** and enter **5.5cm (2.1in)**; set the same in the **Cell** tab. Click **OK**. Click and drag on the cross symbol to centre the table.

● Printing and cutting your cards

Print your business cards on the heaviest weight of paper that's compatible with your printer (check your printer's manual), matching the colour and texture of your letterhead if possible. To add cutting guides, choose **Table Properties** from the **Table** menu. In the **Table** tab, click **Borders and Shading**. Under **Setting**, click **All**, then choose the second **Style** (fine dotted line), and click **OK**. Print the page and cut along the lines with a craft knife and metal ruler. Alternatively, buy perforated sheets of business cards from brands such as Avery, www.avery.com, and use matching Word templates available online.

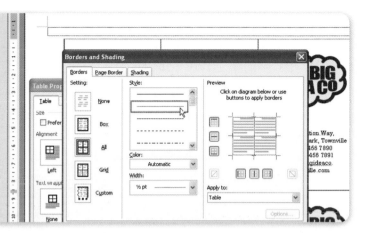

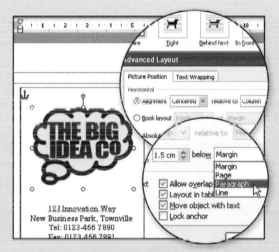

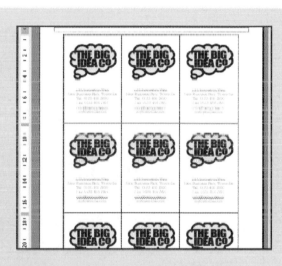

Copy text from your letterhead

3 From the **Window** menu, switch to your letterhead document. Drag to highlight the company details and press **Ctrl+C** (Copy). Switch back to your business card document and press **Ctrl+V** (Paste). Edit the text as necessary to fit on the card, not too near the edges. Click at the start of the text; hold **Shift** and press **Return**, then press the up arrow key to move back up onto the blank line.

Copy the logo from your letterhead

4 Switch to the letterhead, click the logo, and press **Ctrl+C** (Copy). Switch back and press **Ctrl+V** to paste it in above the text. Right-click and choose **Format Picture**. In the **Size** tab, set **Width** to **4.5cm**. In the **Layout** tab, click **Advanced**. Under **Picture Position, Horizontal**, set **Alignment** to **Centred** relative to **Column**. Under **Vertical** set **Absolute** position to **1.5cm** below **Paragraph**. Click **OK** twice.

Repeat the design

5 Click at the start of the text and press **Shift+Return** to move the text below the logo. Triple-click the last line of text and drag up to highlight the whole card. Press **Ctrl+C**. Click at the top of the next card along and press **Ctrl+V**. Repeat for each card. Choose **Save** from the **File** menu and save as a **Word document (*.doc)**. See the box, above, for tips on printing and cutting out the cards.

Prize giving

Reward achievements with an impressive certificate

A colourful printed certificate is a fitting reward for something well done, whether at work or a local event, or even at home. To make the recipient feel really proud, it must look the part: professional, authoritative and with a touch of class. Here's how to create a simple but effective certificate using Microsoft Word. By choosing different pictures and adapting the words, you can produce an award to suit any occasion.

PROJECT TOOLS: Microsoft Word ● Colour printer
SEE ALSO: Font basics explained, page 326 ● Printers and printing, page 312

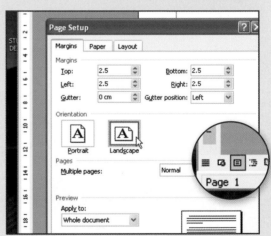

Prepare the page

1 Run Microsoft Word to start with a blank page. On the **View** menu, choose **Print Layout** to show your page as it will look when printed. In the **File** menu choose **Page Setup**. You may have to select the double-arrow symbol at the bottom of the menu to make this option visible. In the **Page Setup** box, set all the margins to **2.5cm** (1in). Click **Landscape** to make your page wide rather than tall. Click **OK**.

DESIGN WISE

● Free Microsoft clip art

Word comes with its own collection of clip art and photos, but what you get depends on which version of the program you have, and whether you bought it as part of Microsoft Office or by itself. You'll get the widest choice of graphics if you have an internet connection and **Web Collections** is ticked on the **Search in** pop-up menu in the **Clip Art** panel (see step 3). This downloads free graphics from Microsoft's website.

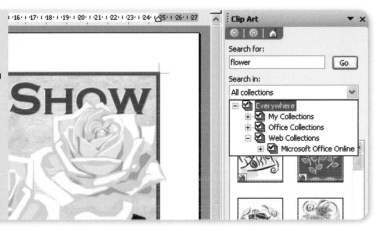

● Selecting items in Word

Once you've added several items to your page, such as a picture, a border and a text box, you may find that when you try to click on something, another item that's overlapping it gets selected instead. One solution is to move the overlapping item out of the way while you edit the other. Alternatively, use the **Tab** key on the keyboard. Pressing **Tab** selects each item in turn: just stop when you get to the one you want.

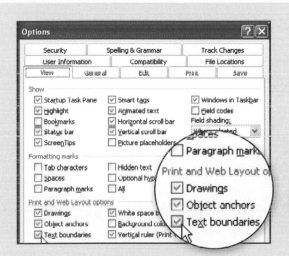

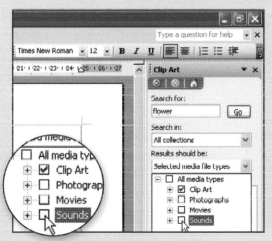

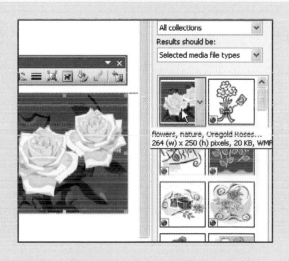

Display the margins

2 In the toolbar at the top, click the triangle next to the zoom percentage to pop up a list of **Zoom** options. Choose **Whole Page** to adjust the magnification so that the whole page is visible on screen. If you don't see the margins shown as dotted lines, go to the **Tools** menu and choose **Options**. Click the **View** tab, then tick **Text Boundaries**, shown under **Print and Web Layout options**. Click **OK**.

Add a picture

3 From the **Insert** menu, choose **Picture**, then **Clip Art**. If asked whether you want to organise your clip art, click **Later**. In the **Clip Art** panel on the right, in the **Search for** box, enter a word describing the kind of picture you want, in this case flower. In the **Search in** pop-up menu, tick **Everywhere**, showing **All collections**. Click the arrow next to **Results should be** and untick all the options except **Clip Art**.

Find a suitable image

4 Click **Go** to search Word's collection of clip art. The results may vary depending on your installation of Word. These pictures are stored as Windows Meta File (WMF) drawings, which means you can use them at any size – unlike photos, they won't become fuzzy if printed too large. Click the picture seen here, or any you prefer, to add it to your page. It appears at the top left corner.

● Adding a border

Setting wide margins, as in step 1 of this project, helps prevent the certificate getting damaged when handled, and looks good if it's framed. If your printer can print right to the edges of the page ('borderless'), you could add a texture to the margins. Draw a rectangle as in step 13, this time making it fill the whole page. Give it a different texture to your existing background (see step 14). Send it behind the text as in step 15, then from the same menu choose **Send to Back**.

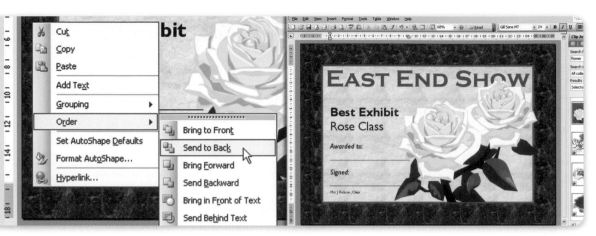

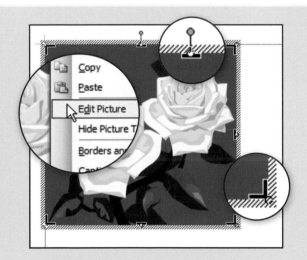

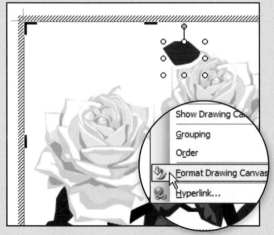

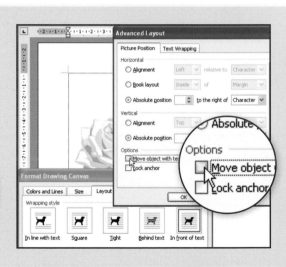

Edit your picture

5 Click the picture to highlight it. Drag the bottom right corner to enlarge it. For your certificate, it's best to have a cutout picture – something without a background. To remove the solid green background in this picture, right-click it and choose **Edit Picture** from the pop-up menu. A shaded border indicates that the picture is ready to edit. Click on the green background – a handle at the top shows it's selected.

Remove the picture's background

6 Press the **Delete** key to remove the background, leaving the rest of the drawing intact. Click and delete any other shapes that you don't want, such as the leaves at the top. If you delete too much, press **Ctrl+Z** to undo. When you're happy with the picture, right-click it and choose **Format Drawing Canvas** from the menu. If you haven't edited your picture, choose **Format Picture**.

Set the picture layout properties

7 When you insert a picture in Word, it's 'anchored' to a certain position within the text. As you haven't any text yet, the picture is fixed at the beginning of the page. In the **Format Drawing Canvas** box, click the **Layout** tab and choose **In front of text**. Click the **Advanced** button, below. In the box that appears, click the **Picture Position** tab and untick **Move object with text**. Click **OK** to close each box.

DESIGN WISE

● Word toolbars to suit

If the toolbars in Word don't appear the same as those seen in this project, it's because you have them arranged differently. Go to the **View** menu, choose **Toolbars**, and pick any toolbar to turn it on or off. To move a toolbar on screen, drag the dotted bar at its left (**1**). Click the symbol at the right (**2**) to see any buttons that don't fit on the screen, or to display the toolbar on two rows to fit all the buttons in.

● Precise positioning

When you move a picture around in Word, it 'snaps' to predefined positions, which helps line up items to make your page appear neat. But sometimes you'll need to override this to position something more precisely. Hold the **Alt** key while dragging a picture around to prevent it snapping. Or instead of dragging with the mouse, 'nudge' the picture with your keyboard's cursor keys (the up, down, left and right arrows). Hold the **Ctrl** key while nudging to move in smaller steps.

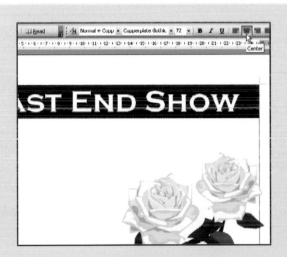

Write a heading

8 Move the picture to the bottom right of the page by clicking its shaded frame and dragging. Now click back at the top left corner. A flashing text cursor appears. Type a heading, in this case the name of the organisation awarding the prize. Drag over your text to highlight it and, from the **Formatting** toolbar at the top, pick a font. Here it's **Copperplate Gothic Bold**, often used for official documents.

Colour and style your heading

9 In the toolbar, click the centred text button to position the heading in the middle. Choose a size that almost fills the space. For more text style options, go to the **Format** menu and choose **Font**. Click the pop-up menu labelled **Font color** to pick a colour. You can add one of the **Effects** listed below: here it's **Emboss**. Click **OK**, then press the right cursor arrow key to move to the end of your heading.

The award title

10 Press **Return** to move onto a new line. In the **Formatting** toolbar, click the **Align Left** button to position your text at the left margin. Type the title of the award being given. Here there are two parts to the title, so press **Return** for a new line. Highlight the title. Then go to the **Font** box as before; choose a different font to the heading and a smaller size, and make the text plain black. Click **OK**.

● A traditional certificate with an 'olde worlde' look

For a more formal document, reminiscent of a college degree or professional qualification, here's how to adapt the tutorial on these pages.

Set up your document as in step 1 but choose **Portrait** format. In step 3, enter ribbon in the **Clip Art** search box to find a picture of a seal. Edit the seal as in steps 5 and 6. As well as deleting unwanted shapes, you can click any shape and recolour it: use the **Drawing** toolbar for this, as in steps 13 and 14. Continue from step 8 to add your text. For the full 'olde worlde' look, choose the **Old English Text** font. Use a script font like **Blackadder** for details such as the recipient's name.

In step 14, use the **Stationery** texture but set the **Line Color** to white. Choose a thick, plain **Line Style**, then click the **Dash Style** button in the **Drawing** toolbar, and pick the second option, **Round Dot**. This gives the effect of a rough uncut edge.

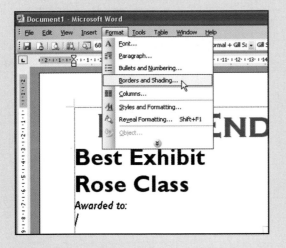

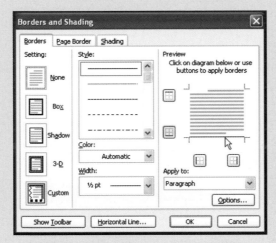

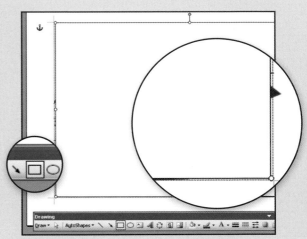

The prize goes to…

11 Press **Return** at the end of your title. In the **Formatting** toolbar, set a smaller text size and vary the style by choosing **Italic** (click the 'I' button). Type Awarded to:. You now need a horizontal line or 'rule' where the recipient's name will be added by hand. Press **Return** twice, then press the cursor up arrow to move one line back up. In the **Format** menu, choose **Borders and Shading**. A dialogue box appears.

Make a line for the name

12 The **Style** option, under the **Borders** tab, sets the type of rule. Pick the first option, a plain line. Leave **Width** set to ½ **pt** (half a point). Under **Preview** on the right, the grey lines represent the paragraph of text you're adding a border to. Click below them to make an underline. Click **OK**. Press the cursor down key, then type Signed:. Press **Return** twice, press the up arrow, and add a rule as before.

Add a background

13 Press the cursor down key. Type the name of the person awarding the certificate. Press the **Page Up** key to go to the top of the page. In the **Drawing** toolbar (if it isn't visible, in the **View** menu choose **Toolbars** then **Drawing**), click the **Rectangle** button. Ignore the box that appears on the page. Click at the top left margin and drag down to the bottom right to draw a rectangle across the whole page.

Printing and saving

Save your certificate as a Word document by choosing **Save As** from the **File** menu. To print it, choose **Print** from the **File** menu. In the **Print** dialogue box, make sure that your printer is selected at the top, then click **Properties**. Check that the printing mode is set to colour at best quality. If there's a choice of 'photo' or 'business graphics' modes, business graphics will usually give best results with a layout that includes text and clip art.

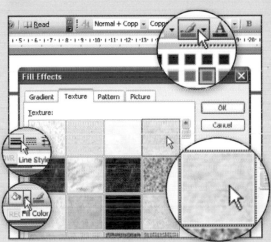

Choose a border and texture

14 In the **Drawing** toolbar, click the **Line Color** button (paintbrush) and choose a similar colour to your headline. Click the **Line Style** button (horizontal lines) and choose a **6pt** plain line from the options that pop up. Then click the **Fill Color** button (paint bucket) and choose **Fill Effects** from the menu. In the **Fill Effects** box, click the **Texture** tab and choose a subtle texture. Here it's **Stationery**.

Arrange your graphics

15 Click **OK**, then right-click your rectangle. In the pop-up menu, choose **Order, Send Behind Text**. Click your picture. Right-click its shaded border and choose **Show Drawing Canvas Toolbar**. In this toolbar, click **Scale Drawing**. By dragging its top-left corner handle, resize the picture to fill the space available. It's a nice touch to let it slightly overlap the heading and margin.

Final touches

16 Using the **Formatting** toolbar and **Font** box (as in step 9), adjust the text to fit neatly, adding extra line spaces where needed. Now highlight all the text that's aligned to the left, click the lowest segment of the marker at the left of the ruler bar at the top and drag it to the right, moving the text away from the margin. Shorten the rules by dragging the marker at the right towards the left.

Say it with style

Create your own greetings cards for that personal touch

There are ready-made cards for just about all occasions. But one you've designed will be more appreciated than any shop-bought card, and save you money. You can use family photos, children's artwork or pictures chosen specially for the event you're celebrating, then add your own verse to complete the greeting. In this project you'll make a simple card in Microsoft Word, then an even more creative one using Photoshop Elements.

PROJECT TOOLS: Microsoft Word ● Photoshop Elements ● Photos ● Colour printer (optional)
SEE ALSO: Automate your Christmas list, page 194 ● Produce a poster, page 84

Cards the easiest way

Many free greetings cards templates are available from Microsoft for use with Word. Choose **New** from the **File** menu, then in the **New Document** pane that appears on the right look for the **Templates** section. Here you can find templates already installed on your PC, plus more online. Type a word into the **Search online for** box, or click **Templates on Office Online**, to show a web page to browse for designs.

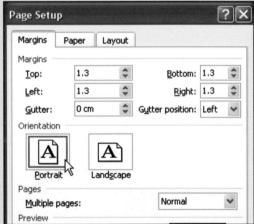

Choose the page size

1 Run Microsoft Word, which opens with a new blank document. From the **File** menu, choose **Page Setup**. In the **Paper** tab, set **Paper Size** to **A4**. In the **Margins** tab, set all margins to **1.3cm (0.5in)** and **Gutter** to **0**. Set **Orientation** to the opposite of the card format you want – **Portrait** for a wide card folded at the top, or **Landscape** for a tall one folded at the left.

Children's artwork

Children will enjoy helping to design their own cards and party invitations. It's more fun than sending bought cards or ones supplied by party venues. If you have a flatbed scanner, import your child's artwork from a painting or collage and use it on the front of a card, adding text inside using your PC. Or make the whole card by hand, complete with message, and scan it ready for printing.

Professional printing

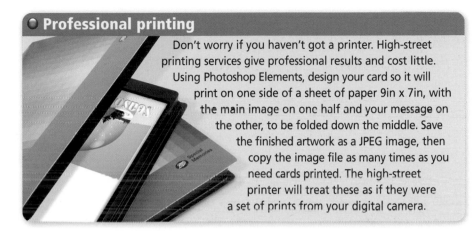

Don't worry if you haven't got a printer. High-street printing services give professional results and cost little. Using Photoshop Elements, design your card so it will print on one side of a sheet of paper 9in x 7in, with the main image on one half and your message on the other, to be folded down the middle. Save the finished artwork as a JPEG image, then copy the image file as many times as you need cards printed. The high-street printer will treat these as if they were a set of prints from your digital camera.

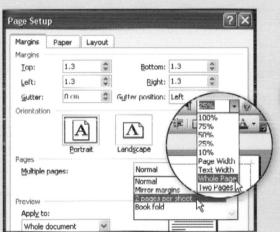

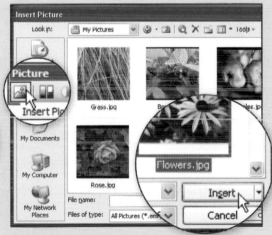

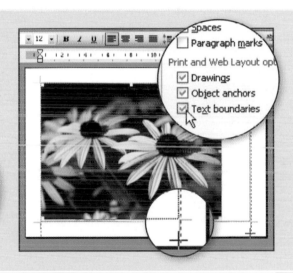

Set two pages to a sheet

2 Under **Pages**, set **Multiple pages** to **2 pages per sheet**. Click **OK** – the first page of your blank document appears. From the **View** menu, choose **Print Layout** to see your page as it will appear when printed. Also on the **View** menu, choose **Toolbars**, and turn on the **Formatting** and **Picture** toolbars. In the **Standard** toolbar at the top, adjust the **Zoom** percentage and select **Whole Page**.

Choose a picture

3 In the **Insert** menu, choose **Picture**, then **From File**; or click the **Insert Picture** icon in the **Picture** toolbar. In the **Insert Picture** box, navigate to the image file you want to use and click to highlight it. At the bottom right, ensure the button above **Cancel** is labelled **Insert**; if not, click the triangle next to it and choose **Insert** from the menu that pops up. Click this button to import the picture into Word.

Size the picture to fit

4 Your picture is fixed at the top left of the page. The margins you set up in step 1 will be visible on the page as dotted lines. If not, go to the **Tools** menu and choose **Options**; click the **View** tab, then under **Print and Web Layout** options tick **Text boundaries**. Click **OK**. Click and drag the square handle at the bottom right corner of the picture to enlarge it until it hits the right and bottom margins.

● Special occasion cards

Greetings cards aren't only for birthdays and festive holidays. You can make a personalised card to announce your change of address, congratulate someone on an achievement or thank a person for a gift. Choose from Photoshop Elements' readymade templates (see 'Instant cards with Photo Creations', page 111). Use one of these as the basis for your design by adapting the snow-globe project shown in steps 10 to 22 or borrow tips from other projects in this book to create artwork.

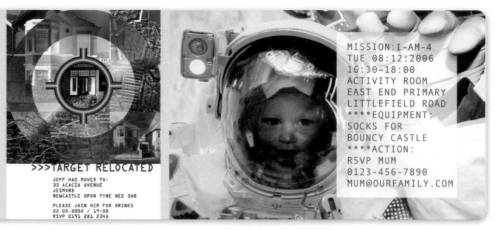

Troubleshoot picture sizing

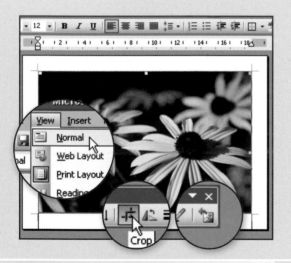

5 When a picture goes over the bottom margin it's trimmed automatically. If it goes over the right margin, click the **Crop** icon in the **Picture** toolbar and drag a side handle to trim it. If the handle is off the edge of the page, choose **Normal** in the **View** menu, drag a handle to reduce the picture's size, then switch back to **Print Layout** view. If you make a mistake, click the **Reset Picture** icon at the end of the **Picture** toolbar.

Add more pages to your document

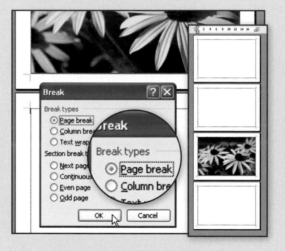

6 Once you're happy with the picture, press the left cursor arrow key, then press **Return**. A new blank page appears before the one containing your picture. Now press the right cursor arrow key, and **Return** again. A third page appears after the picture. From the **Insert** menu, choose **Break**. In the **Break** dialogue box, click **Page Break**, then click **OK**. A fourth page is added at the end.

Write a greeting inside the card

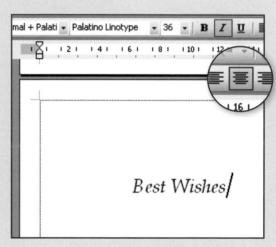

7 In the **Formatting** toolbar (normally shown at the top), choose a font suitable to the mood of your greeting. Here it's **Palatino Linotype Italic**. Set the size to **36pt**, and click the second of the four alignment buttons on the right, for centred text. Press **Return** a few times so the text cursor is halfway down the card, then type your message. Don't include 'To' and 'From' lines – write them by hand.

Microsoft Word print settings

If Word documents containing images print with poor quality, check your print options. From the **File** menu, choose **Page Setup** and click **Print Options**, or select **Print** and click **Options**. The **Print** dialogue box appears. Under **Printing options**, untick **Draft output**. Under **Include with document**, tick **Drawing objects** and **Background colours and images**; untick **Field codes** and **XML tags**. Also check your printer's settings by clicking **Properties** in the **Print** tab.

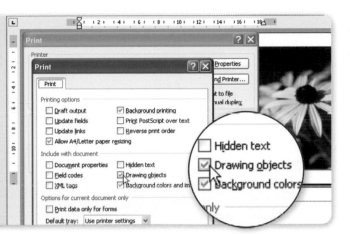

Choosing envelopes

You'll need to buy envelopes to fit the cards you make. The international A series of paper sizes matches the C series of envelopes. A half-page card printed on A4 paper, folded to A5 size, will fit a C5 envelope. A quarter-page card, folded twice, will fit a C6 envelope.

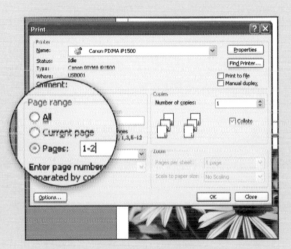

Choose printer settings

8 Print your card on greetings card paper or thick photo paper (see box, page 110). Word won't correctly preview a document with multiple pages per sheet, so select **Print** on the **File** menu (or press Ctrl+P). Choose your printer at the top, and click **Properties** to adjust its settings. Click **OK**. Under Page Range, next to **Pages**, type 1-2. Click **OK** to print the first sheet, with the picture at the bottom.

Print on both sides of the paper

9 Feed this printed sheet back into the printer, turning it around so that the blank side is uppermost with the printed picture edge fed into the printer first. (This is the correct way up for most inkjet printers.) Go back to **File**, **Print** (or press Ctrl+P) and set **Pages** to 3-4. Click **OK**. Fold your card in half with the message inside. Click **File**, **Save** and choose where to save your card.

Create cards in Photoshop Elements

10 Elements includes card templates (see 'Instant cards with Photo Creations', page 111), but with limited options. To be more creative, make a blank **Photo Creation** and edit it yourself. Run Photoshop Elements and from the **Welcome** screen click **Start from Scratch**. In the **New** dialogue box, choose **Preset**, **Default Photoshop Elements Size** and **Background Contents**, **White**. Click **OK**.

● Adjusting layers

If you apply a **Layer Style** (as in step 22) and the result isn't what you expected, try changing the document resolution. In the **Image** menu, choose **Resize** then **Image Size**. Untick **Resample Image**, change **Resolution** to 72 pixels/inch and click **OK**. Then choose the same **Layer Style** again. If it's still wrong, try different values. Once the **Style** looks right, remember to go back and reset the **Resolution** to **300 pixels/inch**, always keeping **Resample Image** unticked.

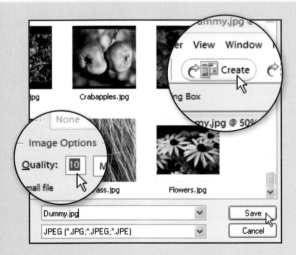

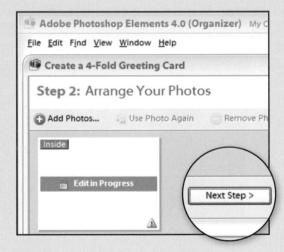

Make a blank image

11 Choose **Save As** from the **File** menu. Type Dummy, choose **JPEG** format, then click **Save**. In the **JPEG Options** box, set **Quality** to 10 and click **OK**. With your blank canvas open, click the **Create** button in the main toolbar at the top of the Elements window. In the **Creation Setup** screen, choose the option to **Create a 4-Fold Greeting Card**, which will print on a single side of paper. Click **OK**.

Follow the Elements steps

12 In Photoshop Elements the **Photo Creation** process is divided into stages, named 'Step 1' through to 'Step 5'. (Don't confuse these with step numbers in this project.) In Elements' **Step 1**, choose **Snowglobe** from the card designs displayed on the right. Click **Next Step** at the bottom of the screen. In **Step 2**, ignore any warnings about your photo, which is blank, and click **Next Step**.

Remove text

13 In Elements' **Step 3**, editable text is added to the front of the card. If you try a different template, the steps will be similar but the items on the card may be arranged differently – for example, your picture may appear on the front and the text inside. You'll type in your own text later, so click the text box shown and press **Delete** to remove it. Click **Yes** in the warning box. Click **Next Step**.

Mixed media cards

Incorporate real objects into a card design using a scanner. Find an object that suits your theme, and scan it as explained on page 322. If you're using Photoshop Elements, scan straight into the program: choose **Import** from the **File** menu and pick your scanner from the list. Make a selection to cut out the scanned object (see step 17). Press **Ctrl+N** to create a new blank document, and in the **New** box choose A4 from the **Preset** menu. Click **OK**. Using the **Move** tool (press **V**), drag your cutout object onto the blank document. Size and position it according to whether you want to make a single-fold, double-fold or full-page card. Add your text, then print. Here the dragon and cloth were scanned separately, and the dragon was cut out and moved to the top.

Printing from Elements

When you've finished your card (steps 10 to 22), choose **Save As** from the **File** menu and save as a **Photoshop** file. To print, choose **Print** from the **File** menu. Click **Page Setup**, set your paper size and click **Printer** to check settings. Click **OK** to get back to **Print Preview**. If you're using A4, choose **Fit On Page** from the **Print Size** menu. To finish, you'll need to trim the ends of the printed card with scissors or a craft knife.

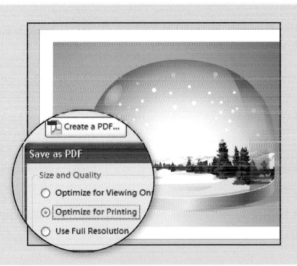

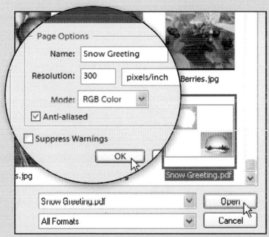

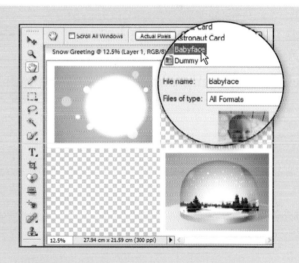

Save and export your card

14 In Elements' **Step 4** you're invited to save your work. Type in a suitable name and click the **Save** button. This file can only be opened as a **Photo Creation** in Elements' **Organizer Workspace**; you can't edit it directly. To make an editable image file of your card, click **Create a PDF** in Elements' Step 5. In the **Save as PDF** box, choose **Optimize for Printing** and click **OK**. Click **Save**.

Open your PDF

15 When asked if you'd like to view the PDF, click **No**. Click **Done**. If an information box appears, click **OK**. Press **Alt+Tab** to switch back to the Elements **Editor Workspace**. Choose **Open** from the **File** menu, and in the **Open** box go to the folder where you saved your PDF. Highlight it and click **Open**. In the **Import PDF** box, set **Resolution** to 300 pixels/inch, mode to **RGB Color** and tick **Anti-aliased**. Click **OK**.

Add your own photo

16 The PDF is imported as a full-page image showing the front and back of the card, arranged for printing and folding. The unused area is transparent (shown as a checkerboard pattern). Select **Open** from the **File** menu to load a portrait photo to use on the card. Zoom into it so that you see the head and shoulders clearly – press **Ctrl** and **+** to magnify, hold the **Space Bar** to move the image.

● Paper weight and thickness

Paper, an important part of your design, is classified by weight. A typical greetings card is around 200 grammes per square metre (gsm). Alternatively, the thickness may be quoted in microns (thousandths of a millimetre). Your printer's manual should say what thicknesses of card are recommended for your printer. You can buy greetings card paper pre-creased to fold into a half-page card. If you have a laser printer you must only use paper suggested by the manufacturer, but with an inkjet printer you can try almost any kind. Avoid very thin or soft papers that may disintegrate, or anything with applied effects, such as sparkles, that might come off inside the printer and cause damage.

● Mounting onto card

There are two different card formats in this project: half-page, single-fold, to be printed on thick paper, and quarter-page, double-fold, which will work with thinner materials. If you want an A4 card, design the front with a fairly large border – about an inch – and print it out onto high-quality paper. Cut it out, then paste it onto a double-size (A3) sheet of card, available from stationers or art shops. For the neatest finish, instead of scissors use a craft knife and a metal ruler to make exact cuts. Or invest in a table-top paper trimmer – the kind with a rotary blade is inexpensive and helps avoid cut fingers.

Cut out part of the photo

17 Press **L** for the **Lasso** tool. In the **Options** bar at the top, pick the last of the three lasso icons on the left, **Polygonal Lasso**. Set **Feather** to 8 for a soft edge. Click on the edge of the area to be cut out, release the mouse button and move to make a straight line. Move further along the edge and click again. Continue around the head and shoulders, taking care to follow the outline closely.

Move the face over

18 Double-click to finish – your selection is outlined with flashing dots. Press **V** for the **Move** tool. Click within the selection and drag onto your greetings card. Hold **Shift** and drag any corner handle to resize the image to fit within the snow globe. Press **Return** to finish. Press **M** for the **Marquee** tool. In the **Options** bar choose **Elliptical Marquee**, set **Feather** to 0 and **Mode** to **Normal**.

Distort the face

19 Click and drag to draw a circle around the head and shoulders. In the **Filter** menu choose **Distort**, then **Spherize**. Set **Amount** to 50% and **Mode** to **Normal**, and click OK. The face is distorted as if through glass; the bottom of the photo curves to match the globe's base. Use the **Move** tool to adjust the position, then switch back to the **Elliptical Marquee** (or press **M**).

○ Instant cards with Photo Creations

Run Photoshop Elements and choose **Edit and Enhance Photos**. In the **File** menu, choose **Open** and browse to the images you want to use. Click **Create**, then click **4-Fold Greeting Card** for a quarter-page card ready to print and fold, or **Photo Greeting Card** for a flat design to cut out and stick (see 'Mounting onto card', page 110). Click **OK**, then choose a layout style for the main image. Click **Next Step**. The photos you opened are shown. At the left is the image selected for the front of the card. Drag a different photo into place if you prefer. Click **Next Step** to preview your card and edit the text. There are more steps if the design has an inside message. Finally, give your creation a name, click **Save**, then click **Print**.

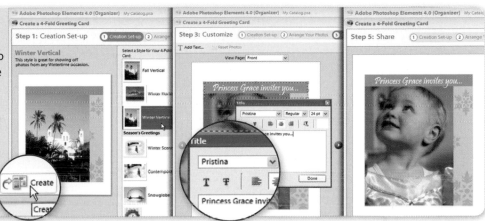

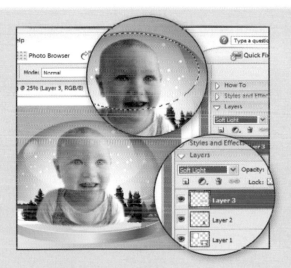

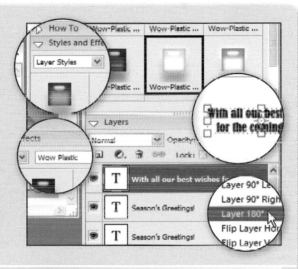

Add a highlight effect

20 Draw an oval within the top part of the globe. In the **Layers** palette on the right (choose **Layers** from the **Window** menu if you can't see it), click **Layer 1**, the original card. Press **Ctrl+J** to copy the selected area and create a new layer. In the **Layers** palette, drag it (**Layer 3**) to the top. Use the pop-up menu at the top left of the palette to set the **Blending** mode from **Normal** to **Soft Light**.

Type your message

21 Press **T** for the **Text** tool. In the **Options** bar at the top, choose a suitable font, set the size to about **48pt**, and click the button for **Centred text**. You'll find more tips on text formatting on pages 85 to 86, steps 3 to 6. Click halfway across the card below the snow globe, and type a message. Click twice on the **Move** tool, at the top of the toolbox, and drag the text into position.

Complete your card

22 In the **Styles and Effects** palette, pick **Layer Styles** in the first menu, **Wow Plastic** in the second. Click **Wow-Plastic White**. With the **Text** tool (press **T**) add plain black text to the inside of your card at the top left. From the **Image** menu, choose **Rotate, Layer 180°**. The upside-down text will be the right way up when your card is folded. From the **File** menu choose **Save** to save your card.

This is your life
Make someone's day with an album to treasure

A 'This is your life' album, telling someone's history in photos and mementos, is the perfect gift for a special birthday, anniversary or retirement. Family photo albums can be treasured forever, but when you've stuck a photo into one, it can't also feature in another. Digital albums are more flexible – once your photos are stored on your PC, you can reorganise them whenever and however you like, and produce albums for all occasions that include any pictures you please.

PROJECT TOOLS: Google Picasa • Microsoft Word
• Colour printer • Scanner • Photographs and mementos
SEE ALSO: Get creative with your scanner, page 322

○ Organising photos with Picasa

Picasa, from Google, is an easy-to-use digital photo manager. Go to www.picasa.com and click to download the software. Click **Save** in the warning box and choose where to save the software, for example on the **Desktop**. Double-click the file you've downloaded to run the installer, click **Run** in the warning box, and follow the steps. Picasa offers to 'scan' (automatically find) pictures on your PC. Choose what folders you want to be included in the scan. See 'Organising your digital images', page 324, for more on Picasa.

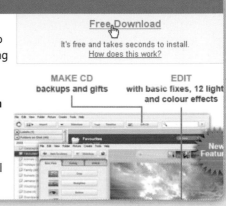

Organise your photos

1 Run Picasa (see box above). On the left is displayed a list of the folders containing images. They're arranged by date, with the most recent photos at the top. This is handy for planning a 'This is your life' album, where most of your photos of the subject are digital. Work your way back through the years, opening each folder to view the images on the right.

Start to choose photos

2 To put a photo aside to use in your album, drag it from the main window onto the **Photo Tray** at the bottom left. Notice that each photo appears in the **Picture Tray** when you click it, but it will only stay there if you drag it in or click the **Hold** button. Adding a photo to the **Picture Tray** doesn't remove it from its original folder but creates a link reference to it. You can add any number of photos.

Change the date of a folder

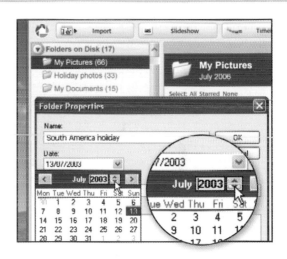

3 Some folders may contain pictures from different occasions and dates. To sort them into batches correctly organised by date, hold the **Ctrl** key while clicking to select the photos in the main window, then right-click and choose **Move to New Folder**. In the **Folder Properties** box, give the folder a name, set the approximate date when the pictures were taken and add any extra information.

A team effort

Get your family and friends involved in the project. Ask them to contribute their own photos and mementos to scan in, and their own quotes and comments to add to captions. They can also email you their digital photos for inclusion. You may even want them to collaborate on the album itself – set up your album, then email it to anyone who has Word and let them add their own pages before sending it back.

Make the most of type

It's best to devote your album mostly to pictures – keep the words short and sweet. But ensure your captions are large enough to be read comfortably by all members of the family – at least 14pt in size – and in a clear font, preferably the same one throughout. You may want to use different styles, such as bold and italic, for the dates and places where pictures were taken and relevant quotations and reminiscences from family members.

Pictorial milestones

If your album chronicles someone's life, it makes sense to arrange the pictures in date order. But you can vary this. Certain themes run through everyone's life – for example, an accomplished musician probably started displaying talent at an early age, so allot a spread to musical milestones through the years. If your subject is married, show photos of parents' and grandparents' weddings alongside your subject's wedding.

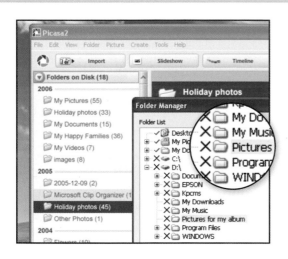

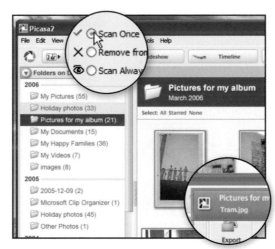

Add a folder to Picasa

4 If there's a particular folder of pictures that you want to use for your album, and you don't see it listed in Picasa, you need to add it. Go to the **File** menu and choose **Add Folder to Picasa**. In the **Folder Manager** box, browse the folders on your computer. Find the folder you want and click to highlight it. A cross indicates that Picasa hasn't been told to import photos from it.

Let Picasa scan the folder

5 Pick **Scan Once** to get pictures from this folder now. If you pick **Scan Always**, Picasa will also import any pictures that may appear in it in the future. Click **OK** to import the pictures into Picasa, where your folder's name appears in the list. You may need to adjust its date, as in step 3. Click the folder, click any picture in it, or press **Ctrl+A** to select them all. Click **Hold** to put them in the **Picture Tray**.

Importing scanned photos

6 If you have photo prints you want to import for your album using your scanner, you can do so from within Picasa. Click the **Import** button at the top to open the **Import Tray**. Click **Select Device** and choose your scanner to open its software. Perform a scan as explained in your scanner manual. Set the resolution to **300dpi** to reproduce items at actual size. For more scanning tips, see page 322.

● Fake photo borders

Unlike traditional photos, digital image files don't have white borders. In an album, borders help to separate each picture from the background and from other items it may overlap. To add a white border to any picture in Word, right-click it and choose **Format Picture**. In the **Colors and Lines** tab, under **Line**, set **Color** to **White**. Choose a solid line from the **Dashed** menu and set **Weight** to about **12pt**. Click **OK**.

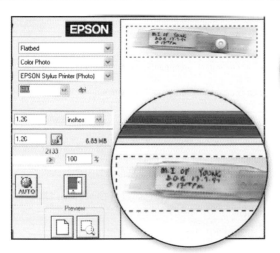

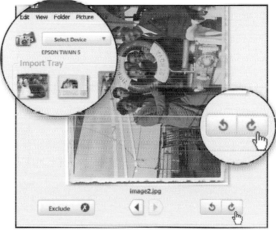

Scan objects, too

7 The scanned image opens in Picasa, behind your scanner window. Continue and scan any other items you want; not just photos but anything that reminds you of an event or milestone, as long as it's small enough to fit on the scanner glass and doesn't have sharp corners that might scratch it. Use a higher resolution, such as **600dpi**, when scanning smaller items, so you have the option of enlarging them.

Check your scans

8 When you've finished scanning all the items you need for the moment, close your scanner software. If you're not returned back to Picasa, choose it from the **Windows Task Bar** at the bottom of the screen, or press **Alt+Tab** to switch to it. The scanned items appear in the **Import Tray**. If you've scanned something the wrong way round, use the arrow buttons below the **Preview** to rotate it.

Exclude unwanted items

9 Remove any unwanted items or failed scans by selecting them and clicking **Exclude**. Click **Finish** to bring your scanned images into Picasa. The **Folder Properties** dialogue box appears, where you can name a new folder for the files and add other information for your own reference. Change the date to the date of origin of the items you scanned, so they'll be correctly ordered in time. Click **Finish**.

● Share your album online

To display your album on a website, choose **Web Preview** from the **File** menu. The album appears in Internet Explorer; scroll down to see all your pages. As the margins of the pages overlap vertically, if one of the pictures goes over the top margin, it will overlap pictures on the page above so your album appears like a continuous vertical banner. You may need to move captions away from the bottom of the page to avoid bits getting sliced off. Use only standard web fonts (Arial, Comic Sans, Courier, Georgia, Times, Trebuchet and Verdana) to make sure other users see your text as intended. Choose **Save As Web Page** from the **File** menu to save your web album. See also 'How to show off your website', page 263.

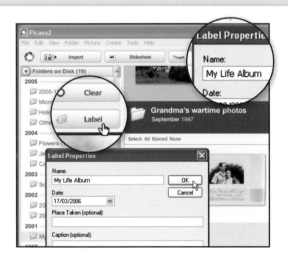

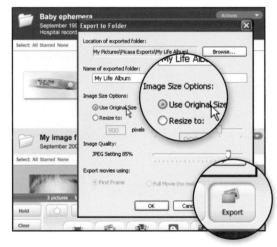

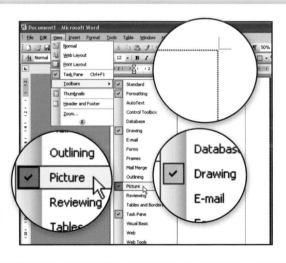

Label your photos

10 Back in Picasa's main screen, your new folder of scanned images appears in the list on the left. Click it to see your scans, then select them and drag onto the **Picture Tray**. When you've collected all the photos you want, click the **Label** button at the bottom. Click **New Label** in the **Label Properties** dialogue box and type a description such as My Life Album. Click **OK**.

Export your photos

11 Click the **Export** button at the bottom right to copy the pictures listed in your **Photo Tray** to a new folder on your hard disk. In the **Export to Folder** box, choose where to store this and give it a name. Below, pick **Use Original Size**, to keep your pictures unaltered. Leave **JPEG Setting** at **85%** for good picture quality. Click **OK**. Now exit Picasa; there's no need to save since it updates automatically.

Set up Word to work with graphics

12 Run Word, which opens with a new blank document. From the **View** menu, choose **Print Layout**, to see your page as it will appear when printed. Also on the **View** menu, choose **Toolbars** and turn on the **Formatting**, **Drawing** and **Picture** toolbars. If you don't see margins shown as dotted lines, choose **Options** from the **Tools** menu, click the **View** tab and tick **Text boundaries**, under **Print and Web Layout**.

● Improving poor photos

While browsing for photos in Picasa, you may find some of the shots you want to use don't look as good as you'd like. To make adjustments, double-click a photo in the main window. The **Basic Fixes** tab (**1**) has options to crop or straighten (useful for scans), remove red-eye from flash photos, or auto-correct colour or contrast. Try the button marked **I'm Feeling Lucky** to improve a dull photo. The **Tuning** tab (**2**) has alternative colour and lighting controls, while the **Effects** tab (**3**) offers instant fun effects. Later, when you've imported your images into Word, you can make basic adjustments using the **Brightness** and **Contrast** buttons in Word's **Picture** toolbar (**4**).

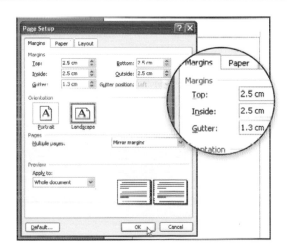

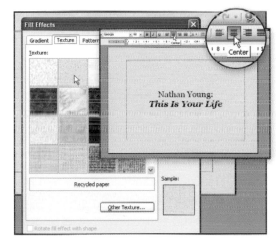

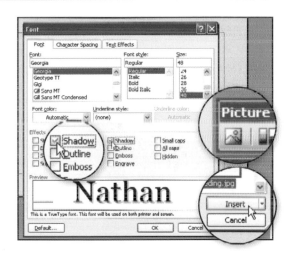

Set your album page size

13 From the **File** menu, choose **Page Setup**. In the **Paper** tab, set **Paper Size** to A4. In the **Margins** tab, set **Multiple pages** to **Mirror margins**. Set all margins to **2.5cm** (1in) and **Gutter** to **1.3cm** (0.5in); this allows extra space for the binding. Set **Orientation** to **Landscape** for wide pages, a good choice for albums and scrapbooks. Click OK. Your first blank page appears.

Pick a background effect

14 In the **Format** menu, choose **Background**, then **Fill Effects**. Click the **Texture** tab and choose an effect that won't distract from the photos, such as **Recycled Paper**. Click OK. Press **Return** a few times to move to the middle of the page, and type the title of your album. Highlight the text and, in the **Formatting** toolbar, choose a suitable font and size, here **48pt Georgia**. Choose **Center** alignment.

Add your first picture

15 With the text highlighted, choose **Font** from the **Format** menu. In the **Font** tab, tick **Shadow**. Click OK. At the end of your title press **Return** until a new page appears. Click the **Insert Picture** icon at the left of the **Picture** toolbar and browse to the pictures exported from Picasa. Click a picture. If the button at the bottom right doesn't say **Insert**, click the triangle and change it to **Insert**.

Binding and finishing

There are many ways to bind your album. For a small number of pages, stack them correctly and staple through the left side, about 1.3cm (1/2in) from the edge. Doing so means you won't obscure any of the photos inside, because you left a 'gutter' on the binding side when you set your margins (step 13). Use about half a dozen staples in a neat line. You may stick tape or glue ribbon over the stapled edge. If you want to bind larger numbers of pages, stationers can supply slip-on plastic binder bars, or binders consisting of a spine with slide-out paper clamp and transparent front cover sheet (left).

Nathan Young:
This Is Your Life

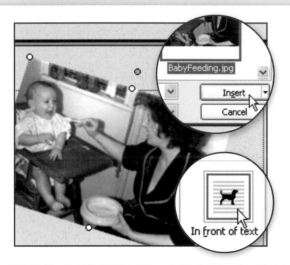

Resize and rotate

16 Click the **Insert** button to bring the picture onto the page. Right-click the picture and choose **Format Picture** from the menu that pops up. In the **Layout** tab, choose **In front of text**. Click **OK**. A box with white 'handles' appears around the picture. Drag the picture to reposition it, and resize it by dragging any corner handle. Drag the green handle at the top to rotate it at an angle.

Arrange your pictures

17 Add more pictures in the same way. As you set each picture to **In front of text**, it'll overlap the previous picture. To bring a previous picture in front, right-click it to pop up a menu and choose **Order**, **Bring Forward**. If you need to trim a picture, click the **Crop** icon in the **Picture** toolbar, then drag the middle handle on any edge and pull it inwards. Arrange your pictures within the margins.

Use shadows to add depth

18 To give the pictures a slight shadow, hold **Shift** and click each picture in turn to select them all. Click the **Shadow** icon second from the end of the **Drawing** toolbar. Choose **Shadow Style 6**, a semi-transparent mid-grey shadow falling diagonally to the right. To adjust the effect, click **Shadow Settings**. To adjust the shadow's position, click the icons with arrows in the **Shadow Settings** palette.

Printing your album

To print your album, choose **Print** from the **File** menu. Select your printer at the top, and click **Properties** to adjust its options: set the type of paper you're using and choose high-quality colour printing. Click **OK** to return to the **Print** dialogue box. Under **Page range**, pick **All**. Below, click the **Print** menu and choose **Odd pages**. Click **OK** to print pages 1, 3, 5 and so on. Take the pages out of the printer, check that they're dry, and feed them back in so that the other side will be printed (which way up they need to go depends on your printer). Go back to **File**, **Print**, and change **Odd pages** to **Even pages**. Click **OK** to complete your double-sided pages.

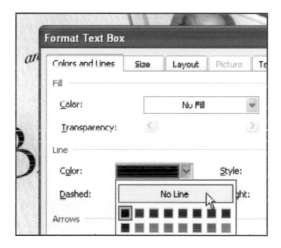

Write a caption

19 Click on the page to see the text cursor, then click the **Text Box** icon in the **Drawing** toolbar. The first time you click the **Text Box** icon you may see a shaded frame labelled **Create your drawing here** – if so, press **Ctrl+Z** to remove it. Then click anywhere on the screen and drag to make a box for your caption. Choose a font and size in the **Formatting** toolbar and type some text.

Make the text box transparent

20 Right-click the edge of the text box and choose **Format Text Box** from the menu that pops up. Click the **Colors and Lines** tab. Under **Fill**, click the **Color** menu and choose **No Fill**. Under **Line**, click the **Color** menu and choose **No Line**. Click **OK**. Now click at the bottom right of the page to see the flashing text cursor, then press **Return** to create a new page. Add pictures and a caption in the same way.

Preview your album

21 To check how your album looks, choose **Print Preview** from the **File** menu. In the toolbar at the top, set **Zoom** to about **25%** to fit several pages at once. Word shows your pages facing each other, as they will in your printed album. If you don't see your backgrounds and/or pictures, read 'Microsoft Word print settings', page 107. Print your finished album as explained in the box above.

Wrap it up

Make a gift special with some personalised wrapping paper

Design your own wrapping paper using any kind of artwork – scanned photos or objects, pictures from a clip-art collection, graphics drawn using your software's built-in tools to create shapes, or text in a dynamic font. Here's a way to turn a collage of photos into a seamless repeating pattern to print as many times as you want, to make enough gift wrap for even the largest present.

PROJECT TOOLS: Photoshop Elements ● Photos
SEE ALSO: Restore an old photo, page 20 ● Award certificates, page 98

⊙ Instant patterns

You can fill a page with texture or repeating patterns in Photoshop Elements, to create quick and easy wrapping paper. Open a blank canvas (**Ctrl+N**) and choose **A4** from the **Preset** drop-down box. Set **Resolution** to **100 pixels/inch** then click **OK**. From the **Edit** menu, choose **Fill Layer**. In the dialogue box, under **Contents**, **Use** choose **Pattern**. In the **Custom Pattern** drop-down, below, select a pattern then click **OK**.

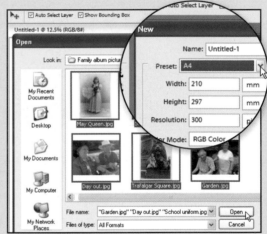

Open some photos

1 Run Photoshop Elements. From the **Welcome** screen click **Start From Scratch**. In the **New** box, click the **Preset** menu and choose **A4**. Set **Resolution** to **300**, **Color Mode** to **RGB Color** and **Background Contents** to **White**. Click **OK**. Choose **Open** from the **File** menu. Navigate to the folder containing the photos to open. **Ctrl+click** on each photo to select several at once, then click **Open**.

● Inspired by nature

Close-up photos of tree bark, grass, leaves or flowers make striking designs. Take your digital camera outdoors to look for subject matter. Point the camera skywards and photograph cloud formations. Copy and repeat the texture, as in steps 11 and 12. The abstract texture will conceal any rough edges. Alternatively, tile (see box, page 123) different textures for a patchwork effect.

● Enhancing old photos

To commemorate a major event in someone's life, it's great to combine recent photos with older ones from the family album, as in this project. Applying a tint to all the pictures (step 13) will help to make them look consistent, but if some of your photos are faded or damaged, you may wish to improve them before adding them to your gift wrap. See 'Restore an old photo', page 20, for tips on enhancing and repairing.

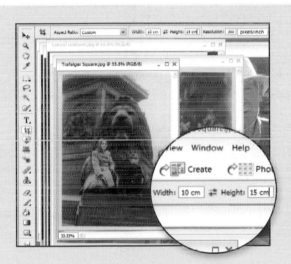

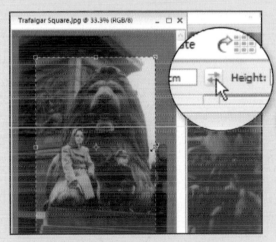

Set a crop size

2 Crop each photo to a consistent size for use on your gift wrap. Press **C** for the **Crop** tool. In the **Options** bar, set **Width** and **Height** according to the number of photos you're using. For example, if you have six photos and you're working on A4, each picture, allowing for some overlap when you arrange them, must be more than a sixth A4 size – a quarter (15x10cm), for instance.

Crop your photos

3 In the **Options** bar, set **Resolution** to **300 pixels/inch**, matching your blank canvas. Click and drag on your first photo to draw a crop box. Adjust it to contain the part of the photo you want. Double-click to crop the photo to this area. Crop the next photo in the same way. Differently sized photos may need the **Width** and **Height** values swapped, by clicking the two-way arrow symbol between them.

Add the photos to your canvas

4 Press **V** to activate the **Move** tool. From the **Window** menu, choose the name of your blank canvas to bring its window to the front. Then choose the window containing each photo in turn (do this from the **Window** menu if you can't see the window itself). Click on the photo and, holding down the mouse button, drag it onto the blank canvas. Don't worry about size or position yet.

● Choosing paper

Gift wrap is usually quite thin, because thick paper would be difficult to wrap around awkwardly shaped objects. Choose the lightest paper that's compatible with your printer. The printer manufacturer may not have an own-brand lightweight paper, but the printer's manual will list the minimum thickness that it can use. You can then buy paper of that thickness from a stationery supplier.

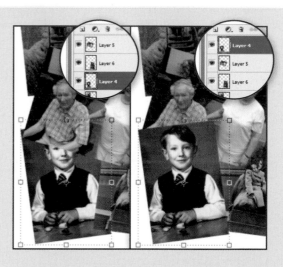

Plan your photo collage

5 When all the photos are on the canvas, move them around into a rough arrangement. Think about which parts of each photo need to be seen in the finished design, such as faces or costumes, and which can overlap parts of other pictures. Don't resize or rotate the photos at this stage, just plan the arrangement in your head. Repeatedly resizing or rotating will degrade picture quality.

Make an overlapping arrangement

6 Using the **Move** tool, resize and rotate each picture to fit. In the **Options** bar, make sure **Auto Select Layer** and **Show Bounding Box** are ticked. Click any photo on the canvas to show its bounding box. To prevent the photo changing shape, hold **Shift** while resizing. To rotate, move the mouse pointer slightly away from the handle so it shows a turning arrow symbol, then click and drag.

Finish off your collage

7 After moving or resizing, press **Return** (or double-click) to apply the changes. To alter the way pictures overlap, press **Ctrl+]** to bring a picture forward (on top of others) or **Ctrl+[** to send it back (underneath). When finished, your canvas should be mostly filled, with no gaps between pictures. But keep all the pictures away from the edges, leaving a clear border around all four sides.

● Check your pattern matches

Repeating a pattern by placing copies next to each other, as you'll do with your finished printed sheets, is known as 'tiling'. If, after completing step 12 of this project, you're not convinced that you have a seamless repeating pattern, use the **Offset** filter again to check your tiling. No matter what amounts you enter for the **Horizontal** and **Vertical** offsets, you shouldn't see any discontinuity in the image. This proves it will tile correctly.

● Working with offsets

The **Offset** filter (see step 10, below) is useful for repeating patterns because it moves the edges of your artwork into the middle, where you can fill any gaps. The exact amount that you offset doesn't matter as long as it brings the problem areas – in this project, the blank white parts – well away from the edges of the canvas. The amount of offset also governs which parts of the underlying photos show through. If you're not happy with the appearance after step 12, undo (press **Ctrl-Z**), then go back to **Filter**, **Other**, **Offset** and try a slightly different number of pixels.

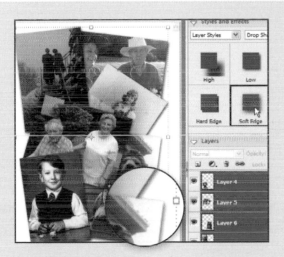

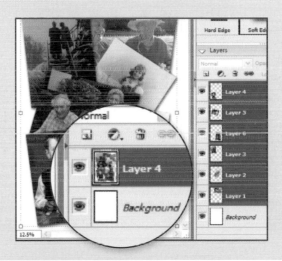

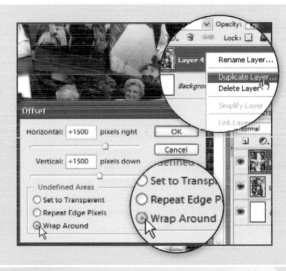

Add soft shadows

8 Shadows give the impression of scattered photo prints. In the **Layers** palette (choose **Layers** from the Window menu if you can't see it), click the top layer, containing a photo, then hold **Shift** and click the lowest layer above **Background** so that all your photos are selected. In the **Styles and Effects** palette, choose **Layer Styles** in the first menu and **Drop Shadows** in the second, then pick **Soft Edge**.

Merge your layers

9 Give your collage a final look over – check that there are no gaps between pictures, or any pictures or shadows going off the edges of the canvas. When you're happy with it, make sure all your picture layers, but not the **Background**, are selected in the **Layers** palette (see previous step), then press **Ctrl+E** to merge all the selected layers. You now have just the **Background** layer and the collage layer.

Duplicate and position the collage

10 Right click the collage layer (here it's **Layer 4**; yours may have a different name) and choose **Duplicate Layer** from the menu that appears. Click **OK** in the next box to make a copy of your collage, with 'copy' added to its layer name. Now go to the **Filter** menu and choose **Other**, then **Offset**. Enter 1500 into both boxes, and under **Undefined Areas** choose **Wrap Around**. Click **OK**.

● Printing your gift wrap

Choose **Print** from the **File** menu (or press **Ctrl+P**). Click **Page Setup**, choose the paper size that matches your printer and click **OK** to return to the **Print Preview** dialogue box.

When you click **Print**, you may be warned that the image is larger than the paper. This is because many printers can't print a full sheet, right to the edges. Even those that do offer 'borderless' printing often don't recommend it with non-glossy paper. Tick **Scale to Fit Media** to reduce your artwork so that nothing gets missed off. Click **OK** to print, then trim the white borders off the printed sheet with scissors or a craft knife.

Because you've created your photo background as a repeating pattern (see steps 10 to 12 of this project), you may stick multiple sheets together to make a larger piece of gift wrap. The edges will match up seamlessly. Place the sheets next to each other, face down, then apply sticky tape along the join.

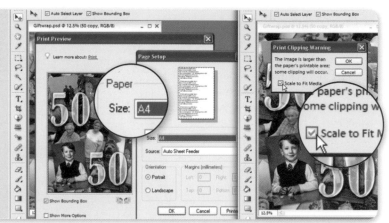

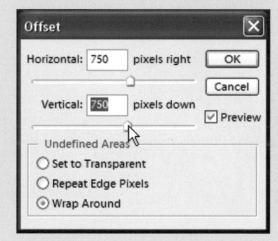

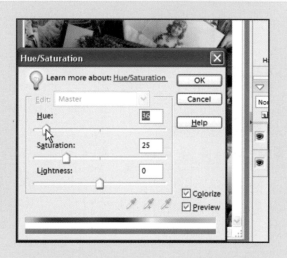

Repeat the patterns

11 The copy of your collage appears a few inches across and down. The parts that are moved off the edge come back on the opposite side. So you're still seeing the whole collage, but the gaps that were at the edges of the canvas are now in the middle. Underneath, the original copy of the collage shows through, filling the gaps. This is the secret of creating a seamless repeating pattern.

Merge and duplicate the layers

12 There will still be four unfilled areas; these were the sides of the original canvas. To fill them, press **Ctrl+E** to merge the two collage layers into one, then duplicate this as in step 10. Again, go to **Filter**, **Other**, **Offset**. Enter a different value into both boxes — say, half the previous amount (750). Click **OK**. You should now have a completely filled canvas. Press **Ctrl+E** to merge one last time.

Tint your photos

13 You can leave your photos as they are, but for a more consistent look, similar to commercial gift-wrap designs, tint them all the same colour. Open the **Hue/Saturation** box (**Ctrl+U**). Tick **Colorize** to remove any existing colour rather than adjusting it. Then set **Hue** to about **36** for a sepia effect, or whatever colour you prefer. Saturation is automatically set to **25** for a subtle tint. Click **OK**.

● Painting with text

Many gift wrap designs are based on text rather than pictures. Make your own with the **Text** tool in Photoshop Elements, or even using Microsoft Word. It's more difficult to make a repeating pattern with writing, but it's not essential that your gift wrap has a seamless repeat; just stick sheets together without worrying about the pattern matching up. See 'Award certificates', page 98, for tips on using text and backgrounds in Word.

● Saving your work

Choose **Save** from the **File** menu (or press **Ctrl+S**) to save your finished artwork as a Photoshop (.PSD) file. You'll then be able to hide or delete the layers containing your message and reuse the photo collage in future projects. If you want to send the artwork to someone else, use **Save As** to resave the file in JPEG format, choosing a high-quality setting (**9** or **10**), or a lower quality (**3** or less) to reduce the file size for emailing.

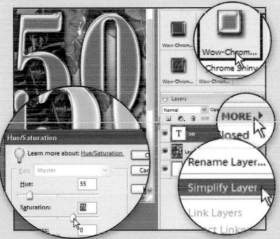

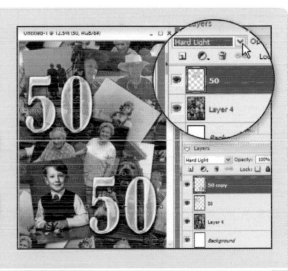

Add a message

14 Press **T** for the Text tool and type a message relevant to the occasion. For tips on entering and formatting text, see steps 4 and 5, page 182. Add as much or as little text as you like, perhaps a full-length message such as Best Wishes on your Golden Wedding Anniversary, or a brief word or phrase. To finish entering text, click twice on the **Move** tool button at the top of the main toolbox on the left.

Style your text

15 Drag the handles of the text box to adjust the position and size of the text. In the **Styles and Effects** second menu, choose **Wow Chrome** and click **Wow-Chrome Shiny Edge** from the options below. Now convert the text to an image by choosing **Simplify Layer** from the **Layer** menu (right). If necessary, use **Hue/Saturation** as in step 13 to alter the colour of the converted text.

Make the text translucent

16 In the **Layers** palette, change the blending mode from **Normal** to **Hard Light**, to make the text see-through. Repeat the text by holding **Alt** while dragging it to make a copy. Position copies so that the distance between them roughly matches the total of the distances between each copy and the edge, both horizontally and vertically. Finally, save your wrapping paper design (see above).

Boxing clever
Make a present extra special by designing an exclusive gift box

A carefully chosen gift deserves thoughtful wrapping. For small, delicate or awkwardly shaped objects, the ideal solution is a customised gift box. Create one sized and decorated to fit a special present, or make up a whole batch for a promotional gift or for festive tree-hanging. Use this project to draw a template in Photoshop Elements, add colours or graphics, then print it out and fold into a neat gift box.

PROJECT TOOLS: Photoshop Elements ● Colour printer
SEE ALSO: Wrapping paper, page 120 ● Turn a digital photo into a work of art, page 74

● Decorating your box with photos

Brightly coloured images and pictures of loved ones will make your gift box unique and personal. The box on the far right makes use of Pop Art effects described on page 81. To add images, click one of the white squares, as in steps 15 to 16 of this project, but instead of using **Fill Layer** to colour it, press **Ctrl+O** and open a photo. Press **Ctrl+V** for the **Move** tool, then click and drag the photo onto your box artwork (right). Press **Ctrl+G** to group it with the previous layer. The photo is cropped within the white square. Adjust its size and position. Do the same for the other sides.

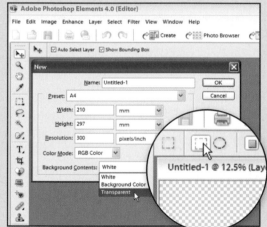

Make a transparent canvas

1 Run Photoshop Elements and from the **Welcome** screen click **Start from Scratch**. When the **New** dialogue box appears, click the **Preset** drop-down menu and choose your paper size (A4). Set **Color Mode** to RGB Color and set **Background Contents** to Transparent. Click **OK** to make a full-page blank canvas that's transparent, indicated by a checkerboard pattern.

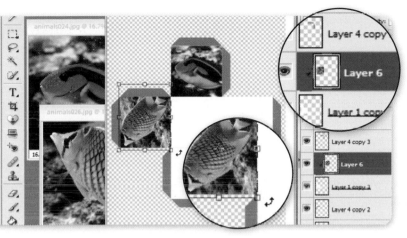

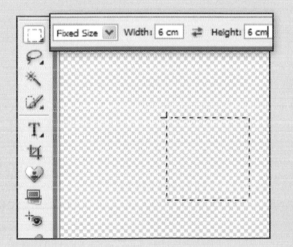

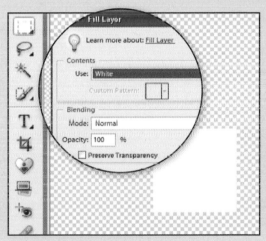

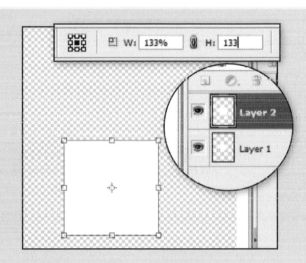

Draw a square

2 Press **M** to activate the **Marquee** tool. In the **Options** bar at the top choose **Rectangular**. Set **Feather** to 0 then click **Mode** and choose **Fixed Size**. Set both **Width** and **Height** to **6cm** (type the letters cm after the number to set the units to centimetres). Now click and drag near the middle of the canvas and draw a square. The selection marquee is shown as a flashing dotted outline.

Fill the square with white

3 From the **Edit** menu, choose **Fill Selection**. In the box, set **Contents** to **White**, then **Blending Mode** to **Normal** and **Opacity** to **100%**. Untick **Preserve Transparency**. Click **OK** to fill the square with white. Make sure the whole canvas is visible – press **Ctrl+0** (zero) to fit the canvas on screen. Press **Ctrl+X** (cut), then **Ctrl+V** (paste). This cuts the square then pastes it back in the exact centre of the canvas.

Duplicate and resize the square

4 Press **Ctrl+V** again to make a copy of the square. It appears as a new layer, **Layer 2**, in the **Layers** palette (choose **Layers** from the **Window** menu if it isn't visible). Press **Ctrl+T** to **Transform** (scale) the layer. In the **Options** palette, make sure the **Reference Point**, in the diagram at the left, is set to the middle. Set both **W** (width) and **H** (height) to **133%**. Press **Return** twice to confirm.

● Make a gift tag

A gift tag is usually a small folded card. In Elements press **Ctrl+N** for a new blank file. Set **Width** and **Height** to the size you wish, not allowing for folding – **4cm (1.5in)** is adequate. Set **Resolution** to **300 pixels/inch**, **Color Mode** to **RGB Color**, **Background Contents** to **White**. Click **OK**. Add a colour or pattern using **Fill Layer** (see step 16) or a photo (see box, page 126). Press **Ctrl+A** (**Select All**) and from the **Image** menu choose **Crop**. Then from the **Image** menu select **Resize**, **Canvas Size**. Set **Width** to **200 percent** and click the middle right **Anchor** position. Set **Canvas extension colour** to **Other** and pick a colour for the back. Click **OK** twice. Print on thick glossy paper, cut out and score down the middle. Write your message on the reverse of the tag, then fold in half. Using a hole punch, make a hole near the top left corner. Thread ribbon through and tape the ends to your gift box.

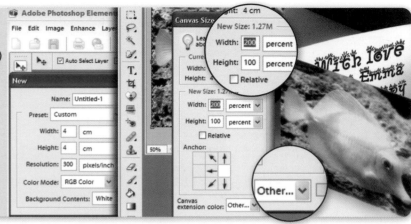

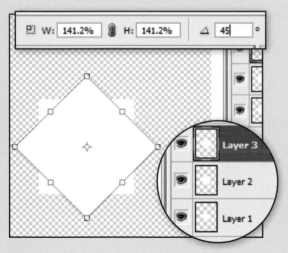

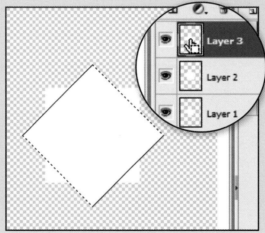

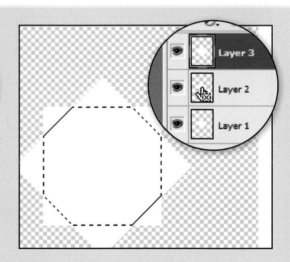

Create a rotated copy

5 You now have an 8cm square, giving a 1cm border all around your original 6cm square. Cut off the corners to leave mitred tabs on each side of the square by pressing **Ctrl+V** to paste another copy of the original square, which appears in a new layer, called **Layer 3**. Press **Ctrl+T** to **Transform** (rotate) the layer. Now set **W** and **H** to 141.2%. Set **Angle** to 45. Press **Return** twice to confirm.

Select the rotated square

6 This makes a diamond shape, the sides of which touch the corners of the original square (**Layer 1**), although you can't see this at the moment since it's covered by the larger copy (**Layer 2**). Now combine **Layers 2** and **3** to leave only the intersection of the two shapes by first holding **Ctrl** then clicking the thumbnail image next to the name **Layer 3** in the **Layers** palette.

Intersect the two shapes

7 This selects the contents of the layer (the diamond), shown by a dotted outline. Hold the **Shift**, **Ctrl** and **Alt** keys and click the thumbnail for **Layer 2**. The mouse pointer shows a hand with a crossed box, indicating that the new selection will be intersected with the existing selection. The dotted outline now shows a square with its corners cut off. Press **Shift+Ctrl+N** to make a new layer, and click **OK**.

Assembling the base

Print the box base at actual size on thick glossy paper. Cut around the outline, then score lightly along all the folds using a craft knife and metal ruler. Apply glue to the four side tabs, on the printed side, then fold the box into shape and press the tabs into place. Now glue the end tabs on the unprinted side, fold them back inside the box and stick down, making a strong lip.

Assembling the lid

When printing the lid, set **Scaled Print Size** to **105%** in **Print Preview**, which allows it to fit over the base. If a warning says the image will be clipped, untick **Scale to Fit** and click **OK** (do the same for the box if this appears). Cut around the outline and cut in where the tabs abut the sides. As with the base, glue the small side tabs to join the sides, then glue the end tabs back for strengthening.

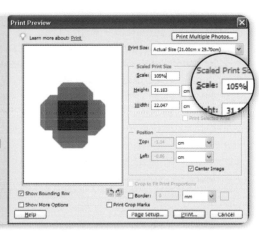

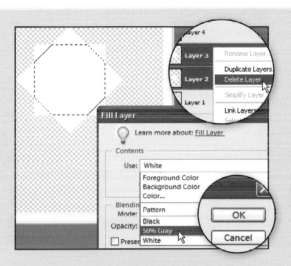

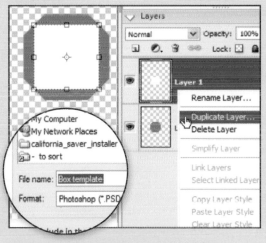

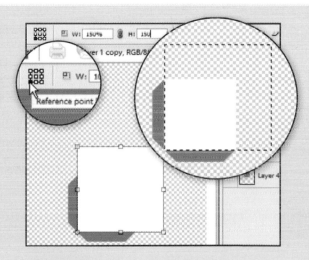

Discard the unwanted layers

8 From the **Edit** menu, choose **Fill Selection**. Set **Contents, Use** to **50% Grey**. Click **OK** to fill the selected area. **Layer 4** now contains a grey square with mitred corners. You don't need **Layers 2** and **3** any more. Click **Layer 2** in the **Layers** palette, then hold **Shift** and click **Layer 3** to select both at once. Right-click to pop up a menu and choose **Delete Layer**. Click **Yes**. Press **Ctrl+D** to deselect.

Send the grey shape behind

9 In the **Layers** palette, click **Layer 1** and drag it to the top of the list, above **Layer 4**. You now have a white square with grey tabs all around. From the **File** menu choose **Save** and save as a **Photoshop** (.PSD) file, naming it Box template. Click **Save**. You can use this later to make different boxes. Here you need to remove two of the tabs. Right-click **Layer 1** and choose **Duplicate Layer**. Click **OK**.

Cut off the unwanted tabs

10 Press **Ctrl+T** to **Transform**. In the **Options** bar, click the bottom left point in the **Reference Point** diagram and set **W** and **H** to **150%**. Press **Return** twice. In the **Layers** palette, Ctrl+click the **Layer 1 copy** thumbnail to select the large square area. Right-click its name and choose **Delete Layer**. Click **Yes**. Click **Layer 4** and press **Delete** to erase the selected area. Press **Ctrl+D** to deselect.

● Build a house-shaped box

For an interesting variation, turn your box into a house. Print another copy of your box and lid – you might first like to colour them red, to look like bricks (see step 16). Print and assemble the box and lid as before. Now open the **Box Template** file that you saved in step 9. This contains a white square with grey tabs on all sides. Choose **Save As** from the **File** menu and call the new file Roof.

Press **V** for the **Move** tool, click on the white square (**1**) and, using **Fill Layer** as in step 16, fill it with a dark greyish colour, for roof tiles. Holding down the **Alt** key, click the square and drag to snap a copy into place immediately above. Then hold **Alt** and drag again to make a copy below (**2**). Next, click and drag the grey tab shape to copy it onto the top square. Finally, release the **Alt** key and drag the original grey tab shape down onto the lower square. You now have something like a dumbbell (**3**).

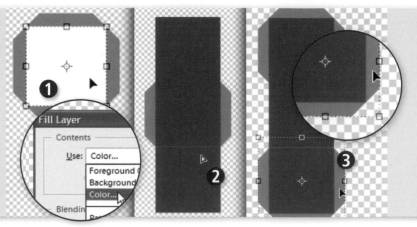

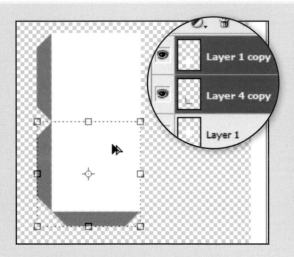

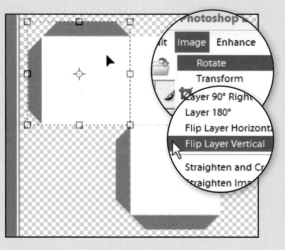

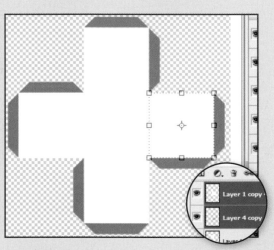

Add the other sides of the box

11 In the **Layers** palette, hold **Shift** and click **Layer 1** so that both layers are highlighted. Press **V** for the **Move** tool. Holding the **Alt** key, click on the white square and drag to make a copy of the square with its grey tabs. Position it directly below so it snaps into place, abutting the original square. Holding **Alt**, click and drag again to place a copy to the left of the original square.

Rotate to position the tabs

12 In the **Image** menu, choose **Rotate**, **Flip Layer Vertical**. The bottom tab on this copy of the square swaps to the top. Without holding **Alt**, drag the shapes back into position so the squares line up. Now **Alt**+drag the shapes to make a copy at the top centre. Swap the tab to the right using **Image**, **Rotate**, and **Flip Layer Horizontal**. Drag this copy into place, then **Alt**+drag to place a final copy on the right.

Complete your base

13 Swap the tab on this copy from top to bottom using **Image**, **Rotate**, **Flip Layer Vertical**, then drag into position. You will end up with a windmill-like pattern, as seen here. Choose **Save As** from the **File** menu and save with a new name, Box base. Click **Save**. Next, adapt it for the lid. In the **Layers** palette, click the top layer, then **Shift**+click the layer below so both are highlighted.

Click the middle square again and press **Ctrl-T** to **Transform** it. Click just off a corner of the square (the pointer shows a turning arrow) and, holding **Shift**, rotate it **45 degrees**. Drag it to the right so it snaps into place along the edges of the other squares (**4**). Press **Return** to apply this, then **Ctrl-T** to **Transform** again. In the **Options** bar, set **W** to **124%** and **H** to **70.5%**. Click the tick button. Holding **Alt**, drag your diamond shape to copy it onto the left side, completing the roof.

Press **Ctrl-S** to save. Print your roof, crease all the tabs and fold the sides (**a**) up to form a peak, sticking the side tabs inside the triangular sides (**b**) and the two top tabs back to back inside the top. Glue the roof to the top of your lid.

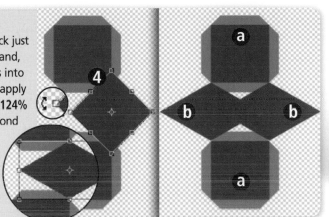

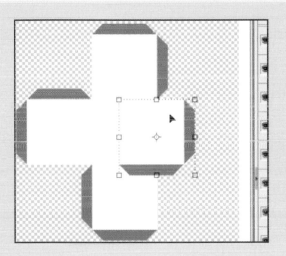

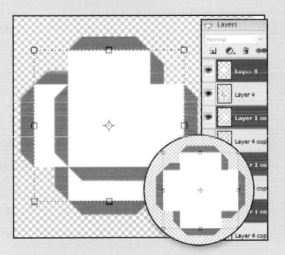

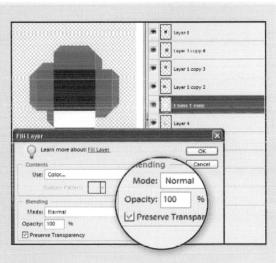

Reduce the sides

14 On the canvas, drag the selected shapes towards the centre. Snap them into place where the centre of the selection hits the edge of the centre square. Press **Shift+Ctrl+[** to send these layers to the back. In the **Layers** palette, click the layer that's now at the top, then **Shift**-click the one below. On the canvas, move the shapes towards the centre in the same way.

Your box lid

15 Repeat for all four sides. Finally, in the **Layers** palette, click the top layer, then hold **Ctrl** and click every alternate layer (the layers containing white squares). Press **Shift+Ctrl+]** to bring them to the front. Choose **Save As** from the **File** menu and save with a new name, Box lid. Now to add some colour. Click in the transparent background to deselect, then click the central white square.

Add colour

16 Go to **Edit**, **Fill Layer**. Tick **Preserve Transparency**. Choose **Color** from the **Contents, Use** menu, then pick a colour. Click **OK** twice. Select the side rectangles and colour them in the same way. Press **Ctrl+O** and open your **Box Base** file. Click each of the white squares and use **Fill Layer** to colour them. If you wish, colour the tabs, too. Choose **Save** from the **File** menu to finish.

All year round

Make a personal calendar with a new photo for every month

Don't settle for a shop-bought calendar when you can easily make your own. Select twelve favourite images – anything from picturesque landscapes to snapshots of family or friends – and create a calendar that's personal to you and unique. It can also make a great present. Using Excel, you'll adapt a Microsoft Office calendar template. Most of the work is already done – just add photos and other personal touches, then print your calendar, bind it and hang it up.

PROJECT TOOLS: Microsoft Excel ● Photoshop Elements ● Photos
SEE ALSO: Charts and graphics with Excel, page 300

● Personalising templates

Microsoft's calendar templates are great timesavers but it's worth including your own touches. As well as adding photos, change the typeface. Highlight the text and select a font from the drop-down menu in the toolbar. For the sake of consistency try to keep it the same for the month and day of the week headers. Change the colour scheme by highlighting cells and selecting a new fill colour from the toolbar.

Go to Office Online

1 Start Excel and click **Connect to Microsoft Office Online** in the **Getting Started** task pane, right. This opens the Microsoft Office Online website in your web browser. Click the **Templates** link (top left of the home page), then the **Calendars** link in the **Browse templates** section of the next page. Here you'll find a variety of calendar templates for Excel as well as for other Office applications.

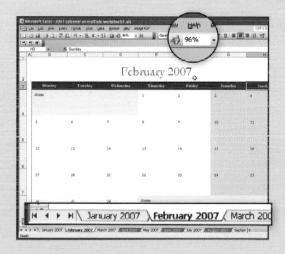

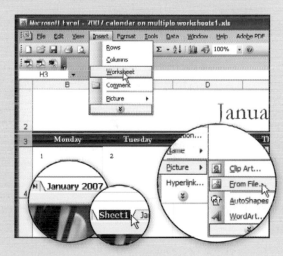

Download a template

2 Click the **2007 Calendars** link. Click **Next** for the second page of templates and select **2007 calendar on multiple worksheets (12-pp, Mon-Sun)**. Then click the **Download Now** button. Read the **End User Licence Agreement** and click the **Accept** button to agree to the terms and download the template, which is automatically loaded into Excel. Choose **Save As** from the **File** menu to save it.

Time to zoom in

3 If you don't see the whole page, choose a lower magnification view from the **Zoom** drop-down menu on the toolbar. Each month in this calendar template occupies a separate worksheet. The worksheet tabs for each month are at the bottom of the screen. To view a particular month, click on its tab. Not all the templates are organised in this way – some have all of the months on one worksheet.

Make a photo page

4 The active worksheet is displayed in bold. Click the **January 2007** worksheet tab to make it active and select **Worksheet** from the **Insert** menu to add a new worksheet in front of the January one. It will contain the January photo. Double-click the **Sheet 1** tab and name it Jan photo, and press **Return**. From the **Insert** menu, select **Picture**, **From File**. Browse your hard drive to find a photo to use.

Doing it in Word

You'll find similar calendar and planner templates for Microsoft Word on the Office Online website. Start Word, then click **Connect to Microsoft Office Online** in the **Getting Started** task pane (press **Ctrl+F1** if you don't see the task pane). Choose and download a template as in step 1. Adding your own images and customising templates is as easy as the Excel example in this project.

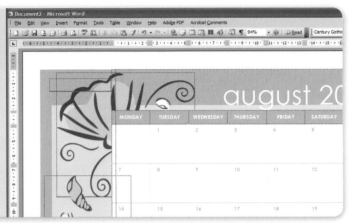

A quality feel

Printing on special paper will make a huge difference to your calendar. As well as making photo-quality inkjet paper, printer manufacturers produce matte and heavyweight papers that will give your calendar a professional look, as well as being durable. For a touch of class, consider using fine art papers from a specialist paper manufacturer such as Lyson, www.lyson.com.

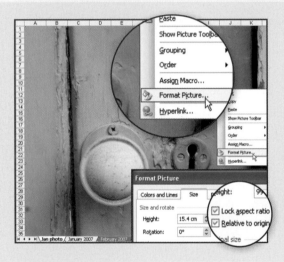

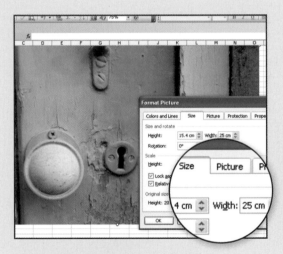

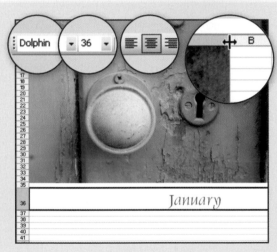

Resize the photo

5 Unless you've previously resized the photo it may appear very large on screen and you'll only be able to see a part of it. Right-click on it and choose **Format Picture** from the pop-up menu. Click the **Size** tab in the **Format Picture** dialogue box. By default, the **Lock aspect ratio** box is ticked so that when you change the width or height, the other dimension is also changed by the same amount.

Select the orientation

6 Landscape-format photos will work best with this template. To fit the photo on an A4 landscape page, resize it to no wider than **26cm** or no taller than **15cm**. Using the default cell sizes of this template, it will fit within columns **A** to **O** and rows **0** to **35**. If you want to use a portrait-format shot, use the cropping tools on the **Picture** tab of the **Format Picture** dialogue box to make it fit.

Name the month

7 Click in the first available cell in the **A** column below the photo and type in January. Select a font from the drop-down menu at the top, set the size to 36pt, and choose a colour. It's best to use the same colour throughout or match a predominant colour from the photo. Click the **January** cell followed by the **Align Centre** button on the toolbar. Click and drag to resize the **A** column to the photo width.

Producing a year planner

If you want your own year planner, have a look at the other templates on the Microsoft Office Online website. Go to www.microsoft.com, then click the **Templates** link. In the next page, click **Calendars** from the **Browse templates** section, followed by the required year. You'll find one-year-to-a-page calendars, which are the closest thing to a year planner template. There are also school and academic calendars, which run from the autumn term through to the summer term of the following year.

If you're looking for a more conventional year planner with days arranged on the horizontal axis and months vertically, there are some commercially available templates. Type Excel "year planner" into www.google.com.

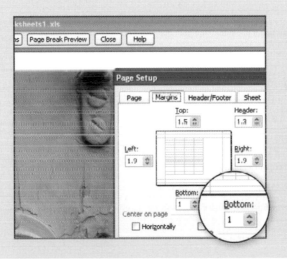

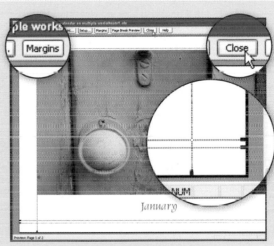

Preview before you print

8 Click the **Print Preview** button on the toolbar at the top to see how the calendar will appear on the printed page. Don't worry if it doesn't look quite right at this stage. Click the **Setup** button on the **Print Preview** window toolbar, and on the **Page** tab of the **Page Setup** dialogue box change the orientation to **Landscape** and set the paper size to **A4 210x297 mm**.

Adjust the margins

9 Click the **Margins** tab and reduce the bottom margin to **1cm**. You can also reduce the top margin but, remember, you'll need to fix the finished calendar to the wall at the top edge. Check your printer's manual to ensure you can print this close to the edge. Click **OK** to see how the changes affect the layout. Aim to fit both the photo and month name on the page.

Fine-tuning in Print Preview

10 A quicker alternative to using the **Page Setup** dialogue box is to click the **Margins** button and drag the markers in the **Print Preview** window. If you can't fit both the photo and month name on the page, go back and make the picture smaller (see step 6). Centre everything horizontally by dragging the left-hand margin to adjust it, then click the **Close** button.

● The online option

Internet sites such as Google, www.google.com/calendar, Yahoo, http://calendar.yahoo.com, and AOL, http://calendar.aol.co.uk, all provide online calendars where you can input appointments and events, set up reminders or send out invitations. All work in similar ways. You'll need to sign up with the site, but registration is free. Your diary can be private or public, so you can share calendar information with any people you choose – their appointments appear alongside your own. You can also print out a copy to create a traditional calendar.

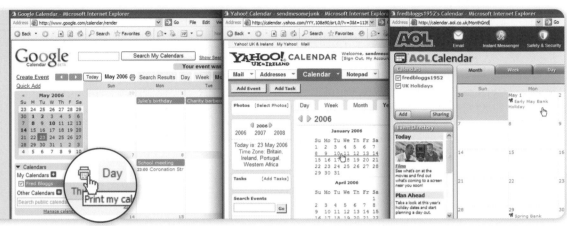

Move onto the next month

11 Right-click the **Jan photo** tab and select **Move or Copy** from the pop-up menu. Select **February 2007** from the **Before sheet** list and tick the **Create a copy** box. The new sheet appears before the **February 2007** page, called **Jan Photo (2)**; rename it **Feb photo**. Click on the original photo and press **Backspace** to delete it. Now click in the **A1** cell and insert a new photo as you did in step 4.

Completing the whole year

12 Resize and, if necessary, crop the photo to the same dimensions as the January one and overwrite the January text with **February**. Now repeat the process from the previous step, copying the worksheets, replacing the photos and changing the text so that you have a photo page worksheet preceding the calendar worksheet for every month of the year.

Birthdays and special occasions

13 To illustrate events such as birthdays or special events, add photos to the main calendar pages. You can resize large photos in Excel but it's easier to resize them first in Photoshop Elements (see page 57, step 4). Make them no bigger than a few inches or 600 pixels wide. Return to Excel, select the date cell to add the photo to, and choose **Picture, From File** from the **Insert** menu.

Best ways to bind a calendar

If you're producing a small number of calendars for family and friends, consider having them professionally bound. The two most common options are plastic comb binding and 'Wire-O' binding. Small print and copy shops offer this service at reasonable prices. An inexpensive option is to buy plastic sleeve binders from a stationer.

For a more attractive finish, use a three-hole punch. If you don't have one, use one hole of a two-hole punch to make three equally spaced holes in the same position along the top of each page. Loosely tie the pages together with three lengths of fancy string or ribbon. Finally, punch a single hole horizontally centred at the bottom of each page, then use it to hang or pin the calendar to the wall.

Protective measures

One way to make your calendar durable is to cover it, and there are a variety of materials you can use. The best known is 'Fablon', which comes in transparent and printed styles and is available from DIY stores. Another option is 'Transpaseal', which you can buy from graphics suppliers. Plastic coverings will make it difficult to write on your calendar with a ballpoint pen or pencil, and you may have to use a special felt-tipped pen instead.

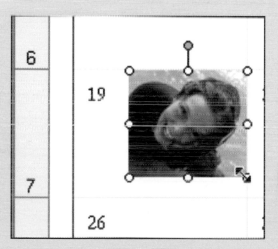

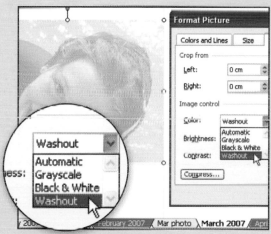

Resize the photo

14 Click and drag on a corner handle to resize the photo. Hold down the **Shift** key at the same time to constrain the proportions as you're resizing. Rotate the photo by clicking and dragging the green handle above the top of the photo. Alternatively, size the photo to fill the cell and reduce its opacity so that you can print text or write in details by hand on top of it.

Fade the photo

15 Right-click the photo and select **Format Picture** from the pop-up menu. Click the **Picture** tab. Under **Image control**, select **Washout** from the **Color** drop-down menu. This reduces the brightness and contrast of the photo. Click **OK** to see the result and, if you wish, reopen the **Format Picture** dialogue box and use the **Brightness** and **Contrast** sliders to adjust the appearance of the picture.

Print your calendar

16 Select **Print** from the **File** menu to print the calendar. In the **Print** dialogue box tick the **Entire workbook** button. If you later make changes, you can print individual pages by ticking the **Active sheets** button. Staple the calendar together along the top edge and pin it to the wall, or use a more sophisticated binding technique (see 'Best ways to bind a calendar' box, above).

Tough at the top
Can Hancock hack it?
Page 2

New kid on the block
Dwight makes his debut
Page 2

THE ⚽ EASTIE

EAST END WANDERERS INDEPENDENT FAN MAG

18 OCTOBER 2006

Coach reckons 5-a-siders will be 'ready...

BY EASTIE STAFF

With three fresh faces, a new strip, and sponsorship courtesy of All Star Glazing, this should be the Easties' moment. Yet as John Hancock begins his third term as coach, some say his biggest challenge is to lay the ghosts of missed opportunities.

Hancock himself is determined to focus on the future. 'The problems of the past are just that, in the past. Now we've got a keen line-up and the lads are ready for anything,' he told the Eastie before last Sunday's League match against North Village.

Hopes dashed
Solid performance in Sunday's game would have boosted the East Enders' hopes for the season, but sadly it was not to be (see match report, page 2). It remains to be seen if Hancock can motivate his team and resolve the attendance issues that have plagued us in recent years. On the plus side, All Star's generous sponsorship will

allow investment in the Fa... ground and improver... facilities, which in turn sh... the club get 100% from its p...

New signing Dwight Gor... the coach his full ba... exciting for me to m...

FORTHCOMING FIXTURES
West Field Rovers
Sunday 22 October
...ck-off 3pm

...TOBER 2006

The lads have silverwar...

CH REPORT
...ST END WANDERERS 1
...RTH VILLAGE 4

East End go down fighting

BY ANDY ROBINSON

...he first game of the season it may ...ve been, but there was little sign of beginner's luck for the crew during ...Cup tie with the Villagers. ...a sterling effort on all parts, ...e home team was manifestly ...from the start, and the ...ast count themselves lucky ...ot to have conceded two or three ...ecially in the second half. ...or condition of the pi... ...ential rain was no exc... ...not brilliance, the... ...ence did giv... ...the weathe... ...ful, b...

Smith's shot in the 15th minute was sadly off-target. **PHOTO: BEN FRITH**

to warm up in the chilly conditions, a series of early throw-ins introduced something of a random element into play and Village were arguably fortunate to find their way through the East End defence after just eight minutes, Tony Hopkirk's improvised scissor kick grazing Calum Higgins' outstretched fingers on its way to the back of the net.

From then on it was all downhill, and while neither team particularly distinguished itself on this occasion, slightly less scrappy play from the men in yellow was rewarded with two more goals before the...

...ird time...

mark courtesy of John Garton and Vernon Heckle.

In the second half, Gordon came out fighting and almost immediately caught the opposition off guard, smashing the ball into the net from little closer than the half-way mark. This performance was not to be sustained, and the match petered out, with all players looking fatigued (and wet), enlivened only by Garton's second successful strike five minutes from full time. Not the start we might have wished for, then, but leaving the door open for better results as the season progresses.

The stats as they stand

LATEST MATCH STATS
15 OCTOBER
EAST END WANDERERS 1
NORTH VILLAGE 4
VENUE FACTORY ROAD GROUND
REFEREE DAN MASON
ATTENDANCE 49
MAN OF THE MATCH DWIGHT GORDON
GOALS HOPKIRK (8 MINS), GARTON (24 MINS, 86 MINS), HECKLE (32 MINS), GORDON (47 MINS)

MEGA MOTORS LOCAL LEAG...

TEAM	P	W	D
South Fork Utd	2	1	1
North Village	1	1	0
West Field Rvrs	1	1	0
Near Bye	1	0	1
Far Aweigh	1	0	1
...d W'ers	1	0	0

Hold the front page
Bring everyone up to date with a newsletter in Word

Whether you're running a voluntary organisation or a coffee club, managing a sports team or masterminding a political campaign, it's vital to keep people informed about news and upcoming events. Or perhaps you just want to keep distant friends and family up to date. Emails are quick and easy to send, but not everyone has a computer or is connected to the internet. A newsletter, on the other hand, can be read by all. And by giving the newsletter a professional look using your PC, you enhance the image of your organisation at the same time as delivering information.

The simplest and often the best format for a newsletter is a single sheet of A4 paper, printed both sides. Here's how to create one in Microsoft Word.

PROJECT TOOLS: Microsoft Word ● Photoshop Elements ● Digital photos
SEE ALSO: Create a 'This is your life' album, page 112 ● Desktop publishing with Word, page 328

Desktop-publishing software

Microsoft Word has all the features that you need to create professional-looking pages. But dedicated programs such as Microsoft Publisher, http://office.microsoft.com/publisher, and Serif PagePlus, www.serif.com/pageplus, are even more intuitive and offer greater accuracy and control over text and pictures. You can download a free copy of PagePlus SE – a 'light' version of PagePlus – as well as full versions of other Serif graphic-design programs, from www.freeserifsoftware.com.

PagePlus SE - Desktop Pul
● Ads & Broch
● Business St
● Flyers & For
● Invitations
● Greeting Ca
● Over 500+

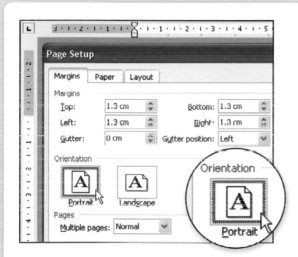

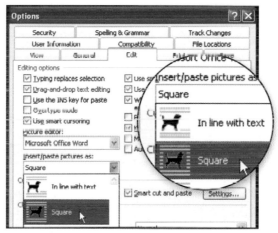

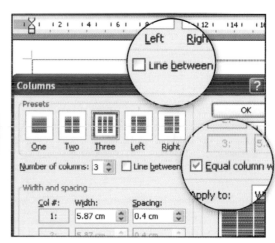

Create a blank document

1 Run Microsoft Word, which opens with a new blank document. From the **File** menu, choose **Page Setup**. In the **Paper** tab, choose **A4**. In the **Margins** tab, set all margins to **1.3cm (0.5in)** and **Orientation** to **Portrait**. Set **Multiple pages** to **Normal**. Click **OK**. Go to the **View** menu and choose **Print Layout**. Click the **Zoom** percentage in the **Formatting** toolbar and choose **Whole Page**.

Set up Word for desktop publishing

2 Under **Toolbars** on the **View** menu, make sure **Formatting**, **Drawing** and **Picture** are turned on. Choose **Options** from the **Tools** menu. In the **View** tab, tick all the **Print and Web Layout** options. In the **General** tab, untick **Automatically create drawing canvas**. In the **Edit** tab, click the **Inset/paste pictures as** box and choose **Square**. You can ignore the other settings on this tab. Click **OK**.

Make newspaper-style columns

3 From the **Format** menu, choose **Columns**. In the box, click one of the **Presets** to choose the number and width of columns. For a newsletter, three equal columns are best. Tick **Equal column width**. The **Spacing** option sets the gap between columns, which should be just enough to keep them clearly separated; set this to **0.4cm (0.15in)**. Untick **Line between** (this doesn't work correctly with complex layouts). Click **OK**.

Straight and curly quote marks

The quotation marks found on your PC keyboard (' and ") are really 'primes', used to denote imperial measures. But Word can convert them to 'curly quotes'. Choose **AutoCorrect Options** from the **Tools** menu, click the **AutoFormat As You Type** tab, and tick **Straight quotes with smart quotes**.

Use primes for feet and inches, as in 4' 6"; press **Ctrl+Z** to undo when Word converts them. You can add other special characters by choosing **Symbol** from the **Insert** menu. Click the **Special Characters** tab, then double-click a symbol to insert it. For example, a hyphen (-), found on your PC keyboard, is used in double-barrelled words, but a dash – used to separate whole phrases – is longer.

Order of importance

A big picture should usually be near the top of the page, accompanying your main or 'lead' story. This has the largest headline. Any other stories have smaller pictures and headlines, but the same size text, although you may vary the font, for example between serif and sans serif, or bold and normal. To make a page look balanced, try diagonal symmetry, for example where a picture at the top right is balanced by one at the bottom left.

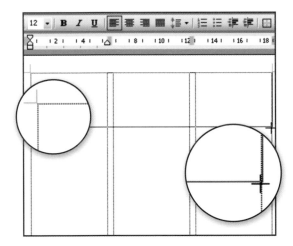

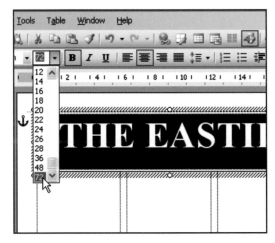

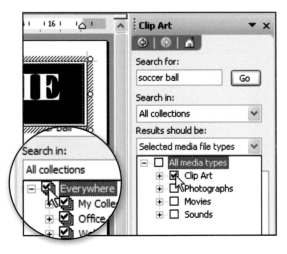

Add a text box

4 You'll see your page divided into columns. Above them, you'll need a 'masthead' – the title of your newsletter – across the front page. Create a text box to contain this. Choose **Text Box** from the **Insert** menu; the mouse pointer turns into a crosshair. Click at the top left of the page, in the corner of the margin, hold down the mouse button, and drag across to the right margin and down to draw a box.

Format your masthead text

5 Type the title of your newsletter, then click and drag over it with the mouse to select all the text. Using the **Formatting** toolbar, choose a suitable font – here it's **Times New Roman Bold**, making the masthead reminiscent of *The Times* newspaper. Set the alignment to **Center** and choose a size that makes the text nearly fill the space available, leaving spare room for a graphic.

Choose a graphic

6 *The Times* has a coat of arms between the words 'THE' and 'TIMES'; choose a theme appropriate to your newsletter. From the **Insert** menu, choose **Picture**, then **Clip Art**. Under **Search for** in the **Clip Art** panel, type in a word for what you're looking for, in this case soccer ball. Click the **Search in** menu and, in the drop-down list, tick **Everywhere**; for **Results should be**, tick only **Clip Art**. Click **Go**.

DESIGN WISE

● Lining up the text

Text in newspaper columns is often 'justified', meaning that the spacing between letters and words is adjusted so that everything lines up at both the left and right sides of the column. Word has a **Justify** option but lacks the features found in desktop-publishing programs to fine-tune spacing, so text can sometimes look 'gappy'. If that's the case, choose **Align Left** instead, for a less formal style that appears neat.

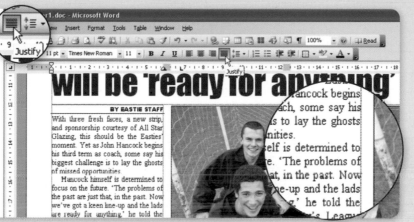

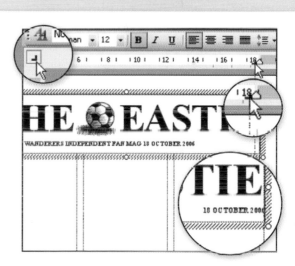

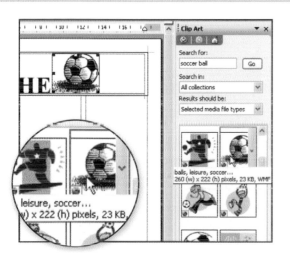

Add a picture to the masthead

7 In the search results, find something suitable – here, a drawing of a football. At the top of your page, click between 'THE' and 'EASTIE' to place the text cursor within the masthead, then click your chosen clip-art graphic to insert it. Don't worry if it pushes out the end of your text. Click the top right corner of the box around the graphic and drag to make the image smaller.

Adjust the picture's position

8 If the graphic doesn't line up with the text, choose **Font** from the **Format** menu. In the **Character Spacing** tab, change **Position** from **Normal** to **Lowered**. Increase the **By** setting to move the graphic downwards. You don't see the result until you click **OK**, so it may take a few tries. Click and drag to select all the text, and adjust the font size to fill the whole width.

Describe your newsletter

9 Click at the end of the text, then press **Return**. Change the text size to **12pt**, **Left** alignment. Type a phrase describing your newsletter. This is called the 'strapline'. Press **Tab**, then type the publication date. Now click the symbol at the top left until it shows a backwards 'L', for a right tab stop. Click in the white ruler across the top, then drag the mouse pointer over to the right margin to place the tab stop there.

● Wraps and overlaps

Both picture and text boxes have text wrap settings, accessed by double-clicking the item (use the edge of a text box) and going to the **Layout** tab in the **Format Picture** or **Format Text Box** dialogue box. **Square** is the usual choice, making text on the page flow around the box. If you want one box to overlap another, and it won't, click the **Advanced** button in the **Layout** tab and, under **Picture Position**, tick **Allow overlap**; do this for both boxes.

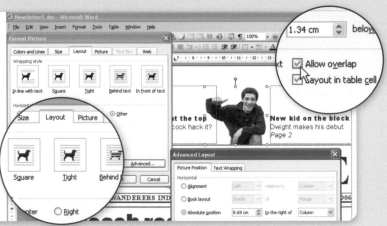

● Commercial printing

If you need more than a few copies of your newsletter, it makes sense to have it printed by a copy shop rather than trying to do it yourself. Many local services have colour laser printers or digital printing presses that will run out any quantity, from one to thousands, at a reasonable price per copy. Just ask if they can work from Word files.

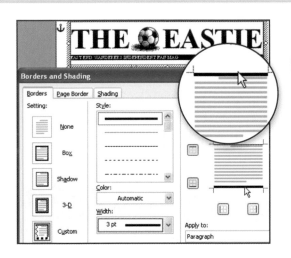

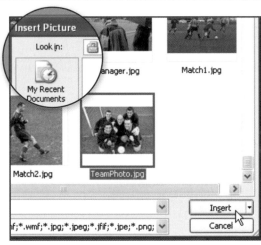

Add emphasis using rules

10 With the text cursor in the strapline, choose **Borders** and **Shading** from the **Format** menu. In the **Borders** tab, click the first option under **Style** for a plain line (or 'rule'), set **Color** to **Automatic**, and set **Width** to **1pt** (one point). In the **Preview** diagram, click above the text (grey lines) to add a line here. Change the **Width** to **3pt** and click below the text to add a thicker line here. Click **OK**.

Insert a picture

11 Now click on the page outside the text box you just made. Click the **Insert Picture** button at the left of the **Picture** toolbar, or go to the **Insert** menu and choose **Picture, From File**. In the box that appears, click to highlight the image file you want to use. If the button at the bottom right doesn't say **Insert**, click the triangle and change it to this. Click the button to bring the picture onto the page.

Crop pictures tightly for impact

12 Click on the picture to select it, then click on the **Crop** button in the **Picture** toolbar – the box around the picture changes. Drag the 'handle' in the middle of any side to crop off that edge. Try to leave only the significant elements in the frame. Click the **Crop** button again to finish, then drag the picture over to the right margin. Drag the bottom left corner to resize it to fit across two columns.

● Giving credit where it's due

Newspapers usually credit journalists and photographers. In the example layout here, the writer is credited with a 'byline' at the top of each main story – align this **Right** and add a ¾**pt** rule below using **Borders and Shading** (see step 10). Use your chosen sans serif font (such as **Arial**), in bold, slightly smaller than the story text; in the same style, credit the photographer at the end of each picture caption.

● Headers and footers

Each page should show the title of the publication, date and page number, either in a 'header' at the top or a 'footer' at the bottom. Word's **Headers and Footers** will repeat the same text on every page, with the correct page number.

Choose **Header and Footer** from the **View** menu to display the header and footer boxes, which start off empty. Click in either; for a newsletter, a footer is best. Type some text – THE EASTIE, for example – at the left, then press **Tab**. In the centre box you can add more text. Press **Tab** again. In the right-hand box, type PAGE then, instead of typing a page number, click the **Insert Page Number** button in the **Header and Footer** toolbar. Click and drag to highlight your text and format it in the usual way.

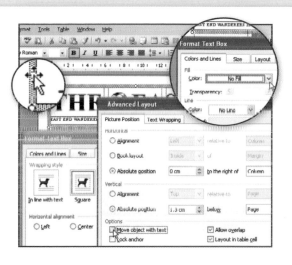

Set text wrapping

13 Before typing a headline, place the mouse pointer at the edge of the masthead's text box (the pointer shows crossed arrows) and double-click to show **Format Text Box**. In the **Colors and Lines** tab, set **Color** to **No Fill**. In the **Layout** tab, set **Wrapping style** to **Square**. Click **Advanced**, and untick **Move object with text**. Click **OK** twice. Click anywhere on the blank page.

Type a headline

14 The flashing text cursor appears below the masthead. Type a headline for your first story, then press **Return** and type the first sentence of the story. Click and drag to highlight just the headline, then choose **Columns** from the **Format** menu and set **Number of columns** to 1. Click **OK**. Highlight the headline text again and use the **Formatting** toolbar to set it larger and in a suitable font, such as **Impact**.

Write your lead story

15 Click the photo and drag it downwards to let the headline run right across the page. Adjust the size of the headline text, and rewrite it, if necessary, to fill the space. Click and drag to highlight the story text and format it in a serif font – for example, **Times New Roman**, **11pt**, **Left** aligned. Press the right arrow key to go to the end of the text, then type more of your story. You needn't finish it yet.

● Making use of Word's paragraph styles

Paragraph 'styles' provide a quick way to apply fonts and formatting. When you're happy with a paragraph of text, click within it and choose **Styles and Formatting** from the **Format** menu. In the **Styles and Formatting** panel, click **New Style**. Give it a name and click **OK**. Click the **Styles** picker at the left of the **Formatting** toolbar (it usually shows **Normal**) and choose the new name.

To apply the same formatting to another paragraph, click in it and then choose the style. To change this style throughout, alter one paragraph to which you've applied the style, then choose **Styles and Formatting** from the **Format** menu. In the **Styles and Formatting** panel, right-click the style and choose **Update to Match Selection**. The new formatting is applied to all other text to which you've applied the style.

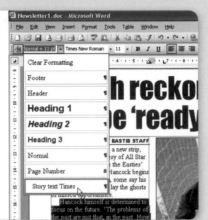

● Printing and paper

Print your pages as explained in the 'Printing your album' box on page 119, turning over page 1 to print page 2 on the back. For inkjet printing, choose a fairly thick paper so that the printing doesn't show through, but avoid glossy photo paper because it makes text hard to read. Instead, choose a high-quality matt paper. If you're using a laser printer, whether black and white or colour, then good-quality copier paper is fine.

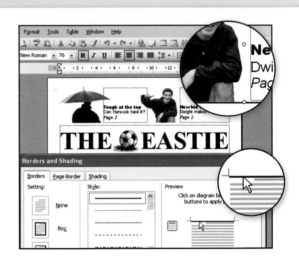

Liven up your front page

16 Many newspapers now make space above their mastheads to present titbits of what's inside, known as 'teasers'. This can liven up your front page. Click on the edge of your masthead text box, then hold **Shift** and click on your photo, selecting them both at once. Drag them downwards to leave a space about the same depth as the masthead. The headline pops up to the top.

Fill the space with pictures and text

17 Ignore this and add some teaser pictures, as in step 12. It's best to make these cutouts (see box, page 145). For each picture, add a text box, as in step 4, and format it with no colouring and a text wrap, as in step 13. Format your text in a sans serif font – for example, **Arial**, **13pt**. When you fill the space above the masthead with pictures and text boxes, the headline is pushed back into place.

Draw a rule below the teasers

18 Click within the masthead text, then use **Borders and Shading**, as in step 10, to add a 1½pt line above it. Position your teaser text boxes so that they sit above the line, with a gap about the height of one line of text. Position your pictures exactly on the line. Hold **Alt** while dragging to move items in smaller steps, or hold **Ctrl** and nudge a selected item with the cursor arrow keys.

● Making cutouts

Cutout photos look good over the masthead (see step 17). To make a cutout, open your photo in Photoshop Elements and make a selection around an object or person. There are various ways to do this, including the **Lasso** tool (see page 320). Fill the rest of the picture with white: press **D** to set the background colour, invert the selection (press **Shift+Ctrl+I**), then press **Delete**. Save the image with a new name, then insert it in Word.

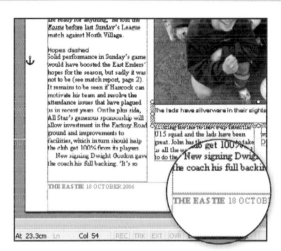

The final elements of your page

19 Add a footer (see 'Headers and footers', page 143), plus a text box for a caption (see step 4) below the picture. Make the text the same size as your story, but in a sans serif font. If the story disappears from the last two columns, it'll come back if you nudge the caption up to touch the picture. Adjust the bottom of the caption's text box to make the story text line up across all three columns.

Create a tint box

20 At the bottom left, add one final text box for a useful bit of information. Double-click it and use **Format Text Box** (see step 13) to give it a 'tint'. In the **Colors and Lines** tab, pick a light **Fill Color** so that black text will show up easily over it. In the **Text Box** tab, set an **Internal margin** of about **0.2cm** (0.08in) to move the text in from the edges of the box.

Edit your story to fit

21 Now you can see how much space is left for your story. Don't change the font size to make it fit – text should be the same size throughout your publication. Instead, rewrite the story to fit. At the end of the page, press **Return** to create a new page, for the back. Lay it out using the same techniques, but with two stories and one or more boxes. Add any further pages in the same way, then save the Word file.

Grand designs
Plan your kitchen revamp with the help of Excel

Remodelling your kitchen adds value to your home as well as increasing your enjoyment of it. Planning the job can be complicated, but using Microsoft Excel it's easy to draw a scale diagram of your kitchen and add cabinets, appliances and other furniture to figure out what will fit where. By working to a grid, you can create a neat plan that you can discuss with family members or your builder. Or print out your plan and cutout furniture for coffee-table planning sessions.

PROJECT TOOLS: Tape measure ● Appliance catalogues ● Microsoft Excel ● Photoshop Elements
SEE ALSO: Children's story book, page 180 ● Charts and graphics with Excel, page 300

Pick a shape

Using the **Select Objects** option (see step 2) makes it easier to work with shapes. When it's turned on, indicated by the white arrow button highlighted in the **Drawing** toolbar, you can click on a shape to resize or move it. You may also replace a text label by clicking the shape and typing. To edit text in the normal way using a text cursor, or to select cells for spreadsheet work, you'll need to turn this option off.

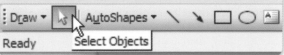

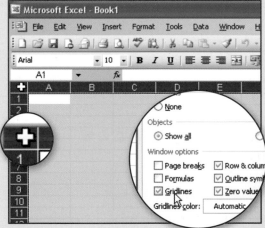

Set up a grid in Excel

1 Run Excel. If you don't see a grid of cells, choose **Options** from the **Tools** menu, click the **View** tab and tick **Gridlines**. First, you need to make the cells exactly square. The height of a cell is set in a different way to the width (see 'Excel cell sizes', page 149, for more detail). Click the rectangle in the top left corner of the spreadsheet, above '1' and to the left of 'A', to highlight all the cells.

● A lick of paint

You can give your kitchen a fresh look just by redecorating – painting the walls, choosing new floor covering or replacing the worktops. Take a digital photo of the room – use your camera's wide-angle setting, and fit as much of the interior as possible into the shot. Transfer the image to your PC and open it in Photoshop Elements. Use the **Lasso** tool (see 'Making selections', page 320) to draw around the area you want to recolour, using **Shift** or **Alt** to add or subtract tricky areas (see 'Children's story book', steps 7 to 8, and 'How to lasso', page 183). You needn't be too precise, since it's just for a quick impression. Press **Ctrl+U** to open the **Hue/Saturation** box. Tick **Colorize**, then adjust the **Hue** slider to set the colour, and use **Saturation** and **Lightness** to fine-tune it.

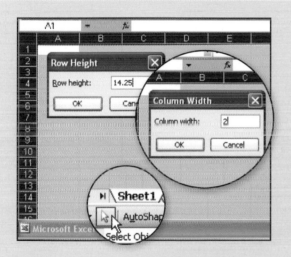

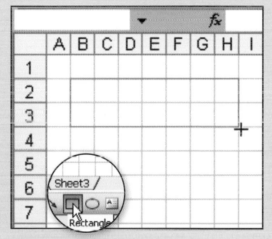

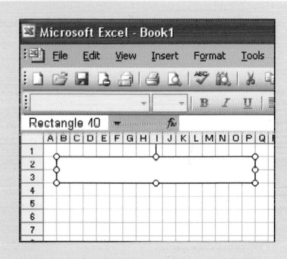

Resize the spreadsheet cells

2 From the **Format** menu, choose **Row**, then **Height**. Enter 14.25 and click **OK**. Back on the **Format** menu, choose **Column**, then **Width**. Enter 2 and click **OK**. The cells now look square. Look for the **Drawing** toolbar, usually displayed at the bottom left of the window. If you don't see it, go to the **View** menu and choose **Toolbars**, then **Drawing**. In this toolbar, click the white arrow button (**Select Objects**).

Start drawing your plan

3 Further along the toolbar, double-click the **Rectangle** tool. The first task is to draw the kitchen walls (see 'Measuring your room', page 148). You're going to represent everything schematically within the grid. Hold the **Alt** key to draw exactly on the gridlines. Start by clicking one square in from the top left corner and, holding down the mouse button, drag to draw a rectangle.

Draw walls as rectangles

4 Draw the wall to the length you measured, stopping at any opening. Count the squares as a guide to length – each square represents 10cm. Unless your measurements show otherwise, make the wall one square thick if it's an internal wall, usually made of wood and plaster 'stud', or two squares thick for a solid external wall. Keep the **Alt** key held down to finish on a gridline.

● Measuring your room

Unless you're building a new kitchen, you will need to plan within the existing walls. With a paper and pencil, sketch the shape of the room, not exactly to scale. Measure each wall and write the measurement on the sketch. Don't forget to mark and measure the positions of doors, windows, fireplaces, alcoves and any other openings. Your plan needs to be accurate to 10cm or 3in; double-check exact sizes before going ahead with your project.

● Printing your plan

First choose **Page Setup** from the **File** menu. Then in the **Paper Size** tab, set **Paper size** to **A4**, and **Print quality** to **High**. Choose **Portrait** or **Landscape** according to the shape of your plan (tall or wide). Set **Scaling** as explained in 'Printing to scale', page 151, or choose **Fit to**. Click **Print Preview** to check how your plan fits on the page. If necessary, click **Margins** and drag the margins (see right) to make more room. Click **Print**.

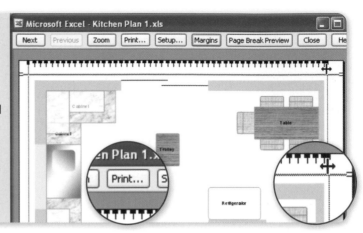

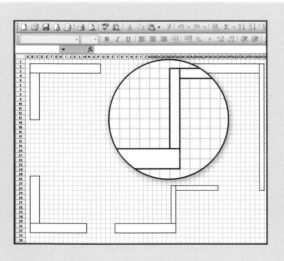

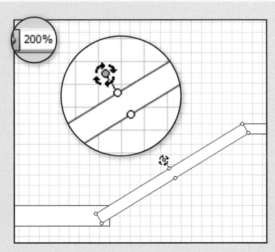

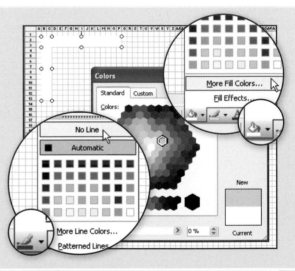

Keep to the grid

5 If the measurement of your wall isn't an exact multiple of 10cm, just draw it to the nearest gridline. This may seem quite a wide margin of error, but keeping to the grid will make your kitchen plan neater and easier to draw. Rechecking the exact dimensions and making sure it all fits will be a task for a later stage in the project. Draw your other walls in the same way.

Drawing diagonal walls

6 If you have a wall that runs diagonally, first draw it straight, then rotate it by dragging the green handle at the top centre of the shape. If you don't see the handle, zoom in, using the setting in the top toolbar. Click within the shape and drag it into place. This may take trial and error, but if you draw neighbouring walls first, based on your measurements, you'll see how the angled wall should fit.

Shade the walls

7 When all your walls are done, hold **Shift** and click each in turn to select them all. In the **Drawing** toolbar, click the triangle next to the **Line Color** button (paintbrush) and pick **No Line** from the menu that pops up. Click the triangle next to the **Fill Color** button (bucket) and pick a colour. If you wish, choose a colour that you might use to paint the walls. Click **More Fill Colors** for a wider choice.

Preparing a schedule

A 'schedule' lists what you'll need to buy. Click the **Sheet2** tab at the bottom of the sheet, and in the **Drawing** toolbar turn off **Select Objects**. Click in cell **A1**. Pressing **Tab** between cells, type Item, Quantity, Cost and Total. Click in **A2** and fill in the details for your first item. Under **Total**, press =, click the cell under **Quantity**, press *, then click the cell under **Cost**. Press **Return**. Click the row number (**2**) to highlight the whole row, then hold **Ctrl** and drag the black border to copy it to the next row. Edit this for your second item, leaving the **Total** to calculate itself. Repeat to complete your list. Click the cell under the last **Total**, click the **AutoSum** button in the top toolbar, and press **Return**.

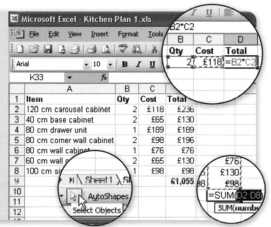

Excel cell sizes

Spreadsheet cells are designed to hold numbers, not to represent physical space. So you can't set their width and height in inches or centimetres. The width of cells is set in arbitrary units representing how many numbers will fit in. This has some odd consequences – for example, if you double the **Column Width**, the cell doesn't get twice as wide. Use the settings shown in step 2 to get 0.5cm square cells.

DESIGN WISE

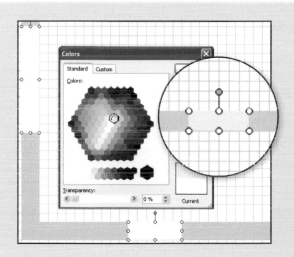

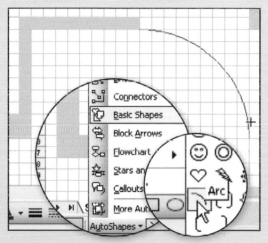

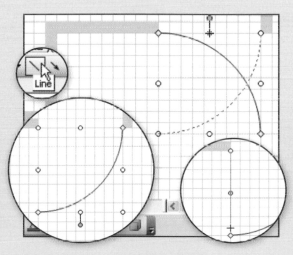

Add windows

8 Where you've left gaps for window openings, draw rectangles to indicate the windows. Holding down the **Shift** key, click each in turn to select them all and then colour them in. There's no need to use an architectural symbol for windows – just make them clearly distinct from the walls by choosing a different **Fill Color**. Again, choose **No Line** in the **Line Color** pop-up menu.

Add doors

9 For doors, use the conventional architectural symbol (an arc), because it shows what part of the floor must be kept clear for the door to open. In the **Drawing** toolbar, click **AutoShapes**, choose **Basic Shapes** and pick **Arc**. Hold down the **Alt** and **Shift** keys, to snap to the grid and prevent the shape squashing. Click on the corner of the wall at one side of the doorway and drag across to the other.

Complete the door symbol

10 Depending on the position of your doorway, you may find the arc won't go the right way. So make it the right size, then flip it over – hold the **Alt** and **Ctrl** keys, click on one of the shape's side handles and drag it to the opposite side. Next, in the **AutoShapes** toolbar, click the **Line** button. Holding **Alt**, click and drag to join the loose end of the arc to the doorframe.

● Planning with paper shapes

Make paper cutouts to plan with when you're not sat at your PC. Hold **Ctrl**, click the **Sheet1** tab at the bottom of the sheet and drag it to the right to copy the whole sheet. Repeat for another copy. On **Sheet1 (2)**, click each of the windows, walls and doors, and remove them (press **Delete**). Rearrange the furniture into groups, and make extra copies of cabinets. Print the sheet and cut out the items with scissors. Click the **Sheet1 (3)** tab, and delete all the furniture. Print with the same scaling and lay your cutouts on top.

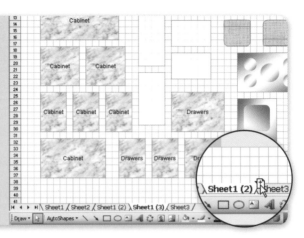

● Printing gridlines

The gridlines shown in Excel's window are just for display and don't normally print out when you print the document. In step 1, you can see how to turn gridlines on or off in the on-screen display. If you want gridlines to appear on your printed plan too, click the **Sheet** tab in the **Page Setup** box (see 'Printing your plan', page 148) and, under **Print**, tick **Gridlines**. The grid will now be printed along with your plan.

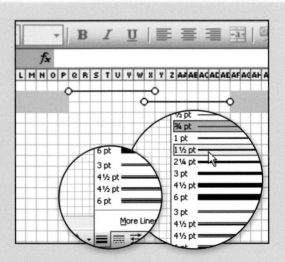

Add sliding doors

11 Double doors or french windows can be indicated with two arcs. For sliding patio doors, use straight lines instead (as above), again using the **Line** tool. When you've added all the doors, **Shift**+click to select all the lines you've drawn. In the **Drawing** toolbar, click the **Line Style** button and change the thickness from ³/₄pt to 1¹/₂pt so that your lines will be clearly visible when the plan is printed.

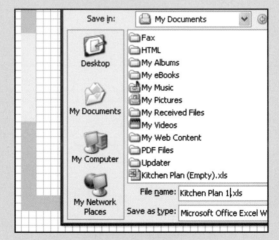

Save your plan

12 With your existing kitchen plan complete, choose **Save** from the **File** menu (or press **Ctrl+S**) and save your workbook in Excel (*.xls) format, naming it Kitchen Plan (Empty). From the **File** menu choose **Save As** and save it again under a new name, Kitchen Plan 1. This ensures you don't accidentally spoil your basic plan while experimenting with new kitchen layouts.

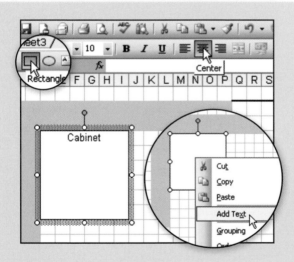

Start adding furniture

13 In the **Drawing** toolbar, choose **Rectangle** again. Holding **Alt** and **Shift**, draw a shape six cells square. This is a standard European cabinet size. To remind you that it's a cabinet, right-click the shape and choose **Add Text** from the menu that pops up. A shaded border appears around the shape and a text cursor flashes inside it. Type in Cabinet. In the **Formatting** toolbar, click the **Center** button.

Printing to scale

Use the **Scaling** factor in **Page Setup** to determine the scale at which your plan is printed. If you've followed the steps shown to create a metric plan, then each cell is 0.5cm square and represents 10cm square in real life. So if you print at **100%** size, the scale will be 1:20, which happens to be a standard choice for house plans. For a large room that doesn't fit on one sheet, scale to **80%** for 1:25 scale, or **40%** for 1:50.

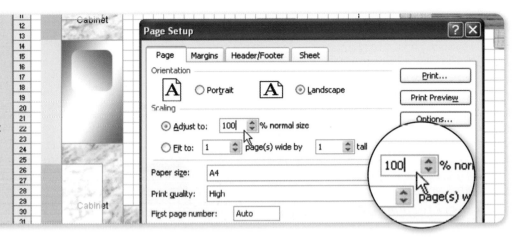

Format the text label

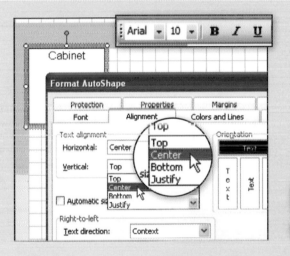

14 To style the text, click on it, then set the font, size or other attributes in the **Formatting** menu. Right-click on the shape and choose **Format AutoShape**. In the **Alignment** tab, set **Vertical** to **Center**. Click **OK**. Using the **Line Color** and **Fill Color** menus on the **Drawing** toolbar, change the shape's outline from black to grey, so it's less distracting, and fill it with a colour.

Set the cabinet's appearance

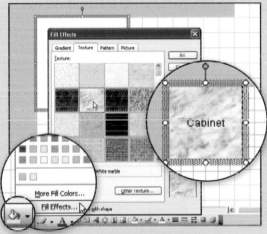

15 From the **Drawing** toolbar, click the **Fill Color** options (down arrow) and choose **Fill Effects** from the pop-up box. In the **Texture** tab, choose a finish such as wood or marble, to help visualise the new kitchen cabinets. Click **OK**. To make more cabinets, hold the **Ctrl** key (the mouse pointer shows a plus sign) and the **Alt** key, then click on the cabinet and drag to a new position.

Add more cabinets

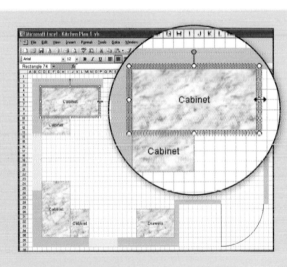

16 For narrower or wider cabinets, hold **Alt** and drag a side handle. Common sizes are 40, 50, 60, 80, 100 and 120cm, all 60cm deep. In corners, you'll need a carousel (usually 120cm) to get at the cupboard contents. Use the same cabinet shape to represent a drawer unit; click the text and type Drawers over it. Don't place drawers in a corner where a cabinet would open onto them.

Planning a kitchen the Ikea way

Ikea provides a free program that you can use to plan your kitchen then visualise it in 3D. Although designed for Ikea units, the program is useful regardless of the brand of kitchen furniture you're interested in, as sizes are fairly standard.

Go to www.ikea.com/ms/en_GB/complete_kitchen_guide/planner_tool/download, click the **Download now** link and then save the file **ihp_Kitchen.exe** to your desktop. From the **Download Complete** dialogue box, click **Run**, then follow the instructions.

When the program loads, it displays the first of the four main 'views' – **Room Design** (right). If your kitchen is not the plain rectanglular shape shown, click the **Room shape** box on

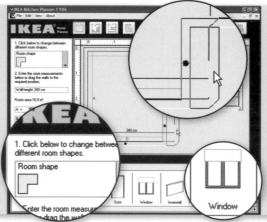

the left and choose a new shape from the drop-down list. Adjust the room's shape by clicking and dragging walls – sizes are shown as you drag. Below are main fixtures such as doors, windows, radiators, water, gas and electric points. Drag these into place on the walls. You can change dimensions of doors or windows in the boxes at the left, or delete unwanted items by pressing **Delete**. When you're happy with the basic plan, click the next button – **Furnish**. At the bottom

---

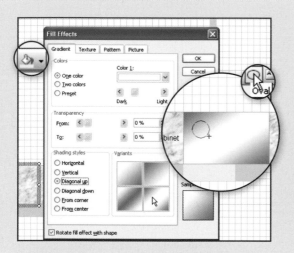

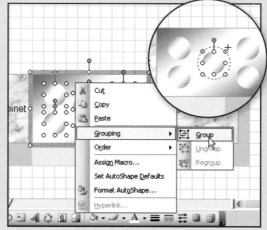

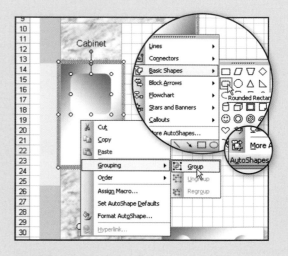

Draw a hob

17 For a hob, stove or cooking range, adjust a cabinet shape to size (from 50 to 100cm wide). Double-click the text to highlight it and press **Delete**. Choose **Fill Effects**, click the **Gradient** tab and pick a **Diagonal** style – for stainless steel. Click **OK**. In the **Drawing** toolbar, click **Oval**. Holding **Alt** and **Shift** click and drag to draw a circle to represent a cooker ring. Give this a similar fill effect.

Duplicate and adjust the rings

18 Holding **Alt** and **Ctrl**, drag the circle to duplicate the cooker ring. To move the rings apart, select one and use the cursor keys to nudge it; nudge each the same number of times for equal spacing. To enlarge a centre ring, hold **Ctrl** and **Shift** and drag a corner handle. Holding **Shift**, click each of the circles and the rectangle to select them all, then right-click and choose **Grouping**, **Group**.

Draw a sink

19 Copy a cabinet, adjust its size (sink units are usually 100 or 120cm wide), delete its text label and set a fill (see step 17). On the **Drawing** toolbar, click **AutoShapes**, then **Basic Shapes**, and pick **Rounded Rectangle**. Holding **Alt**, click and drag to draw the sink bowl. Give this a suitable fill. For multiple bowls, copy and resize. Group the bowl(s) with the underlying rectangle as before.

left of the screen are listed the ranges and models of kitchen unit Ikea sells. Click the + sign to expand each heading. Right of this are thumbnail images of units, which you can drag into place on your plan. **Rotate left** or **Rotate right** buttons let you rotate individual units. For an idea of what everything will look like, in realistic perspective, click the next button at the top **3D View**. Here you can zoom in or out, and rotate or tilt your kitchen by clicking the arrow buttons. You can even look inside cupboards by clicking the **Hide fronts** button, at the left. In **3D View** you can still drag items to reposition them or add new units. The fourth button at the top, **Item List**, shows which units you've used, together with product numbers, quantities and prices. Click **Save**, at the top right, to save a copy of your plan, or print out the current view by clicking **Print**.

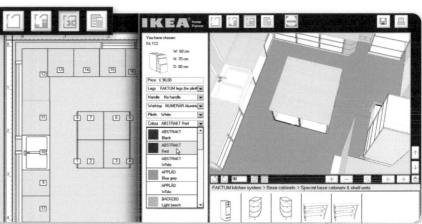

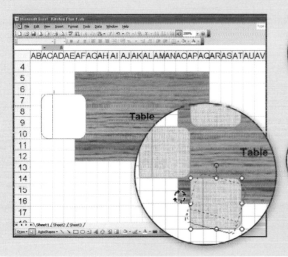

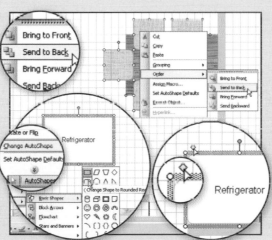

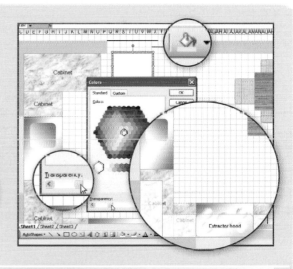

Draw a table and chairs

20 For a table, copy a cabinet and resize it – about 120x80cm will seat four to six people. Change its text and apply a **Fill Effect** (see step 17). For a chair, draw a **Rounded Rectangle** four cells square (40x40cm), then add another, one cell wide, for the back. **Shift**+select both, group them and apply a **Fill**. **Ctrl+Alt**+drag to make more chairs; use the green handle, holding **Shift**, to turn some around.

Draw a refrigerator

21 **Shift**+click each chair to select them all, then right-click and choose **Order**, **Send to Back**. Drag the chairs under the table. To make a fridge, copy and resize a cabinet, change the text label and set **Fill Color** to **White**. In the **Drawing** toolbar, click **Draw**, **Change AutoShape**. Choose **Basic Shapes** and click the **Rounded Rectangle**. Drag the yellow handle to adjust the roundness of the shape's corners.

Add wall cabinets

22 Wall cabinets 40cm deep can be fitted above base cabinets. Copy a cabinet and delete the text. Click the **Fill Color** button and choose **More Fill Colors**. Pick **White** and increase **Transparency** to 33%. Click **OK**. Holding **Alt**, drag your cabinet into place. Duplicate as required. With all the elements of the kitchen drawn, use them to create your ideal plan. Choose **Save** from the **File** menu to finish.

Happy families

Use your family members as characters in a deck of cards

Card games are even more fun with personalised cards. Here's how to make Happy Families cards featuring your own family. Traditionally, each family in the pack has a different profession or hobby. Take photos of yourselves acting these out or use pictures from your family album, then turn the photos into wacky caricatures. Add text and a background, and your cards are complete.

PROJECT TOOLS: Photoshop Elements ● Family portrait photos
SEE ALSO: Draw a comic strip, page 32 ● Photo filters and special effects, page 316

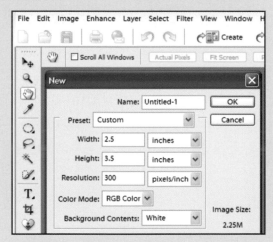

Choose a size for the cards

1 Run Photoshop Elements and from the **Welcome** screen choose **Start From Scratch**. The **New** dialogue box appears. Set **Width** to **2.5 inches** (6.35cm) and **Height** to **3.5 inches** (8.9cm), or choose a different size if you prefer (see 'Size and shape' box, page 157). Set **Resolution** to **300 pixels/inch** and **Color Mode** to **RGB Color**. Ignore **Background Contents** for now and click **OK**.

Rules of the game

To play Happy Families, shuffle and deal the cards (up to 48, or 12 families) to three or more players. The first player asks an opponent for a specific card, say 'Mr X'; the person asking must already hold at least one card of that family. If the opponent has this card, it must be handed over, and the player continues by asking the same or another opponent for a different card. If the opponent doesn't have the card, it's that player's turn. When all the families are complete the player with the most families is the winner.

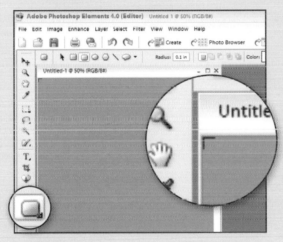

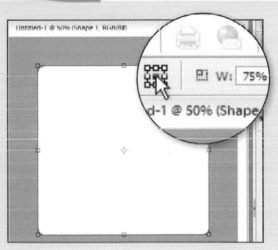

Pick a background colour

2 Go to the **Edit** menu and choose **Fill Layer**. In the **Fill Layer** box, set **Mode** to **Normal** and **Opacity** to **100%**. In the box labelled **Use**, choose **Color**. The **Color Picker** appears. Choose a colour you like from the spectrum in the middle, then click on the palette on the left to set the exact shade for the cards. Choose something vibrant but not too vivid. Click **OK**, then click **OK** in the **Fill Layer** box.

Make a picture frame

3 Choose the **Shape** tool by clicking the third icon from the bottom in the toolbox on the left, or press **U**. From the **Options** bar at the top, choose **Rounded Rectangle**, set **Radius** to **0.1in** (2.5mm), click the arrow next to **Color** and choose white. Now click at the top left corner of your canvas making sure you're on the canvas, not the edge of the window. The mouse pointer should show a crosshair.

Adjust your picture frame

4 Pressing **Shift**, click and drag diagonally down and to the right until the shape reaches the right side of the canvas, then release the mouse button. To keep the shape centred, highlight the middle square (anchor point) in the small diagram to the left, then go to the **Image** menu and choose **Resize**, and **Scale**. In the **Options** bar at the top, set both **W** and **H** (width and height) to **75%**. Press **Return**.

Shadow effects

You can make the characters look as if they're sitting behind a window in the card by adding a shadow within the picture frame. In the **Layers** palette, click the text layer. In the **Styles and Effects** palette (choose its name in the **Window** menu if you can't see it), pick **Layer Styles** from the first menu at the top, then **Drop Shadows** from the second. Below, select **Low**. Click the **Shape** layer, switch from **Drop Shadows** to **Inner Shadows**, and pick **Low**. Do this on your first card, and the effects will apply to all the rest.

Other card games

Use the techniques in this project to make a pack of cards for the game of Snap. You could alter the pairs in **Liquify** to make it harder to spot a match, or use different photos of each person for each pair. If you're really ambitious, design a standard 52-card pack, substituting your friends and family for the picture cards – the king, queen and jack of each suit and, of course, the joker.

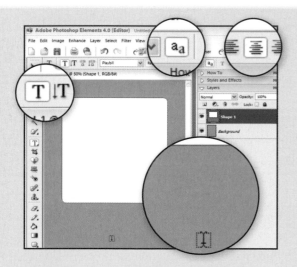

Type in a family member's name

5 With the centre square resized, press **T** for the **Text** tool. In the **Options** bar, choose the first of the four icons on the left for **Horizontal Type**, then choose a suitable font and size. The icon labelled 'aa' must be highlighted for **Anti-aliased** (smooth) text. From the three buttons showing horizontal lines, click the middle one to centre the text. Click on your canvas below the shape.

Type the longest title first

6 Happy Families members are traditionally titled Mr, Mrs, Master and Miss. Think of a name for your family and type Master (the longest title) followed the family name. Highlight the text by dragging over it, then adjust the size in the **Options** bar. As 'Master' is the longest title, you now know that the others will fit. Click the **Move** tool (top button of toolbox on the left) twice, then drag the text to position it.

Open a photo to edit

7 If the first card you want to design isn't 'Master', click back on the text with the **Text** tool and change it, but leave the size the same. Now choose **Open** from the **File** menu and open the photo that you want to edit. Press **C** for the **Crop** tool. In the **Options** bar, set **Width** to **2in** – half an inch (1.25cm) less than the width of your card. Set **Height** the same. Set **Resolution** to **300 pixels/inch**.

Size and shape

The size of your cards is your choice. Standard playing cards are 2.5x3.5in ('Poker' size, paper format B8) or 2.25x3.5in ('Bridge' size). Happy Families can be played with up to 48 cards: 12 families, each comprising Mr, Mrs, Master and Miss. If you only have time to design one family, then copy them with different names, and change the background colours by repeating **Fill Layer** (see step 2). Or you could use the same set of photos from one family, but process them differently using **Liquify** to create a series of imaginary families.

Why stop at cards?

Card games aren't the only kind you can personalise using image-editing software. You could also make a Snakes and Ladders board. Choose **A4** or **Letter** from the **Preset** menu in the **New** dialogue box (see step 1) to make a full page. Draw the squares using the **Rounded Rectangle** tool (see steps 3 and 4) and label them using the **Text** tool (steps 5 and 6). Browse the **Custom Shapes** (see step 15, 'Draw a comic strip', page 37) for animals and other fun symbols you can add.

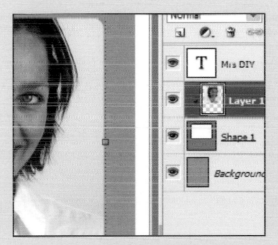

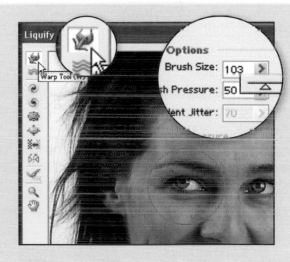

Size the photo to fit

8 Click near the top left of the canvas and drag to draw a crop box. Adjust this by dragging the corner handles to surround the area of the picture you want to use. Double-click or click the tick icon to finish. Press **V** for the **Move** tool. Now click on the photo and drag it across onto the window containing your card design. Drop it onto the card, then drag to position it over the shape you made.

Place the photo in the frame

9 In the Layers palette, drag the photo's layer one step down, so it's below the text but above the shape. Now press **Ctrl+G**. This groups the selected layer (the photo) with the one below (the shape), meaning that the photo is only visible within the shape. To turn the photo into a caricature, go to the **Filter** menu and choose **Distort**, then **Liquify**. The **Liquify** box appears, showing only the photo (the current layer).

Choose a tool and brush size

10 On the left are the eight distortion tools. Below them is **Reconstruct**, which undoes changes, then **Zoom** and the **Hand** tool (for moving around the canvas when zoomed in). Using **Zoom**, click the face to enlarge it, then click the top tool icon, **Warp**. Move the mouse over the photo, then adjust the **Brush Size**, on the right, so it's about a third of the width of the face. Set **Brush Pressure** to 50.

◉ Printing out your cards

From Photoshop Elements click **File**, **Open** and then open the JPEG files of all the cards to print. Click **File**, **Print Multiple Photos**. The **Organizer** module opens and shows the **Print Photos** dialogue box, with thumbnails of your cards on the left. On the right, choose your printer and paper. Click the menu labelled **Select Type of Print** and choose **Individual Prints**, then click the menu **Select Print Size and Options** and choose **Custom**. In the dialogue box that opens, set the same **Width** and **Height** as you used to create your cards. Click **OK**, then untick **One Photo Per Page**, so your cards are arranged automatically on as many pages as necessary. Finally, click **Print**. For best results, print on the thickest glossy card that your printer manufacturer recommends. Cut out your cards with scissors or a craft knife.

Raise the cheekbones

11 Caricatures generally exaggerate facial features. For results even your subject will appreciate, accentuate the positive and don't make changes too extreme. Here, the mother's smile is crinkling up the eyes, so emphasise this. Click with the circle centred on the right pupil, and drag gently to move the eye slightly inwards. Do the same with the left. Then click each cheekbone in turn and pull it up.

Get a nose job

12 Female noses tend to be smaller than male, so exaggerate this. Choose the fifth tool in the toolbox, **Pucker**. Place the circle over the nose, then click and hold down the mouse button briefly to suck the area into the centre. If you make a mistake at any point, press **Ctrl+Z** to undo, or choose the **Reconstruct** tool, then click and hold anywhere on the photo to return that area to normal.

Working on teeth and hair

13 The mouth is hardest to alter without looking unnatural. With the **Pucker** tool, click just above one corner of the mouth and squeeze it slightly, then do the same the other side. This will also flare the nose a little. Switching back to the **Warp** tool, drag the hair bit by bit down towards the face, making a lower hairline. Use a small **Brush Size** to pull some of the flyaway ends further out.

● Professional printing

For a high-gloss finish, use a high-street or online digital photo service. For example, go to www.kodakgallery.com and click **International Sites** at the bottom and choose **United Kingdom**. Follow the instructions to upload files and order prints.

A good option is to print two cards side by side as a single 6x4in photo and cut it in half. Make your cards 3x4in (step 1). Open one of your finished JPEG files in Photoshop Elements. From the **Image** menu choose **Resize**, then **Canvas Size**. In the dialogue box that opens, set **Width** to **200 percent**, leave **Height** alone and click the middle left **Anchor** position. Click **OK** to make a space. Open another finished card. With the **Move** tool (press **V**), drag this onto the first and position it in the space. Press **Ctrl+E** to merge them together. Go to **File**, **Save As**, and save in **JPEG** format with a new file name. Repeat to pair your other cards.

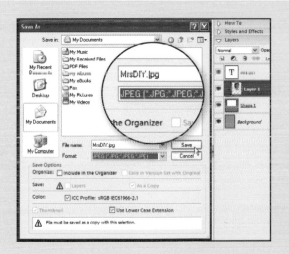

Save the project

14 Finish tweaking, then click **OK**. Choose **Save** from the **File** menu and browse to a folder to save your card in. Enter a file name such as Card Template, and leave **Format** set to **Photoshop (*.PSD)**. Click **Save**. Go back to the **File** menu, choose **Save As** and enter a file name for this particular card. Set **Format** to JPEG. Click **Save**. Set **Quality** to 8, then click **OK** to save a copy of the file for this card.

Design a second card

15 For your next card, repeat steps 7 and 8: alter the text, open another photo, crop it, drag it onto your card and position it on top of the previous photo. In the **Layers** palette, click the eye icon next to the previous photo's layer to make it invisible. Drag the new photo down so it's directly above the shape layer. It groups automatically, fitting within the shape. Use **Liquify** as before to create the caricature.

Complete the family

16 As before, update your Photoshop file using **File**, **Save**, then save a copy of the second card as a new **JPEG** file using **Save As**. Add your third photo in the same way. Create as many cards and families as you wish, ending up with one layered Photoshop file (useful for later editing) and individual **JPEG** files of all the cards. For tips on printing your cards, see boxes on pages 158 to 159.

Fancy dress
Try on a new face with a party mask

Wearing masks is a party tradition with kids and adults alike, whether it's comical masks for a social get-together or scary ones for Halloween. To create a mask, all you need is a digital or scanned photo or drawing of a face. A great twist is to mirror one side of the face to make it symmetrical. Try using animals, famous faces – perhaps found on the internet – or even the faces of your party guests.

PROJECT TOOLS: Photoshop Elements ● Digital photos
SEE ALSO: Children's story book, page 180 ● Virtual family portrait, page 46

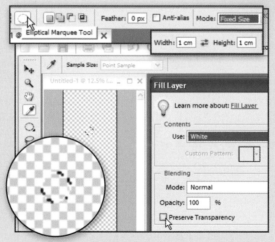

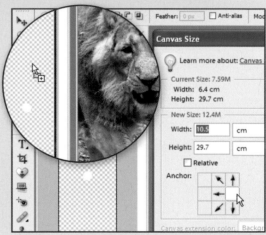

Create a template

1 Run Photoshop Elements and click **Start from Scratch**. In the **New** box, choose your paper size (A4) from the **Preset** menu. Change the **Width** to the distance between the mask's eye holes – **6.4cm (2.5in)** for adults or **5cm (2in)** for children. Set **Background Contents** to **Transparent**. Click **OK**. Press **Ctrl+0** to see the whole of your blank canvas. Press **M** for the **Marquee** tool.

Draw an eye hole

2 In the **Options** bar at the top, choose **Elliptical**. Set **Feather** to **0** and untick **Anti-alias**. Set **Mode** to **Fixed Size**, and both **Width** and **Height** to **1cm (0.4in)**. Click anywhere on the canvas to select a circular area. Choose **Fill Selection** from the **Edit** menu. Set **Contents** to **White**, **Mode Normal**, **Opacity** **100%**, and untick **Preserve Transparency**. Click **OK**. Press **Ctrl+C** to cut the circle, then **Ctrl+V** to paste it.

Add a picture

3 The white circle is now centred within the canvas. From the **Image** menu, choose **Resize**, then **Canvas Size**. Change the **Width** to half the width of your paper: **10.5cm** for A4. Click the right **Anchor** position. Click **OK**. Now go to **Open** on the **File** menu and open the photo you want to use. Press **V** for the **Move** tool, then drag the photo onto your blank template.

● Mirror, mirror...

Mirroring is a good way to create a symmetrical mask. But the results may be very different depending on which half of a particular face you choose to mirror. Before dragging a photo onto your mask template (see step 3 of this project), look at it and decide which is the better side of the face. If it isn't on the left of the photo, flip the face over – go to the **Image** menu and choose **Rotate, Flip Horizontal**. Mirroring different sides of the same face can produce unexpected and humorous results (see right), so experiment.

● Masks without mirrors

Some faces don't mirror well, especially if they're very asymmetrical to start with. Rotating slightly (as in step 4, below) often helps. Alternatively, use a photo without mirroring it. After resizing the canvas in step 3 of this workshop, skip to **Select All** in step 6. Click **OK** to resize the canvas again, add your photo and adjust its size and position (as in step 4) to fit the two eye holes. Draw around the whole outline and delete the background (steps 5 to 6).

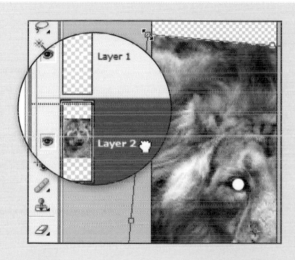
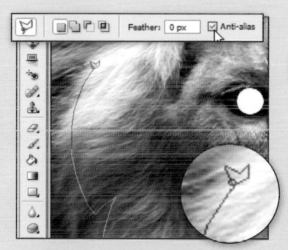
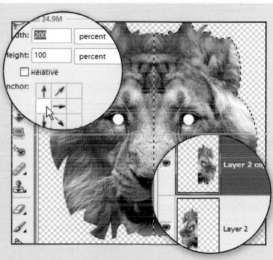

Size the picture to fit

4 In the **Layers** palette (choose **Layers** from the **Window** menu if you can't see it), drag your picture, **Layer 2**, to below **Layer 1**. The white circle appears over the photo. Resize, rotate and position the photo (see 'Moving objects around', page 182) so the eye meets the eye hole, the centre of the face is aligned with the right edge of the canvas, and the face fills the canvas as well as possible. Press **Return**.

Cut around the edges

5 Press **L** for the **Lasso** tool. In the **Options** bar at the top, click the rightmost of the icons on the left, for **Polygonal Lasso**. Set **Feather** to **0** and tick **Anti-alias**. Click on the canvas at any point along the proposed edge of the mask, then at short intervals right around your planned cutout line, back to the position you started at. Press **Shift+Ctrl+I** to invert your selection, then **Delete** to erase the background.

Mirror your mask

6 Press **Ctrl+A** (Select All) and choose **Crop** from the **Image** menu, then press **Shift+Ctrl+E** to merge the layers. Go to **Canvas Size** as in step 3; set **Width** to **200 percent** and **Anchor** to the left. Click **OK**. In the **Layer** menu, choose **Duplicate Layer** and click **OK**. Press **Ctrl+A**, and go to **Image, Rotate, Flip Selection Horizontal**. Finally, save your mask as a **Photoshop** (.PSD) file.

Party time

Help your get-together go with a swing with personalised props

There's nothing like a party to bring everyone together. Whether it's a special dinner for friends or a grand birthday bash, your PC can help you celebrate in style with custom menus, place mats, invitations and more. From neat name cards to a colourful banner that spells out the occasion in big letters, here's how to tailor everything not just to your event but to each guest, so that every piece becomes a souvenir of the occasion.

PROJECT TOOLS: Photoshop Elements ● Microsoft Word
SEE ALSO: Gift box and tags, page 126 ● Produce a poster, page 84 ● Family card game, page 154

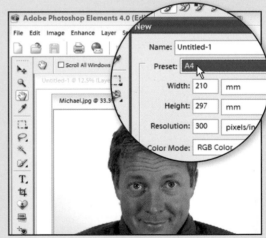

Place mats – Prepare your canvas

1 Run Photoshop Elements. From the **Welcome** screen click **Start From Scratch**. In the **New** box, **Preset** menu select **A4**. Swap the numbers in **Width** and **Height** to turn the page sideways. Set **Resolution** to **300 pixels/inch**, **Color Mode** to **RGB Color** and **Background Contents** to **White**. Click **OK**. Choose **Open** from the **File** menu, or press **Ctrl+O**, and open a photo of one of your guests.

● Making place cards in Photoshop Elements

To create place cards, follow the method in 'Making a gift tag', page 128. In the **New** dialogue box, set **Width** to **14.75cm** and **Height** to **5.25cm**. After filling with colour (see step 5), add a name as for the place mat (see step 6). In **Image**, **Resize**, **Canvas Size**, double the **Height** and choose the bottom **Anchor** position. Press **Ctrl+S** and save as a **JPEG (.JPG)** file. Press **Ctrl+Z** to restore the original canvas size, then change the guest's name. If you want to change the colour, click **Fill Layer** in the **Edit** menu. Double the canvas again and save with a new filename. Repeat for all your guests, then open all the JPEG files. Press **Ctrl+N** and make a full-page sideways blank canvas, as for the place mat. With the **Move** tool (press **V**), drag up to four cards onto the canvas and snap into place. Print, cut out and fold in half.

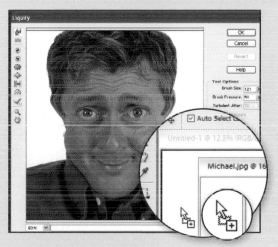

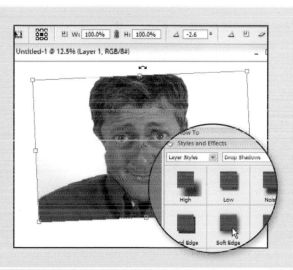

Crop a photo

2 Press **C** to activate the **Crop** tool. In the **Options** bar at the top, set **Width** to **24cm** (9.5in) and Height to **16cm** (6.3in). Set **Resolution** to **300 pixels/inch**, matching the resolution of your blank canvas. Click at the top left of the photograph and drag to draw a crop box around the part that you want to use. Double-click or press **Return** to confirm your selection.

Create and place a caricature

3 From the **Filter** menu select **Distort**, **Liquify** to change the photo into a caricature (see 'Family card game', pages 157 to 158, steps 9 to 13). Press **V** for the **Move** tool. Click on the photo and, holding down the mouse button, drag it onto the blank canvas. Click on the photo and drag it into position, leaving an equal margin on each side, a small gap at the top and extra space at the bottom.

Rotate and add a shadow effect

4 Place the mouse pointer just off one of the 'handles' around the photo, showing a turning arrow, and drag to rotate the photo slightly. Press **Return** to confirm. Choose the **Styles and Effects** palette from the **Window** menu. Now choose **Layer Styles** in the first menu and **Drop Shadows** in the second, then pick the **Soft Edge** style in the options below.

MICHAEL GREEN

JORDAN MAGENTA

JENNIFER BROWN

Door signs

You may want to direct your guests to certain areas of the venue and politely prohibit them from others. Using the same approach as for the place mats (see steps 1 to 7 of this project) make a sign for the door of each room. Print the sign on card. Use a hole punch and string to hang the sign, or fix to a door using sticky tape.

Debbie's 21st
Off Limits!

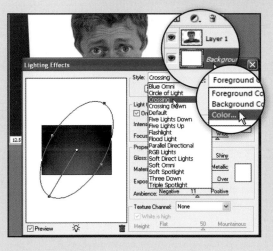

Add a background

5 In the **Layers** palette (choose it in the **Window** menu if you don't see it), click the **Background** layer. From the **Edit** menu, choose **Fill Layer**. In the **Use** dialogue box, choose **Color**, then pick a colour. Set **Mode** to **Normal** and **Opacity** to **100%**. Click **OK** in each box. From the **Filter** menu, choose **Render**, then **Lighting Effects**. In the **Style** menu at the top, choose **Crossing**. Click **OK**.

Write a guest's name

6 Press **T** for the **Text** tool. In the **Options** bar at the top, select the first of the four icons, the **Horizontal Type** tool. Choose a fairly plain font and set the size to about **60pt**. The icon labelled 'aa' will be highlighted for anti-aliased (smooth) text. At the far right, click the triangle next to the **Color** swatch and choose **White**. Click below the photo and type in the name of one of your guests.

Print the place mat

7 To finish typing, click twice on the **Move** tool at the top of the main toolbox. Drag the text into position in the middle. Add a shadow to the text (as in step 4). Save your work (press **Ctrl+S**) and print it (**Ctrl+P**). For tips on printing, see 'Printing your story book', page 187. If your printer won't print right to the edge, scale to about **90%** to fit in everything, then cut off the borders.

DESIGN WISE

Protect your place mats

For waterproof and tear-proof place mats try lamination, or encapsulation, which seals printed paper between two sheets of plastic. If you laminate your customised place mats, guests can take them away and reuse them, which is great for children's parties. Most high-street print shops will laminate items for you. You can even buy a laminating machine, for example at www.the-laminator-warehouse.com. 'Cold lamination', using self-adhesive pouches, available from most high-street stationers, gives a less durable finish.

Get the accent right

The names of dishes are often in French or another foreign language, so you may need to use accented characters. Place the text cursor in the word where you want to add a special character. From the **Insert** menu choose **Symbol**. In the **Symbol** dialogue box click the **Symbols** tab and, from the **Font** drop-down menu, select **(normal text)**. Scroll down to find the character you want, and double-click it to insert it. Click **Close** to finish.

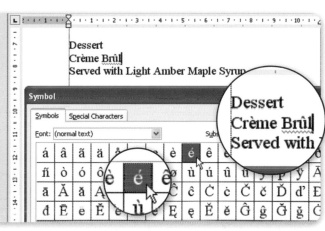

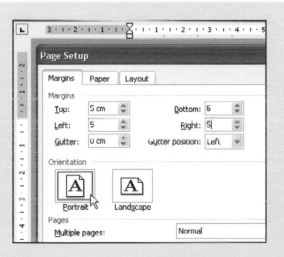

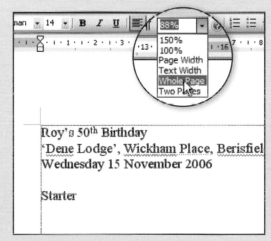

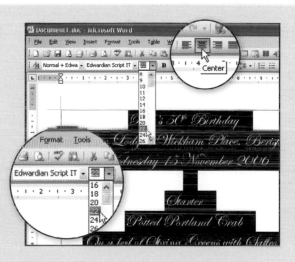

The menu – Set up the page

1 Run Microsoft Word, or if the program is already running press **Ctrl+N** for a new blank document. From the **File** menu, choose **Page Setup**. In the **Paper** tab, choose your paper size (A4). In the **Margins** tab, set a wide margin of **5cm** (2in) all round. Set **Gutter** to 0, **Orientation** to **Portrait** and **Multiple pages** to **Normal**. Click OK. From the **View** menu, choose **Print Layout**.

Give a date and time for the meal

2 Click the **Zoom** drop-down in the top toolbar and choose **Whole Page**. If you don't see the margins, go to the **Tools** menu and choose **Options**; click the **View** tab, then tick **Text Boundaries**. Start by typing in the title of the event. Pressing **Return** between lines, continue with the venue and the date. Press **Return** twice to make a gap, then type in Starter (or however you prefer to name the first course).

List the courses

3 Press **Return** and type the name of the dish, then press **Return** twice and type Main Course. Continue through all your courses. Press **Ctrl+A** to select all the text. In the **Formatting** toolbar, click the **Center** button to centre the text on each line. To the left of this, choose a font. **Edwardian Script** looks good, but to make it readable increase the size to about **22pt**, checking that everything still fits.

⦿ You are cordially invited

To make party invitations, follow the same steps as for the menus (pages 165 and 166). In **Page Setup**, set all margins to **3.5cm (1.4in)** and **Orientation** to **Portrait**. Set **Multiple pages** to **2 pages per sheet**. Enter full details of the event and to whom the invitee should reply ('RSVP'). To save time, you could copy and paste the text from your menu, then edit it. Add a fancy **Page Border** as in step 5 below. Set **Vertical alignment** to **Bottom**, then click at the end of the text and press the **Delete** key to remove any extra returns (blank lines). Press **Ctrl+A** to select all the text, then **Ctrl+C** to copy it. Press the right cursor arrow key, choose **Break** from the **Insert** menu, pick **Page break** and click **OK**. Press **Ctrl+V** to paste a copy of your text onto the second page. Delete any extra returns. Print half as many copies as you need invitations, and cut the sheets neatly in half. Write each guest's name by hand in the top left corner.

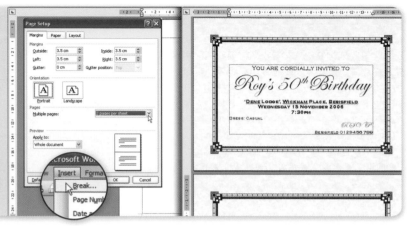

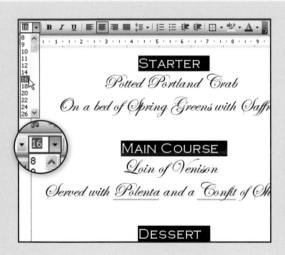

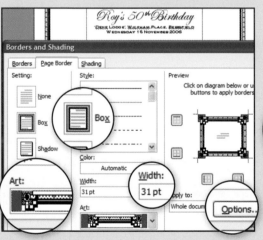

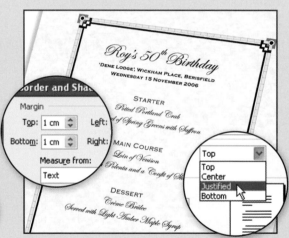

Format the headings

4 Highlight the first heading, **Starter**, by clicking three times quickly. Hold the **Ctrl** key and click the next heading to select it, too. Repeat for the other headings. Choose a plainer font, preferably a 'titling' font, which is designed for headings and has only capital letters – here it's **Copperplate Gothic Light**. Since the letters are larger, make the font smaller, about **16pt**.

Add a border

5 Select and style the main heading using similar fonts in different sizes. Finish off with a border. From the **Format** menu, choose **Borders and Shading**. Click the **Page Border** tab. Under **Setting**, click **Box**. From the **Art** drop-down, choose a border design. In the **Width** box, type 99 and press **Tab** to see a close-up preview on the right. Set the **Width** to **31pt** (the maximum), then click the **Options** button.

Adust the layout

6 In the **Measure from** box, choose **Text**, then set all the margins to **1cm (0.4in)**. Click **OK** twice. To make your text fill the page, go to **Page Setup** on the **File** menu, click the **Layout** tab, and set **Vertical alignment** to **Justified**. Click **OK**. You may wish to add a textured **Background**, as shown in step 14 on page 117, or print on subtly coloured paper. Select **Print** from the **File** menu.

○ Say it loud

An alternative to printing and tiling a banner (see step 3, below) is to print single giant letters – each on a single sheet of A4 paper. You can print characters as large as you like. If you don't need anything fancy, print out your characters using Microsoft Word. An 800pt letter 'A' will fill the page, but you'll need to adjust the margins so that it sits in the middle of the sheet. Attach the printed pages directly to a wall, or tape them to a string in sequence to form a banner that you can drape.

○ Customised napkins

To fully accessorise your party, print napkins with your own design. Most printing services only handle orders in the thousands, but a few suppliers such as www.i-candi.co.uk will print your design onto any quantity of napkins in a range of colours. Alternatively, try local printers that specialise in wedding stationery. If you only have a few guests, use a t-shirt transfer kit (see 'Print a t-shirt', page 200) to print your design and iron it onto linen or heavy-grade paper napkins.

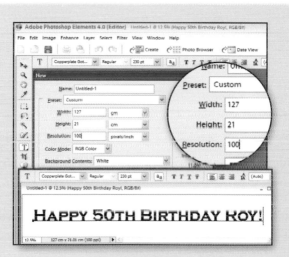

Party banner – Set up the canvas

1 In Photoshop Elements, press **Ctrl+N** for a blank document. The maximum size that Elements will print is **127cm** (**50in**); set this as the **Width**. Set **Height** equal to the short side of your paper – **21cm** for A4. Set **Resolution** to **100 pixels/inch**. This is fine for printing to be read from a distance. Click **OK**. Use the **Text** tool to type your message (see step 6, page 164).

Style your text and background

2 Size your message to fill the banner. In the **Styles and Effects** palette (see step 4, page 163) choose **Layer Styles** in the first menu, **Wow Plastic** in the second. Below, click **Wow-Plastic Red**. Follow step 5, page 164, to colour the **Background** layer and add a **Lighting Effect**. In the **Lighting Effects** box, click the **Style** menu and select **Five Lights Up**, to vary the background shading. Click **OK**.

Print on multiple sheets

3 Press **Ctrl+P** to print. Set **Print Size** to **Actual Size**. Click **Page Setup**, then click **Printer** to set your printer's options. If it doesn't offer tiling or banner printing, click **OK** twice to get back to **Print Preview**. Untick **Center Image**. Drag the preview image to show the left end of your banner. Print it, then press **Ctrl+P** again and drag to the next part of the banner, and so on. (See 'Printing a multi-sheet poster', page 88.)

Words in a flash

Create visual aids to help you or your children learn a language

Flash cards are a great teaching aid. Not only do they help children with literacy and numeracy, they're also ideal if you're trying to learn a foreign language, or for any kind of study. Here's how to design effective flash cards using Photoshop Elements. You can use the same techniques to put together full-page worksheets with several pictures and captions. Alternatively, combine this project with 'Produce a poster', page 84, and make an educational wall chart.

PROJECT TOOLS: Photoshop Elements
SEE ALSO: Produce a poster, page 84 ● Draw a comic strip, page 32

Get your colours right

When using **Paint Bucket** (see step 5), check the **Options** bar settings. Tick **Anti-alias** for smooth edges, and set **Opacity** to 100%. **Tolerance**, usually **0**, can be increased to let colour spread more widely; it makes no difference when filling in a solid outline. Ensure **Contiguous** is ticked (otherwise, when you click with the **Paint Bucket**, all areas the same colour as the one you clicked on will change to the current colour).

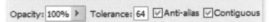

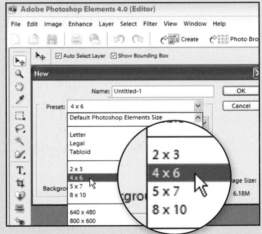

Set up your card size

1 Run Photoshop Elements and from the **Welcome** screen click **Start From Scratch**. In the **New** dialogue box, set **Width** and **Height** or choose a format from the **Preset** menu. The standard photo print size, 4x6 – 4in wide and 6in high – is probably best (see box, page 173). Set **Resolution** to **300 pixels/inch**, **Color Mode** to **RGB Color**, and **Background Contents** to **White**. Click **OK**.

● Working with layers

Each of the shapes you create occupies its own layer, visible in the **Layers** palette. If you have trouble colouring or editing a shape, check that you're working on the right layer: click the name of the layer you want to edit. When using the **Move** tool, ticking **Auto Select Layer** in the **Options** bar means you just click on the shape you want on the canvas, without having to select it first in the **Layers** palette.

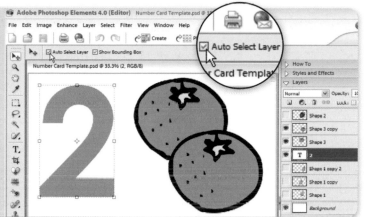

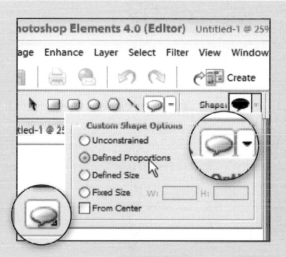

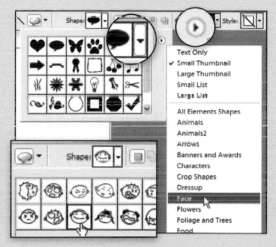

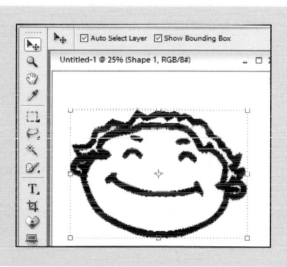

Add a symbol

2 Flash cards usually feature simple line drawings that are clear and legible from a distance. Photoshop Elements has many built in as **Custom Shapes**. Click the **Shape** icon, third from the bottom in the toolbox on the left, or press **U**. In the **Options** bar at the top, choose the last of the seven icons from the left for **Custom Shape**. Click the triangle next to this and, in the pop-up box, click **Defined Proportions**.

Choose a Custom Shape

3 Click the triangle to the right, next to the current **Shape**, to pop up a palette of shapes. Now click the blue triangle at the top right of this for a menu listing sets of shapes. Choose a set appropriate to the theme of your flash cards – here it's **Face**. The shapes in this set now appear in the palette; click one of them. Before you draw it, press **D** (for default colours) to choose black.

Draw the shape

4 Now click near the top left of your blank canvas and drag to draw out the shape. Because you set **Defined Proportions**, the symbol will stay the right shape as you resize it. Make it large enough to fill most of the width of the card. Release the mouse button, press **Return** to finish, then press **V** for the **Move** tool. Click on a black area of the shape and drag to position it.

● Pictures and copyright

It's possible to make flash cards using any kind of picture. Choose **Open** from the **File** menu to load an image file into Photoshop Elements, then use the **Move** tool (press **V**) to drag it onto your card. To find pictures on the internet, try www.google.com/images. For any use other than strictly personal, including school or college teaching, stick to pictures that are cleared for copyright. This will usually mean paying, either for a collection on disc or at a site such as www.istockphoto.com. Check for copyright notices on the website before you download. Cheap royalty-free photo collections are also available, offering thousands of images you can use in any way you wish. Visit www.amazon.co.uk and type photo clipart into the search box to find collections from companies such as Greenstreet, GSP and Hemera. If you have a digital camera, you can take your own photos for your flash cards. Suitable subjects for language learning are all around, and it only takes a moment to snap a hand, an eye or a pair of shoes. It's free and you won't have to worry about copyright.

eye

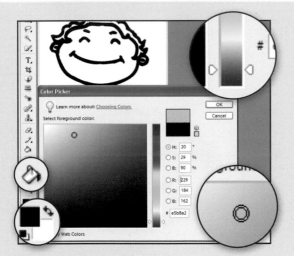

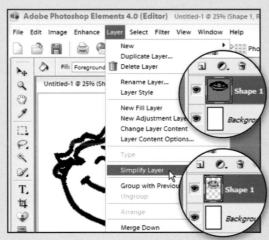

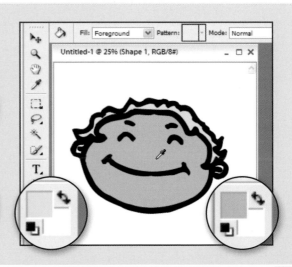

Set the fill colour

5 To add some colour, use the **Paint Bucket** tool from the toolbox on the left or press **K**. Click the **Foreground Color** swatch – the upper square at the foot of the toolbox (currently black) – to open the **Color Picker**. On the spectrum in the middle, click between red and orange as most flesh tones are found here. In the larger box on the left, click to choose the exact shade you want. Click **OK**.

Colour in your drawing

6 To colour in the drawing, you first need to convert it from a vector shape to an ordinary image layer (see 'Smooth lines and curves' box, page 35). Go to the **Layer** menu and choose **Simplify Layer**. Now click with the **Paint Bucket** anywhere inside the face. The colour fills the area within the outline. Click the **Foreground Color** swatch again to pick a colour for the hair, then apply it.

Matching colours

7 Have you missed any bits? Here, the ears should match the face. To copy a colour used previously, hold the **Alt** key while using the **Paint Bucket**. The mouse pointer turns into an eyedropper, looking like the one used to apply eyedrops. Click the eyedropper on the colour you want to copy, here the face. It's copied to the **Foreground Color** swatch. Release the **Alt** key and click in the ears to apply the colour.

Typography for learning aids

Take extra care when formatting text for learning aids. Use large font sizes, especially for flash cards and other items to be viewed from a distance.

Materials aimed at children are usually written in a sans serif typeface (see 'Font basics explained', page 326). You can use Arial or Verdana, but you may prefer a font that has the simpler 'single storey' forms for letters such as 'a' and 'g', for example Century Gothic or Futura. For teaching literacy or foreign languages to adults, it may be more appropriate to use a serif typeface such as Times or Georgia, which reflects the typography of books and newspapers.

When writing single words, as on flash cards, write the whole word in lower case unless it's a word that always has a capital letter, such as a name or an acronym, like USA. Finally, for obvious reasons, watch your spelling.

Arial Verdana
Century Gothic
Futura Futura
Times Georgia

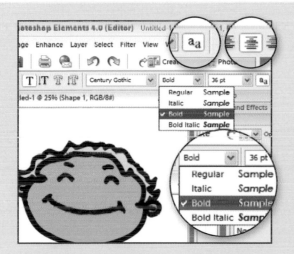

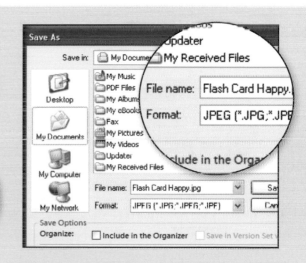

Get ready to add words

8 Press T for the **Text** tool. In the **Options** bar, make sure the first of the four icons on the left is highlighted, for **Horizontal Text**. Choose a suitable bold font – see the 'Typography for learning aids' box above. Set the **Size** to about **36pt**, and ensure the icon labelled 'aa' is highlighted for anti-aliased (smooth) text. Of the three icons showing horizontal lines, pick the middle one for centred text.

Type in text

9 Press D to choose black. Click halfway across your card below the picture and type a word. A set of flash cards works best with the same size text throughout, so try your longest word to see if it fits. If necessary, double-click on the word to highlight it and adjust the font **Size** in the **Options** bar. When finished, click twice on the **Move** tool at the top of the toolbox, then use it to position your text.

Save your template and card

10 In the **File** menu, choose **Save** and pick a folder for your cards. Enter a file name such as Flash Card Template, and leave **Format** set to Photoshop (*.PSD). Click **Save**. Back in the **File** menu, choose **Save As**. Enter a file name for the individual card, such as Flash Card Happy. Set **Format** to **JPEG**. Click **Save**. Set **Quality** to 8, then click **OK** to save a copy of this card, leaving the Photoshop file open.

● Learning materials online

Look up 'flash cards' on an internet search engine such as Google, www.google.com, and you'll find an amazing variety of education resources. At www.flashcardexchange.com, for example, there are more than three million flash cards ready to download and print. The only catch is that there's no guarantee of their quality or accuracy. More consistent materials are available for a small fee from subscription sites such as www.eslkidstuff.com, which specialises in language learning.

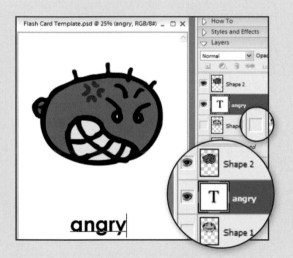

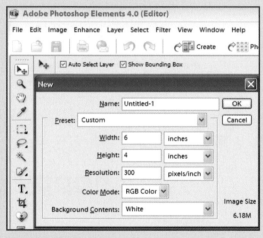

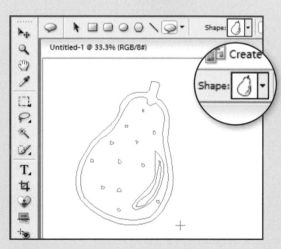

Make another card

11 Go to the **Layers** palette on the right (choose **Layers** from the **Window** menu if you can't see it) and click the eye icon next to the shape layer, making it invisible. Go back to step 2 – draw a new shape and colour it in. Using the **Text** tool, click on your text and change the word. Update your Photoshop file using **File**, **Save**, then use **Save As** to save the card as a new **JPEG** file.

Pick a number

12 Cards showing a number rather than a word may work better in 'landscape' format: wide rather than tall. To set up landscape, create a new document by choosing **New** from the **File** menu. In the **New** box, set the **Width** to the longer side of the format you want to use, such as **6in**, and the **Height** to the shorter side, such as **4in**. Set the other options as in step 1 and click **OK**.

Draw a shape

13 Follow steps 2 to 4 to draw a shape. Then duplicate the object enough times to match the number you're illustrating, so make the shape small enough to fit enough copies into about half the card's area. (Overlap objects rather than showing them separately so they can be bigger.) Then colour your shape as in steps 5 and 6. Switch back to the **Move** tool by pressing **V**.

DESIGN WISE

● Printing your flash cards

To print flash cards using your own colour printer, either buy paper that's pre-cut to the right size, such as 4x6in photo paper, or print two cards on a standard A4 sheet and cut them out yourself.

To print a single card, open its JPEG file in Photoshop Elements and from the **File** menu choose **Print**. In the **Print Preview** box, click **Page Setup**. In the **Page Setup** box, click **Printer** to select your printer. Click **OK** twice to return to **Print Preview**. For **Print Size**, choose **Actual Size**, or **Fit On Page** to make the card fill the paper. Click **Print**. To print two cards on a page, open both JPEG files. From the **File** menu choose **Print Multiple Photos**. The **Organizer Workspace** loads, showing **Print Photos**. Under **Select Type of Print**, choose **Picture Package**. The cards are fitted to your page size. Click **Print**.

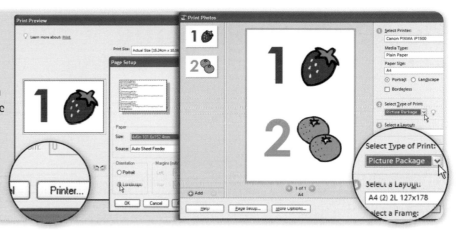

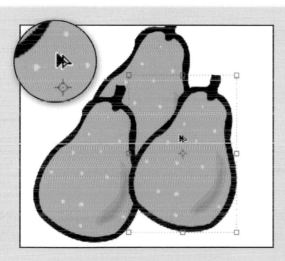

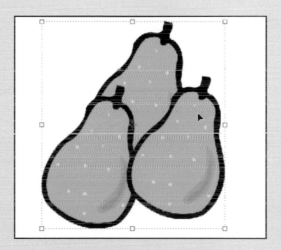

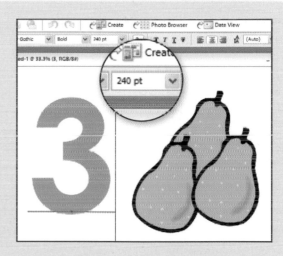

Copy your shape

14 Hold down the **Alt** key so the mouse pointer shows a double arrow. Click on your coloured shape, drag a short distance and release the mouse button to make a copy. Click on this one in turn and drag to make another. When you have the number of shapes you require, arrange them neatly using the **Move** tool. To change how shapes overlap, click on a shape and press **Ctrl-]** to bring it to the front.

Position your shapes

15 To position all the shapes on the card, hold **Shift** and click on each shape in turn until they are all selected. Another way to do this is to hold **Ctrl** and click on all their names in the **Layers** palette. Now reposition them all at once on the canvas. If necessary, resize them as a group: hold **Shift** and drag any corner handle. Place the shapes on the right-hand side of the card.

Add a jumbo number

16 Use the **Text** tool as in steps 8 and 9 to add a number on the left. Make it large enough to fill the space – type the size into the **Font Size** box in the **Options** bar instead of choosing from the preset sizes. Try about **240pt**. To make your card more cheerful, choose a colour instead of black but ensure it's deep enough for the number to be easily read. **Save** and repeat your card as in step 11.

The generation game
Put faces to names with your own photo family tree

Researching your family's history can provide unexpected insights into the lives of your ancestors. You'll not only discover who they were, but where they lived, what they did, and the personal and historical events that shaped their lives. There's a wealth of research resources that you can take advantage of, many of which are now online. When you've completed your research, you can use Microsoft Excel to produce an illustrated family tree.

PROJECT TOOLS: Microsoft Excel ● Family photos
SEE ALSO: Restore an old photo, page 20 ● Charts and graphics with Excel, page 300

● Dedicated family history software

A number of database programs are available that make the task of collating and organising your family research data easier. They generate charts automatically, including family trees, and some also produce web pages. Popular packages to consider are **Family Tree Maker**, www.familytreemaker.com, **Family Historian** www.family-historian.co.uk, and **Legacy Family Tree**, www.legacyfamilytree.com. All three are available as demo downloads to try out for free.

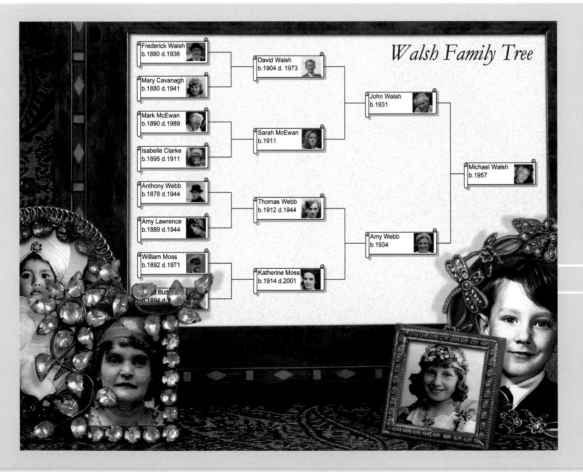

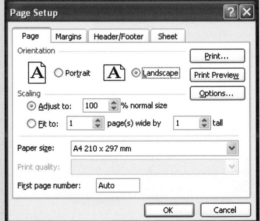

Create a new Excel workbook

1 Launch Excel. A new blank workbook appears (see 'Charts and graphics with Excel', page 300). The family tree is going to be landscape format, so select **File, Page Setup,** choose the **Page** tab and click the **Landscape** button. Set the **Paper size** to A4 and click **OK**. In your spreadsheet you'll now see the automatic page break dashed lines displayed after column N and row 35.

Research begins at home

While you can find out much about your family online, it's best to start with what you already know: the names and dates of birth of your immediate family. You may already have copies of birth, marriage and death certificates that can tell you facts you might not be aware of. For example, your mother's birth certificate will tell you the maiden name of her mother and so your grandmother's surname. Also, talk to your older relatives about what they remember of their parents and grandparents.

Preparing your photos

Crystal-clear high-resolution images of relatives and ancestors aren't essential for your family tree. But it's worth adjusting colours and contrast so that the small images stand out clearly when you incorporate them into the chart. A quick fix that works effectively on scanned-in faded prints is **Auto Levels** (press **Ctrl+Shift+L**). When you scan in old prints, set the scanner resolution to **600dpi** (dots per inch) or greater, especially where the original is small. See 'Restore an old photo', page 20.

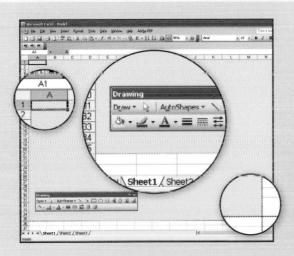

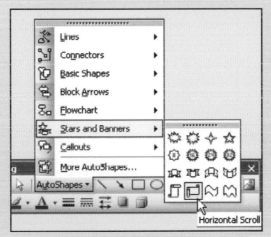

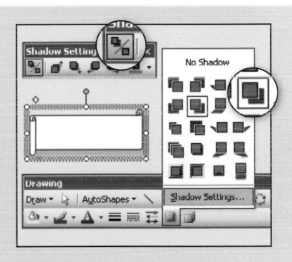

Colour the background

2 Click in cell **A1**, then **Shift**-click cell **N35** to select all the cells in between. Click the arrow next to the **Fill Color** bucket on the **Formatting** toolbar to select a pale colour to fill the cells and create a background. If the **Drawing** toolbar isn't displayed, right-click in the toolbar area and select **Drawing**. If you prefer, drag it away from its docked position, to leave it 'floating' in the main window.

Select an AutoShape scroll

3 From the **AutoShapes** drop-down menu on the **Drawing** toolbar, select **Stars and Banners** and choose the **Horizontal Scroll** shape. Then click and drag anywhere on the green background to create the banner shape. Don't worry about the size for now, but for a four-generation family tree you'll need to fit 15 of these on the page (eight-deep for the fourth generation – see opposite).

Add a drop shadow

4 With the shape still selected, click the **Shadow Style** button (the first green box) on the **Drawing** toolbar and choose **Shadow Style 6** with the drop shadow to the bottom right of the object. Click the **Shadow Style** button again and select **Shadow Settings** from the pop-up menu. Use the nudge buttons in the **Shadow Settings** toolbar to move the shadow up and to the left a little.

● Online research

Where you look for information about relatives will depend on where they were born, lived and died. A good starting point is www.familyrecords.gov.uk, the official UK government source for family records. As well as information and advice on how to go about your research, the site has links to public record and archive sources not only in the UK, but all over the world. In the UK these include birth, marriage and death certificates from the Family Records Centre; census data and immigration and emigration records from the National Archives; and military records from the Imperial War Museum.

Other useful research and advice websites include Ancestry.co.uk, www.ancestry.co.uk, RootsWeb.com, www.rootsweb.com, and Genes Reunited, www.genesreunited.co.uk (a family-based spin-off from Friends Reunited).

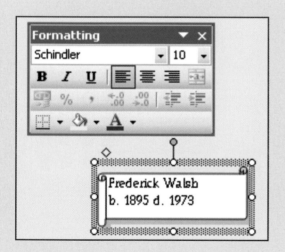

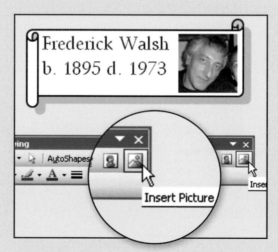

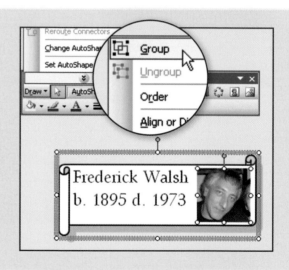

Add a name

5 Select the scroll shape and start typing to add text to it. Use dummy text at this stage and add the real text later, or use the longest name in your family tree so that you know you won't have problems fitting in the others. Select a font and type size from the **Formatting** toolbar. Formal serif-style fonts or italics look best (see page 326). Unless your family has particularly long names, use **10pt** text.

Choose your first picture

6 Click outside the scroll box, then on the **Insert Picture From File** button on the **Drawing** toolbar. Locate the first of your family photos and on the **Insert Picture** dialogue box click the **Insert** button. Position the photo in the white space to the right of the text in the scroll shape and drag a corner handle to resize it proportionally. Use the arrow keys on your keyboard to finally nudge it into position.

Group the photo and scroll

7 **Shift**-click on the photo and then the scroll shape to select both. Click the **Draw** button on the **Drawing** toolbar and select **Group** from the pop-up menu. The photo and the scroll are now 'grouped' or locked together and behave as a single object. Click the scroll/photo group to select it and choose **Copy** from the **Edit** menu or press **Ctrl+C** to copy it to the Windows clipboard.

Online resources from Office

The Microsoft Office Online website has family history templates. These include a family-tree template in Excel and Word templates for requesting family records from churches and other organisations. Launch Excel, then, in the **File** menu, select **New**. Then, in the **New Workbook** pane on the right, click **Templates on Office Online**. The Microsoft Online website loads in your web browser. In the **Search** box, type family tree then click **Go**. Alternatively, type http://office.microsoft.com into the address bar of your web browser. Select **Templates** and, in the **Home and Community** section, click **More…**, then under **Crafts, Hobbies, and Collections** choose **Genealogy**.

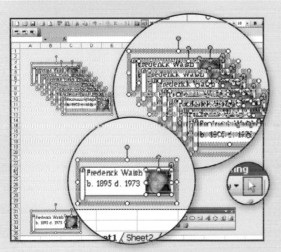

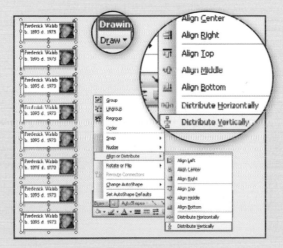

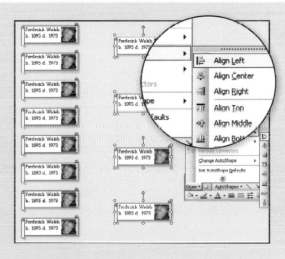

Duplicate the scrolls

8 In the **Edit** menu, select **Paste**, or press **Ctrl+V**, to paste the grouped object. Repeat this six times to create eight scroll boxes. Select the scroll at the front and drag it to the bottom left of the coloured background, roughly aligned with the top box. Click the **Select Object** tool (the pointer) on the **Drawing** toolbar and drag a marquee around the scrolls to select them all.

Get in position

9 Click the **Draw** button on the **Drawing** toolbar and select **Align or Distribute** from the pop-up menu, then from the sub-menu choose **Align Left**. All of the boxes are moved so that their left sides align with the top one. Do the same again, only this time choose **Distribute Vertically** from the sub-menu. The scroll boxes are now positioned equally down the left-hand side of the page.

Create more scrolls

10 Paste four more scroll boxes and click and drag to roughly position them in a column to the right of the others. Position each box vertically as accurately as possible between a pair of boxes in the left-hand column — use the cell row numbers as a visual guide. Left-align the new scroll boxes using **Align or Distribute** from the **Draw Button** pop-up menu as you did in the previous step.

Make your own family crest

When people talk of 'family crests', they are usually referring to a 'coat of arms', of which a crest is only a part. A coat of arms is granted to individuals rather than families. In England you must be a direct male-line descendent of the original bearer to have a legal right to bear a coat of arms. Find out more from the College of Arms site, www.college-of-arms.gov.uk.

Yet there's nothing to prevent you from creating your own coat of arms based on that of someone with a shared family name, or from designing a new one from scratch. Companies that will do this for you include www.fleurdelis.com and www.houseofnames.com.

A good source of free heraldry clip art, including coats of arms catalogued alphabetically by surname, is www.freecoatsofarms.com/catalog.html.

Different tree types

The family tree in this project is an 'ancestor tree'. This means that the subject, usually you, appears at the top, or to one side, and preceding generations branch out from that point. Another popular format is a 'descendant tree' (right), also known in the UK as 'dropline' format, in which an ancestor appears at the top and descendants branch off, down to the present generation.

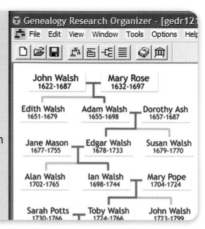

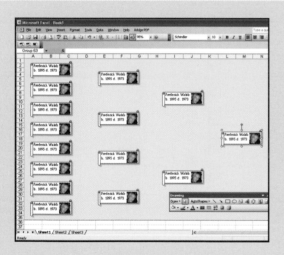

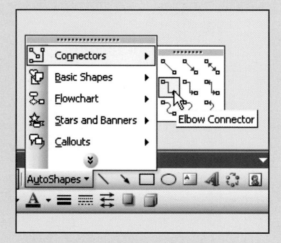

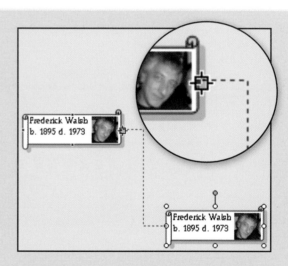

Bridge the generation gap

11 Repeat the process described in the previous step, pasting new scroll boxes and aligning them, to produce two more columns of boxes with two and one boxes respectively in each column. Now you have 15 boxes (from left to right – eight, four, two and one) arranged over four columns, representing your great-grandparents, grandparents, parents and yourself.

Choose a connector style

12 Click the **AutoShapes** button on the Drawing toolbar and select **Connectors** from the pop-up menu. From the flyout, select the **Elbow Connector**. Place the cursor over the first generation scroll/photo box on the far right; you'll see the cursor change to a square box 'target'. Blue dots called 'connection sites' will appear on the object showing you where you can attach the connector.

Make a connection

13 Click the connection site on the left side of the first generation box and drag to one of the parent boxes to the left. The cursor will change to the square box target again and you'll see a dashed line representing the shape of the connector. Left-click again when the cursor is over the connection site on the right side of the parent box to add the connector between the two boxes.

Share it on the web

Having made your family tree in Excel you can print it out and even frame it. But one way many people can get to see it and explore the information and pictures is to save it as a web page. In the **File** menu choose **Save As**. In the **Save as type** drop-down box select **Web Page**. Excel creates a web-page document and a folder containing images for the web page. You can then upload these files to your web space and add a link to it from your home page (see 'Your home page', page 256).

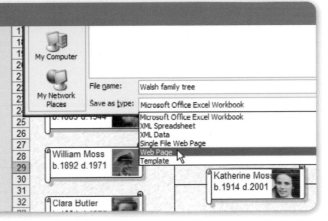

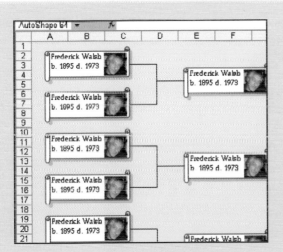

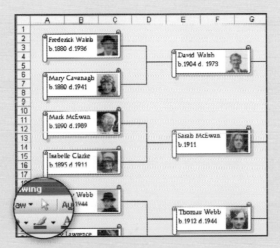

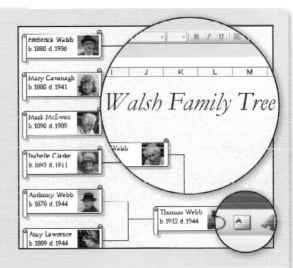

Linking parents and children

14 Repeat step 13 adding connectors between each child box and its two parent boxes. The advantage of using connectors rather than lines is that they move with the objects to which they are attached, enabling you to reposition any of the boxes without redrawing the lines. To resize the connectors, or make them a different colour, right-click them and select **Format AutoShape**.

Substitute with real people

15 Make sure the **Select Objects** button (arrow) in the **Drawing** toolbar is off (if the background is orange it's on – click to turn it off). Select the text in each box and overwrite it. Click on each box in turn to ungroup (click **Draw**, then **Ungroup**, in the **Drawing** toolbar). Then select each placeholder photo and delete it. Insert, size and position the correct photos as you did in step 6.

Add a title and a background

16 Click the **Text Box** button on the **Drawing** toolbar. Click and drag to create a text box, then type in your title. Format it using the options on the **Formatting** toolbar. To replace the background with a texture, click the **Insert Clip Art** button on the **Drawing** toolbar. Right-click on the clip art and choose **Order** then **Send to Back** to place it behind everything else. Save your file.

Once upon a time
Make a children's book starring the people they know

A storybook is a marvellous project to do with children, or to make as a gift for them. Drawing skills are not needed, because you work from photos, and you don't have to write a lot unless you want to – the main aims are to tell a good story and make it look great. If you have photos of the children concerned, they'll love to see themselves in the story.

This project takes you through the process of creating an eight-page storybook. You can adapt the ideas using your own theme and photos. Create as many pages as you wish, so long as it's a multiple of four if you're going to bind your book (see box page 187).

PROJECT TOOLS: Photoshop Elements ● Photos ● Colour printer
SEE ALSO: Flash cards for learning, page 168 ● Draw a comic strip, page 32

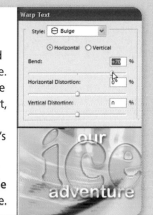

● Design a cover

A storybook cover often features one of the illustrations from inside. Make a new blank file and drag in a picture from one of the pages you've made. Choose a picture that can fill the page, then use the **Text** tool (press **T**) to add your title. For extra impact, add a warp effect. In the **Layers** palette, select the layer containing the text you want to warp; here it's only the middle word of the title, which has been created separately from the others. From the **Layer** menu, choose **Warp Text**. Pick a shape from the **Style** menu and adjust the **Bend** slider for an effect you like.

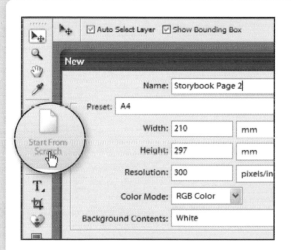

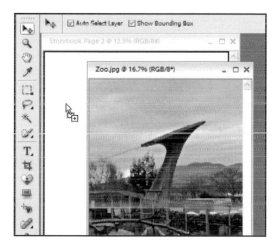

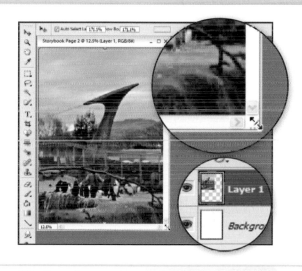

Create your first page

1 Run Photoshop Elements and click **Start From Scratch**. From the **File** menu, choose **New, Blank File** (or press **Ctrl+N**). In the **New** box, **Preset** menu, choose **A4**. Set the **Color Mode** to **RGB Color** and **Background Contents** to **White**. You'll create your storybook one page at a time, leaving the cover until last – so page 2 is the first. Type Storybook Page 2 in the **Name** box at the top. Click **OK**.

Open a picture

2 Choose **Open** from the **File** menu (or press **Ctrl+O**). In the **Open** dialogue box, select a photograph that you would like to use for the beginning of your story and click **Open**. One way to think of your story is as if it were a movie. In films an 'establishing shot', usually a long shot, is used to set the scene. Here we are using a long shot of the zoo where this story is set.

Fit the picture to your page

3 Press **V** for the **Move** tool. Click on the photo and drag it onto the blank page. Release the mouse button, then drag the photo to the top left corner of the page. Resize it by dragging the bottom right corner handle, making it cover the whole page. Hold down the **Shift** key to prevent the photo from changing shape. Press **Return** to finish, then drag the photo to adjust its position if necessary.

● Moving objects around

The **Move** tool works on the layer that's highlighted in the **Layers** palette, or the part of it within a selection you've made (shown by a flashing dotted outline). When you activate the **Move** tool (press **V**), a 'bounding box' surrounds the affected area. If you don't see this, tick **Show Bounding Box** in the **Options** bar. Drag within the box to move it, drag a corner to resize, or place the mouse pointer just off a corner and drag to rotate it.

● Preparing to lasso

Before starting a **Lasso** selection (see box, page 183), press **Z** for the **Zoom** tool, and drag a rectangle around the objects you want, so they're visible at a good size. Start lassoing, and once you're nearly all the way around, double-click to finish. If you double-click too soon by accident, deselect (**Ctrl+D**) and start again. Alternatively, finish by returning to your start point – the mouse pointer shows a tiny circle – then click once.

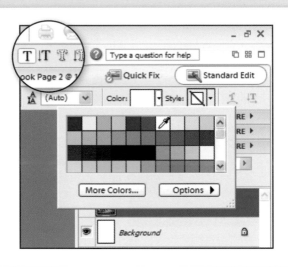

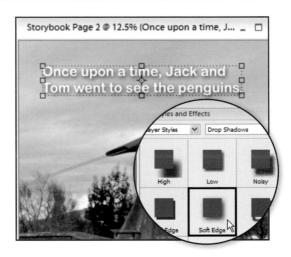

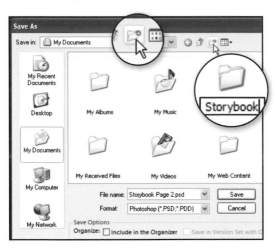

Add some text

4 Book text is usually black – but you can use any colour you like. Use white text on a dark background. Press **T** for the text tool. In the **Options** bar, ensure the first of the four icons at the left is highlighted for **Horizontal Text**. Choose a font and size (see 'Typography for learning aids', page 171), then click the triangle next to **Color**, at the right, and choose **white**.

Use a shadow to emphasise the text

5 Click near the top of the page and type some text. To finish, click twice on the **Move** tool at the top of the toolbox on the left. Position your text well away from the edges of the page. In the **Styles and Effects** palette (choose its name in the **Window** menu if you don't see it), select **Layer Styles** in the first menu and **Drop Shadows** in the second. From the options below, choose **Soft Edge**.

Make another page

6 Choose **Save** from the File menu, (or press **Ctrl+S**). In the **Save As** box, choose where to save your storybook, then click the **Create New Folder** icon at the top. Type Storybook as the name of the new folder, then click **Open**. Click **Save** to store the page you've made. Now press **Ctrl+N** to make a new blank page. Set it up the same as before (step 1), naming it Storybook Page 3. Click **OK**.

How to lasso

You can use the standard **Lasso** tool to draw around an object freehand – hold down the mouse button and keep dragging. But you'll need a steady hand. It's easier to use the **Polygonal Lasso** (see step 7) to draw a series of straight lines; for more precision, draw short lines. For a storybook, draw very roughly with longer lines, leaving a gap around the objects you're selecting so it will look as if you cut them out with scissors.

Create a photo collage

7 Open two photos that can be put together to make a scene. Here, the boys will make perfect penguins. To cut them out, use the **Polygonal Lasso** tool. Press **L** for **Lasso**. In the **Options** bar, click the last of the three icons at the left for **Polygonal Lasso**. Set **Feather** to **0**. Click on the edge of the area you want, release the mouse button, move to draw a straight line, then click again to position it.

Move the cutout

8 Continue all around the outline, and join your line back to the beginning or double-click to finish. Press **V** for the **Move** tool, and drag your cutout onto the penguin photo. Position the boys to fit in with the group and press **Return** to confirm. In the **Layers** palette on the right (choose **Layers** in the **Window** menu if you can't see it), click the eye next to the top layer to hide the cutout.

Duplicate some picture elements

9 Click **Background** to edit the background layer. Press **L** for the **Polygonal Lasso**, and then draw around your chosen elements – here, two penguins. When you've completed your selection, press **Ctrl+J** to copy this area into a new layer, which appears in the **Layers** palette as **Layer 2**. Press **Shift+Ctrl+]** to bring it to the front, or drag it to the top of the list in the **Layers** palette.

Jazzy effects

A quick way you can spice up a photo to use on a storybook page is to apply a colour effect. There are several under **Adjustments** on the **Filter** menu. Choose **Photo Filter**, then pick from the **Filter** menu and adjust the **Density** to set the strength of the effect. Choose **Posterize** and set a small number of **Levels** for a Pop Art effect. Or for a psychedelic image, choose **Gradient Map** and pick a colourful gradient from the menu.

Enlarge the elements

10 Now click the eye to show the boys' layer again. The elements you copied are now in front of them. Press **V** for the **Move** tool – a dotted box appears around the penguins, since their layer is currently selected in the **Layers** palette. Holding **Shift**, drag a corner of the box to enlarge the penguins, so they look as if they're in the foreground. The box's dotted line becomes a solid line.

Flip the elements

11 Press **Return** to confirm the changes. To make it less obvious that the penguins are repeated, in the **Image** menu choose **Rotate, Flip Selection Horizontal**. In the **Layer** menu choose **Flatten Image**. Everything is merged onto the **Background** layer. With the **Move** tool, drag the picture onto your blank page 3. Resize it, holding **Shift**. You'll need to adjust the shape to fit on the page.

Complete your page with text

12 Drag the bottom right corner of the window containing page 3 to make it larger than the canvas, revealing a grey background. Drag a corner of the picture to resize it bigger than the page, cropping off the edges. Leave a space at the bottom to put your text. Press **Return** to finish, then add text as in step 4. This time set **Color** to black. Save your page using **File, Save**.

● Matching colours between photos

To use two photos within a story that are differently exposed, tint one to match the other. On the stronger coloured picture, choose **Blur** from the **Filter** menu, then **Average**. It fills the canvas with a single colour. Press **V** for the **Move** tool and drag the block of colour onto your other picture. In the **Layers** palette, set blending mode to **Color**, and adjust **Opacity** percentage to get the desired colour match.

● Large images and memory

An A4 page of images at 300dpi (see 'Size matters', page 311) makes a large file of around 25Mb (megabytes) and it grows if you add layers. If you have a few files of this size open at the same time, as you will when creating the pages of your book, Photoshop Elements may get short of memory (RAM). You'll hear the hard disk whirring and your PC will slow down. To avoid this, close any pages or photos you're not currently working on.

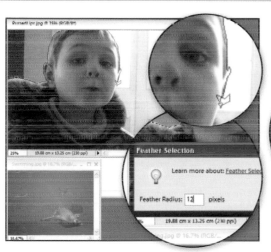

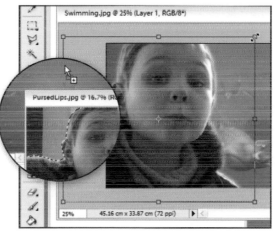

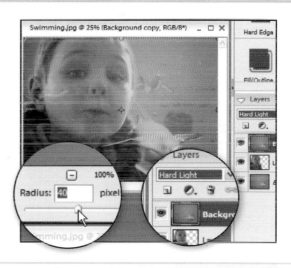

Cut out a face

13 Make another new page (see step 1), and name it Storybook Page 4. Again, open the two photos you want to combine. Here, one of the boys will join the penguins underwater. Draw around the boy's head and shoulders with the **Polygonal Lasso** (press **L**), and join your line back to the beginning. Choose **Feather** from the **Select** menu, enter **12** in **Feather Radius** and click **OK**.

Sizing and positioning the cutout

14 Press **V** for the **Move** tool and drag the face onto the underwater photo. Feathering (see step 13) gives it a soft edge. Enlarge the window, as in step 12, so you can size and position the face beyond the edges of the canvas. Press **Return** to finish. Now to make the face look as if it's underwater. In the **Layers** palette, right-click on the **Background** layer. Choose **Duplicate Layer**.

Blend to combine layers

15 Click OK to make a copy of the underwater scene in a new layer, called **Background copy**. Drag it to the top of the list in the **Layers** palette, bringing it in front of the face. Now click the **Blending Mode** menu at the top left of the **Layers** palette and change it from **Normal** to **Hard Light**. From the **Filter** menu, choose **Blur**, then **Gaussian Blur**. Set **Radius** to 40 and click **OK**.

● Turn a photo into a colouring picture

To convert a photo into a black and white line drawing use filters such as **Photocopy** (see steps 17 to 18, page 38). Children prefer a drawing divided into distinct areas that are easy to colour in. You can create this by tracing over the photo manually, using straight lines. Open a photo and press **Shift+Ctrl+N** to make a new layer. Press **U** for the **Shape** tool and in the **Options** bar choose the straight line. Set **Weight** to **6px** and **Color** to **Black**. To draw a line, click, drag and then release the mouse button. Without moving the mouse, click again to start the next line. Draw just the main features. When finished, scroll down the **Layers** palette – you'll have a lot of layers – and click **Background**. From the **Edit** menu, select **Fill Layer**. Choose **White**, **Normal**, 100%, and click **OK**. Choose **Flatten Image** from the **Layer** menu.

Copy the text

16 The large blur you just created removes details while preserving the water's colour. Choose **Flatten Image** from the **Layer** menu, then use the **Move** tool (press **V**) to drag the picture onto your blank page 4, positioning it similarly to page 3 – move the windows side by side to compare. Drag the text from page 3 to page 4 to copy it, then use the **Text** tool to edit it. Save your page.

Build a colouring page

17 Make a new page, calling it Storybook Page 5. Here we are going to create an interactive colouring page. As described on page 169 in steps 2 to 4, use the **Custom Shape** tool to draw some objects relevant to the story. As the shapes are black and white outlines, they are ideal for colouring. Using the **Move** tool, size, position and rotate each shape, leaving space for text.

Reuse your page layout

18 Drag text from page 4 onto this page and edit it with the **Text** tool (press **T**). Save Storybook Page 5 using **File**, **Save**. This will also form the basis for a blank drawing page at the back of the book. In the **Layers** palette, **Shift+Click** all the shape layers to select them. Right-click one and choose **Delete Layer**. Click **Yes** in the box to remove all the shapes.

● Printing your storybook

Start by opening all your finished pages, and choose **Print** from the **File** menu. Click **Page Setup** and choose your paper size, then click **Printer**. Select your printer and click **Properties** to adjust its settings, including the paper type you're using – a good-quality glossy photo paper gives best results. Click **OK** twice to return to **Print Preview**. Click **Print** to print the current page. Close it and repeat for the next. Alternatively, click **Print Multiple Photos**. The **Organizer Workspace** opens and shows the **Print Photos** dialogue box. Under **Select Type of Print**, choose **Individual Prints**. Click **Print** to print all your photos.

● Bind your book

To give your book a professional touch, buy sheets of heavy art paper and stick your printed pages to them. Use sheets slightly larger than your pages, sticking one page to each side of each sheet. Leave an extra-wide margin at the front left and back right of each sheet, then lie all the sheets flat in the right order and staple through the margin. Cut a strip of paper and glue it over the staples.

Alternatively, use sheets at least double the size of your pages. Take one-quarter as many sheets as you have pages, fold each neatly in half and crease. Unfold the sheets and lay them neatly on top of each other. With a needle and thread, stitch along the fold. Stick your pages onto the sheets.

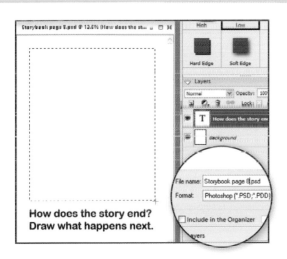

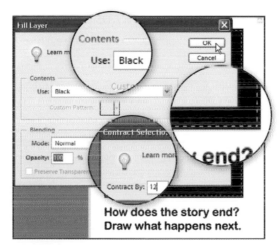

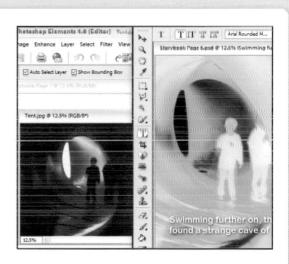

Construct a drawing page

19 Edit the text to invite readers to draw their own picture. Choose **Save As** from the **File** menu. Change the file name to Storybook Page 8 and click **Save**. Press **M** for the **Marquee** tool, and in the **Options** bar click **Rectangular Marquee**. Click a little way in from the top left corner of the canvas and drag to draw a box to frame the reader's art. In the **Layers** palette, click the **Background** layer.

Add a border

20 From the **Edit** menu, choose **Fill Selection** (the **Fill Layer** dialogue box appears). Under **Contents**, **Use** choose **Black**. Set **Blending**, **Mode** to **Normal**, **Opacity** to **100%**. Click **OK**. Go to the **Select** menu and choose **Modify**, then **Contract**. Type 12 and click **OK**. Go back to **Fill Selection** and, in the **Use** box, change **Black** to **White**. Click **OK** to leave a black border. Save your page.

Design the remaining pages

21 Add pages 6 and 7, using **Ctrl+N** (see step 1), or reuse an existing page – save with a different name, as in step 19, then edit the text and drag in a new picture. Here, a photo taken inside a tent will represent the Snow King's palace. To turn the warm red scene to icy blue, press **Ctrl+I** to make a negative. Add a cover (see box, page 181) and print your book as explained in the box above.

Yours sincerely...

Discover how to create a font out of your signature

Transform your own scanned signature into a font character and you can avoid all the hassle of signing letters by hand. Creating new characters isn't difficult and the program you need, Private Character Editor (PCE), is included in Windows XP. You can start from scratch, or make changes to characters from the fonts you have installed already on your computer.

PROJECT TOOLS: Private Character Editor (PCE) ● Photoshop Elements ● Scanner
SEE ALSO: Font basics explained, page 326

● Customise your Windows fonts

You can modify existing characters in Private Character Editor (PCE), for example to create symbols for a school science project, or just to make a fun symbol like a smiley face. To copy an existing character grid to use as a starting point for your own character, run PCE (see step 9), select **Reference** from the **Window** menu and click on a character to select it. Click **OK**, then select the shape in the **Reference** window with the **Rectangular Selection** tool, and press **Ctrl+C** followed by **Ctrl+V** to copy and paste it into the **Edit** window.

Sign here, please

1 You'll need a signature to scan in. Sign your name on a plain white sheet of paper. If possible, use a fountain pen or a good-quality ball-point with black ink. Try and keep your signature as clean and simple as you can. Make several attempts on the same sheet and when you have one you are happy with, place the page face-down on the scanner bed.

● Ready-made symbols you can use or adapt

The Wingdings font, included with Windows, is full of useful symbols that you can use in your documents – as bullet points, for example, or even as a quick and ready source of clip-art images. You can also use Wingdings symbols as a basis for fonts that you create yourself, using Private Character Editor (PCE) – see 'Customise your Windows fonts', page 188. To help you find which Wingdings characters relate to which keys on your keyboard, Windows has a software utility called Character Map (see step 13). You can preview any font you have installed, and copy characters directly into your documents. To use Character Map, click the **Start** menu, click **Run**, then type charmap and click **OK**. For some fonts, Character Map shows keyboard shortcuts to type individual characters. This isn't the case for Wingdings, so you'll need to click on a character, click the **Select** button, then click **Copy**. Finally, switch to your word processor or other program you want to use the character in, and paste it (**Ctrl+V**).

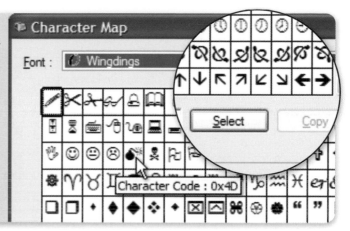

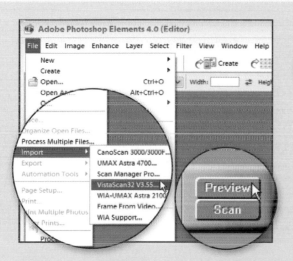

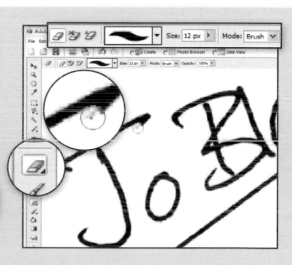

Setting up the scanner

2 Launch Photoshop Elements and click the **Edit and Enhance Photos** button on the **Welcome** screen. When the program has loaded, select **Import** from the **File** menu and choose your scanner from the sub-menu. Click the **Preview** button. After a rough 'preview' scan, select the best signature by clicking and dragging to highlight the area. (The procedure may vary, so check your scanner's user manual.)

Scan your signature

3 In the scanner settings, choose **B/W Photo** (on your scanner it may be called 'greyscale' or something similar). Don't select 'Bitmap, Document' or 'Fax' options as you won't be able to edit them in Photoshop Elements. Set the resolution to **300dpi** and the size to **100%**. Press the **Scan** button. When the scan has finished, it will open in Photoshop Elements. Exit the scanner software to continue.

Clean up the edges

4 In Elements, press **D** to set the background colour to white, then press **E** for the **Eraser** tool. In the **Tool Options** at the top, click the **Eraser Tool** option (leftmost in the group of three erasers). Select **Brush** from the **Mode** drop-down menu. Set the brush **Size** to **12px** (pixels). Zoom in by holding down **Ctrl+Space** and clicking in the image, then use the eraser to clean up any blotches and messy edges.

● Choose the right drawing tool

Private Character Editor (PCE) has a basic set of tools to help you draw new characters or adapt existing ones. These include freehand pencil and brush tools, elipses and rectangles. To select a tool, click in the toolbox on the left side of the window. Press the left mouse button to draw in black or the right button to erase. You can rotate or flip parts of your creation, or copy and paste inside the grid or from another Windows program. If you want to compare your character side by side with a character from any Windows font – useful for 'borrowing' bits of characters or symbols – select **Reference** from the **Window** menu.

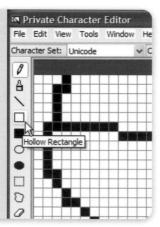

● Making fonts out of pictures

Even photographs can be converted to font characters. Select your starting photos carefully – high-contrast images work best, and remember that the character grid is just 64x64 pixels, so choose a subject that's recognisable even at a very small size.

Run Photoshop Elements and, from the **Welcome** screen, choose **Edit and Enhance Photos**. Press **Ctrl+O** then browse to the folder containing the image you want to use. Select the image and click **Open**. Click the **Crop** tool in the toolbar on the left. In the options at the top, set **Aspect Ratio** to **Custom**, and type 64 px into the **Width** box and 64 px into the **Height** box. Click and drag over the part of the image you want to crop.

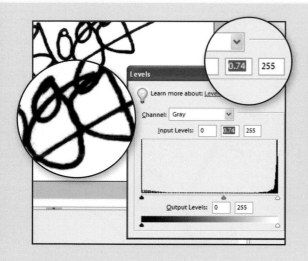

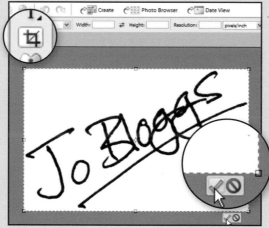

Thicken up the lines

5 In the **Enhance** menu, choose **Adjust Lighting** then **Levels** (or press **Ctrl+L**). Drag the central grey slider underneath the chart to the right. You'll see the signature thicken and become darker. Beyond a certain point black dots start appearing everywhere. When this happens, somewhere between **0.8** and **0.6** in the middle **Input Levels** box, drag the slider back until the dots disappear, then click **OK**.

Crop the signature

6 The font character you are about to make is based on an image that is only 64 pixels square. To obtain as much detail as possible you need to devote all of those pixels to the signature and not on surrounding white space. From the tool box, left, select the marquee **Crop** tool (or press **C**), then click and drag around the signature as close as possible. Then click the green **Tick** button.

Remove the grey tones

7 The image needs to be made up of just black and white pixels (no grey tones) to work in Private Character Editor (see step 9). To convert it, select **Image**, **Mode** then **Bitmap**. Don't change the figure in the output box but choose **50% Threshold** from the **Method** drop-down menu. This converts all the dark-coloured pixels in the image to solid black and all the light-coloured pixels to pure white.

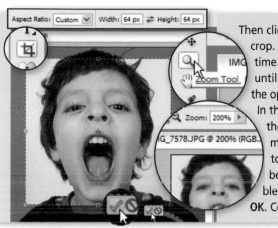

Then click the tick icon to perform the crop. The image is resized at the same time. Press **Z**, then click in the image until the zoom percentage (displayed in the options bar at the top) is **200%**.

In the **Filter** menu, choose **Adjustments** then **Threshold**. In the dialogue box, move the white slider at the bottom to the left or right until the image becomes most recognisable (not too bleached out and not too dark). Click **OK**. Continue from step 7 of this project.

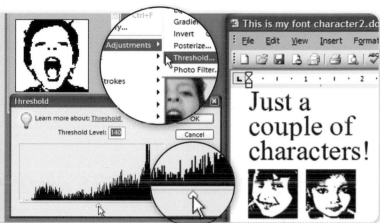

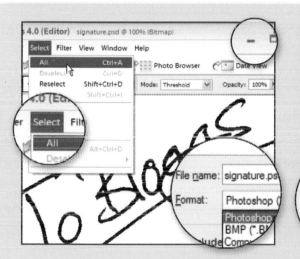

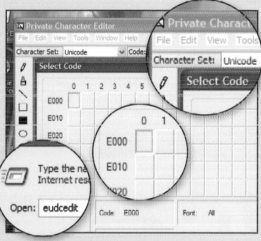

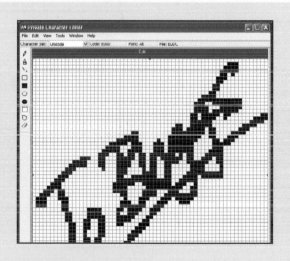

Copy and save

8 Choose **All** from the **Select** menu, followed by **Ctrl+C** to copy the signature to the Windows clipboard. Press **Ctrl+S** to save, give your signature a name, and choose **Photoshop (*.PSD,*.PDD)** from the **Format** drop-down menu. Click **Save** to save the file to your hard drive. Click the **Minimise** button (it looks like a hyphen at the top right of the screen) to minimise the Photoshop Elements window.

Run the PCE program

9 Click the Windows **Start** button, bottom left, and select **Run**. Type eudcedit and click **OK**. PCE will launch displaying the **Select Code** grid. Each box in the grid represents a character. Unless you've used PCE before they will all be empty. The numbers down the side and along the top are 'Unicode' values (unique reference numbers assigned to each character). The first available position, E000, is already selected.

Paste the signature

10 Click **OK** to accept the E000 code and the empty grid for that character will be displayed. Press **Ctrl+V** to paste the signature into the grid. If the pasted signature file isn't square it will be squashed to fit into the 64x64 pixel grid. If you have a very long signature, consider signing only your initials, or using an abbreviated form of your full signature.

● Finding your characters on the keyboard

Your keyboard displays the letters of the alphabet, as well as numbers from 0 to 9 and some commonly used symbols. But there are many characters you won't find printed on the keys, including any special characters that you've designed yourself. You could use Character Map (see step 13) each time to copy a character (**Ctrl+C**) then paste it (**Ctrl+V**) into your document, but there is an easier way.

In Character Map, click to select a character in the main display. At the bottom, you'll see the character's name and, on the right, its 'keystroke' (**Alt** plus a four-digit number). For example, the copyright symbol © is **Alt+0169**. To enter this character in Word, or any another application, first make sure the **NumLock** key is activated (there's usually an indicator light on your keyboard) then hold down the **Alt** key and type 0169 on the numeric keypad.

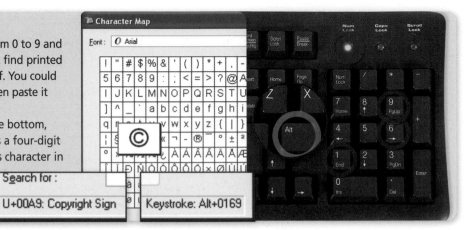

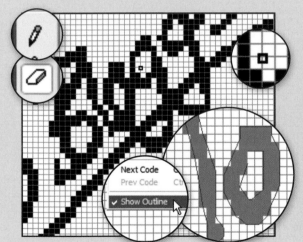

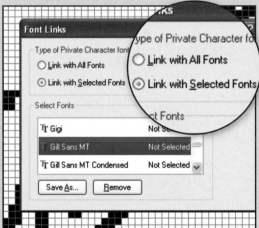

Clean up the signature

11 Click the **Pencil** tool and add black pixels where lines are broken, or use the **Eraser** to delete pixels that shouldn't be there – for example, where the circles of characters are filled in. The pixels are just a guide for the actual outline of the character shape, which you can see (but not edit) by selecting **Show Outline** from the **View** menu. When you're happy with the character, press **Ctrl+S** to save it.

Link the character to certain fonts

12 If you only want special characters added to some but not all of the fonts on your PC, select **Font Links** from the **File** menu. Tick **Link with Selected Fonts**, then select the fonts you want to add the character to, and click **Save As**. Name the file in the **Modify Private Character Filename** dialogue box and click **Save**, then click **OK**. Select **Exit** from the **File** menu to close PCE.

Open the Character Map utility

13 To use the new character in documents, you need to open the **Character Map** utility. Click the Windows **Start** button, then click **Run**, type charmap and click **OK**. In **Character Map**, make sure **Advanced view** is ticked. Type your character's Unicode value – here it's E000 – in the box labelled **Go to Unicode**. If the character is available it will be displayed in the top left box.

● More advanced font-design tools

Private Character Editor (PCE) provides a quick and easy way to produce a special character or symbol. If you want to take things further and design a complete font of your own, you'll need dedicated font-design software.

The best-known font-design programs are Fontlab Studio and Fontographer, www.fontlab.com. They are both aimed at professional typographers and designers, but Fontlab also publishes TypeTool – a cut-down, modestly priced version for beginners. Another good budget font editor is High-Logic's Font Creator, www.high-logic.com/fontcreator.html. All of these programs allow you to draw characters using smooth curves, or 'vector outlines', so that the fonts produced can be used at any size, without losing any detail or smoothness. Your creations are then saved as standard Windows fonts.

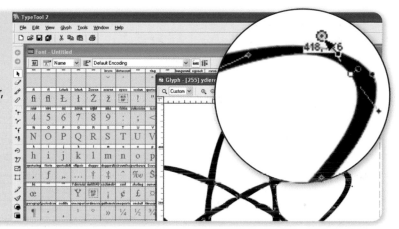

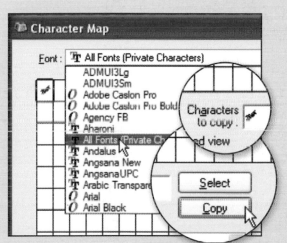

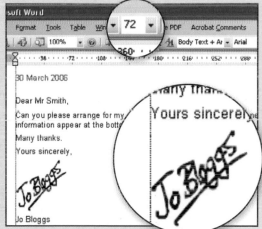

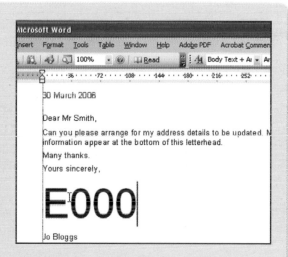

View all new characters

14 If you're having problems finding your new character, click on the font drop-down menu at the top of the **Character Map** dialogue box and select **All Fonts (Private Characters)**. This is a special font created by PCE that contains only the new characters you have created. Click on the box containing your signature character and click the **Select** button, followed by the **Copy** button.

Sign your document

15 Open your Word document, click in the text where you would normally sign and press **Ctrl+V** to paste in the signature character. Because a whole signature is contained within the space of a single character, you will need to increase the size to at least **72pt** – select the size from the drop-down menu on the **Formatting** toolbar – so the signature displays actual size.

Add a signature from the keyboard

16 If your copy of Microsoft Office is version 2002 or later, you can enter special characters directly onto the page – in Word, for example – and you don't have to select them using the Character Map. You just have to type the Unicode number, here it's E000, then, without typing a space or anything else, press **Alt+X** and the number will be replaced with your signature character.

Seasonal greetings
Cut the hassle of sending your Christmas message

When you have a large family or lots of friends, writing and addressing Chrismas cards can be a real chore. Your PC can help, by taking names and addresses straight from your Microsoft Outlook address book or from a list in Excel, then printing personalised envelopes or address labels. And, to keep everyone abreast of your news, you can design a simple Christmas newsletter to accompany your cards.

PROJECT TOOLS: Microsoft Word ● Microsoft Excel
SEE ALSO: Make your own greetings cards, page 104 ● Charts and graphics with Excel, page 300

The principles of mail merge

When you need to write the same letter to many different people, you can include special 'form fields' within the text of a Word document. These link to a list of names and addresses – in Outlook or Excel, for example – so that, when the letter is printed, a personalised copy is made for each person on the list. So, instead of 'Dear sir' or 'Dear friends', you can write 'Dear', followed by a name 'field' that will automatically include the first name of each recipient. Word's **Mail Merge Wizard** (see step 7 onwards) helps automate the task, complete with printed envelopes with all the addresses for your mailing.

Choose a theme for your stationery

1 Launch Microsoft Word and create a new blank document by pressing **Ctrl+N**. Select **Theme** from the **Format** menu, and choose a theme from the list on the left. You'll use this on the envelope as well as the letter, so pick one of the lighter, more subtle themes so it doesn't obscure the address. For example, **Blends** is a good choice. Click **OK** to apply the theme to your document.

● Find free templates

If you want the fastest possible way to produce an attractive Christmas letter, then browse the free, well-designed templates that Microsoft makes available online. Launch Word, click **File** and then **New**. Type Christmas in the **Templates** search box, and click **Go**. The list of results contains everything from simple watermarked stationery to full newsletters; click on anything that sounds interesting to see a preview, then click **Download** to use it.

● Mail merge with Outlook

If you use Microsoft Outlook, and your address book already contains details of everyone on your Christmas list, there's no need to type them in again. Outlook must be set as the default mail program for this to work, so click **Tools**, **Options**, **Other** and tick **Make Outlook the default**. When you reach the **Select recipients** step of the mail merge (see step 8, page 197), tick **Select from Outlook contacts**, then click **Choose Contacts Folder**.

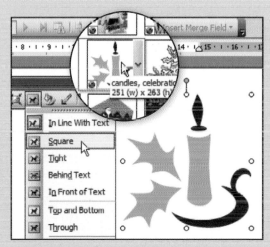

Browse the Christmas clip art

2 The theme that you've chosen needs to be made more seasonal. So connect to the internet and then, in Microsoft Word, on the **Insert** menu select **Picture** then **Clip Art**. In the **Clip Art** task pane on the right, type in an appropriate word, such as Christmas or Holly, in the **Search for** box, and click **Go** to see matching pictures. It may take a few seconds to download all the thumbnail images.

Position images on the page

3 Click on an image you like and it will appear on the page. Double-click the image on the page. The **Format Picture** dialogue box appears. Click the **Layout** tab and choose the **Square** wrapping style. Click OK. Drag the corner handles to resize the picture, or click on the image and drag to reposition it. Repeat the process to add more images but don't overdo it – one or two pictures is usually enough.

Write your Christmas news

4 Click on the white page to place the text cursor. Then press **Return** twice to make space for the name and write a letter with your general news. Leave space below for a personalised greeting to be added later (see 'Personalise a letter', page 197). Press **Ctrl+S** to save the letter. In the **Save As** dialogue box, name the file Christmas news and click **Save**. Quit Word by choosing **Exit** from the **File** menu.

Add a return address

Word can automatically print a 'return address' – your own address – on an envelope, as well as that of the recipient. Click **Tools**, **Options**, select the **User Information** tab, then enter your address in the **Mailing address** box. The next time you see the **Envelopes and Labels** dialogue box, untick the **Omit** box to see the return address appear in the **Preview** window.

Build an address book in Excel

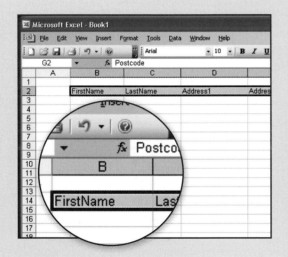

5 Word can't customise your letters without knowing the names and addresses of all the people you wish to send Christmas cards to. So now open Excel (see page 300) and type some column headings. Type in FirstName in cell **B2**, LastName in **C2**, then Address1 and Address2 (the first and second lines of the address), City and Postcode in **D2** through **G2**. Add a Country column if you're sending abroad.

Type in names and addresses

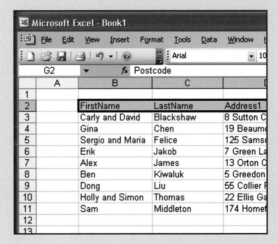

6 Click and drag the mouse across the column headers to highlight them. Right-click on a header and select **Format Cells**. Click the **Patterns** tab and choose a light colour. The shading helps Excel separate the header from your addresses (the data). Now fill the columns with the names and addresses you want. When you've finished, choose **Save** from the **File** menu and **Quit** Excel.

Use mail merge

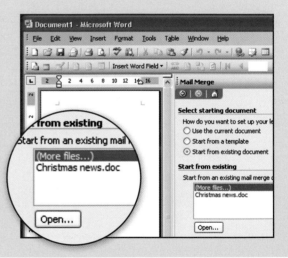

7 Open Word. Click **Tools**, **Letters and Mailings** then **Mail Merge**. In the **Mail Merge** task pane, under **Select document type**, tick **Letters**. Then click **Next: Starting Document** at the bottom. Now tick **Start from existing document**. In the list below, select **Christmas news** then click **Open**. Or, if your file isn't shown in the list, click **More files**, then **Open**; navigate to the file, select it and click **Open**.

Personalise a letter

It's easy to add extra, personal touches to your Word mail-merge letters. Work your way through the **Mail Merge Wizard**, up to the final **Complete the merge** step, (see step 10, below) and click **Edit individual letters**. Word will create and display a single document containing all your merged letters. Browse through the pages, making any changes you'd like, adding new comments and images, then print the document when you're done.

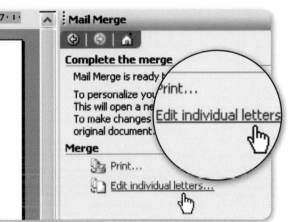

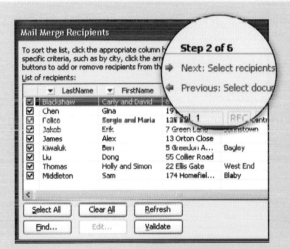

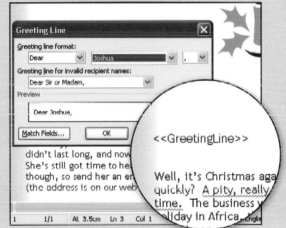

Open your Excel address book

8 Click **Next: Select recipients**, choose **Use an existing list**, then click **Browse**. Pick **Excel Files** in the **Files of type** box, then browse to the Excel file you created earlier. If asked to select a table (from **Sheet1$**, **Sheet2$** and so on), choose the first one and click **OK**. In the **Mail Merge Recipients** dialogue box, you'll see a table of the names and addresses you created earlier. Click **OK**.

Add a personalised greeting

9 Christmas letters are friendlier if you add individual greetings. At the bottom of the task pane click **Next: Write your letter** (Step 3 of 6). Click at the top of the document where you want the greeting to appear, then click **Greeting line** and choose a format for the name and greeting. Click **OK** and the 'GreetingLine' placeholder appears. It will be replaced with the real greeting when the letter is printed.

Preview and print your letters

10 Click **Next: Preview your letters** (Step 4 of 6), to see how they'll appear. To alter the font and size of the greeting, click **Previous: Write your letter**, make your changes then click the **Preview** step again. If all is fine, click **Next: Complete the merge**. Click **Print**. In the **Merge to Printer** dialogue box, tick **All** then click **OK**. In the **Print** dialogue box, set your print options and click **OK**.

Print perfect envelopes

Ensure great results when printing envelopes, by following a few simple rules.

- Choose your envelopes carefully. For example, don't opt for very thick envelopes, or cheap ones with thin edges, as they won't feed into the printer correctly. Never use envelopes with clasps or tie strings, which will jam and may damage the printer.

- Keep envelopes in a cool, dry place. It's more likely they'll feed through the printer properly if they're crisp, clean and free of creases.

- If your printer has a lever that sets paper thickness, then use it whenever you print envelopes (see your printer manual for instructions). Forget and it will assume you're still printing single paper sheets, perhaps resulting in the envelope getting jammed.

- Use the lowest acceptable print-quality setting. This means each envelope is produced as fast as possible, which will also save you money on printer ink or toner.

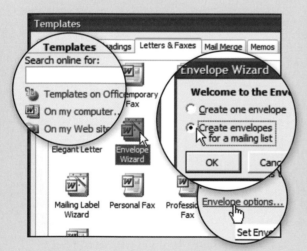

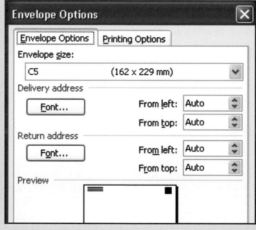

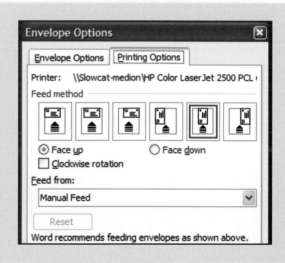

Create an envelope document

11 In Word, click **File** and **New**. In the **New Document** task pane on the right, select **On my computer** from the **Templates** section. In the **Templates** dialogue box, click the **Letters & Faxes** tab, then the **Envelope Wizard** icon. Click **OK** and the wizard appears. Choose **Create envelopes for a mailing list** and click **OK**. Click the **Envelope options** link in the **Mail Merge** task pane.

Select the envelope size

12 In the **Envelope Options** dialogue box click the **Envelope Options** tab and choose from the list (see the 'Choosing envelopes' box, page 107). Most standard sizes are listed, so choose a size closest to the envelopes you want to use. You can also specify the delivery address font and position, but it's best to accept the default settings until you can judge how they look.

Set printing options

13 Click the **Printing Options** tab. Here you choose whether to load the envelopes manually into your printer or from the paper tray, and which way round the address will be printed. Many printers have a straighter 'paper path' for sheets fed in manually. This avoids paper jams with thicker items such as envelopes. For now, accept the default settings and click **OK**.

Create custom labels

If you're printing lots of envelopes, perhaps 50 or more, it may be faster to use labels instead. You'll get several on each sheet, and they'll automatically feed through most printers without difficulty, ensuring you get good-quality finished results at top speed.

Word supports label sheets from most manufacturers, including Avery, Formtec and Rank Xerox. Click **Tools**, **Letters and Mailings**, **Envelopes and Labels**, then click the **Labels** tab, click **Options** and browse **Label products** for the full list. If your label sheet isn't included, click **New Label** instead. In the **New Custom laser** dialogue box enter the width and height of each label, distance between labels and so on, allowing the sheet to be printed correctly. Then choose **Labels** instead of **Envelopes** during a mail merge to enjoy faster print times.

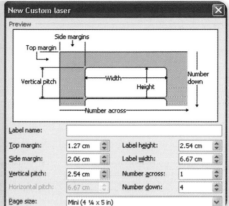

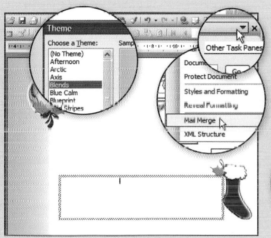

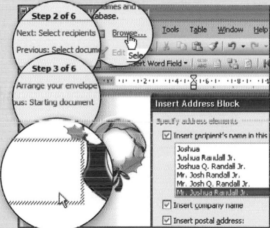

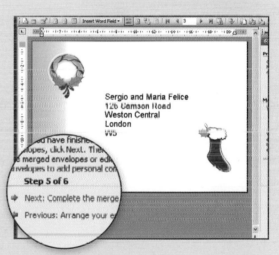

Design an envelope

14 Click Format, Theme and choose a theme such as Blends to match your letter. Click OK. Click Insert, Picture, Clip art, search on the key word Holly, and click on an image. Position it as you did with your letter but don't cover the rectangular address block, which you'll find by clicking around the envelope. Click the **Other Task Panes** button in the top-right corner and choose **Mail Merge** from the list.

Choose the recipients

15 At the bottom, click Next: Select Recipients. Choose Browse, and open your Excel address list just as in step 8. Then, click Next: Arrange your envelope. Click inside the address block area of the envelope (you'll see a striped border if you've clicked in the right place), then click **Address block** in the task pane on the right. In the dialogue box, choose a format for the names, then click OK.

Ready to print

16 To see the completed envelopes, click Next: Preview your envelopes. If the address text is too small or in the wrong place, then return to the previous step and reformat it by selecting the **AddressBlock** placeholder and choosing a new font, or click and drag the address block border to resize it. When all is fine, click **Next: Complete the merge** then **Print** to produce the envelopes.

Wear it with pride
Create a t-shirt for your club or team

You can design and print your own t-shirt with nothing more than your PC, an inkjet printer, a household iron, photos, clip art, plain text and special transfer paper. Personalised t-shirts are inexpensive and a great way to publicise your company, sports club or charity event, or even give as a present. You can also put your own design on almost anything else – from mugs to fridge magnets, and even jewellery and underwear.

PROJECT TOOLS: Photoshop Elements ● Photos ● T-shirt ● Inkjet printer ● Iron ● Transfer paper
SEE ALSO: Font basics explained, page 326 ● Produce a poster, page 84 ● Party kit, page 162

How transfer printing works

To print your design or photo, using a standard inkjet printer, you need special transfer paper, which, rather than absorbing the printed ink, holds it on the surface. The image is printed 'back to front' and, once the ink has dried, the paper is placed face down over the garment. Using a hot iron, the image is transferred from the paper onto the cloth. Once dry, the garment should be washable, just like commercially printed clothing. Light colours work well, although transfer paper is also available for printing on dark colours.

Set the page size

1 Launch Photoshop Elements and click the **Start From Scratch** button on the **Welcome** screen. Select the **A4** preset in the **New** dialogue box. If your inkjet transfer paper is not A4, choose the appropriate size from the **Preset** drop-down menu. At a resolution of **300 pixels/inch** the file is quite large. You don't need this level of detail for t-shirt printing, so reduce it to **200** and click **OK**.

Where to get printing supplies

You can buy inkjet transfer paper for t-shirt printing from almost any printer supplies shop. Epson and Hewlett Packard sell direct from their websites at www.buyepson.com and www.hp.com. A variety of products are also available at online sites such as www.photopaperdirect.com and www.consumables.co.uk. Another good source for t-shirt transfer paper and a host of other specialist materials designed for inkjets is www.folex.com.

You don't need special inks to print on t-shirt transfers, or specialist papers and materials. But you'll get better results if you run the printer through a cleaning cycle beforehand (see your printer's manual to find out how to do so).

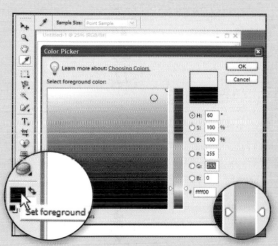

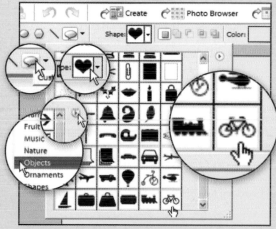

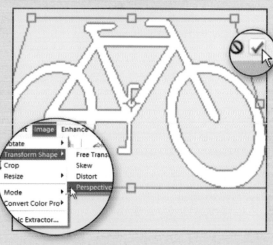

Colour the background

2 The main design here will feature a cycle club logo that incorporates type, a bicycle graphic adapted from one of Photoshop Elements' **Custom Shape** tool presets, and a road surface texture (see box, page 202) for the background. Click the **Set foreground color** swatch at the bottom left, select a bright yellow in the **Color Picker**, click **OK**, then press **Alt+Delete** to fill the **Background** layer with the colour.

Draw a bicycle

3 Press U for the Shape tool. Click the **Custom Shape** tool in the options at the top. Right-click on your canvas. In the pop-up palette, click the small button at the right and choose **Objects** from the list. Scroll down the objects until you see the bicycle shape, then select it. Press **X** to swap the foreground and background colours. **Shift**+drag on the background and draw a white bicycle shape in the centre of the page.

A new perspective

4 From the **Image** menu, select **Transform Shape** then **Perspective**. Drag the top left corner handle of the bounding box towards the top centre handle. The top of the bicycle is squeezed inwards from both sides, simulating perspective. Release the handle when the top of the bounding box is roughly three-quarters as wide as the bottom and click the tick button on the **Tool Options** bar.

Printing a t-shirt online

If you don't have an inkjet printer, you can upload your design to a print website such as TShirt Studio, www.tshirtstudio.com (right), Bonusprint, www.bonusprint.com, or Spreadshirt, www.spreadshirt.co.uk. Choose a size and fabric colour, and the printed t-shirt is sent in the post. You can upload a photo, or a finished design such as the one in this project. Most sites include a simple on-screen designer that lets you compose a slogan, choose fonts and colours, and add an image from a selection of clip art.

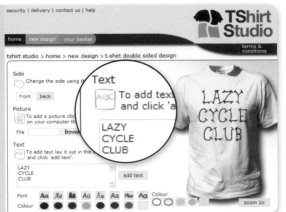

Make a background texture

The simplest way to obtain a road-surface texture, such as the one used in this project, is to photograph a patch of tarmac using a digital camera. Take the shot from a position close to the ground with the camera pointed almost horizontally, so the stones in the foreground are noticeably larger than those further away, to emphasise the perspective.

If you don't have access to a digital camera, or a suitable patch of tarmac, you can create your own texture in Photoshop Elements. Press **Ctrl+N** and create a new document the same as in step 1.

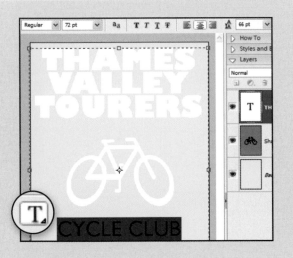

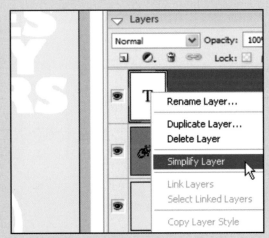

Type in a name

5 From the toolbox, left, select the **Horizontal Type** tool. Click and drag to create a large text box covering the whole page. Type in the club name in capitals, pressing **Return** at the end of each word to create separate lines. Press **Return** again between lines to create space above and below the bicycle. In the **Tool Options** bar, top, choose a bold typeface and a large type size, here **Gill Sans, 72pt**.

Convert the text to an image

6 To add perspective to the type, first 'simplify' the layer. This means turning the layer into an image, so you can apply filters and effects to it including changes to perspective. Simplified layers are no longer editable, so double check that you haven't made any spelling errors or other mistakes, then, from the **Layers** palette, right-click the type layer and choose **Simplify Layer** from the pop-up menu.

Add perspective to the type

7 From the **Image** menu, select **Transform Shape**, then **Perspective**, and drag the top left handle of the type bounding box towards the centre handle, as you did in step 4 for the bicycle. Match the perspective on the bike so that both appear to be on the same surface – wider at the bottom than at the top. You can drag the bottom handles outwards, if needed, to achieve this. Press **Return** to finish.

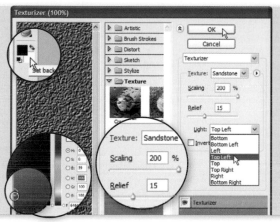

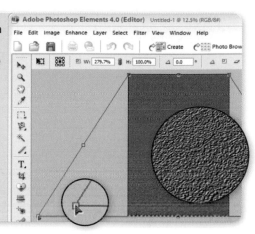

At the bottom left, click the background colour swatch and pick a mid grey colour, then click **OK**. Press **Ctrl+Delete** to fill the page with the background colour. In the **Filter** menu, choose **Texture** then **Texturizer**. On the right, set **Texture** to **Sandstone**, **Scaling** to **200**, **Relief** to **15** and **Light** to **Top Left**. Click **OK** to create the texture on your page. Press **Ctrl+A** to select the whole page and, in the **Image** menu, choose **Transform** then **Perspective**. Grab the bottom right handle and drag it to the right until the base of the selection is three times its original width. Press **Return**. To save your texture, press **Ctrl+S**, then choose a name and location for the file. Set **Format** to **JPEG** and click **Save**. In the **JPEG Options**, set **Quality** to **6** and click **OK**.

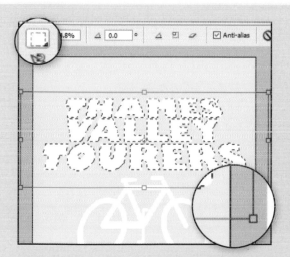

Enlarge the type

8 The top section of your type may now appear too small. Press **M** to select the **Rectangular Marquee** tool, then click and drag around the text. Select the **Move** tool (or press **V**), then click on and drag a corner handle while holding down the **Shift** key to resize the text while maintaining its original proportions. Press **Return** to confirm. In the **Layers** palette, click the **Background** layer.

Add the road

9 Select **Place** from the **File** menu to add the road texture (see box, above). **Shift**+drag a corner handle to resize the texture so it fills the page, then press **Return**. To make space for additional text at the top, press **M** for the **Rectangular Marquee** tool. Drag to select roughly the top fifth of the page, then press **Delete**. In the same way, remove a strip at the bottom, one-eighth of the page height.

Blend the graphics into the road

10 Click the cycle layer in the **Layers** palette, then **Shift**+click to add the type layer. Select the **Move** tool (or press **V**) and drag the top centre handle downwards to squash the graphic, then press **Return**. To make the graphics appear as if they're painted on the road, click on each layer in turn and choose **Blend mode**, **Overlay** from the drop-down menu in the **Layers** palette.

● Print on anything

You don't have to limit your designs to t-shirts. Visit Avery (right), at www.averyinspired.co.uk/products, for a range of creative project kits that come with everything you need to produce fridge magnets, stickers, translucent decals for applying to windows and mirrors, and cotton fabrics that you can print directly onto then sew together to make personalised bags, cushion cases or clothing.

Bonusprint, www.bonusprint.com, will print your design onto mugs, mouse mats, jigsaw puzzles, and even engraved glass and jewellery. At www.kodakexpresscamden.com you can print your photos and designs onto candles, jigsaw puzzles, mouse mats, mugs, coasters, bibs, aprons, key rings, pillow cases, fridge magnets, t-shirted teddies, clocks and even underwear.

To buy transfer paper for a temporary inkjet tattoo, go to http://craftycomputerpaper.co.uk. Instead of ironing the design on, the process involves an adhesive layer applied to the printed sheet, which is then applied to the skin. The sheet is dampened then peeled off, leaving your tatoo design in place.

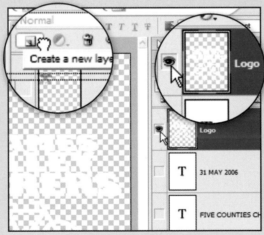

Advertise the event

11 Click the **Set foreground color** swatch in the toolbox and pick a contrasting colour to the background – red on yellow stands out well. From the toolbox, select the **Horizontal type** tool (or press **T**), and add additional text to the top and bottom. To be legible on a t-shirt the type needs to be big, here **72pt**, **Gill Sans**, **Centred**, and the message short, here name of event and a date.

Create a smaller stand-alone logo

12 In the **Layers** palette, **Shift**+click the bicycle and logo type layers, and drag them onto the **Create a new Layer** button to duplicate them. Right-click on one of the new layers' thumbnail and choose **Merge Layers**. Double-click the new layer name and rename it Logo, and press **Return**. Drag the 'logo' layer to the top of the stack, and **Alt**+click its eye icon to turn it on and all the other layers off.

Colour and resize the logo

13 Click on the **Lock** button at the top of the **Layers** palette – a padlock indicates that the transparent pixels in the logo layer are locked and can't be edited. Press **Alt+Delete** to fill all the white pixels in the logo layer with the red foreground colour. From the toolbox select the **Move** tool (or press **V**), then **Shift**+click the bottom right corner handle, and drag to resize the logo smaller.

Transfer paper for lasers

The process for laser printers is almost the same as with inkjet printers, but the transfer paper is more expensive and less readily available. Crafty Computer Paper, www.craftycomputerpaper.co.uk, sells transfer paper suitable for laser printers. You'll need to change the printer settings to 'coated paper' mode and feed the sheets in manually to avoid paper jams. Print your design, then peel off the backing paper and iron the image onto the fabric. The results are washable just like any shop-bought t-shirt.

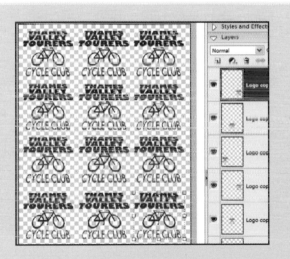

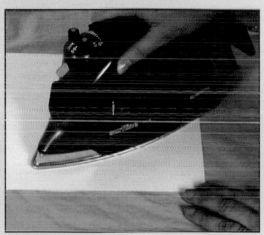

Duplicate the logos

14 Select the **Move** tool (or press **V**) while holding down the **Alt** key and click on and drag the logo to duplicate it. Arrange the copies in a grid on the page. To print a page of logos, turn on those layers using the layer visibility toggle (the eye icon). Use these logos to print on club caps, shirt pockets, and wherever a smaller or more subtle version of your design is called for.

Choose settings for reverse printing

15 Read the instructions that came with your transfer paper and load a sheet into your printer. In Elements, choose **Print** from the **File** menu. Tick **Invert Image** in the **Print Preview** dialogue box so the transfer doesn't come out back to front when ironed on. If it's greyed out, click **Print**, then click the **Properties** button in the **Print** dialogue box to see if your printer provides a 'reverse' or 'mirror' option.

Iron on the transfer

16 Print your images, then allow time for the transfers to dry before ironing them on (follow the instructions supplied with the transfer paper). It's important to have no creases in the t-shirt, so get it as flat as you can on the ironing board and apply the iron, at the temperature specified in the transfer instructions, at equal pressure and for an equal length of time to the whole transfer area.

Sound and vision

Bring out the performer in your PC, make movies and slideshows, digitise your music collection, compose a masterpiece and compile a celebration CD

Home cinema studio
Turn your family video memories into a polished movie

If you own a camcorder it's likely that you have hours of family memories stored away on numerous tapes. The chances are that some bits are less interesting than others, making unedited footage a mixed viewing experience.

But by following this project you can make a movie of edited highlights, complete with titles, clever effects and a music backing track. It can be great fun to do, and everyone who watches will benefit from your efforts. Windows XP includes software called Movie Maker 2 that allows you to edit footage with professional-looking results.

You'll also need a digital camcorder and a cable to connect it to the PC's 'FireWire' socket (sometimes called an 'IEEE 1394 port'). If you have an older camcorder or want to transfer VHS footage, see the 'Digitising old film and video footage' box on page 215.

PROJECT TOOLS: PC with a FireWire port ● Movie Maker 2 ● Digital camcorder and FireWire cable
SEE ALSO: Interactive DVD menu, page 248 ● Sound and vision with Media Player, page 330

Other software

Budget-priced video-editing software provides similar editing tools to Windows Movie Maker, and more. As well as movie editing, programs such as Ulead VideoStudio, www.ulead.com/vs, Pinnacle Studio, www.pinnaclesys.com, and Roxio VideoWave, www.roxio.com/en/products/videowave, allow you to create DVD videos, though you'll need a DVD writer to take advantage of this. Professional packages such as Adobe Premiere Pro and Sony Vegas offer more advanced editing and production tools at a price.

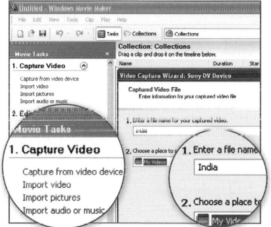

Connect your camcorder to your PC

1 Plug one end of the FireWire cable into the DV socket on your camcorder and the other into the FireWire port on your PC. Power the camcorder using the mains adaptor and not the battery, turn it on and select **Playback**, or **VCR** mode. Using the **Playback** buttons, cue the tape at the beginning of the first scene you wish to capture. Rewind it to the beginning if you want to capture a whole tape.

Start Movie Maker

2 Launch Movie Maker and in the **Movie Tasks** pane on the left of the screen select **Capture from video device**. You'll see the **Video Capture Wizard**, which displays a list of available video devices. Select your camcorder and click the **Next** button. Type in a file name for your captured video clips and choose a destination folder if you want to save them somewhere other than the **My Videos** folder.

Set the video quality

3 Select a video quality setting for your final movie. If you plan to record the finished project back to your camcorder, which you can then connect to your TV for viewing, or if you are going to make a DVD video, select **Digital device format (DV-AVI)**. To produce a lower-quality video, say for emailing or uploading to a website, you should choose the **Other settings** option.

● The timeline and the storyboard

Windows Movie Maker offers two ways of working: the **Storyboard** and **Timeline**. The Storyboard (below right) is the simplest. It provides a thumbnail image for each clip in your project and a transition cell (see step 9) in between. The Timeline (below left) is more complex but gives greater control, with three separate tracks: one for video that can be expanded to show the track's audio and transitions, one for backing music and another for title overlays.

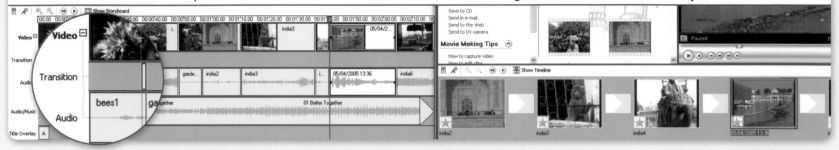

Transfer footage from the camcorder

4 Choose whether you want to capture all of the tape automatically or only parts of it. If your PC is generally quite slow, turn off **Show preview during capture** to improve performance; you can still monitor video capture using the camcorder's LCD panel. Click **Next** to display the capture screen and use Movie Maker's VCR-style buttons, **Start Capture** and **Stop Capture**, to capture clips from the camcorder.

Organise your video clips

5 To stop capturing, click the **Finish** button. Movie Maker then analyses the footage and splits it into a collection of clips, each given a date stamp. Right-click on the clips, select **Rename** and overwrite them with more meaningful names. Choose **Select All** from the **Edit** menu, drag the clips from the **Collection** pane and drop them onto the **Storyboard** area beneath.

Play the Storyboard

6 Each of the clips now occupies its own 'cell' in the **Storyboard**. The thumbnail images show each clip's first frame. To play the entire movie, press the **Play** button underneath the main video **Monitor** panel. To play a particular clip in the **Storyboard**, either click on it or drag the 'seek' bar above the **Monitor** panel's VCR controls until the clip comes into view. Save the project if you haven't done so already.

Marking time

Your digital camcorder automatically writes a time code stamp to the tape as you shoot, showing the elapsed time in hours, minutes, seconds and frames (there are 25 frames per second) in the format hh:mm:ss:ff. Capture and editing software uses the time code to keep track of where everything is. Windows Movie Maker uses its own time code with hundredths of seconds replacing frames. When filming, be careful to shoot each new clip on the tape where the previous clip ended. Leaving gaps (blank tape) breaks the sequence and the time code then resets.

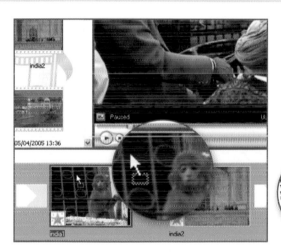

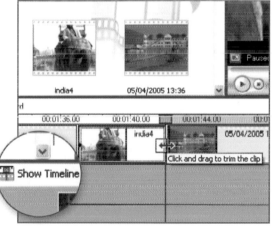

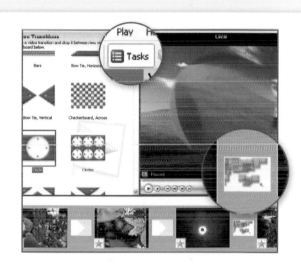

Rearrange the order

7 Drag and drop clips in the **Storyboard** to rearrange their order. When you drag a clip, the cursor changes to a pointer with a rectangle below it, and a vertical blue bar appears in front of clips showing where you can place them. Dragging to the edge of the **Storyboard** causes it to scroll automatically to the left or right if the place you want to drop your clip isn't currently visible.

Trimming your clips

8 To trim clips, switch to the **Timeline** (see box opposite) by clicking the **Show Timeline** button on the button bar above the **Storyboard**. Zoom in using the **Zoom** button or the **Page Down** key, and select the clip to be trimmed. Hover the cursor over the beginning or end of the clip and when the red double-headed arrow cursor appears, drag to shorten the clip. The trim point is shown in the **Monitor** panel.

Add transition effects between clips

9 Click the **Show Storyboard** button to switch back to the **Storyboard**. The small boxes, or cells, between the clips are where you place transitions. If a transition cell is empty you get a straight cut, and one clip cuts directly to the next. Click the **Tasks** button on the toolbar above and select **View Video Transitions** in the **Tasks** pane. Double-click on any of the transitions in the **Content** pane to see a preview.

● Keep your titles simple and clear

A Passage to India

Adding titles to your video makes your film more interesting and gives it a professional feel. Keep things simple. Plain white text on a black background for a few seconds at the beginning of your movie is stylish, easy to produce and tells your audience clearly what they are about to see.

If you overlay titles on the first few seconds of your movie a lot of detail or movement in the scene will make the words difficult to read, so choose your opening footage with this in mind. Don't restrict titles to the beginning of your movie; you can use them for captions and subtitles, too.

back on the streets

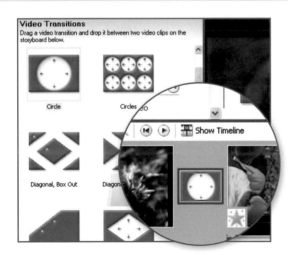

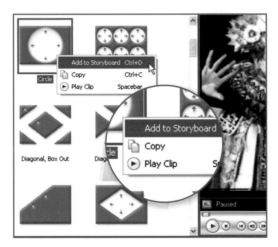

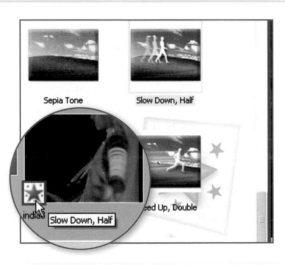

Watch a preview

10 Drag the **Circle** transition from the **Content** pane and drop it onto the empty transition cell displayed between the first two clips in the **Storyboard**. Movie Maker automatically cues the movie 'play head' to the position just before the transition starts, so that you can preview it in the **Monitor** panel by pressing the **Play** button or the **Space Bar**.

Choose transitions

11 You can use a different transition for each clip, but it's best to stick to one or two. Adding transitions individually is laborious if you have a lot of clips. To add the same transition between every clip in the movie, select any clip in the **Storyboard** then choose **Select All** from the **Edit** menu. Right-click the transition in the **Content** pane and choose **Add to Storyboard** or press **Ctrl+D**.

Add a video effect

12 To add a video effect to a clip, select **View Video Effects** from the **Movie Tasks** pane. Scroll down until you see the **Slow Down, Half** thumbnail. Drag this and drop it onto one of the clips in the **Storyboard**; the star icon changes colour from grey to blue to show that an effect has been applied. As the name suggests, **Slow Down, Half** reduces the speed of the clip and doubles its length.

Say it large

Keep titles big and use plain, preferably sans-serif fonts (see page 326) such as Arial. Small type and fonts with narrow strokes are difficult to read on a TV screen. If you're overlaying your title on video footage, choose an animation style (see step 17) that features a drop shadow or places the text in a coloured panel. Keep titles away from the screen edges or you may find them cropped when your movie is viewed on TV.

Mobile phone shots

You can add to your video projects still photos and movie clips shot with most recent models of mobile phone. (Movie clips must be in AVI, ASF, MPEG-1, MPEG-2 or WMV format, so check the phone's user manual.) Plug in the PC-connection lead that came with your phone and start the phone's PC-synchronisation program. Copy the images or clips to your hard disk. Then, in Movie Maker's **Movie Tasks** pane, click **Import Pictures** or **Import Video**. Drag the clips into the storyboard as described in step 5.

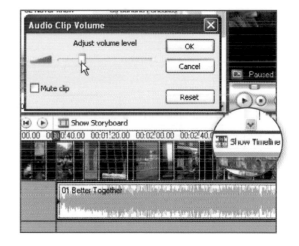

Multiple effects

13 You can add up to six video effects to a clip. Drag the **Brightness, Increase** and **Watercolor** effects from the **Content** pane and drop them on the same clip to which you applied the slow-motion effect. A drop shadow appears behind the star icon to show that the clip has multiple effects applied to it. Hover over the star with your cursor to see what effects have been applied.

Cue the music

14 To add a music backing track, select **Import audio or music** in the **Movie Tasks** pane. You can add audio files in MP3, WAV and many other audio formats (see page 332) from your hard drive. A good place to look for audio files is the **My Music** folder or, if you use Windows Media Player, the location you specified for copied music. Click **Import** to add the audio files to your collection.

Adjust the volume

15 Click the **Show Timeline** button to switch to **Timeline** view, then drag the audio clip from the **Content** pane to the **Audio/Music** track that runs horizontally just below the **Video** track. To fade the audio clip in and out, right-click it and choose **Fade in** or **Fade out** from the pop-up menu. To adjust the volume of the whole audio clip, choose **Volume** and drag the volume slider, then click **OK**.

Adding music and narration

You can add most kinds of audio file as a backing track, but if you want to add music from an audio CD you'll first need to copy and convert it using Windows Media Player (see page 330). Adding voiceover narration in Movie Maker is simple: connect a microphone to your PC and click the **Narrate Timeline** button.

Adjust the balance between the audio from your video clips and any backing track by clicking the **Set Audio Levels** button at the top left of the **Timeline** or **Storyboard**.

Email your movies

To email a video you need to reduce the file size as much as possible without losing too much quality. To save a movie for email in Movie Maker, choose **Send in email** from the **Movie Tasks** pane and the program then does everything for you.

If the resulting video quality is too poor or the file is too big, try choosing **Save to my computer** and experimenting with the **Other settings** in the **Save Movie Wizard**. They offer a variety of size and compression options for different devices and internet connections. Among others, **Video for dial-up access (38kbps)** and **Video for ISDN (48kbps)** will both create files suitable for emailing.

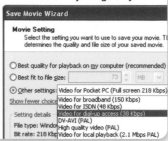

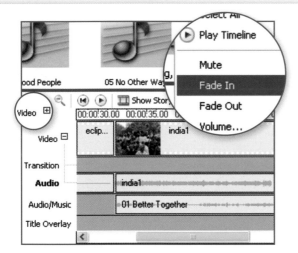

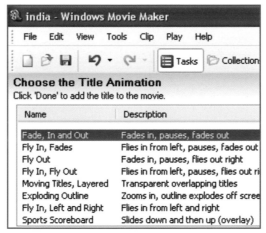

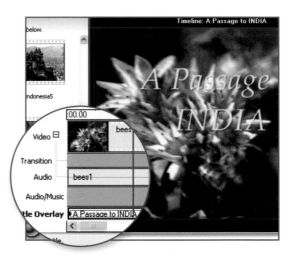

Strike a balance

16 You may want to adjust the volume of the video's sound so that it balances with the backing music; this is called 'mixing'. Click the small plus symbol next to the video track to display the audio track for the video. Each video clip has an accompanying audio clip that appears underneath it. Right-click the audio to access the same fade and volume controls you just used for the backing music.

Write an opening title

17 Click the **Tasks** button and select **Make titles or credits** from the **Movie Tasks** pane. Choose **Add title at the beginning of the movie** and, on the next screen, enter your title text. Use the options at the bottom of the **Title** pane to set the text font and colour and to choose the animation style. There are many animation options, but **Fade, In and Out** is simple and elegant. Click to select it.

Superimpose the title

18 Click **Done, add title to movie**. At this stage the title is on a plain background, and Movie Maker places it at the start of the video track in the timeline. For a more professional look you can superimpose the title text over a video clip. Drag the title from the video track and drop it at the start of the **Title Overlay** track below. You can edit the title at any time by right-clicking it and choosing **Edit title**.

● Digitising old film and video footage

Your old movies needn't gather dust. There are companies that will convert your 8mm film into digital footage; try typing 8mm film transfer into Google, www.google.com, to find one. If you have an 8mm analogue (non-digital) video camcorder you can capture footage from it provided your PC's graphics card has composite video-in or S-Video-in sockets (check your PC's manual). If your PC doesn't have these, you can buy an inexpensive video digitising card, such as Pinnacle's Dazzle DVC 90, www.pinnaclesys.com. Once the video is digitised and on your hard drive, you can edit it in the same way as footage from a digital camcorder.

● Burning questions

Movie Maker allows you to create video CDs using Microsoft's HighMAT format, which is supported by many DVD players. But if you have a DVD burner, a better option is to produce a DVD video. Windows Movie Maker doesn't include tools to produce DVD video, but such software is inexpensive and often included in other budget video-editing applications. DVD video offers the best quality and most reliable way to share your movies with others (see pages 248 to 253).

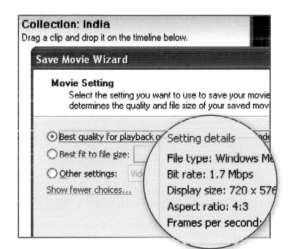

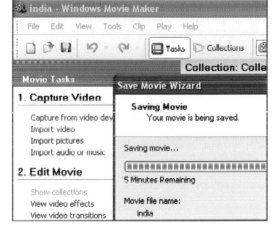

Save your movie

19 You're now ready to export your movie. Movie Maker offers different output options based on how you intend to show the finished movie. In the **Movie Tasks** pane, under the **Finish Movie** section, select **Save to my computer**. This option will create a movie file that you or anyone you give a copy to can play back using Windows Media Player. The **Save Movie Wizard** appears.

Choose a quality setting

20 Type in a name for the movie, choose a location to save it to, then click **Next**. Tick the **Best quality for playback on my computer** option. Movie Maker chooses quality settings best suited to your PC's capabilities. **Setting details** and **Movie File Size**, shown at the bottom of the box, provide information about the movie file, including how much space it will take up on your hard drive.

Create the final file

21 Click **Next** to start producing the file. The time this takes depends on the length of your movie, the number of effects and transitions you've used, and the speed of your PC. The progress bar lets you know approximately how long you'll have to wait. If your movie is more than a few minutes long, you may want to go away and do something else while you wait.

Scratch free

Learn how you can digitise and clean up your old music collection

While they may hold some of your most treasured musical memories, cassette and vinyl recordings are delicate and don't last long. Unless you take great care, records get scratched, tapes stretch or get chewed. Yet by recording them onto your PC, you can enjoy them for longer and also improve their sound quality by removing any annoying hisses, pops and crackles. With the help of your PC, preserve your tapes and LPs and breathe life back into your old music collection.

PROJECT TOOLS: PC with recordable CD drive ● Blank CDs ● Home stereo with either a record deck or cassette player ● Microsoft Analog Recorder

● All about Analog Recorder

Microsoft Analog Recorder is part of the Plus! Digital Media Edition. This is a collection of Microsoft add-ins for Windows XP that includes photo-sharing programs, skins for Windows Media Player, CD Label Maker, alarms, juke-box programs and more. For a nominal fee you can download Plus! Digital Media Edition from Microsoft's website at www.microsoft.com/windows/plus/dme.

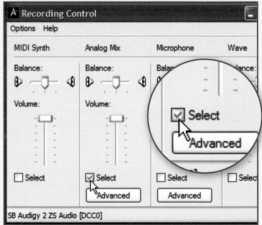

Prepare your PC for recording

1 Having connected your audio equipment (see box, page 217), click the Windows **Start** button, choose **All Programs**, **Accessories**, **Entertainment** then **Volume Control**. When the program loads, click **Options** then **Properties**. Click **Recording**, then **OK**. Make sure the correct recording source is selected (marked **Line in** or **Analog Mix**) with a tick. Click the **X** to close the **Recording Control** program.

Connecting your audio equipment

Your record deck or cassette recorder may have 'Line-level' outputs (**1**), which carry a signal of sufficient strength to be recorded properly. If so, you can connect a cable directly to your PC's soundcard – look for the 'Line-in' socket (**4**) on the back of your PC. If not, you'll need to connect first to an amplifier or preamp (**2**) using standard phono connectors, then connect a cable from your amplifier (**3**) to your PC (**4**). You'll need a cable with two phono plugs at one end (for the Audio Out connectors on the amp) and a single stereo mini-jack (for the soundcard's Line-in socket) at the other.

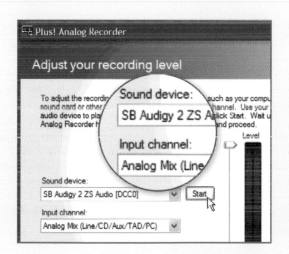

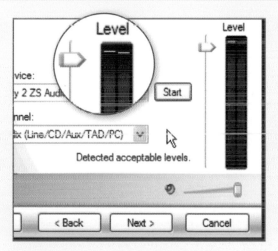

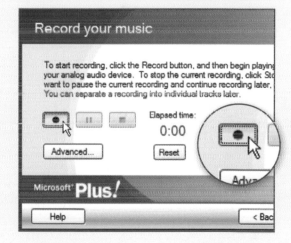

Start the Analog Recorder program

2 Once you've installed Analog Recorder, click on the Windows **Start** button and choose **All Programs**, followed by **Plus!** and then **Plus! Analog Recorder**. After a moment the program appears and displays the welcome screen. Click the **Next** button. Analog Recorder selects the appropriate sound device and input channel. Start playing your cassette or LP and click the **Start** button.

Check your recording levels

3 Leave the sound source playing for now and watch what happens. Analog Recorder listens to what's being played in order to work out the optimum volume level at which to record, so that you get a good, loud result, with little interference. When Analog Recorder is satisfied with the signal, it will stop the test and display a message saying 'Detected acceptable levels'. Click **Next** to continue.

Record side 1...

4 Rewind your cassette to the beginning (or lift the needle up and pop it back onto the beginning of track 1) and then press the play button or lower the needle. Click the red record button in the Analog Recorder program window just before the sound starts playing again. Whatever now plays on your turntable or cassette deck will be recorded onto your home PC by Analog Recorder.

Clean up first

Before you start an electronic clean-up, remove any physical dirt you can see on the record or cassette tape, as well as the player. Cassette player head cleaners are simple to use and effective. Consider replacing the stylus on your record deck. If you're still unhappy, a better-quality connecting cable makes a big difference.

Vinyl records can be washed in warm water with a mild detergent to remove dust and grit from within the grooves. Try to avoid wetting the label too much. After washing the record, rinse it in warm running water then dry thoroughly using a soft lint-free cloth.

Make a test recording

Although Analog Recorder does a good job of looking after all the settings for you, it pays to make a few trial recordings first. After a preliminary listen, you may find that you need to adjust the level of the source recording for some tracks to compensate for varying volume levels. You may also get better results by tweaking the treble and bass controls on your amplifier.

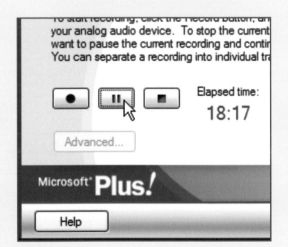

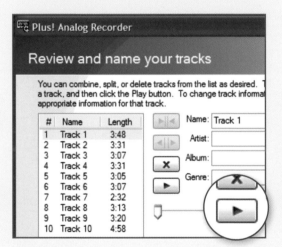

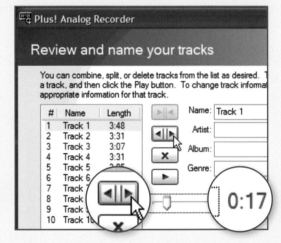

And record side 2…

5 Listen for when side 1 is about to end and then click the **Pause** button in the Analog Recorder program window. Turn the tape or LP over then click the red **Record** button to continue. When the source has finished playing, click the **Stop** button. Don't worry about any gaps between tracks or sections at the beginning or the end where there's no sound; you can sort that out in a minute.

Complete your recording

6 Click the **Next** button. Analog Recorder has not only recorded everything on this particular cassette, but also divided it up into 10 tracks, noted the length of each one and put them in the correct order. To see how any of the tracks turned out, click on them once and then click the **Play** button. To rewind a track to the beginning, click and drag the slider back to the left.

Silence isn't golden

7 Listening back, it's obvious there's a gap at the start of the recording before the music starts. To remove this, select **Track 1** then click **Play**. When you reach the point where the music begins, note the number of seconds; in this example it's 17. Next, drag the slider back to that point and click the button with the two arrows pointing away from each other; this splits track 1 at that precise point.

SOUND AND VISION

Don't break the law

Always stay on the right side of the law by respecting the copyright of others. Making a single copy of a recording that you have paid for, for personal use only, is generally tolerated by record companies, although it's a bit of a grey area. Making any copy for any purpose is, strictly speaking, an offence under UK law. Use Analog Recorder's copy protection feature (see step 12) to ensure that the resulting copy only plays back on your own PC or digital music player and can't be distributed to other people.

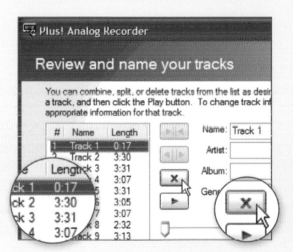

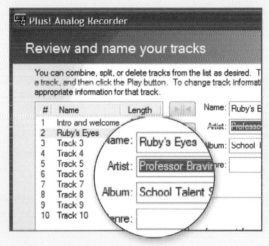

Remove long silences

8 Click the **Next** button and you'll see that Analog Recorder has split the first track into two at exactly the point you specified in the previous step. You now have 11 tracks instead of 10, but the first track is 17 seconds of silence, so it's best to remove it. Click on it once to select it and then click the **X** button to remove it. A small box pops up asking you if you're sure. Click **Yes**.

Name track 1

9 Click on the first track and, in the box to the right, type in a name for it. In the box below, type the artist's name and, below that, a name for the album. You can add a genre of music if you wish. Click on **Track 2** and repeat the process. Unless the artist, album and genre are different from those on track 1, you need only type in a new name for each track.

Finish adding names to every track

10 Carry on adding track and artist names until the list on the left is complete. You could skip this stage, but it's important if you're creating a library of recordings as it allows you to tell one song from another more easily. Every song from the original recording now has a proper name and track length, and you're now ready to check the recording quality. Click the **Next** button to move on.

Alternative cleaners

Magix Audio Cleaning Lab 10 Deluxe, www.magix.net, includes many extra features for making great recordings, including an analogue sound simulator that adds warmth to digital recordings. LP Recorder, www.cfbsoftware.com, also does the job and is available as a free trial. Audacity, http://audacity.sourceforge.net, is free and an excellent general purpose audio-recording program that includes a range of noise removal features (right).

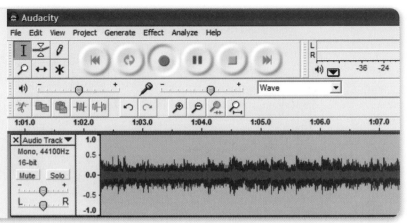

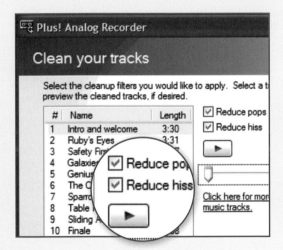

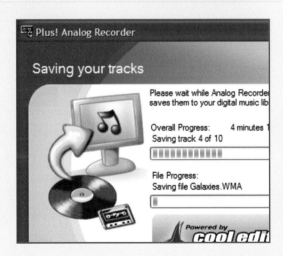

Reduce noise on your tracks

11 Here you can apply Analog Recorder's noise reduction to any of your tracks. Click on the track name and then tick either or both of the empty tick boxes next to **Reduce pops** and **Reduce hiss**. Click the **Play** button to listen to the track. Note that whichever noise reduction options you choose at this stage will be applied to all of the tracks in the list. Click **Next** to continue.

Protect your music

12 The **Content Protection Options** dialogue box appears. If you select the first option, Analog Recorder will protect the music that you've recorded, making it difficult for others to create and distribute copies. You can still play tracks on your PC or portable player. Tick the box below to confirm that you understand your responsibilities regarding copyrighted music. Click **OK** to continue.

Save your finished tracks

13 Leave all the settings in the next dialogue box as they are and click the **Next** button. Now sit back and wait while Analog Recorder converts all the tracks that you've recorded into the WMA format used by Windows to play music on your PC (see page 332). The tracks, together with the information that you typed in, will be saved automatically to your music library.

A finishing touch

To give your CD a professional look, create a great-looking cover for it. The Plus! Digital Media Edition includes the CD Label Maker program, which is the quickest way to make and print out a cover. Click on the **Start** button, choose **All Programs**, then **Plus!** and then choose **CD Label Maker**. Follow the prompts to select the album you created and Label Maker will do the rest.

Alternatively, if you have Microsoft Word and access to the internet, there are some great free CD cover templates provided by Microsoft that you can download. Connect to the internet and start Word. Choose **New** from the **File** menu and when the task pane on the right opens, click **Templates from Office Online**. This will load Microsoft's website, where you'll find the CD cover templates.

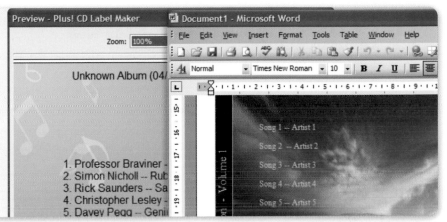

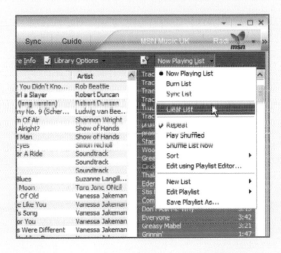

Locate the tracks with Media Player

14 Analog Recorder displays a box telling you that the tracks have been recorded. Click the **Finish** button to close the program. Click the **Start** button, choose **All Programs** then **Windows Media Player**. When the program loads, click the **Library** button. If any tracks are listed in the right-hand window, click the down arrow by the **Now Playing List** heading to open the menu and choose **Clear List**.

Assemble your album in Media Player

15 Double-click on the **Album** heading in Media Player's left-hand column to open the list of albums. Scroll down the list until you find the one that you've created – here it's called 'School Talent Show'. Click on the name once. Find the button along the top marked with a green plus sign and click on it. This moves all the tracks on your selected album into the **Now Playing** list.

Burn a CD

16 Put a blank CD in your drive and click the **Start Burn** button. The screen above shows the CD being 'burned' or created. The amount of time it takes varies, depending on the speed of your recordable CD drive and the number of tracks that you're trying to burn. When it's done, you'll have an audio CD that you can play without the hisses and pops of the ancient original.

Storytelling in pictures

Create slideshows that bring your digital photos to life

Digital photos look great on your PC screen. But how do you share your digital photos of holiday snaps and happy memories with other people? One way is to create a slideshow to give someone on disc or via email. Microsoft's free Photo Story software turns digital still photos into movies, complete with special Hollywood-style effects and music soundtrack. The finished slideshow movie will play back on a PC, a Windows 'smartphone' or DVD player.

PROJECT TOOLS: Microsoft Photo Story
SEE ALSO: Make a movie, page 208 ● How to shoot great photos, page 304

Create your own personal storybook

1 First, install Photo Story. In Internet Explorer, go to www.microsoft.com/windowsxp/using/digitalphotography/photostory and click **Download Photo Story**. When the security warning appears, choose **Save**, and pick somewhere to put a file on your hard disk, such as the **My Documents** folder. Wait for the file to download. It should only take a few minutes, depending on your internet connection.

SOUND AND VISION

Add visual impact between photos

Rather than just switching from one picture to the next as your slideshow progresses, Photo Story and other slideshow programs let you choose from a range of transition effects (see step 15). In most cases, a moving line or shape 'wipes' between one image and the next. Alternatively, the first image may move or distort to reveal the second, as with Photo Plus's **Flip and Page Curl** transitions, shown right. Avoid using too many transitions as they can become distracting.

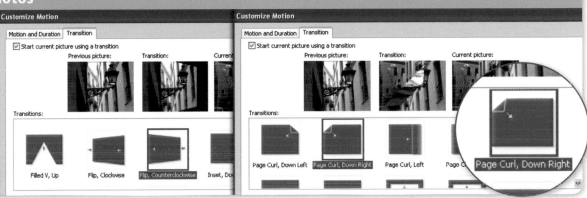

Run Microsoft Photo Story

2 The installer file you've downloaded is called PStory.msi. Double-click this in Windows Explorer, then follow the instructions. You're now ready to run Photo Story. Double-click its icon or, if you don't see it, go to **All Programs** on the **Start** menu and select **Photo Story**. The program opens with a box asking what you want to do. Choose **Begin a new story** and click **Next** at the bottom.

Choose your favourite photos

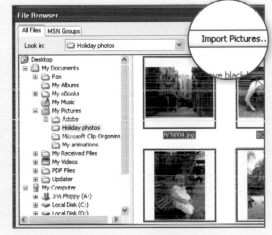

3 Click the **Import Pictures** button and use the **File Browser** dialogue box to navigate to the folder containing the pictures you want. Highlight a folder on the left to see the pictures in it displayed on the right. Then click individual pictures to highlight them, holding **Shift** or **Ctrl** to select several at the same time. Press **Ctrl+A** if you wish to select them all. Click **OK** to import the highlighted pictures.

Organise your pictures

4 Pictures appear as a strip of small 'thumbnail' images. To remove an image from your project, click on its thumbnail then click the button marked with a cross. Don't worry; your original picture file isn't deleted. To add more pictures, click **Import Pictures** again. Arrange your pictures into the order you want. Click a thumbnail, holding down the mouse button, and drag it left or right.

● Make a slideshow from just one photo

A slideshow usually displays a collection of pictures, but you get great results using just one. The trick works best with a detailed high-resolution picture, perhaps from a digital camera with 5 megapixels or more (see page 311). Cityscapes and crowded places work well.

Start Photo Story as in the project, and at step 3 import your picture. Click **Import Picture** again and choose the same one. Repeat to get, say, half a dozen copies. Press **Next** until you reach **Customize Motion** (see step 12). For the first picture, tick **Specify start and end position** and then make the **Start** box quite small. Make the **End** box the same size by clicking **Set end position to be the same** but drag the box to a different position. This gives a 'pan' effect, like a film camera moving across the picture.

Working through all the picture copies, combine pans with zooms for variety. Untick the box at the top of the **Transition** tab for each picture, so there's no transition effect.

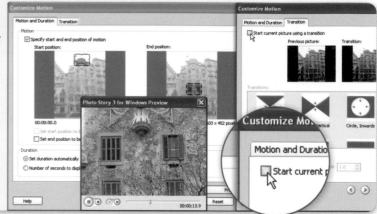

Dealing with red-eye and rotation

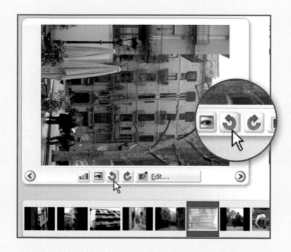

5 Notice that whenever you click a picture it's shown larger at the top left of the screen. The frame around it has buttons to alter the picture. For example, if you turned the camera sideways to take a photo, it may appear the wrong way round. Click one of the green arrow icons to rotate it clockwise or anti-clockwise. If someone in your picture has 'red-eye', click the eye icon to correct it.

Correct and enhance images

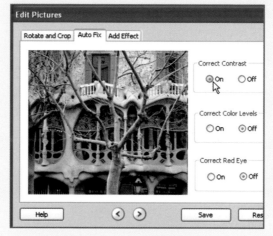

6 Click the **Edit** button for more ways to change a picture. In the **Edit Pictures** box, click one of the three tabs at the top for more options. On the **Auto Fix** tab, you'll find options to correct **Contrast** and **Color Levels**, as well as the same **Red Eye** correction. All of these work automatically with one click. Here, a photo that appears a little dull is improved by clicking **Correct Contrast**.

Add special effects to your images

7 Try the **Add Effect** tab if you want to get more creative. You can turn your photo into a watercolour or pencil sketch, tint it to appear like an old sepia print and so on by choosing different effects from the **Effect** menu. Only one effect can be applied to each picture. If you want a special effect for your whole slideshow, tick the option **Apply the selected effect to all of the pictures in your story**.

Titles and captions

To add personality to your stories, Photo Story lets you give a title or caption to any of your pictures (see step 12). Click and type over the default text in the box on the right and then use the buttons above to choose whether it's aligned to the left, centre or right of the picture, at the top, middle or bottom. Click the button showing two letter 'A's to choose the font, size and colour. Keep titles short and simple; also make sure the text is big and clear enough to read. Choose the colour to contrast with the photo. For creative titles, perhaps to introduce a section of your show, add an effect to the picture (see step 7), such as **Washout**, to let the text stand out.

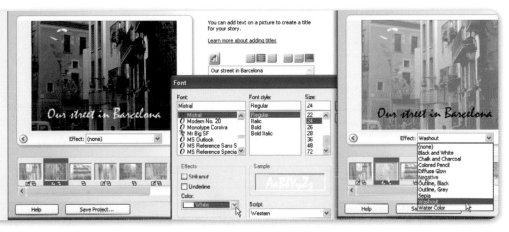

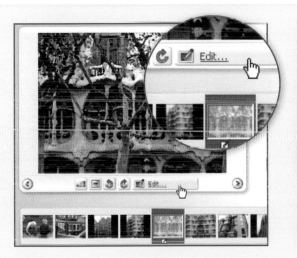

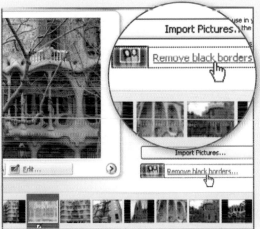

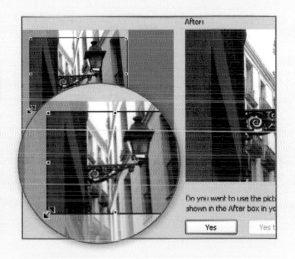

Save or reset your changes

8 Before clicking **Close** to finish editing, click on either **Save** to save or **Reset** to keep the picture the way it looked originally. If you save changes, the picture's thumbnail includes a pencil symbol to show it's been changed. You can undo or alter your changes later by selecting the picture and clicking **Edit** again. The changes apply only within Photo Story; your original photo files aren't affected.

Avoid black borders

9 Any pictures that aren't the same shape, or 'aspect ratio', as a standard (non-widescreen) PC monitor are given black borders to make them fit. This includes portrait photos taken with the camera held sideways. If you prefer, you can cut out or 'crop' part of a picture to the right shape; it's then enlarged to fit without borders. Click the button labelled **Remove black borders** to do so.

Crop your non-standard images

10 Photo Story automatically draws a box of the correct shape somewhere in the middle of the photo. In the right-hand pane you'll see how it will appear when cropped to this box. Sometimes Photo Story doesn't choose the most important part of a picture. Click and drag to move the box around, or change its size by dragging the 'handles' on its corners, to crop to the best part.

Ways to share stories

If you want to share your slideshow with friends and family then saving it in the standard WMV (Windows Media Video) format means anyone with Windows XP can play it back. Email the file to them or give them a recordable CD or DVD that you've copied the file onto (see step 16).

You're not just limited to sharing via a PC. You can save in formats compatible with Pocket PC handheld computers and 'smartphones'. These reduce your pictures to a size suitable for smaller screens, which in turn makes smaller files.

Presenting on DVD or CD

To see your slideshows on a DVD player you need a PC that records CD or DVD discs. Both CDs and DVDs work in the DVD player – you can store moving pictures on CD using the Video CD (VCD) format, although the quality is poor compared to DVDs. Photo Story doesn't have this facility built in but it's included with Plus! Photo Story and in some other slideshow programs (see 'Slideshow software', page 222).

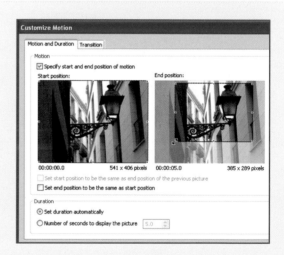

Crop any remaining borders

11 Click **Yes** to set the crop and move on to the next picture. Another box appears, telling you when they're all done. Click **OK**. You may see that some pictures still have borders, where Photo Story couldn't work out how to crop them. To crop a picture, select its thumbnail and click **Edit**. On the **Rotate and Crop** tab, tick **Crop** to show a crop box that you can adjust as in step 10.

Add captions and narration

12 Having arranged and edited your pictures, click **Next**. You're given the chance to add titles to some or all of the images (see 'Titles and captions', page 225). Then press **Next** again. If you want to add narration to your slideshow using a microphone, see 'Once upon a time...', page 227. Now, click on the **Customize Motion** button below the slide preview at the top left.

Make your photos move

13 The **Customize Motion** box has two tabs. **Motion and Duration**, the first, controls an effect that zooms slowly towards or away from a smaller area of each picture – known as a 'Ken Burns' effect, after the US documentary filmmaker. Photo Story sets it up automatically but you can alter it. Tick the box labelled **Specify start and end position of motion**, then click and drag the handles of the two boxes.

Once upon a time...

Telling a photo story in your own words can bring it to life. Photo Story lets you record a voice commentary to describe favorite photos. Make a recording for each picture and the slideshow will play back your voice while it displays the image. You'll need a microphone plugged into your PC. Click the microphone icon in Photo Story (at step 12) to set up and test your microphone. Click the red dot icon to record your message and then click the square icon to stop.

Create an original soundtrack

Generate a mood in your Photo Story slideshows by adding music. When you get to the **Add background music** screen (at step 16), click on the picture where you want a piece of music to start, then click **Select Music** to choose an audio file that's stored on your PC, or **Create Music** to choose from various music styles that are built into Photo Story. You can add any number of songs or music clips, each one starting when a particular image appears in your slideshow.

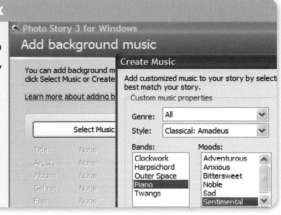

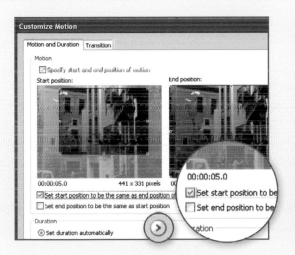

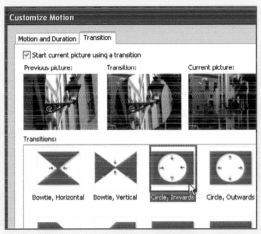

Decide where to start and finish

14 Leave the **Duration** setting on automatic for best results. Click the arrow in the circle below to set up the next picture. It's a good idea to alternate zooming in and out; tick **Set start position to be the same as end position of previous picture** to give you a head start with this. Tick **Set end position to be the same as start position** if you don't want a Ken Burns effect picture.

Choose fades between slides

15 When changing from one photo to the next, Photo Story applies a 'transition' effect, similar to that used in movie editing (see page 211). The transition type is set in the **Transition** tab for each picture in turn. It's preset to **Cross Fade**, so one picture fades out as the other fades in. Set a new transition by clicking on one of the thumbnails; you'll see a preview above. Leave duration on automatic.

Finish and save your slideshow

16 Click **Preview** to check your slideshow and then click **Next**. To add music, see 'Create an original soundtrack', above. Click **Next** again to save your work. First, click **Save Project** to store a Photo Story file that you can edit again later. At the top of the screen, choose how you plan to use your story (see 'Ways to share stories', page 226). Press **Next** to save it in the appropriate format.

Singalong a PC
Turn your PC into a karaoke party machine

Whether you're a good singer or not, karaoke is fun. With the help of Windows Media Player, your PC can be transformed into a karaoke machine – you don't even have to use a microphone. Just add lyrics to any music track, either by typing them or grabbing them from the internet, and change a few settings in Media Player to get song lyrics that appear on the screen, synchronised to the music, so you can sing along. Then add a 'visualisation' light show and the party's ready to begin.

PROJECT TOOLS: Windows Media Player ● PC speakers ● Microphone, if you want to amplify your voice
SEE ALSO: Sound and vision with Media Player, page 330 ● Recording and making music, page 332

SEE ALSO: Sound and vision with Media Player, page 330 ● Recording and making music, page 332

◉ Lyrics the fast way

Save time by getting lyrics from the internet rather than typing them in. Go to www.google.com and type in a phrase from the song – make sure you enclose it in double quotation marks – and click **Search**. When you find the lyric, highlight it with the mouse, right-click on it and choose **Copy**. Return to Media Player and, rather than typing the lyrics (see step 3), click with the right mouse button and choose **Paste**. Remember that lyrics, like the music, are protected by copyright, so only download from websites that respect the law.

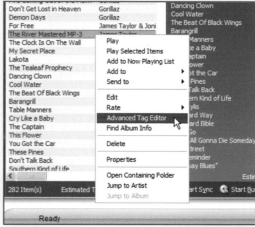

Choose a track for karaoke

1 Load Windows Media Player by clicking the **Start** button, choosing **All Programs** and then selecting **Windows Media Player** from the list. When the player opens, click the **Library** button at the top. Use the mouse to scroll through your library until you find a song you'd like to add karaoke lyrics to, right-click on it with the mouse and choose **Advanced Tag Editor**.

SOUND AND VISION

⬤ Watch the music dancing

To add some visual excitement to your party, Windows Media Player comes with a selection of 'visualisations' – colourful animated light shows that move in time to whatever music you're playing on your PC. To download new ones for free, click the **Now Playing** tab, then click the **Now Playing Options** button just beneath the tab. Choose **Visualizations** and then **Download Visualizations**. When you've downloaded a new one, double-click on its icon to add it to Media Player's **Visualizations** menu, then follow the instructions to view it.

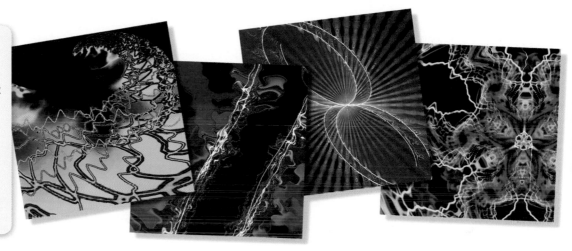

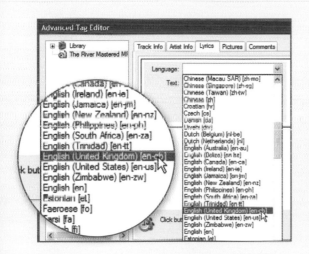

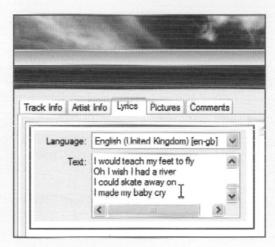

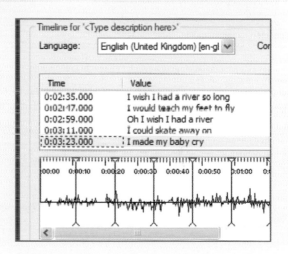

Find your lyrics

2 When the dialogue box appears, find the **Lyrics** tab at the top and click it. This is the screen where you're going to type in the lyrics to the song. Start by clicking the **Add** button. When the empty form appears, click the arrow next to the **Language** box. In the drop-down list of languages, scroll down until you find yours. In this example, it's one of the English variants.

Type in your lyrics

3 Click once in the empty **Text** box and type in the lyrics to the song. As you type, ensure that each line of the song begins on a new line. Otherwise the lyrics won't be displayed properly when the song plays back and you won't get the real karaoke effect. Make sure that you spell everything correctly. If you prefer, you can type the lyrics in your word processor, then copy and paste them onto the screen.

Match the lyrics to the music

4 Click the **Synchronised Lyrics** button in the dialogue box to continue. On this screen you'll see the lyrics you typed in and underneath them a squiggly line that represents the sound of the song. Windows Media Player has guessed where in the song each line appears and these points are represented by vertical lines. It's unlikely that they'll be accurate, so you'll have to change them.

How to make yourself heard

If you have a microphone, plug it into the **Mic In** connector (look for a microphone symbol) at the back of your PC. If you can't hear anything when you speak into the microphone, click the **Start** button and choose **All Programs**, **Accessories**, **Entertainment** and then **Volume Control**. Make sure that the **Microphone input** doesn't have a tick next to the **Mute** setting. Drag the slider up or down to alter the volume at which people sing.

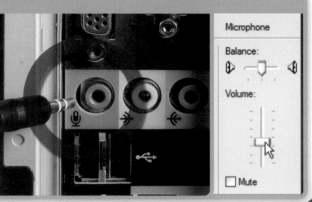

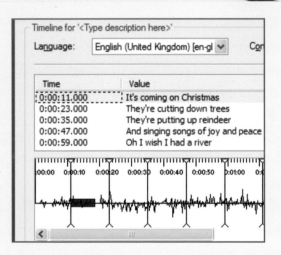

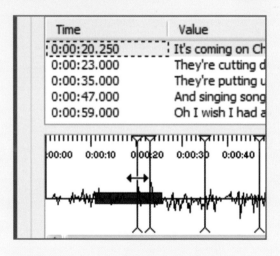

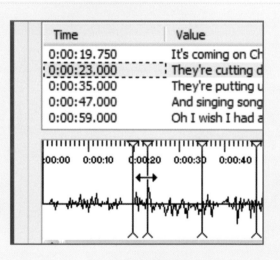

Play back the song

5 Use the mouse to scroll back up the list of lyrics until you reach the first line. Click on it once with the mouse. Click the **Play** button and watch what happens. First, the vertical line in the bottom window that represents the first lyric line starts to blink. Second, as the song plays, the program displays a red progress bar to show you where you are in the song.

Adjust where the singing starts

6 Listen for the first line of the lyric. Move the mouse over the blinking vertical line in the bottom window that represents the first line. The cursor changes from its normal arrow shape to a horizontal line with an arrow at each end. Click on the line and, still holding the mouse button down, drag it left or right, depending on where the line appears in the song.

Synchronise the other lyrics

7 When you've placed the first line where you think it should be, click **Stop**. Click **Play** again and check its position in relation to what you hear playing. If it's not correct, adjust the line by dragging it with the mouse. Now click **Stop**. Click on the second lyric line in the list and repeat the process until it's in the correct position. Repeat for all the lyrics in the song. Click **OK** to close the **Synchronized Lyrics** box.

Real karaoke programs

Media Player is a great introduction to music with singalong lyrics. But, for an even more sophisticated karaoke experience, you need a dedicated program. KaraFun, www.karafun.com, is free and lets you play back lyrics full-screen (see right), displays duet lyrics in different colours and even includes a follow-the-dots melody guide to help you stay in tune. If you want to take it even further, PowerKaraoke, www.powerkaraoke.com, lets you create your own discs that will play back on any PC.

Prepare Media Player for karaoke

8 Back in the **Advanced Tag Editor** box, remove the lyrics you typed in previously. If you don't they will be displayed all at once when the song plays back, instead of one line at a time. So, click the **Delete** button, then click **OK** to return to Media Player. Click the **Access Application menus** button (small triangle at the top-right corner of Media Player), select **Play**, **Captions and Subtitles** then **On if available**.

Set up a visual display

9 For an animated light show to play along with your song and lyrics (see box, page 229), click on the **Now Playing** tab, and then on the **Select now playing options** button to open the **Visualizations** menu. Choose one you think sounds interesting, such as **Smokey Circles** from the **Plenoptic** list. To change it, click the left or right arrows above the main display window to cycle through the available visual effects.

Your PC karaoke machine in action

10 Turn down the lights and turn up the volume. In the bottom-right corner of Media Player, click the **Play** button and your song starts. At the same time, you'll see the visualisation that you chose in the previous step begin to play; the animation pumps and swirls in time to the music. As the first line is sung, the lyric will appear just below the visualisation so you can sing along.

In tempo
Start composing music in minutes with free software

Even if you don't have a musical bone in your body, you can use your home PC and a free program such as ACID XPress to create a song that sounds as good as much of the music you hear on the radio. ACID XPress uses a system of short repeated recordings ('loops') of instruments or vocals. You create an arrangement by positioning loops on a grid that scrolls right to left. After downloading the program be sure to also get the sample projects from the same web page, so you can make music immediately.

PROJECT TOOLS: PC speakers ● ACID XPress ● Microphone, if you want to record your voice
SEE ALSO: Sound and vision with Media Player, page 330 ● Recording and making music, page 332

Loops for free

Collections of loops are available on CD. But there are also hundreds of sites on the internet where you can download them for nothing. Go to www.freeloops.com or www.looperman.com for a good selection of modern dance-related sounds. Elsewhere, www.samplenet.co.uk has interesting orchestral samples, and www.platinumloops.com includes mandolins, sitars and clarinets. Also, ACID's publisher, Sony, makes a new pack of free samples available for download at www.acidplanet.com/tools/8packs **every week.**

Download and install ACID XPress

1 Go to www.sonymediasoftware.com/download/freestuff.asp, register with Sony, and then click **ACID XPress**. In the next window, click **ACID XPress** then click **Save**. In the dialogue box, browse to your desktop, or click the **Desktop** icon on the left of the window. Click **Save** to start the download, go to your desktop, double-click **acidxpress50a.exe**, then follow the instructions.

More instant music software

The eJay family of music programs (see example right) works in a similar way to ACID XPress, with variations available for different types of music. Visit www.ejay.com for free demos and downloads.

If you enjoy unusual instrumental music, try Fruity Loops, www.fruityloops.com, which offers a free demonstration download. Or look at Music Maker music-composition software from Magix, www.magix.net. The results from all these programs are of CD quality.

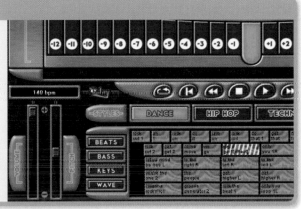

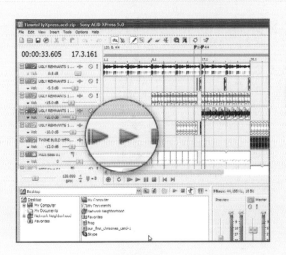

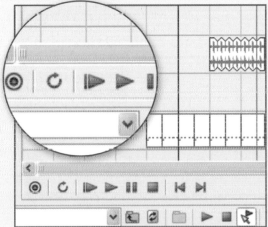

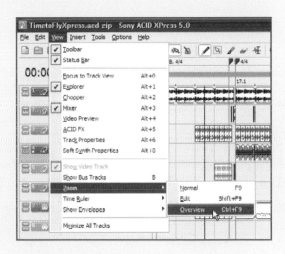

Listen to an ACID XPress song

2 Click the Windows **Start** button and choose **All Programs**, then **Sony** and then **ACID XPress** to start the program. It opens with a song already loaded. Find the CD-style controls in the middle of the screen. Make sure that your speakers are turned on and click the on-screen control that looks like a single arrow pointing to the right. The song will start playing back.

Get to know the play controls

3 Starting from the left, the first button lets you record a live sound – for example, someone singing. The **Loop** button lets you play part of your song over and over again. The third one plays the song from the beginning. The fourth plays from the current position, then come the **Pause** and **Stop** buttons. Finally, the last two move you to the start or finish of your song.

See the whole song

4 Move the cursor to the top of the main window and it turns into a hand. Hold down the left mouse button while you drag the contents of the main window to the left to see the rest of the song. Any composition that is longer than a few bars will need to be scrolled into view in this way. Alternatively, go to the **View** menu, choose **Zoom** and then click on **Overview** to see the whole song.

Other music-making software

For general purpose home use, consider Cubase SE3, www.steinberg.net, or Cakewalk SONAR Home Studio (near right), www.cakewalk.com. Both programs allow you to combine prerecorded samples with original synthesised music and acoustic recordings to produce complete songs. If you're a keyboard player, both Reason (far right), www.propellerheads.se, and Orion, www.synapse-audio.com, let you use thousands of original sounds to create and record original music. Again, expect CD-quality results.

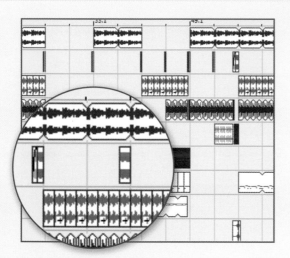

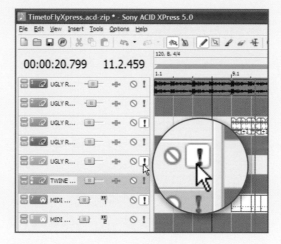

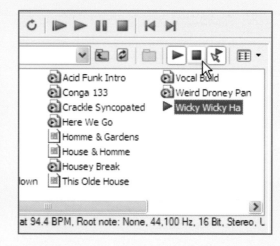

What makes a song?

5 You create songs in ACID XPress by stringing together 'samples' – short clips of music recorded in loops so that each can play in a continuous cycle for short or long notes. These are arranged along tracks that run horizontally across the screen. For example, this song uses nine tracks. The blocks with squiggly lines inside them in the middle of the screen are the actual sampled sounds.

Silencing and soloing tracks

6 Play the song again. Find the nine track headings on the left and notice that each one has a couple of symbols: a circle with a line through it and an exclamation mark. Click the first to 'mute' the track so that you can't hear it. Click the second to 'solo' the track, so that you can't hear anything else. Experiment with these buttons on different tracks as the song plays.

Create a new song

7 Go to the **File** menu and choose **New**. When ACID XPress asks if you want to save changes, click **No**. Give your song a title and click **OK**. Use the **Explorer** window to find the sample projects from the ACID XPress website. Click on any of the sounds there except the ones with the green icons as they don't make any noise. Stop the sound with the **Stop** button at the top of the window.

● Simple guidelines for getting the right results

Start by giving your song a time limit of, say, three minutes. If it's a song with lyrics, stick to the classic format of verse, chorus, verse, chorus, middle eight bars, verse, chorus and chorus end. Modern music tends to be repetitive, so don't use more than ten samples in your first few songs. Instead, concentrate on being creative with what you've got. To add lyrics, burn a copy of the backing music onto a CD to play in the car and try singing over the top of it, so you experiment first. Your lyrics may be wonderfully poignant, but if they're too personal, nobody else will appreciate them, so always try and make what you write accessible to others. If you don't want to write another love song and are stuck for inspiration, look for ideas in a newspaper or magazine.

● Some track tips

Ingenuity and experimentation pay off when it comes to laying down tracks. If you're using two percussion tracks, for example maracas and congas, try panning (see page 237, step 15) one left and the other right to create a broader musical soundscape. Sudden stops, particularly in instrumental music, are also effective. To produce a surprising effect, try reversing a sample. Also change the key of your song for the last chorus to add a 'lift' at the end.

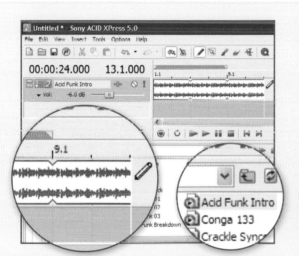

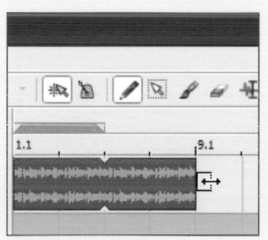

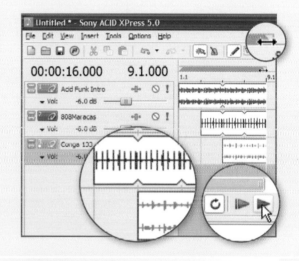

Your first track

8 To create your first track, click on **Acid Funk Intro** in the **Explorer** window, and still holding down the button, drag it up into the main window. Let go of the mouse button. The track is empty, so move the cursor into the main window and, holding down the left mouse button, drag along to your right so it looks like the screen above. Now let go of the mouse button.

How samples work

9 The scale above the track measures the number of bars in the composition. '1.1' indicates the start of the first bar; '9.1' indicates the start of the 9th bar (which is also the end of the 8th bar). In step 8 you 'drew' the sample across 12 bars. Shorten the sample to 8 bars by clicking on the end so the cursor turns into a double arrow and dragging to the left until you reach the '9.1' mark.

Add more tracks to a song

10 Add two more tracks to the song by dragging them out of the **Explorer** window and then moving them onto the screen with the mouse. Now loop the whole song so it keeps playing over and over. Click the yellow corner at the right-hand end of the loop region bar above the main window and drag it so it lines up with the end of the song. Click the **Loop** and **Play** buttons.

Recording your own samples

The professionally prerecorded samples used by programs such as ACID XPress are top quality, but to produce truly original material you may need to record your own. When recording with your PC, use a program such as Audacity – a free download from http://audacity.sourceforge.net – to make the recording; then use its editing tools to define the start and end points for the loop and to add effects. You can treat your recorded loops in exactly the same way as those that come with ACID XPress.

Get the best from your vocals

The human voice is one of the most difficult sounds to record well on a PC. To give yourself the best chance, consider a small 'powered' mixer (a combined mixer and pre-amplifier) – www.behringer.com has some inexpensive ones – and a high-quality microphone – the B1 from Studio Projects, www.studioprojectsusa.com, is good value. Don't use tone controls or effects when you're recording but add them later, and concentrate on getting the highest recording level possible without distortion.

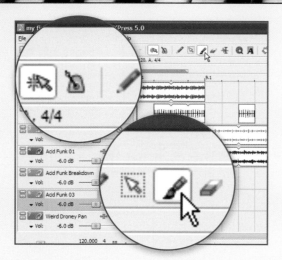

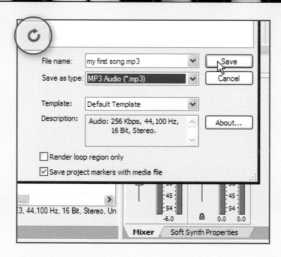

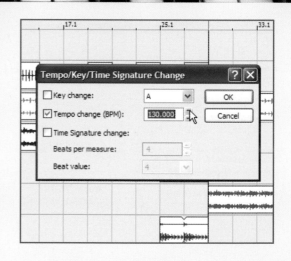

Know your tools

11 Take time to try out the standard tools. **Snap** (arrow and star shape) ensures that samples snap into place. The **Metronome** adds a steady beat behind your music. **Draw** (a pencil) adds a new sample to a single track. The **Selection** (white arrow) tool moves samples around the song. The **Paint** tool lets you add samples across all tracks. Finally, the **Eraser** deletes samples from the song.

Build up a song

12 Click the **Loop** button to turn it off and then continue adding tracks to your song. Notice that everything is in perfect time, in the same key, and plays at the same speed. This is because the people who create samples make it their business to ensure that everything fits together perfectly. Go to the **File** menu and choose **Save**. Type in a name for your song and click **Save**.

Speed up your song

13 Just because everything fits together doesn't mean you won't want to change it. For example, to make the song go faster at a certain point click with the mouse where you want the speed to increase and then go to the **Insert** menu and choose **Tempo/Key/Time Signature Change**. Click the up arrow shown here to increase the speed and click **OK**.

● Mix, master and export your compositions

ACID XPress lets you save your songs as MP3 files so that you can play them back on any PC or digital music player. Go to the **File** menu and choose **Render As**. Give your song a name and then open the drop-down list next to **Save as type** and choose **MP3 Audio**. Click the **Save** button. Now, you can play the finished track back using Windows Media Player. ACID XPress lets you do this 20 times, but after that you have to buy a commercial version of the program.

When ACID XPress has finished rendering the song, click the **Open Folder** button. You'll see an icon representing the song in the window, with the name you gave it. Double-click on the icon and after a moment Windows Media Player loads and begins to play it. If you wish, you can then use Media Player to burn the song to an audio CD (see page 221, step 16).

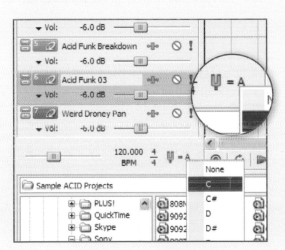

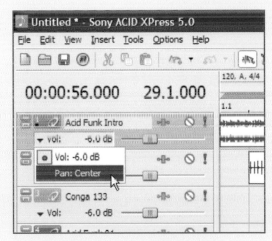

Pick up the tempo or change key

14 To alter the speed of your whole song, look underneath the track headings on the left and you'll see **120.000 BPM**. This is the tempo of the song in beats per minute. Drag the slider left or right with the mouse to slow down or speed up your song. Similarly, click the A next to the tuning fork to pick a new key for your song from those in the pop-up list.

Track volume and stereo settings

15 Each track has a small horizontal slider on the left-hand side that you drag left or right with the mouse to decrease or increase the volume. After you've adjusted the relative volumes, click the little arrow to the left of **Vol** on any of the tracks and select **Pan** from the drop-down list. Now use the same sliders to move sounds between the left and right speakers.

Correct your mistakes

16 As with all good programs, ACID XPress has an undo feature that lets you change your mind and go back to the point before you made the mistake. Open the list next to the **Undo** button on the button bar and pick how many steps you wish to undo with the mouse. Click to confirm. Multiple undos such as this make experimenting with your songs easy.

Name that tune

Download tracks from the internet and make a compilation CD

A music compilation makes a great birthday or Christmas gift. Choose the year, for instance, that someone was born, and use www.google.com to find a list of the top songs from that year. Once you've decided which songs you want, use Apple's free iTunes software and its built-in online music store to buy the songs and create a CD to suit the mood of the occasion. Once you've burned the CD, iTunes provides a cover layout with album artwork and track listings for you to print out and insert in a CD case.

PROJECT TOOLS: Apple iTunes
SEE ALSO: Recording and making music, page 332 ● Produce a podcast, page 286

Tunes for nothing

There's plenty of music that you can download legally for free. Amazon, www.amazon.com (below), regularly showcases new music – in the list on the left, click **Music**, then, at the top right, choose **Free Downloads**. Elsewhere, www.peoplesound.com has thousands of free tracks in all genres to download, while http://music.download.com regularly includes free tracks by named artists.

Visit Apple's music store

1 To download the free iTunes software go to www.apple.com/uk/itunes and follow the on-screen instructions. With iTunes you can make digital copies of music you already own, play songs on your PC and transfer them on and off an iPod portable music player. Here, you use it buy new music from Apple's internet store. Load the program and click **Music Store** in the left-hand column.

SOUND AND VISION

● Watch music videos

You can even use iTunes to catch up on videos of your favourite artists. Go to the **Music Store** and, in the **Inside the Music Store** list, choose **Music Videos**. Here you can search for a specific song, or click on one of the featured titles. When the video appears in the main iTunes window, click the **Preview** button. You'll be able to watch about 20 seconds of the video. You don't need any extra software and you can buy videos in the same way as music tracks.

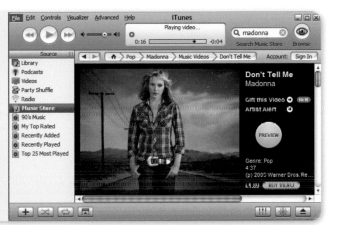

● Know your rights

Be a conscientious music lover and respect copyright. Digital music is protected by 'digital rights management', which places some restrictions on what you can and can't do with the songs you buy from the iTunes store. For example, you can only burn the same tracks seven times. This is designed to protect the copyright of the artist and recording company.

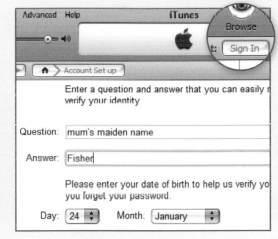

Search for music

2 The iTunes shop has a library of more than two million songs and you can listen to a snippet of any track before you buy it. You'll also find music videos, album art, and background on artists and albums. To find a song you're interested in, type either its name or the name of the band or album into the search box at the top right of the iTunes program window and press **Return**.

Listen before you buy

3 After a while, the iTunes shop displays a list of all the tracks it can find by the particular band that you're looking for, together with albums it has featured on. In this example, it's a group called The 5th Dimension, which had a big hit in 1969 with 'Aquarius'. To see if it's the song you want, click it once in the bottom list to select it and click the **Play** button at the top-left corner of the iTunes window.

Start an iTunes account

4 You'll hear a 30-second clip of the song. Try another if it's not the one you want. When you've found the right one and you're ready to buy, click the **Sign In** button at the top-right corner of iTunes. When the box appears, click the **Create New Account** button and follow the instructions to type in an iTunes account name and password along with your contact and payment details.

Convert your whole CD collection

Audio CDs are convenient and easy to play in any CD player or on your PC. But MP3 or WMA files (see box, right) offer far more flexibility. Programs such as Windows Media Player and iTunes can convert tracks from your audio CDs into these files (the process is called 'ripping'), which you can then play on portable players and mobile phones or directly from your PC's hard disk. It's much easier to search your PC for a particular song than it is to go through all the CDs on your shelves. And you can create compilations, called 'playlists', such as one for female singers, or blues guitarists or movie soundtracks, which you can then play back in any order. Or you can play your whole music library randomly so that the next track is always a surprise.

Now Playing
9 of 13
Just Feel Better
Santana
All That I Am
3:30
-0:49
MENU

Digital music file formats

There are many different digital-audio file types, or 'file formats', and they are not all compatible. MP3 and WMA are the two most widely used (see page 332) and will play back on all modern PCs and portable music players. Some players, including iTunes, have to convert them first, which may affect sound quality. Apple uses its own proprietary format (called AAC) that works only on iTunes and Apple's iPod portable music players.

Buy a song from the iTunes shop

5 On the right-hand side of the iTunes window are displayed the prices for each of the tracks found. Click on the **Buy Song** button and the track is added to your shopping basket. You'll be asked to sign in again for safety purposes and then told that your account (or any other payment method you're using, such as tokens) will be debited immediately. Click the **Get** button to continue.

Narrowing your searches

6 By default, iTunes searches through everything, including talking books, videos and 'podcasts' (see page 286), so if your searches return too many results, filter out the ones you don't want in order to make the list in the bottom window shorter. For example, click the **Music** button if you're looking for a CD, the **Artist** button if it's a band, and the **Song** button if you want a specific track.

Review songs for your compilation

7 Continue picking the songs you want for your compilation. When you've bought enough to fill an audio CD (up to 80 minutes of music), look down the left-hand column in the iTunes window and click **Purchased**. A list appears of all the songs you've bought, ready to be burned to a blank CD. If you want to change the song order, pick tracks up and move them with the mouse.

● Legal music on the go

Apple's iTunes is great but it's aimed mainly at iPod owners. Napster, www.napster.co.uk, on the other hand works with more than 70 different players, and offers more than one million legal music downloads. HMV has a similar service, based around its HMV Digital jukebox software, which you can download from www.hmv.co.uk/pmenu/downloads; while Tesco, www.tescodownloads.com, has a library of 400,000 songs that work with dozens of portable players.

● Why not add a hidden track?

Many audio CDs 'hide' a bonus track that plays long after the others have finished. You can do the same with your compilation by recording five minutes of silence using a sound editor such as Audacity (see page 286), which you can download free from http://audacity.sourceforge.net. Save the file, drag it into iTunes with the mouse, drop it into the playlist before the last track and then burn the CD. This will create the effect of having a hidden track.

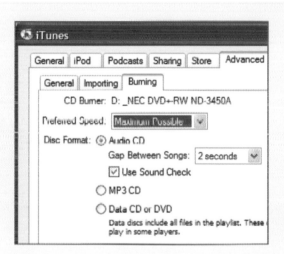

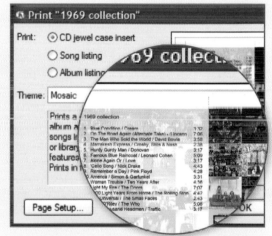

Last-minute checks

8 Before you make the CD, you need to check a couple of settings. Go to the iTunes **Edit** menu and choose **Preferences**. When the dialogue box appears, click the **Advanced** tab at the top, and then the **Burning** tab. Next, select **Audio CD** as the disc format (as opposed to MP3 CD or Data CD) and ensure that there's a tick next to **Use Sound Check**. Leave the other settings as they are and click **OK**.

Create the CD compilation

9 Click the **Burn Disc** icon at the top right hand corner of the iTunes window. The grey circle changes to reveal a black and yellow icon and iTunes ejects the tray of your CD writer. Place a blank CD in the drive – iTunes starts burning your songs onto the disc. The process only takes a few minutes. When it's finished, the CD writer will open and you can take your disc out and play it on any CD player.

Choose some cover art

10 To create a cover for your CD, go to iTunes' **File** menu, choose **Print** and select a design from the **Theme** list. Since this is a compilation, choose the **Mosaic** theme – iTunes arranges cover artwork from the albums your tracks were taken from into a mosaic, complete with crop marks to help you with cutting out. On the reverse is a track listing with duration times. Click **OK**.

Show and tell
Make an interactive presentation you can send to friends or family

Slideshows needn't run in sequence. Create a 'contents' screen with small pictures of each slide in the presentation and you can go to any slide you like depending on where you click on-screen. Or if you're showing famous landmarks, superimpose them on a map so people find their own way through the slideshow. This project tells the story in words and pictures of a year's fishing. Copy it to CD or email it and everyone can share in and explore your show.

PROJECT TOOLS: Writable CD drive (optional) ● Microsoft PowerPoint
SEE ALSO: Creating PowerPoint slideshows, page 302

● Preparing images

When you insert a photo or clip-art image into PowerPoint, it's nearly always the wrong size. Resize it by clicking and dragging the corners with your mouse. Then right-click on it and choose **Format Picture**. When the box appears, click the **Size** tab and make a note of the height and width. Run any subsequent pictures through an image-editing program such as Photoshop Elements (see page 308) and resize them to the correct dimensions before inserting into PowerPoint.

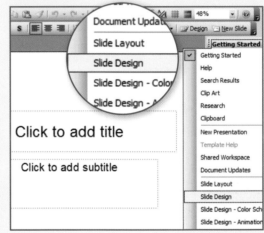

Design your slides

1 Start PowerPoint. When the program loads you'll see an empty white template in the centre of the screen ready for you type in a title and subtitle for your presentation. Before you do, make the background more interesting by clicking the drop-down arrow next to **Getting Started** in the task pane on the right of the screen and then choose the **Slide Design** option from the menu.

SOUND AND VISION

Storyboarding

If your presentation is complex, lay it out in rough first by creating a set of slides that have some text on them describing what the final content will be – for example, Calendar contents goes here or Big picture of fish. Click on the **View** menu and choose **Slide Sorter** to see a bird's-eye view of the whole show. To move slides around, just click and drag with your mouse.

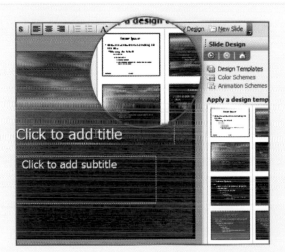

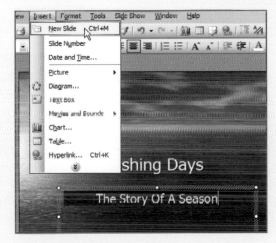

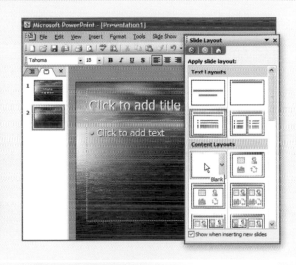

Choose a colour scheme

2 On the right of the main screen you'll see a selection of different colour slides called 'design templates'. You can create your own, but these ready-made schemes will save you time. To apply one to your show, click on it once with the left mouse button. Try out a few different styles until you find one you like. In this example it is a blue sea background (called 'Ocean') to go with the fishing theme.

Add text to your slides

3 The design templates include guide text for headings, sub-headings, bullet points and other text, ready for you to replace with your own. Select **Click to add title** and type your title over the text that's currently there. When you've finished, do the same for the subtitle underneath. Your first slide is complete. To add a second one, go to the **Insert** menu and choose **New Slide**.

Change slide layout

4 Notice there are now two thumbnail slides in the column on the left: the title slide and the one you've created. PowerPoint tries to help you out by automatically formatting new slides, but sometimes you'll want to design them from scratch. The design templates on the right have been replaced by text and content layouts; choose the blank content layout by clicking on it.

Mini movies

To add a short movie to a slide, from the **Insert** menu choose **Movies and Sounds** then **Movie from file**. PowerPoint opens your **My Videos** folder (**1**). Double-click on the clip. PowerPoint then asks you to choose whether the clip should play as soon as the slide appears in the show or when you click your mouse (**2**). The clip is inserted on the slide (**3**) and you can reposition or size it in the same way as a still image (see step 11). For further **Movie Options** (**4**), right-click on the movie clip and choose **Edit Movie Object**.

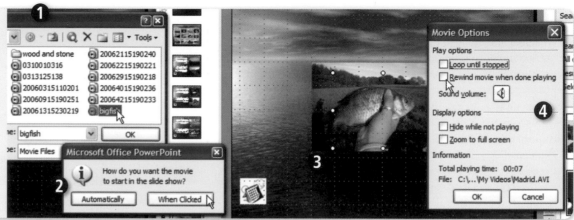

Keep everything lined up

5 Use PowerPoint's grid features to line up your pictures. As well as providing a visual grid, objects on screen will 'snap' into place and line up accurately as you move them near a grid line. Go to the **View** menu and choose **Grid and Guides**. When the box opens leave all the settings as they are but put a tick next to the **Display grid on screen** option. Click the **OK** button to return to your slides.

Create a navigation screen

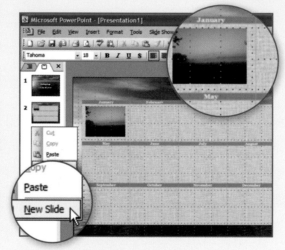

6 This is the contents page. It's a simple calendar, created in Word then saved as a picture. In the **Insert** menu, choose **Picture** then **From File**. Navigate to where the calendar is stored and double-click to add it to the slide. In the same way, add a photo to the first month (see 'Preparing images' box, page 242) and position it with the mouse. Right-click in the left-hand column and choose **New Slide**.

Make your contents interactive

7 When someone clicks on a thumbnail picture within the calendar, you want the slide that relates to that thumbnail picture to appear on screen. Click once on the calendar slide thumbnail to open it in the main window. Next, right-click on the January picture and choose **Action Settings** from the pop-up menu. Click **Hyperlink to** and then choose **Next Slide** from the list. Click **OK** to confirm.

Add links to the web

Providing links to additional resources or extra reading on the topic of the slideshow enhances its value. If you're connected to the internet, you can set up any element in the show, such as a picture, so that when you click on it, a website you've selected appears in your web browser. Right-click on a photo and choose **Hyperlink**. Type in the full address of the web page in the empty address line at the bottom and click **OK**. When you run the show and click that picture, the website appears.

Applause please

PowerPoint comes with a collection of ready-made sound effects such as clapping and drum rolls. You can also add any sound that's stored on your PC or play a music CD along with your show to create atmosphere. To add sounds to a slide, click on the **Insert** menu and choose **Movies and Sounds**. When the sub-menu opens, click the arrow at the bottom to reveal all of the extra menu items. Choose **Sound from Clip Organizer** for a selection of sounds from Microsoft's website. Double-click one to add it to your slideshow.

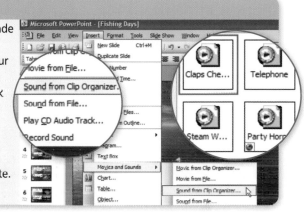

Test the navigation page

8 Go to the **Slide Show** menu and choose **View Show**. After a moment, you'll see the title slide appear full screen on your PC's display. If you haven't changed any other settings, click the mouse once anywhere on the screen to move on to the calendar slide. Move the cursor over the January picture. It turns into a hand. Click once and you'll move to the next slide.

Returning to the navigation page

9 It's important to have a link on each slide to click when you want to return to the navigation page. Instead of adding one to every new slide, add it once to the **Slide Master** and then it will appear automatically. Click the **View** menu; choose **Master** and then **Slide Master**. Hover your mouse pointer over the two thumbnails and click on **Slide Master** to select it.

Use ready-made pictures

10 Right-click on the bulleted text in the main window and choose **Cut** from the menu to delete it. Go to the **Insert** menu and choose **Picture** and then **Clip Art**. Type calendar into the **Search for** box on the right of the main window and click **Go**; PowerPoint will display any calendar-related pictures it can find. Double-click on one you like to add it to the slide.

Use special visual effects

Rather than having your slides flick from one to the next, use PowerPoint's built-in transitions to fade, dissolve or wipe between them. These visual effects work well, but use them sparingly so you don't distract from the show's impact. Right-click on any slide and choose **Slide Transition** from the pop-up menu for a list of available transitions. Click one to apply it to the slide and see a preview in the main window. A dissolve effect is shown right.

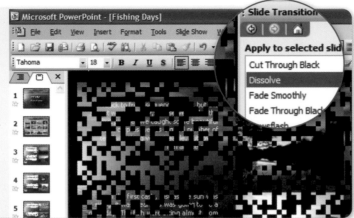

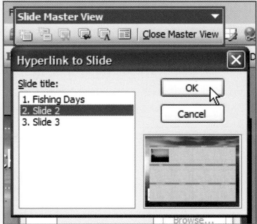

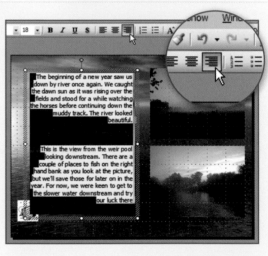

Move pictures

11 To move the picture anywhere you wish on the slide, left-click on it and drag it with your mouse, holding down the mouse button. Similarly, click on one of the small white circles round its edge and hold down the mouse button to make it larger or smaller by dragging in or out. When you're finished, right-click on the picture and choose **Action Settings** from the menu.

Create links

12 Select the **Hyperlink to** option, then open the drop-down list and scroll down until you reach **Slide**. Click on it to see a list of all the slides that you've created so far. When you click on one of them, a thumbnail image appears next to it so you can tell the slides apart. In this example, **Slide 2** is the calendar page, so select it. Click **OK** to confirm and then click **OK** again.

Add content to a slide

13 Click on the third slide in the thumbnail list to select it and add a couple of photographs by going to the **Insert** menu and choosing **Picture** and **From File** as in step 6. Open the **Insert** menu and choose **Text Box**. Use your mouse to draw out a box on the slide. Type in some text and use PowerPoint's formatting buttons to change the font, alignment and other text elements.

Reference material

Research is made easy in PowerPoint. Go to the **Tools** menu and click **Research**. When the **Research** pane opens on the right of the screen, type in a word or phrase you want information on and the program returns a list of web links for you to click. It's a good way to check facts without leaving your presentation. The same **Research** feature is also available in other Microsoft Office programs, including Word and Excel.

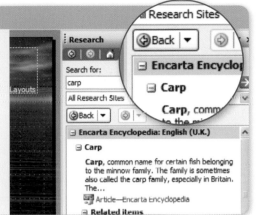

Saving for sharing

You can share your PowerPoint slideshow with people even if they don't have a copy of the program. Go to the **File** menu and choose **Package for CD**. As the name suggests, this can be used to copy a version onto a blank CD that can be played back on any PC. Put a blank CD in your recordable CD drive and click the **Copy to CD** button. PowerPoint does the rest. Alternatively, copy everything someone needs to view your show to a folder and send it to them via email.

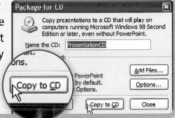

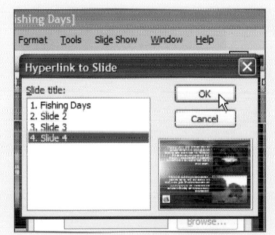

Complete your navigation page

14 Go back to the calendar page by clicking on the thumbnail in the left-hand column and then add more pictures until all the months are filled. Use the grid lines to help you position the pictures so they line up. You may choose to use a map or a family tree instead of a calendar as a way of navigating around a presentation such as this one.

Finishing your navigation controls

15 Carry on adding slides as you've done previously. As you add each slide, you will need to return to the calendar slide and right-click on the picture that relates to the new slide you've added and choose **Action Settings**. Select **Hyperlink to** and then choose **Slide** from the list. Select the new slide in the dialogue box, click **OK** and then **OK** again.

Running your slideshow

16 Go to the PowerPoint **Slide Show** menu and choose **View Show**. Click once to move from the title screen to the main navigation screen (the fishing calendar). Now click on any one of the pictures to jump to the slide for that month. To see a different month, click the picture you added to the **Slide Master** in step 9 – now on each slide – to return to the navigation screen.

Hollywood action

Add a DVD menu and turn your home movie into a blockbuster

Producing a DVD makes your home videos more accessible and enjoyable to watch. You can skip to favourite bits using scene menus and even include 'bonus features' similar to the ones on Hollywood DVD movies. With the right software most of the hard work is done automatically, giving you the opportunity to get creative by adding titles and choosing still images, clips and music for menus. Even better, you can play the DVD in any domestic DVD player and make copies for friends and family.

PROJECT TOOLS: Adobe Premiere Elements 2, www.adobe.com/products/premiereel ● DVD writer
SEE ALSO: Sound and vision with Media Player, page 330 ● Make a movie, page 208

SEE ALSO: Sound and vision with Media Player, page 330 ● Make a movie, page 208

● The software you need

Many PCs with built-in DVD writers come with budget video-editing software already installed, which includes the tools that allow you to create DVD menus and burn a disc. Movie Maker, part of Microsoft Windows XP, doesn't. To carry out this project, you'll need Adobe Premiere Elements 2 video-editing software. To download a free 30-day trial version, go to www.adobe.com/products/premiereel then follow the prompts. Now you have everything you need to start making your own DVDs.

Capture your movie

1 To make a DVD you first need to capture video footage from your camcorder. Launch Premiere Elements. Select **Capture Video** from the **How To** panel of the screen, then choose **Capture multiple scenes from a single tape** and follow the directions. In step 4, you will automatically create a DVD menu button to take you directly to each captured scene, rather than sit through the whole movie each time.

Get your clips in order

As you're creating a menu from which viewers can access any clip and any chapter on your DVD, you might think that the actual order of clips isn't all that important. It is. When a clip or chapter that has been selected from the menu and played reaches its end, the next item in the list plays, and then the next, and so on, right the way through to the end. The only exception to this is if the viewer presses a button on the remote, for example to return to the top menu. Although your main task is to create an easily navigable menu, try and keep in mind how the project as a whole will work when played from beginning to end.

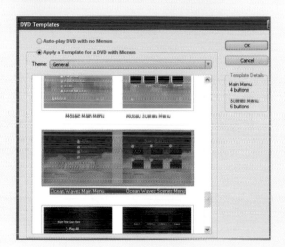

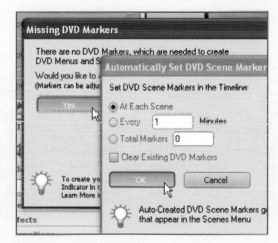

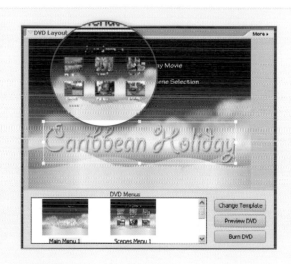

Choose a template

2 Click the **DVD** button on the toolbar. The **DVD Templates** dialogue box appears. Tick the button labelled **Apply a Template for a DVD with Menus**, choose a theme from the pull-down list and select a template. The thumbnails show two templates for each design: **Main** and **Scenes Menu**. Some main menus offer additional buttons, for bonus features and credits – these can be added later.

Make your markers

3 Click **OK** and the **Missing DVD Markers** alert box will appear (providing you have more than one clip captured). Click the **Yes** button and Premiere Elements creates DVD scene markers. You can choose to add markers at each scene, for example for each clip, or at regular intervals. Leave the default setting with the **At Each Scene** button ticked and then click **OK**.

Write a title

4 Premiere Elements creates a main menu and as many scene menus as are needed. You can fit up to six scenes to a scene menu. Here, there are six clips, so only one scene menu is produced. The main menu is displayed in the central DVD layout window with a link to the **Scene Selection** menu. Double-click the **Main Title** text to overwrite it with your own title.

● Careful planning pays

Try and structure your DVD menu so that viewers can quickly select what they want to watch without having to navigate through endless menus. So before you start, think about how you're going to organise your DVD. You may structure it chronologically; for example, a holiday DVD may start with your journey to the airport, followed by arrival at your hotel and then continue with visits to local beauty spots. A promotional DVD may include separate menus for products. With complicated projects that include multiple menus, sketch out a diagram of the menu structure. Premiere Elements 2 includes special markers that allow you to divert the navigation when a particular point is reached. For example, when the end of a scene is reached, a stop marker will return to the main menu instead of continuing to the next scene.

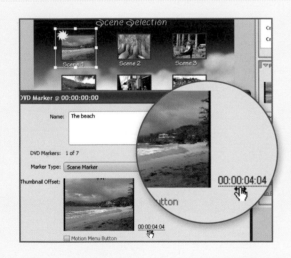

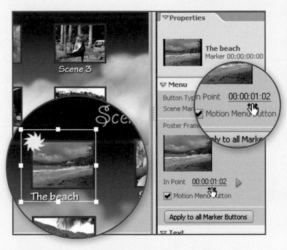

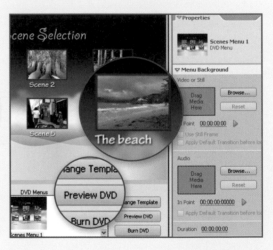

Select a button image

5 Click the **Scenes Menu 1** thumbnail and double-click the thumbnail **Scene 1** to edit it. In the **DVD Marker** dialogue box, type in a name for the scene, which will then appear below the thumbnail. To change the 'poster frame' – the frame from the clip that's displayed on the menu – click and drag the blue time code numbers to the side of the thumbnail until the frame you want is displayed.

Use a movie clip on the button

6 To display a short movie clip, rather than a still frame, on the menu, tick the **Motion Menu Button** box below the thumbnail and click OK. In the **Menu** section of the **Properties** panel, scroll down until you see **Poster Frame**. Set the **In Point** for the thumbnail (where the movie starts playing) by dragging the time code left and right to navigate through the clip.

Preview the button movie clip

7 Click **Preview DVD** to check that your menu button plays correctly. The maximum duration for any clip on a motion menu is 30 seconds. If the clip is longer, it will play for 30 seconds, then loop back to the 'in' point and play again. Click anywhere on the menu background in the **DVD Layout** panel. The background properties are displayed in the **Properties** panel.

No DVD writer?

Even if you don't have a DVD writer in your PC, you can still make a video disc, as long as your PC has a CD writer. Some video and DVD applications – not Premiere Elements 2 – let you create Video CDs (VCDs). The drawbacks are that you can't fit as much video on a VCD as on a DVD, the quality isn't as good and not all DVD players are capable of playing a VCD.

If you've got a lot of video to edit and don't have a DVD writer, you can buy a single-layer version relatively cheaply. If you're not confident enough to install one inside your PC, for a little more you could buy an external drive that connects to your computer using a USB cable (see page 11). Blank DVD discs are inexpensive and hold the equivalent of roughly eight CDs.

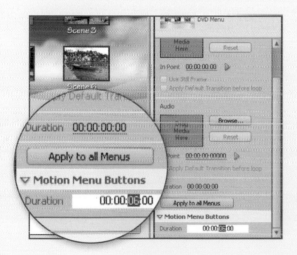

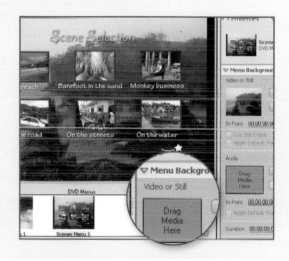

Shorten the loop

8 Scroll down the **Properties** panel until you get to the **Motion Menu Buttons** section. The time code displays the duration of the button clip in hours, minutes, seconds and hundredths of a second. Change from the default of 30 seconds to 6 seconds. You can do this by clicking the time code and dragging to the left to decrease duration or click and overwrite the seconds value.

Set up the other buttons

9 Double-click the **Scene 2** button in the **DVD Layout** panel, rename it and make it a motion menu button using the **DVD Marker** dialogue box as in step 6. Set its 'in' point using the **Properties** panel. The duration will automatically be set to 6 seconds, as applied in the previous step for all newly created motion menu buttons. Repeat this process for every button on the **Scenes Menu**.

Alter your menu background

10 To add a new menu background using a still image, click anywhere on the existing background and drag a photo from the **Media** panel onto the drop zone labelled **Drag Media Here** in the **Properties** panel. Alternatively, click **Browse** in the **Menu Background** panel and navigate to a folder holding photos. You'll see the new background image in the **DVD Layout** panel.

● Adding a black and white effect

Press the **Edit** button at the top right corner. Click the **Video FX** button in the **Effects and Transitions** panel then drag the **Black & White** filter from the **Image Control** section and drop it on the clip in the **Timeline** panel. Drag the ends of the grey 'work area bar' in the **Timeline** to match the length of the clip. Select **File**, **Export** then **Movie**, click the settings button in the dialog box and choose **Work Area Bar** from the **Range** pull-down menu. Enter a file name and click **Save**. The new clip is added to the **Media** panel and you can drag it from here onto your menu background.

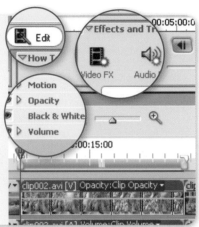

● Avoid motion sickness

Premiere Elements' motion menu buttons and backgrounds (see steps 6 to 8) are fun to watch, but don't overdo them. The brain can only cope with so much information at once, and if you have six small video buttons competing with each other and a longer clip running in the background your audience may switch off altogether rather than attempt to make sense of the video pandemonium. Use motion, but keep it simple. For backgrounds, use soft images with little detail such as a cloudy sky, a river, slow-motion waves or a close-up of a flag. Navigation buttons need to be legible on top of the video background, so choose button clips with care.

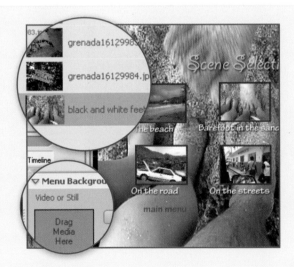

Add a video background

11 You can replace the menu background with a video. Drag a clip from the **Media** panel to replace the still photo thumbnail in the **Drag Media Here** box, or drag directly onto the menu background. If you're short of video footage, apply a filter to an existing clip. Here, a black and white version of one of the clips from the movie is used (see 'Adding a black and white effect', above).

Cue the background clip

12 Set the **In Point** of the menu background video clip by dragging the time code indicator in the **Properties** panel; the thumbnail image updates so that you see what you're getting. Scroll to the bottom of the **Properties** panel to set the duration. Don't get the background duration confused with the duration for the motion menu buttons that appears below it.

Cue the music

13 Add music to your menu by dragging an audio clip from the **Media** panel to the audio drop zone in the **Properties** panel. Or you can just drag an audio file (see page 332) from an open folder on the desktop. Use the **Play** button (the green triangle) in the **Properties** panel to find a suitable **In Point** for the audio – the duration will be the same as for the background video clip.

SOUND AND VISION

Sharing DVDs

If you need to make more than one copy of a DVD to send to friends or family, or for a club or other organisation, most video and DVD applications, including Premiere Elements 2, give you the option of burning multiple DVDs in a single session. This is the quickest method because the time-consuming encoding only needs to be done once and then the file is written to as many discs as you want. But be careful since any mistakes you make will cost you several wasted discs, not just one.

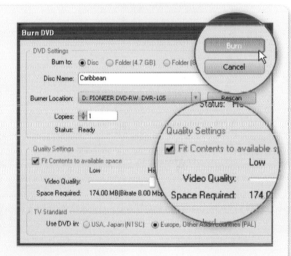

Keep transitions smooth

14 When a motion background or button loops (ends and restarts), the transition, as the clip lurches from the last frame back to the beginning, may jar on the eye. To soften this, apply the default transition by ticking the **Apply Default Transition before loop** box in the **Properties** panel. The default transition is a cross-dissolve. You can change this in the **Effects and Transitions** panel.

The big preview

15 Click the **Preview DVD** button in the **DVD Layout** panel. This launches the Preview panel with playback controls that operate in the same way as a DVD player remote control. Ensure that all the navigation buttons work and everything plays back as you want. The motion buttons and backgrounds may be jumpy at this stage but they should be fine on the finished DVD.

Time to burn

16 Click the **Close** box on the **Preview DVD** dialogue box, followed by the **Burn DVD** button in the **DVD Layout** panel. Insert a recordable DVD in your DVD burner and tick the **Fit Contents to available space** box. Unless you have more than two hours of video this will use the best-quality setting. Click **Burn**. It may take several hours to compress and burn a long project.

Internet active

Play an active part in the World Wide Web with a family home page, an online diary and photo album, free video calls and your own internet radio show

Home sweet home page
Build your own website in no time in Microsoft Word

Make a place on the web that you can call your own, where you can have your say and share news, views and photos with the world. All Microsoft Office programs include a **Save as Web Page** option, so you could design a newsletter-style document then convert it to a web page at the last minute. But the files will be large, and slow to view over the internet. So the best approach is to build your website

from scratch. Microsoft Word includes all the tools you need. Starting with a frames page to set out where the different parts go – heading, menus and the main content – new pages slot into this structure, so you don't have to add headings and menus each time.

The same principles apply whether you're designing a family home page, or a website for a club or local organisation.

PROJECT TOOLS: Microsoft Word ● Photoshop Elements
SEE ALSO: Lay out a newsletter, page 138 ● Online photo album, page 266

● Neat and tidy filing

Your website will expand as you add more pages, new photos and new sections. The number of files involved will increase with every new page, and you could end up with hundreds or thousands of files.

The key to a tidy website is keeping all the files – pictures and web pages – in well-organised folders. Before you even start to create your first page, create a folder for it (see step 1, below). Then, when you come to save for the first time (see steps 5 and 6), make sure the files and web pages are all saved in the same place, ready to be uploaded.

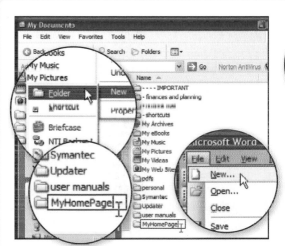

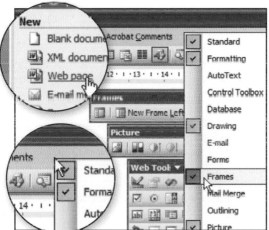

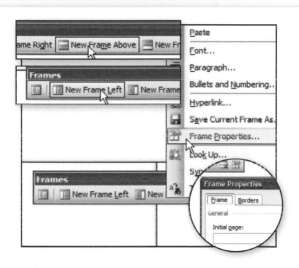

Make a place for your files

1 Click the Windows **Start** button and choose **My Documents**. Right-click on a blank part of the main **My Documents** window and, from the pop-up menu that appears, choose **New** then **Folder**. Type in MyHomePage (no spaces) and press **Return** – you'll see the folder that you've created in the list of folders. Start Microsoft Word. From the **File** menu, choose **New**.

Prepare Word for web editing

2 The **New Document** task pane is displayed on the right of the screen. Click **Web page**. A blank page appears. Right-click in the space to the right of the main menus at the top. From the list of toolbars available, make sure that among those ticked are **Frames**, **Picture**, **Drawing** and **WordArt** (you'll need to right-click each time that you want to tick or untick a toolbar).

Set out a framework

3 The web page will be divided into three areas, using frames – a heading at the top, a list of links to other pages on the left, and a main area in the centre. In the **Frame** toolbar, click **New Frame Above**. Your page splits, vertically, into two parts. Click in the lower part and, in the **Frame** toolbar, click **New Frame Left**. Right-click inside the top frame and choose **Frame Properties**. A dialogue box appears.

● The best fonts for the web

Choosing the right fonts (see page 326) means people will view your site as you want it to be seen. Your web-editing program may let you choose any fonts it finds on your PC, but someone viewing your website that hasn't got those fonts installed will see only an approximate match. For the best results, stick to the core web fonts, Arial, Comic Sans, Courier, Georgia, Times, Trebuchet and Verdana, since almost everyone has these on their computer. Use these fonts and you can be sure pages will appear just as you created them, for almost all visitors to your site.

Arial Comic Sans
Courier Georgia
Trebuchet Times
Verdana

● More ways to style your text

With Microsoft Word as your web editor, you have access to the same set of text formatting tools as you would when writing a letter. Use bold type (press **Ctrl+B**) to pick out key words within the body text, or italic (**Ctrl+I**) for captions. Use colour where it's appropriate, but don't get carried away. It can be effective to subtly colour body text using the very dark (almost black) colours along the top line in the **Font Color** picker.

Don't use very large font sizes (above 16 points), as the text won't display correctly on most PCs when your page is uploaded to the web. If you need to make a very large heading, use **WordArt** (see step 7) or type out and style the text using an image editor such as Photoshop Elements, then save the heading as a JPEG image (see 'Size matters', page 311).

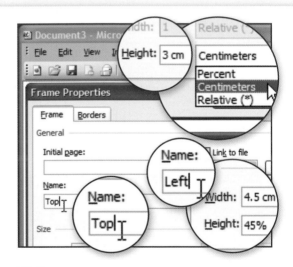

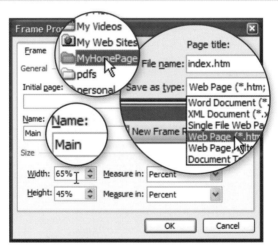

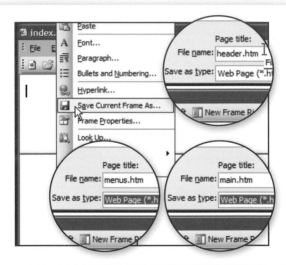

Adjust the frames

4 Click the **Frame** tab. Under **Name**, type Top. In the **Measure in** box, choose **Centimeters** then set **Height** to 3. Click **OK**. Next, right-click in the left frame. Choose **Frame Properties** and name this frame Left. Set **Measure in** (for **Width**) to **Centimeters** then set **Width** to 4.5. Set **Measure in** (for **Height**) to **Percent** then enter 45. Click **OK**. Finally, right-click in the right-hand frame and choose **Frame Properties**.

Save the frames

5 In the dialogue box, name the third frame Main. Set both **Measure in** boxes to **Percent**, then set **Width** to 65, **Height** to 45. Click **OK**. Press Ctrl+S. When the **Save As** dialogue box appears, click **My Documents** on the left, then double-click the **MyHomePage** folder you created earlier. In the **Save as type** box, choose **Web Page** from the drop-down list. By **File name**, type index.htm and click **Save**.

Save the pages of your frames

6 Right-click in the top frame and, from the pop-up menu, choose **Save Current Frame As**. In the **Save As** dialogue box, next to **File name**, type header.htm. Choose **Web Page** from the drop-down box by **Save as type**, then click **Save**. Right-click in the left frame and save that frame in the exactly same way, but naming it menus.htm. Repeat for the main frame, naming that file news.htm.

Build a website for a local club

Your web pages don't just have to be about you and your family. A website is the perfect way to promote your local church, drama group, school or sporting club. The structure of the website and format of the pages needn't change – start with a frames page (index.htm) and add a page for each frame (as in steps 1 to 6). Then, in step 7, choose a **WordArt** style and banner heading that suits the subject of your website and, in step 8, add appropriate menu buttons in the same style. All the remaining steps apply, whatever the purpose of the site. Add more buttons and links to new pages as your site, or your organisation, develops.

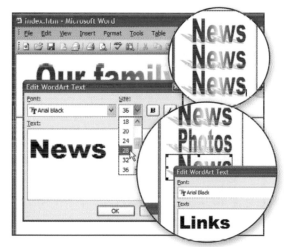

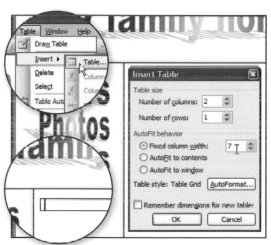

Choose a WordArt main heading

7 Click in the top frame. In the **Insert** menu, choose **Picture** then **WordArt**. The **WordArt Gallery** displays the styles available – choose one that you like, then click **OK**. In the next box that appears, type a heading for your website, such as Our family home page. This will appear at the top of every page. Set a large, clear type style. In the example above it's **Arial Black**, size **36**. Click **OK**.

Add side menu headings

8 Click in the left frame. In the **Insert** menu, choose **Picture** then **WordArt**. Choose the same style, and click **OK**. Type News, set a smaller type size, 28, then click **OK**. Click the **News** heading, then press **Ctrl+C** to copy it. Press **Ctrl+V** three times to paste the heading three times. Double-click the second heading and type Photos. Click **OK**. Double-click the third and type Links, then click **OK**.

Make a table

9 The main text and pictures on the page will be kept neat and aligned using a table. Click in the **Main** (right-hand) frame. In the **Table** menu, choose **Insert**, then **Table**. In the dialogue box, under **Table size**, set **Number of columns** to **2** and **Number of rows** to **1**. Under **AutoFit behaviour**, tick **Fixed column width** and enter **7** in the box to its right. Click **OK**; a blank table appears in the **Main** frame.

○ Preparing pictures for your home page

Photos should ideally be cropped and reduced to the right size for your web page before you import them into Word. (You can adjust them in Word, but the file size remains unchanged, and a large file could take ages to download, making your page slow to view.) Crop and resize your pictures first using an image editor such as Photoshop Elements (see page 308). A good width for photos to be inserted in the table used in this project is 260 pixels, but smaller images can look great too.

Start Photoshop Elements and, on the **Welcome** screen, choose **Edit and Enhance Photos**. Choose **Open** in the **File** menu. Navigate to a photo that you want to use, then click **Open**.

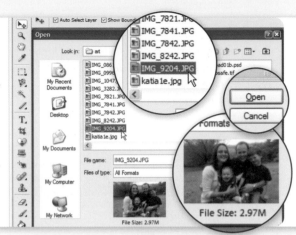

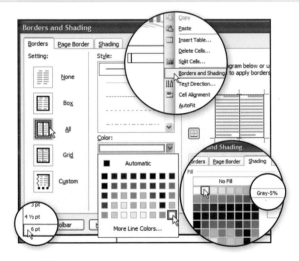

Format the table

10 Right-click in one of the table cells and choose **Borders and Shading** from the pop-up menu. In the dialogue box, click the **Borders** tab, then click **All**. Click the **Color** drop-down box and choose the colour **White**. Just below the **Color** box, click the **Width** box and choose **6pt**. Click the **Shading** tab and choose a subtle shade for the table background, such as **Gray-5%**. Click **OK**.

Remove the frame borders

11 Right-click on a blank part of the top frame, and choose **Frame Properties**. Click the **Borders** tab. On the right-hand side of the dialogue box, you'll see a representation of the arrangement of frames relative to one another. It's neater and more professional-looking not to display any frame borders on a web page so, under **Frames Page**, tick **No borders**. Click **OK**.

Start writing the news

12 The page currently in the **Main** frame will be the first page your visitors see, where they'll find all your latest news. Treat the columns in the table as if they were columns on a newspaper page. You could start with a welcome message and a few words about the site. Then type, or copy and paste, your stories, news and views into the columns to start filling the page.

Click the **Crop** tool in the toolbar on the left, then, in the **Options** toolbar along the top, type 260 px into the **Width** box (leave **Height** and **Resolution** blank). Click and drag to draw a rectangle over the image – this highlights the part to be cropped – then release the mouse button. Click the green tick icon to perform the crop – at the same time, Photoshop Elements resizes the image so it's 260 pixels wide. In the **File** menu, choose **Save As**. In the **Save As** dialogue box, navigate to a folder where you want to save resized images. Type a name for the photo, then, in the **Format** drop-down box, choose **JPEG** and click **Save**. The **JPEG Options** box appears. Under **Image Options**, set **Quality** to 8, then click **OK** to save the file.

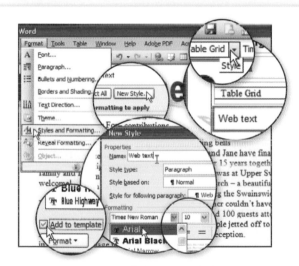

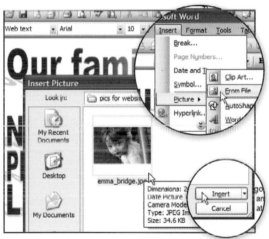

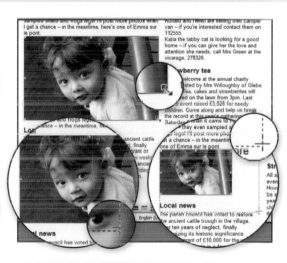

Create a text style

13 Click within the text, then choose **Styles** and **Formatting** from the **Format** menu. In the **Task** pane on the right, click **New Style**. By **Name**, type Web text. Under **Formatting**, pick **Arial** and **10** from the drop-down boxes. Tick the **Add to template** box then click **OK**. Click the **Style** drop-down menu at the top. Choose **Web text** for the body text and **Heading 3** for each story headline.

Add a photo

14 Photos should be the correct size and format for your page (see 'Preparing pictures for your home page', page 260). Click to position the text cursor at the end of a story, then press **Return**. In the **Insert** menu, choose **Picture** then **From File**. In the **Insert Picture** dialogue box, navigate to where you saved your resized photos. Click on the photo you want to use, then click **Insert**.

Adjust the picture to fit

15 The photo is inserted wider than the table cell, and the table column expands to compensate. Click on the picture, then click the square handle at its bottom right corner. Drag up and left to make the picture visibly smaller than you'll need, then release the button – the table returns to normal width. Carefully drag the handle back until the picture fits without stretching the table, then release the button.

○ Bring the background to life

The web pages in this project are on a plain white background. But you can change the colour or even add a texture or photo background to each or all of the frames. Using Windows Explorer, navigate to the **MyHomePage** folder (see step 1). Right-click the file **index.htm** and choose **Edit** from the pop-up menu. When the frames page loads in Word (see step 5), right-click in the top frame and, from the **Format** menu, choose **Background**. A colour picker appears, together with options for choosing further colours and background fill effects. Click **Fill Effects** – in the dialogue box you can choose from gradient fills, photo textures, simple patterns or photo backgrounds using images on your hard disk. Click the **Texture** tab and scroll down to select a texture, then click **OK**. The top frame background changes to the texture you chose. Alternatively, click the **Picture** tab, then click **Select Picture** and browse to a JPEG image file on your PC. If you select an image smaller than the frame, it repeats to fill the area. You may find that your WordArt heading text (see step 7) is hard to read after adding a background. Modify the WordArt style by clicking the heading, then clicking the **WordArt Gallery** button.

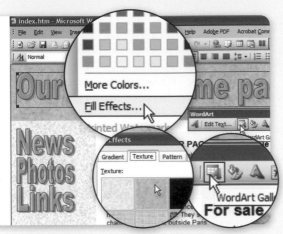

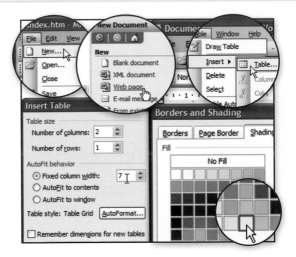

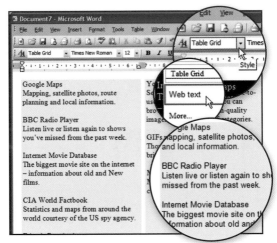

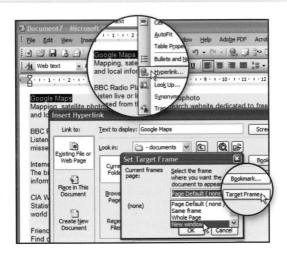

Add a new page

16 Press **Ctrl+S** to save all of the web pages that you're working on. Then in the **File** menu, choose **New** and, in the **Task** pane on the right, click **Web page**. A blank page appears. In the **Table** menu, choose **Insert**, then **Table**. Format the table exactly as you did in steps 9 and 10 but, this time, choose a different table background colour, such as **Light Turquoise**.

Make a favourite links page

17 Click in the left-hand cell and type the name of the first website – for example, Google Maps. Press **Return**, then type a brief description, such as Mapping, satellite photos, route planning and local information. Press **Return** twice, then add a second website. Add all your favourite websites in this way. Highlight and style all the text as **Web text** (see step 13).

Set up link addresses

18 Highlight the first website name – **Google Maps**. Right-click it and choose **Hyperlink** from the pop-up menu. The **Insert Hyperlink** dialogue box appears. In the **Address** box, type the address for Google Maps, http://maps.google.co.uk. Click **Target Frame** and, from the drop-down box, pick **New window**. Click **OK**. Click **OK** again. Add links to each site in the same way.

○ How to show off your website

You've created your web pages, and you want the world to see them, so you need to upload them (copy them from your PC to a computer on the internet, known as a web server, from where visitors can view them). Some web-editing programs will transfer them for you, or you can use a separate file transfer protocol (FTP) program such as SmartFTP, www.smartftp.com, which is free for personal use (see 'Download and install SmartFTP', page 269). Start the program, enter details of your web space, user name and password (your web space provider will give you this information) and a window will open, showing the files currently on the web server. You can drag, or copy and paste, your web-page files from Windows Explorer to the web server – just like copying files from one folder on your PC to another.

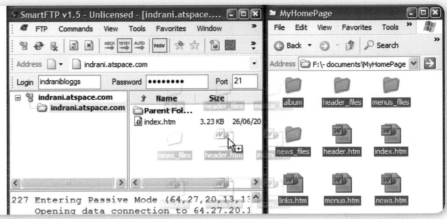

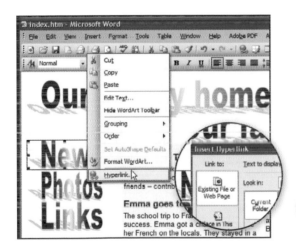

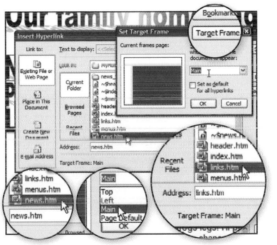

Return to the index page

19 Press Ctrl+S to save the links page. Navigate to the folder that you created in step 1, set **Save as type** to **Web Page** and name the file links.htm. Click **Save**, then press Ctrl+W to close the page. Switch back to your frames pages (index.htm) and click on the top menu button (**News**). Right-click the selected button and choose **Hyperlink**. The **Insert Hyperlink** dialogue box appears, as before.

Configure the menu buttons

20 Navigate to the **MyHomePage** folder, and choose **news.htm** (or **news**) from the file list. Click **Target Frame**, then choose **Main** from the drop-down list. Click **OK**. Click **OK** again. Select the **Links** menu button, then right-click it. Choose **Hyperlink** as in step 19. This time, select **links.htm** (or **links**) in the file list. Set **Target Frame** to **Main**, as above. Click **OK** twice. Press Ctrl+S to save the index page.

View and upload your website

21 Later you could link the **Photos** menu button to an online photo album (see page 271). For now, use Windows Explorer to navigate to the **MyHomePage** folder, then double-click the **index.htm** file. Your web browser loads and you can try out your website 'offline' (from your PC's hard disk). To upload it to the web, where everyone can visit your pages, see 'How to show off your website', above.

See the heartbeat
Build your own small animations to liven up emails and websites

If you want to add some pizzazz to your website, one of the easiest ways is to add an animation. Graphics interchange format (GIF) is a type of image file often used for graphics on web pages. A single GIF file can store several images; when it's viewed in a web browser, these appear one after the other, making an animation. So you can create an animated 'banner' or a moving button that you can turn into a clickable link when you create your website, or simply a fun graphic for decoration.

PROJECT TOOLS: Photoshop Elements
SEE ALSO: Design an illustrated email greeting, page 284

Why small is beautiful

One of the most common uses of animation on websites is in advertising banners, often seen across the top of a page. A standard banner is 468 pixels wide by 80 high. Don't try animating graphics at sizes much larger than this – the GIF file will take too long to download when people view your page, and the animation won't play back smoothly. For the same reason, avoid over-complex graphical effects. Small animated buttons can be just as effective as large banners and are quick to display on your page.

Create an animated graphic

1 Run Photoshop Elements and select **Start from Scratch** from the welcome screen. The **New** dialogue box appears. Enter the width and height you want, in pixels. An animated button would be quite small, so set **Width** and **Height** to **192 pixels**. Then set **Resolution** to **96 pixels/inch**, **Color Mode** to **RGB Color**, and **Background Contents** to **White**. Click **OK** to create a blank image.

Set your background colour

2 If the graphic is for a web page where the background isn't white, make your canvas match. From the **Edit** menu, choose **Fill Layer**. In the **Fill Layer** box, click **Use** and select **Color**. In the **Color Picker** box, copy the background colour code from the program used to make your web page, usually as RGB values (see pages 310 to 311). Click **OK** then **OK** again to close both dialogue boxes.

Select a shape you like

3 Next, draw a simple graphic. Press **U** for the **Shape** tool, then click the **Custom Shape Tool** in the **Options** bar. Click on **Shape**, then on the right pointing arrow and choose **Shapes**, to select the heart. Click and drag on your canvas to draw a heart. In the **Styles and Effects** box on the right, choose **Layer Styles** in the first menu, then **Wow-Plastic** in the second. Select the red style.

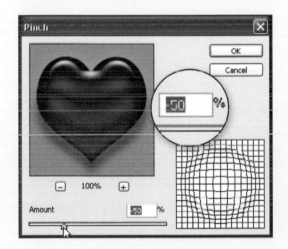

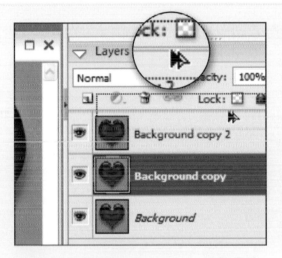

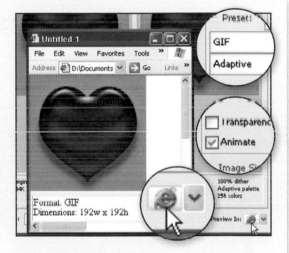

Choose an effect to animate

4 Press **Ctrl+E** to merge the shape with the background. This will be the first image, or 'frame', in your animation. To make another, go to the **Layer** menu and choose **Duplicate Layer**. Click **OK**. For this example, select **Pinch**, found under **Distort** on the **Filter** menu. Drag the **Amount** slider to the left to make the heart bulge, but only go halfway, to **-50%**. Click **OK**.

Add more frames

5 Click **Layer**, **Duplicate Layer** to create a third frame. Look in the **Layers** palette on the right to verify. Holding the **Alt** and **Ctrl** keys, click on the layer named **Background copy** and drag it to the top of the list, then let go. This makes a copy of it called 'Background copy 3'. You now have four frames. To turn them into an animation, go to the **File** menu and choose **Save For Web**.

Save your animation

6 In the **Save For Web** box, below **Preset**, set the first two options to **GIF**, **Adaptive**. Below this, untick **Transparency** and tick **Animate**. At the bottom, **Preview In** should show the Internet Explorer icon. Click on it to play your animation. The heart appears to beat. Close Explorer, and click **OK** to save your animated GIF. For future editing, click **File** then **Save**, to save a Photoshop (.PSD) file.

International gallery

Put your photos on the web where the world can view them

Using Picasa, Google's free photo-management software, you can assemble a professional looking photo album from any collection of images. The album is constructed as a stand-alone web page, which you can view in any browser. Sign up for free web space and you can upload the gallery to the web, where everyone can admire your photos. It's also simple to integrate the gallery into your own website (see 'Your home page', page 256).

PROJECT TOOLS: Picasa, http://picasa.google.co.uk ● Photos ● SmartFTP, www.smartftp.com
SEE ALSO: Your home page, page 256 ● Organising your digital images, page 324

Optimise your images first

Having gathered the image files into one place (step 1), fix any that are faded, too light or too dark. Double-click the thumbnail image in Picasa, click the **Basic Fixes** tab, then try the **I'm Feeling Lucky** button (which fixes most problems at a stroke). If that's not enough, experiment with the other controls here, such as **Auto Contrast**, **Auto Color** and **Fill Light**. When you're finished, click **Back To Library**.

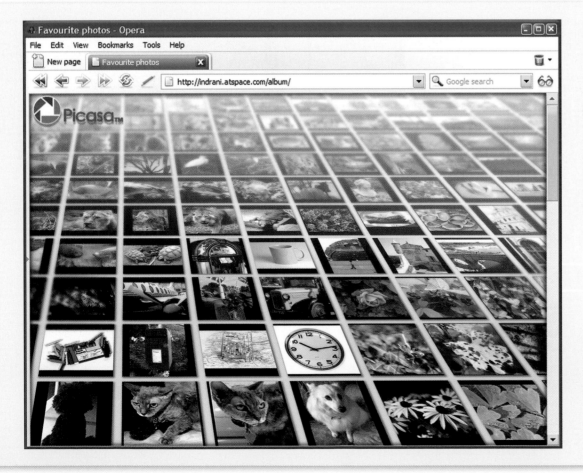

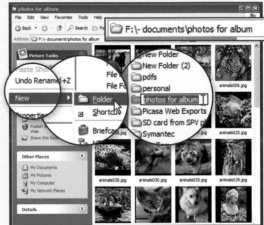

Organise your images

1 Start by gathering into one place all the photos that you want to use. In the Windows Start menu, choose **My Documents**. In the **My Documents** window, right-click the background and choose **New** then **Folder** from the pop-up menu. Name the folder photos for album, then press **Return**. Copy all your photo files into this folder. Don't worry if they are different shapes and sizes.

Album template options

Picasa offers two main types of template (see step 4), with background colour variations in each. The first displays all the thumbnail images in a grid across the page. Click one and the thumbnails are replaced with the photo, shown full screen. The second option (right) creates a frames-based display (similar to that used in the 'Your home page' project, page 256). Thumbnails are in a narrow scrollable frame on the left, with the currently selected photo filling a large frame on the right. Either type will integrate within the frames of your home page (see page 271, steps 14 to 16).

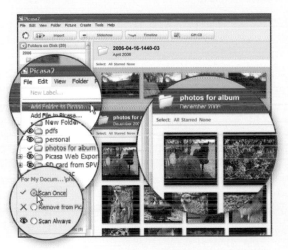

Launch the Picasa software

2 If you haven't got Picasa on your PC, see 'Organising photos with Picasa', page 113, to download and install the program. Then launch **Picasa** and browse to the folder that contains the photos you want to use. If you can't see the folder, click the **File** menu and choose **Add Folder to Picasa**. In the dialogue box, click the **photos for album** folder, tick **Scan Once**, then click **OK**.

Select the photos to use

3 Scroll down the thumbnail images displayed in the main window to find your photos. Just above the thumbnails of your photos, click the button marked **Actions**. In the pop-up menu, choose **Make a Webpage**. The **Export as Web Page** dialogue box appears. Tick **640 pixels** in the size options, and type a title for the web page, such as Favourite photos. Click the **Browse** button.

Generate the album

4 In the **Browse For Folder** dialogue box, click the **MyHomePage** folder in **My Documents**. Or, if it doesn't exist, click **My Documents**, click the **Make New Folder** button, type MyHomePage and press **Return**. Click **OK**. Back in the **Export as Web Page** dialogue box, click **Next**. Choose a template from the list on the left – you can see what each will look like in the panel on the right. Click **Finish**.

Customising your album

Picasa offers few colour or layout options for the photo albums it creates. But, since albums are made up of standard web pages, you can modify every aspect of the finished layout using web-editing software or Microsoft Word. In the **album** folder, right-click the file **index.html** and choose **Edit** from the pop-up menu. Edit the album page as if it were your own home page (see page 256), adding new text, links, colours or background textures.

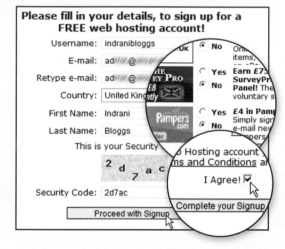

Browse your album

5 Your web browser loads to display the album Picasa has created, so you can see how it will look when it's on the web. Thumbnail images of the photos are displayed. Scroll down to see any that are out of view. Click a thumbnail to see the image full size – in this case, 640 pixels wide. In full-size view, navigation links let you skip forward or backward within the album or revert to the thumbnail view.

Find a web home for your album

6 Your album is ready, but it's on your PC's hard disk. You need somewhere on the web to store the album, known as 'webspace', and a program to transfer files from your PC to that webspace. Your internet provider may offer space for your home pages. But there are free alternatives, such as ATSPACE. In your web browser, type www.atspace.com and press **Return**. When the page loads, click **Sign Up Now Free**.

Sign up for free webspace

7 On the next page, fill in your details and type the security code you see at the bottom of the form. Then click **Proceed with Signup**. Next you'll see a list of offers that you can opt into or out of by ticking **Yes** or **No** boxes. You need to agree to ATSPACE's terms and conditions by ticking the **I Agree** box. Then click **Complete your Signup Now** and in a few minutes you should receive a confirmation email.

○ Download and install SmartFTP

Files are uploaded from your PC to your webspace (see step 6) using a technology known as FTP (File Transfer Protocol). To copy files to the web in this way you need an FTP program such as SmartFTP, which is free for personal use. Start your web browser and type www.smartftp.com, then press **Return**. When the page loads, click **Download SmartFTP 2 Now**. On the download page, click **Download SmartFTP Client (x86)**. On the next page, click **Download Now**. In the next box, click **Save**, then browse to your Windows desktop and click **Save** again. When the file has finished downloading, go to your desktop and double-click its icon, then follow the on-screen instructions, accepting the default options during installation.

To start SmartFTP, click the icon on your desktop, or click the **Start** button, **All Programs**, **SmartFTP Client 2.0**, then **SmartFTP Client**. Each time you run the program you'll see a **Licence Reminder** screen. Personal users can ignore this and click **OK** to proceed.

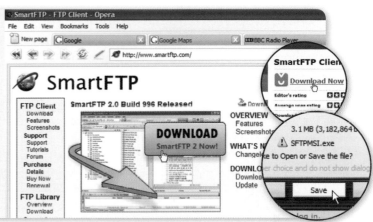

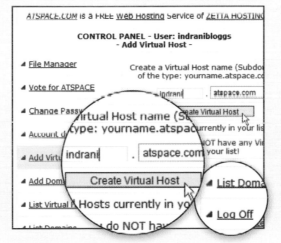

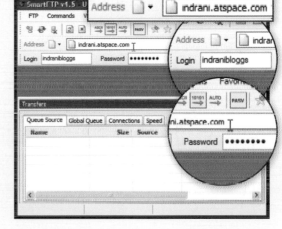

Get your user name and password

8 Check your email at the email address you gave in step 7. An email from ATSPACE gives you a user name and a password. Click the link to the signup web page, www.atspace.com/members, just below. Next, click the button marked **FREE Hosting Control Panel**, enter the user name and password, and click the **Login** button. On the Control Panel page, click **Add Virtual Host**.

Choose your web address

9 In the blank box next to **.atspace.com** type a name – your name, for example. This, added to .atspace.com will be what people need to type in order to get to your website. So, the web address (or URL, which stands for Unique Resource Locator), is http://yourname.atspace.com. Click **Create Virtual Host**. Back at the **Control Panel** page, click **Log Off**. (You can add as many names in this way as you like.)

Log into your web space

10 If you haven't done so yet, download and install SmartFTP (see the box above) to transfer your files. Make sure you're connected to the internet, then start SmartFTP. In the **Address** box at the top, type your URL (without the http://), for example yourname.atspace.com. In the **Login** box, type your user name and, in the **Password** box, type your password (see step 8), then press **Return**.

The Photoshop Elements alternative

In a few clicks, Photoshop Elements also can produce a web-ready photo album with sophisticated buttons and backgrounds. Start the program and, on the **Welcome** screen, click **View and Organize Photos**. In the **Organizer** window, click the **File** menu and choose **Get Photos**, then **From Files and Folders**. Browse to the folder that contains your photos, highlight all the image files you want to use (hold **Ctrl** and click to make multiple selections), then click **OK**. Thumbnail images of the photos appear in the **Organizer** window. In the **File** menu, click **Create** then **HTML Photo Gallery**. On the next screen you'll choose a design theme for the album, add a banner title, and set caption and thumbnail fonts and sizes.

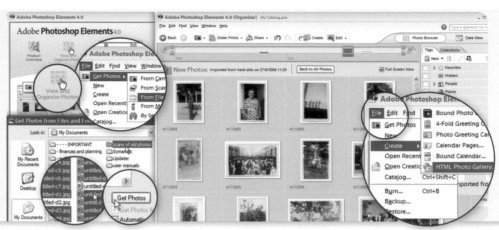

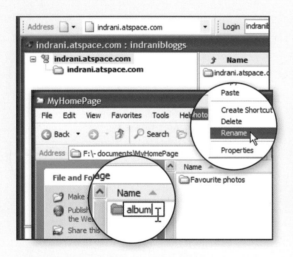

Rename the album folder

11 A window opens in SmartFTP. In the left pane are folders for any webspace names you created (see step 9). Now click the **Start** button, click **My Documents** and double-click **MyHomePage**. You'll see a folder with the same name as the album title you gave in step 3 – for example, Favourite photos. Right-click the folder and choose **Rename** from the pop-up menu. Type album and press **Return**.

Upload your files

12 Click the **album** folder and press **Ctrl+C** to copy it. Then switch back to SmartFTP by clicking its icon in the Windows **Taskbar**. In the left pane, click your webspace folder. Its contents are displayed on the right – just one file to begin with, called **index.htm**. Right-click in the right pane and choose **Paste** from the pop-up menu. After a while, your album folder and its files upload to the webspace.

View your album on the web

13 Launch your web browser. In the address box, type yourname.atspace.com/album (where yourname is the name you gave in step 9). You'll see your album exactly as it was displayed in step 9, but the images are coming from the web, not from your PC – so anyone who types in the address can view your album. You could include a link in emails to let friends know your album is online.

Click the **Gallery Style** drop-down box at the top to select from a long list of themes. Then, in the **Destination** section at the bottom, click the **Browse** button, choose where your album files will be saved (such as the **MyHomePage** folder created in step 4), then click **OK**. Type a name in the **Site Folder** box, such as gallery, and click **Save**. When Elements has finished building the album, you'll see your images displayed in a browser window.

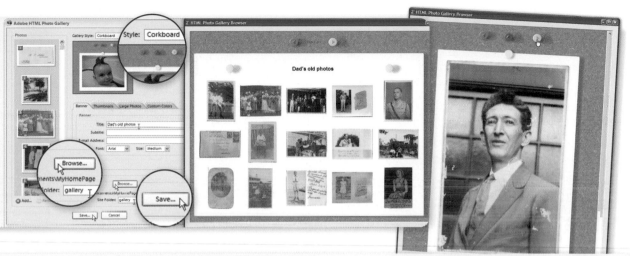

Add a link from your home page

14 If you've built a home page (see page 256), click **Start**, **My Documents**. Double-click **MyHomePage** to see your web-page files. Right-click **index.htm** and, from the pop-up menu, choose **Open With**, then **Microsoft Office Word**. In the 'Your home page' project you made three menu buttons on the left. Click the middle one (**Photos**). Then right-click it and choose **Hyperlink** from the pop-up menu.

Configure the menu button

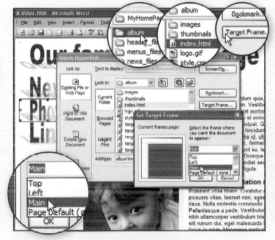

15 In the **Insert Hyperlink** dialogue box, navigate to the album folder and double-click it. Among the files inside the folder, you'll see one named **index.html**. Click it once to highlight the file. Next click the **Target Frame** button. In the **Set Target Frame** box, click the drop-down box on the right and choose **Main**. Click **OK**, then click **OK** again. Press **Ctrl+S** to save your home page files.

View your home page

16 Using Windows Explorer (see step 14), navigate to your home page folder (**MyHomePage**) and double-click the file **index.htm**. Your page loads. Click the **Photos** button on the left – in the main window you'll see your photo album, just as in step 5, but now integrated into the frames of your home page. To upload your home page to the web, see 'How to show off your website', page 263.

World wide diary

Share your thoughts and experiences with the world via a weblog

Want to get creative, share your thoughts on issues you care about, make new friends, and perhaps even earn a little money? Then start a 'blog', which is essentially an online diary or journal, on a hobby or any topic that interests you. It's fun, free and requires no special knowledge or technical expertise. Follow the steps in this project and you can join the millions of people already in the blogging world.

PROJECT TOOLS: MSN Spaces, http://spaces.msn.com
SEE ALSO: Getting started with the internet and email, page 14 ● Your home page, page 256

● Blogging for free

Dedicated 'blog hosting' websites provide a home for your online diary where visitors can read your musings, browse photos, watch videos, and even contribute their own thoughts and ideas. There are many blogging sites where you can sign up for free (see 'Choosing where to blog', right), and most offer simple ways for you to update the content of your blog – by email, for example – while travelling. Blogs are indexed, too, so potential visitors with similar interests can find your blog more easily.

Get some inspiration

1 If you're wondering what to write, and how to write it, explore the blog world for inspiration. Search for blog topics that interest you at Google, http://blogsearch.google.com, and Blog Catalog, www.blogcatalog.com, or explore lists of popular blogs at Technorati, www.technorati.com/pop/blogs, Daypop, www.daypop.com/blogrank, or the blog tracker blo.gs, http://blo.gs/most-watched.php.

● Choosing where to blog

MSN Spaces is used in this project to build a blog, but there are plenty of free alternatives if you'd like to experiment with other solutions. Blogger (far right), www.blogger.com, is a well-established Spaces competitor; BlogSource (near right), www.blogsource.com, has a large and varied range of page-design templates; BlogDrive, www.blogdrive.com, allows multiple authors to work on one blog; and Bloglegion (mid right), www.bloglegion.com, lets you add photo albums, podcasting and friends lists to your blog pages.

Find an online home

2 Setting up and running a blog on your own can be tricky, so as a first-time 'blogger' use a service such as MSN Spaces. It's easy to use, has many powerful features and is free. Visit the Spaces site and follow the **Sign Up** link to begin, then complete the registration form and choose a login password (or you can use your existing Microsoft Passport password, if you have one).

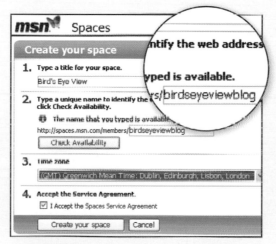

A name to remember

3 You need an imaginative name for your blog, rather than just 'Brian's Blog', for example. The blog shown here is about wildlife, so it's called 'Bird's Eye View'. Pick a variation on that for your web address, 'BirdsEyeViewBlog', and click **Check Availability** to make sure no one else is using it. Finally, select your time zone, read the service agreement, tick **I Accept** and click **Create your space**.

Is your blog public or private?

4 At first, your Spaces blog can only be viewed by people on your MSN Messenger contact list. If you don't use MSN Messenger or want more flexibility, click the **Change Permissions** link. Now you may either select **Public** to let everyone view your blog, or **Private** to restrict it to people you specify. You then enter their email addresses in the box, click **Add** and tick the box next to their names.

● Get paid to blog?

Blogging is about fun, not profit, yet successful blogs can make at least a little cash by including adverts, although these can drive some visitors away and you can't put them on all blogs. If you're interested in using adverts, you can try an advertising scheme such as Google AdSense (right), at www.google.com/adsense, which is supported directly by the blog-creation site Blogger, www.blogger.com.

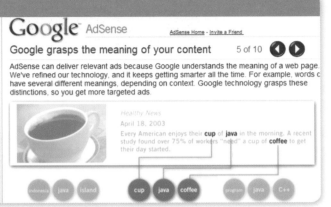

Google AdSense AdSense Home - Invite a Friend

Google grasps the meaning of your content   5 of 10

AdSense can deliver relevant ads because Google understands the meaning of a web page. We've refined our technology, and it keeps getting smarter all the time. For example, words can have several different meanings, depending on context. Google technology grasps these distinctions, so you get more targeted ads.

Healthy News
April 18, 2003
Every American enjoys their **cup** of **java** in the morning. A recent study found over 75% of workers "need" a cup of **coffee** to get their day started.

● Quality over quantity

It's important to update your blog at least weekly, ideally every one or two days, to prevent your audience losing interest and moving elsewhere. But frequency isn't the whole story and it's more important to concentrate on the quality of your content. If you write interesting, informative and detailed pieces then readers will stick around, even if they only visit every couple of weeks or so.

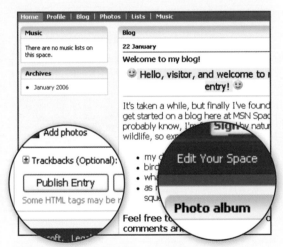

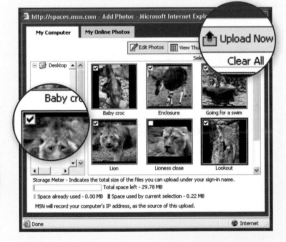

Your first entry

5 Click **Blog**, then **Add Entry**. Enter a title and type your first story in the box: a simple welcome message and details about your blog. The toolbar has options to give the entry a more interesting look – you can make text bold, italic or underlined, set background colours, add emoticons (facial expression icons) and more. Hover your cursor over a button to see an explanation of what it does.

Preview what your visitors see

6 Click **Publish Entry**, then **Preview My Space** on the top right to see how your blog will appear. This is a good start, but adding some digital photos would help give the blog more colour and personality, as well as offering your visitors more content to browse. MSN Spaces allows you to build photo albums accessible from the main blog page, so click **Edit Your Space** then **Create**.

Look for images

7 Enter a descriptive album title such as 'African holiday 2006' and click **Add Photos**. If Internet Explorer displays a warning that the 'MSN Photo Upload Control' is needed, click the yellow bar at the top of the window and select **Install ActiveX Control** then **Install**. Use the Windows Explorer-like window to browse images on your hard drive, tick the box next to any you'd like to share then click **Upload Now**.

Finding readers

A good blog needs great content first but then you must find people to read it. Start by telling your friends and online contacts about the blog. Include the 'URL' (the web address) in your email signature, and spread the word in any web forums you participate in. Submit your web address to as many online blog directories and registers as possible, such as Blogwise, www.blogwise.com, Blog Catalog, www.blogcatalog.com, and Bloghub, www.bloghub.com.

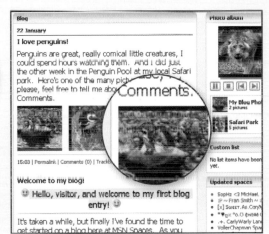

Build a photo album

8 It may take a little while for your photos to upload, especially if you've selected many of them. Drag and drop the thumbnail images in the viewing bar if you wish to reorder them, clicking **Save** and **Close** when you're done. Your photo album automatically appears as a small slideshow whenever people view your blog, or they can use the **Full Size** button to see the complete image.

Add some captions

9 To use images in blog entries, click **Home**, **Add Entry** and then **Add Photos**, browse for some images to include, tick the box to their left and select **Upload Now**. You won't see the images on screen yet, only their names, but they will appear when visitors view your blog. Type in a comment or two about the images and click **Publish Entry** and then **Preview My Space** to see the entry.

Make and add a list

10 Your blog now looks much better, but you can make further improvements. MSN Spaces lets you create 'Lists' on anything you choose, such as favourite books, films or holiday destinations, which is a fun way for your visitors to discover more about you. Think of a topic, click **Edit My Space**, **Edit List**, then click **Add Item** and type in a description for the items you want to list.

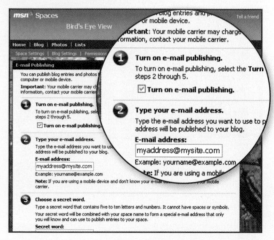

Putting in links

11 By adding links to associated sites, lists can be useful for your audience as well as entertaining. Use Google, www.google.com, to find websites, click **Edit** for each item and add a web address. Click **Rename List** when you've finished and change the current name from **Custom List** to something more descriptive. Click **Preview My Space** to see how the finished list will appear.

The personal touch

12 You're still using the default layout. To give your site a more individual look, click **Edit My Space** then **Customize**. Select **Themes** to choose a new colour scheme and background. Click **Modules** to remove features you don't require, such as **Music List**, and reorganise others by dragging and dropping. Feel free to try out options; Spaces only records your changes when you click **Save**.

Update from almost anywhere

13 Spaces blogs can be updated via email, so you can post entries from a mobile phone that has email. Click **Settings**, **E-mail Publishing** then tick **Turn on e-mail publishing**. Type in the email address you'll use for updates, choose a password then decide whether your entries will be saved as drafts (in which case they won't go online until you return to your PC) or published immediately.

● Advertise your updates

To alert your audience to blog updates as you upload them, rather than relying on random visits to the site in the hope of some new content, try out Real Simple Syndication (RSS). To turn this on in MSN Spaces, check your blog is set up for public access by going to **Settings** and then **Permissions**. Click **Settings, Space Settings** and then tick the **Syndicate** box. To explore the MSN Alerts system further, visit www.alerts.msn.com.

● Stay out of trouble

Blogs are all about free speech but you still need to be careful what you write. If you disagree with someone, by all means say why, but don't libel them by making accusations that you couldn't back up in court. Don't copy text or graphics from other sites and pass it off as your own. Be aware of any other restrictions imposed by your blogging service (see www.spaces.msn.com/coc.aspx for Spaces Code of Conduct).

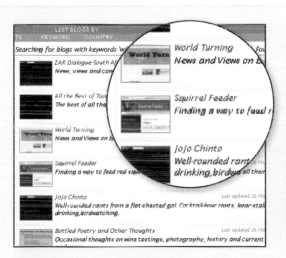

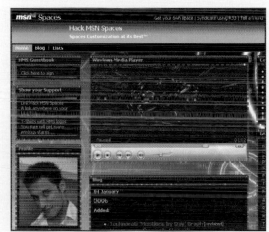

Publish your updates

14 Spaces now displays an email address for updating your blog. Add this to the address book on the mobile phone you'll use. Any emails sent from your nominated email account to that address will go straight to the blog. This is handy, but be careful, especially when using internet cafés, as anyone who discovers the email address will have update access to your blog, too.

Attract visitors

15 By now you have a great-looking blog with plenty of interesting pictures and stories, so the next step is to attract visitors. Try to find blogs you like on the same topic as yours in a directory such as Blogwise, www.blogwise.com, then link to or write a blog entry about them. Send an email to the author, who may then link back to you, so sending some visitors your way.

Get more tips and advice

16 Now that you've seen how to set up and run your own blog, you can pick up advanced tips on blogging by visiting the Hack MSN Spaces blog, http://spaces.msn.com/d3vmax. For more general advice on blogging look at the Blogger Forum, www.bloggerforum.com, Blogger Tips, www.bloggertips.com, and Blogging Pro, www.bloggingpro.com.

Get together

Meet and share ideas and interests in your own online group

The internet lets you keep in touch through emails, instant messages and even talking face to face using webcams. By forming an internet group, you can pull all those things together and create a shared place where you and other people – friends and family, or even strangers who share a particular interest – can exchange messages, swap photographs, chat and arrange meetings. With the help of Microsoft's free MSN Groups service, your group will be up and running in minutes.

PROJECT TOOLS: MSN Groups, http://groups.msn.com
SEE ALSO: Set up a blog, page 272 • Build your own website, page 256

● Ready-made groups

If your group is based around a hobby or interest, visit other groups on the same topic, and make new contacts by posting messages and links to your group home page. Use the **Search** feature in MSN Groups, as well as Google Groups, http://groups.google.com, and Yahoo Groups, http://groups.yahoo.com.

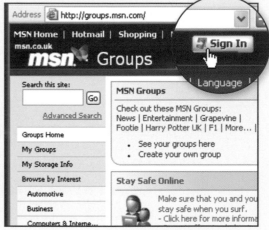

Sign in at MSN Groups

1 Groups can be based on any topic that you're interested in. For this project, it's a place where your family can share memories. MSN Groups is free to use, but you'll need a .NET Passport (see 'Get a .NET Passport', page 16). Start your web browser, go to http://groups.msn.com and click the **Sign In** button at the top. The first time you sign in, the .NET Passport Wizard will start (see box, above right).

○ Running the Passport Wizard

The very first time you click the MSN Groups **Sign In** button, the **Windows XP Passport Wizard** starts automatically. This adds the Passport ID details you chose (see page 16) to Windows on your PC, so you won't need to type them in each time. When the **Passport Wizard** appears, click **Next**. Tick **Yes, use my existing e-mail address** then click **Next**. Tick **Yes, sign in with my Passport Network credentials**. Click **Next**. Type in your Passport email address and password, and tick **Associate my Password Network account with my Windows user account**. Click **Next** then click **Finish**. Back at the MSN Groups home page, you are now signed in. The Wizard is a once-only process – the next time you visit this page, a single click of the **Sign In** button signs you in.

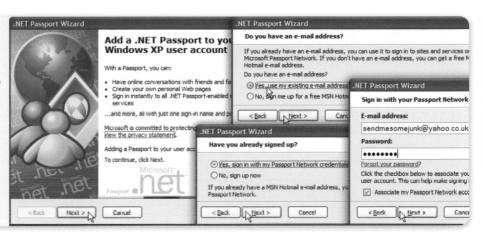

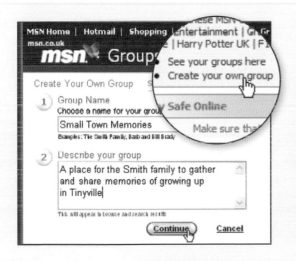

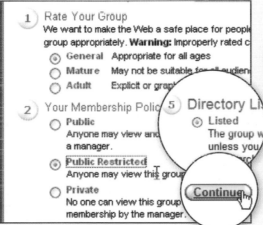

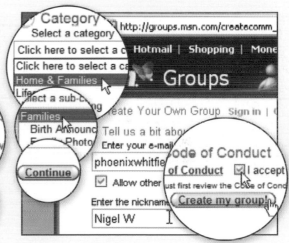

Name and describe your group

2 Click **Create Your Own Group** and start adding your details. You need a short, simple name for your group, then, in the next box, type a description. The words you type here will be found when people search for groups, so include anything important that will help lost relatives find your pages. Be specific, so people will know what the group is for when they join. Click **Continue**.

Choose group settings

3 Next, under **Rate Your Group**, tick **General**, since the content will be suitable for family viewing. This group is for your family members and friends so, under **Your Membership Policy**, tick **Public Restricted** – anyone can view messages, but people need your permission to join. Scroll down and, under **Directory Listing**, tick **Listed**, to include details of your group in the MSN directory. Click **Continue**.

Let them know who's boss

4 Choose a category and sub-category for your group, then click **Continue**. In the next page, choose an **MSN Nickname**, which will be used whenever you post messages in the group. By **Code of Conduct**, tick **I accept**, then click **Create my group** to set up the group with you as the 'manager', which means you add new members, approve messages and make sure the group runs smoothly.

● Organise your page list

Your group website is divided into pages, listed down the left side of the home page. Not all of these will necessarily be of interest to your group – you may, for example, want to remove the **Chat** page. To change the order pages are listed in, or to rename, delete or hide pages, click **Manage Pages** in the **Manager Tools** section of the home page. When you've finished managing the page list, click the **Save Changes** button.

○ Email everyone at once

When you have something urgent or important to announce, click **What's New** to get to the home page. Then, under **Manager Tools** on the right, click **Send an Announcement to All Members**. Type the subject and the message you want to email, then click **Send Message**, below. Every member will receive an email, regardless of their email settings. To avoid emails 'bouncing back', check regularly that your email list is up to date.

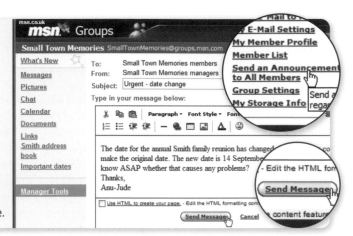

View your group

5 The group's home page is displayed. Make a note of the web address, shown in your browser's address bar, so that you can return when you wish. Tell family members, so they can join up by visiting the home page. Make a note, too, of the email address that's shown below **Group E-Mail Address** – when you send an email to this address, all the members of your group will receive it.

Invite people to join

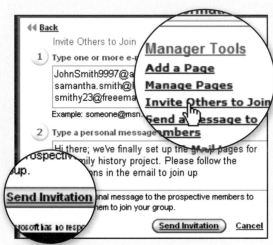

6 Under **Manager Tools** on the right, click **Invite Others to Join**. In the upper box, type the email addresses of any people you want to invite, with a comma between each one. In the box below, type a short message explaining what the group is for, then click the **Send Invitation** button. Your invitees will receive an invitation email with instructions on how to join the group. Click **Go to Home Page**.

Approving new members

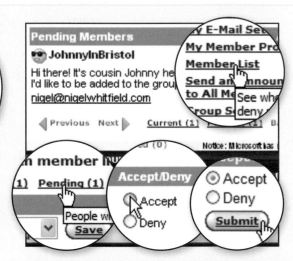

7 In step 3 you opted for visitors to require your permission to become members. So you should check from time to time to see if anyone has asked to join. Under **Manager Tools** on the home page click **Member List**. Next, click on **Pending** to see a list of the people who want to join. Click **Accept** or **Deny** next to their messages, then click **Submit** to update the member list.

○ Using the shared calendar

MSN Groups comes with a built-in calendar that all members can access. The calendar has **Day**, **Week** and **Month** views, accessed by clicking the tabs along the top. To add a new entry, click the **New** tab or double-click on the day of the event or appointment. Then type the **Subject** and **Location**, choose **Start** and **End** times, and add any notes you want. If it's a recurring event, such as a birthday, click **Recurrence** on the right, then choose how often the event repeats and for how long. Click **Save**. To display a personal calendar, for appointments you don't want to share with the whole group, click the **My Calendar** tab.

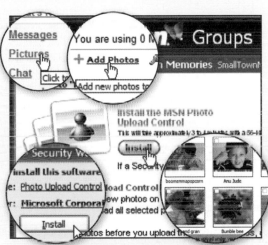

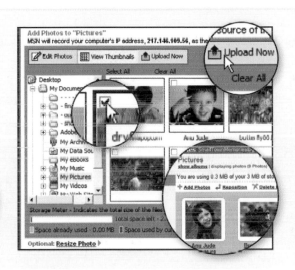

Edit the group's welcome message

8 Click **Back** to return to the group's home page, then click **Edit Welcome Message**. In the text box, type an introduction to the group – use the buttons above to choose fonts and format the text. Click the **Save Welcome Message** button when you're finished, to return to the home page. The new welcome message is displayed and will be seen by anyone who visits the group.

Install the Photo Upload Control

9 Click **Pictures** in the list at the left of the home page, to see the group's photo album. There are no pictures in there yet, so click **Add Photos**. The first time you upload, you'll see a screen like the one shown here. Click **Install** to add the **Photo Upload Control**. When the **Security Warning** box appears, click **Install**. The **Upload Control**'s browser window appears, showing thumbnails of photos on your PC.

Choose photos for the group album

10 Using the folders list on the left, browse your PC's hard drive to find pictures for your group page. Tick the small box at the top left of each picture you want to select, then click **Upload Now**. In a few moments the group's photo album appears, displaying thumbnails of the photos you've uploaded. Visitors can click these to display large-size versions of the photos.

Instant chat with group members

Use your group page as a handy way to keep in touch with friends and family, since the group page tells you which of the members is online and available to chat. Click **Chat** in the list on the left of your group home page. The first time that you access the **Chat** page, the browser downloads and installs MSN Chat Software (click **OK** when you see the security warning, as in step 9). When the **Chat** page appears, type your message in the box at the bottom, then click **Send**. Your message and replies from other members appear in the main window.

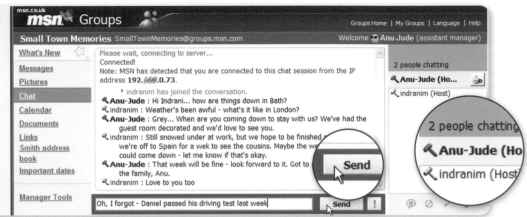

Start a discussion

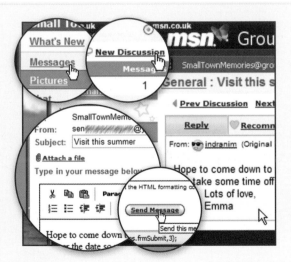

11 You and other members of the group can read messages on the group's pages on the web, as well as by email. Click the **Messages** link at the left of the home page to see the group's discussions. To start a discussion on a new topic click the **New Discussion** button above the messages. In the box that appears, type a subject title and your message, then click **Send Message** at the bottom.

Reply to messages

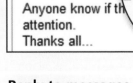

12 To add your response to any message, click the **Reply** button just above it and a text input box will open. As in step 8, you can choose different fonts and sizes and even link a file to the message or include a picture within it. When you've finished composing your reply, click the **Send Message** button at the bottom. The original message is displayed, with your reply beneath.

Add links to websites

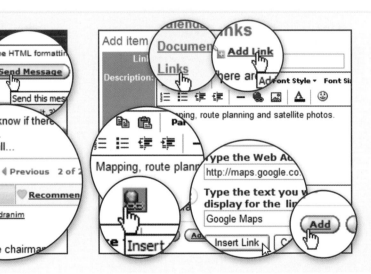

13 If you know websites that may be useful to others in your group, add them to the pages. On the left of the home page, click on **Links**, then **Add Link**. In the **Description** box, add a few words about the site. Then, to the top right of the box, click the small **Insert web link** button. A box appears – type the address of the website and, below, its name, then click **Insert Link**. Click **Add**.

● Alternative places to set up your online group

MSN Groups isn't the only way of setting up a shared space on the internet for you and your family. If you subscribe to AOL, create a group at http://groups.aol.com, and anyone can join, whether they subscribe to AOL or not. Yahoo! provides a group service too, at http://groups.yahoo.com, which anyone can use. Google has a similar free service, which you can sign up to at http://groups.google.co.uk.

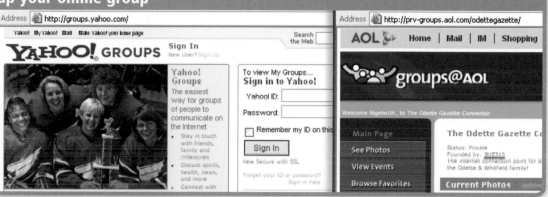

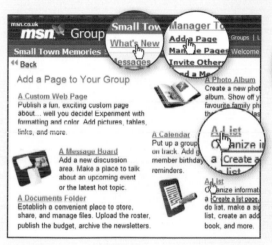

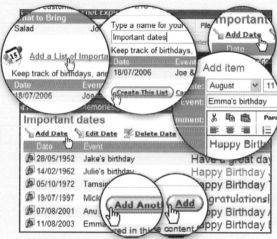

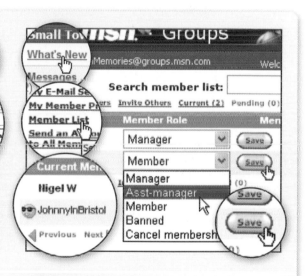

Make a new page

14 MSN Groups lets you add new pages to your group. Among these are lists of various kinds – announcements, recipes, important dates and member contacts – that can help keep the group members organised and in touch. Click **What's New** to get back to the home page, then click **Add a Page** in the **Manager Tools** list on the right. Click **A List** to see the types of list available.

Create a family birthday list

15 Scroll down the page and click **Add a List of Important Dates**. Name your list Important dates, then click **Create This List**. There are no entries yet, so click **Add Date** at the top right of the list. On the **Add item** screen, type the date of birth for the first entry, with the name of the event and a brief comment. Click **Add Another** to add a new entry, or **Add** if you've finished adding to the list.

Promote group members

16 As your group grows, you may want to share the work of managing. Click **What's New** to get back to the home page. Then, below **Manager Tools** on the right, click **Member List**. You'll see a list of the group members and their roles. To promote a member – to manager or assistant manager – click the **Member Role** box and pick a new role from the drop-down list. Click **Save**.

A special announcement
Design an illustrated, animated email greeting

Emails don't have to be just plain text. Software such as Outlook Express, the standard email program that comes with Windows, can send and receive messages that are formatted just like web pages. So you can change the colour and size of text, display pictures within a message, and even incorporate animations and sounds.

PROJECT TOOLS: Outlook Express ● Digital photo ● GIF animation file ● Sound clip

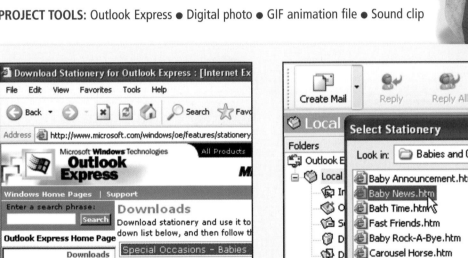

Download some free stationery

1 Run Outlook Express by choosing **E-mail** from the **Start** menu. Select **Options** from the **Tools** menu. Click the **Compose** tab, then click **Download More**. Internet Explorer opens. Click the link to **Download More Stationery**, pick **Special Occasions – Babies** from the drop-down list and click **Download Now**. In the **Save As** dialogue box, browse to your Windows desktop and choose **Save**.

Create a new message

2 On your desktop, double-click the file you've downloaded (**Babies.exe**) to install the new stationery. Go back to Outlook Express. Click the black triangle next to **Create Mail** and choose **Select Stationery**. The stationery templates files are listed here. In the **Special Occasions** folder, in a sub-folder named **Babies and Children**, select your new stationery, then click **OK** to create a new message.

Enter your own text

3 There's a background, a header graphic and some sample text. Highlight the text and type in your own. Stick to common fonts. If you choose one that your recipient doesn't have installed, the message won't display as it should. Those fonts referred to as 'web safe' include Arial, Comic Sans, Times New Roman, Courier New, Georgia, Trebuchet, Impact and Verdana. See page 326 for more on fonts.

Free graphics and sound

Many websites offer free clip-art graphics, animations and sounds you can download and use in your emails. Try entering **"web graphics"**, **"animated gifs"** or **"audio clips"** into a search engine such as Google, www.google.com. To download an image displayed on a web page, right-click on it, then choose **Save Picture As** from the pop-up menu that appears. Useful websites include www.bestanimations.com, www.clubunlimited.com, www.freeaudioclips.com, www.gifmania.co.uk **and** www.wavcentral.com.

How to add a sound clip to your message

You can give your greeting a sound that plays when it's opened. All popular sound types are supported, including WAV and MP3 (see page 332), so you could use anything from a brief sound effect to a complete song. Stick to small sound files, though, as larger than 1Mb may take a long time to download, especially if your recipient has a slow internet connection. In the **Format** menu, choose **Background**, **Sound**. Click **Browse**, select a sound file from your hard disk then click **Open**. Click **OK** to apply and hear the sound.

Add a picture to the email

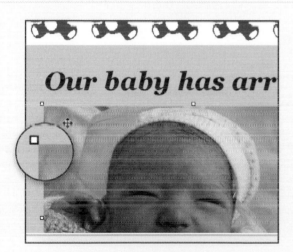

4 Press **Return** after your title to make a blank line, then click the **Insert Picture** button at the end of the toolbar. In the dialogue box, click **Browse**. Double-click an image file then click **OK** to import it. Choose a photo that's not too big (500 pixels wide is ideal). Larger images could mean unnecessary scrolling and long download times. To adjust size, click it, then drag the square handles on the corners.

Complete your message

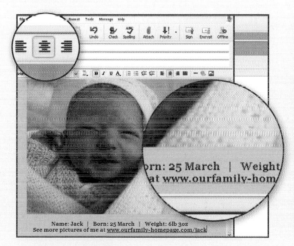

5 Centre everything on the page by pressing **Ctrl+A** and clicking the **Center** button in the toolbar. This helps keep everything aligned whatever screen size or resolution the message will be viewed in. Add any more text you want below the picture. If you enter a web address, for example to your own home page, Outlook Express automatically turns it into an underlined link that the recipient can click.

Insert an animation

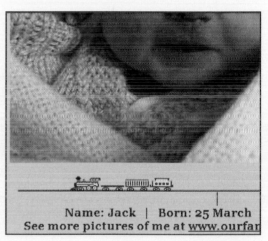

6 Animated graphics in GIF format are widely available (see the box above), so why not use one to jazz up your greeting? Having downloaded a GIF file, add it to your message as you did with the picture in step 4. Make a blank line for it so that it doesn't appear in the middle of a line of text, then use **Insert Picture** as in step 4. Avoid resizing these graphics, as they won't look good.

Hello world

Start your own podcasts and become an internet radio star

If you've ever listened to a radio show and thought 'I could do that', now's your chance. Record your own show – on any subject you feel passionate about – on your PC and then use the internet to broadcast it to the whole world, for free. It's called 'podcasting' and anyone can do it. To record and edit your show you'll use a program called Audacity – a digital sound recorder that you can download free from http://audacity.sourceforge.net.

PROJECT TOOLS: Microphone ● PC speakers ● Audacity sound recorder (see above)
SEE ALSO: Recording and making music, page 332 ● Karaoke party time, page 228

SEE ALSO: Recording and making music, page 332 ● Karaoke party time, page 228

Broadcasting standards

There's more than one way to create and promote your podcast. You can do it for free as this project explains, or you can pay for the privilege. Both have their pros and cons. Start out using the free software and services that are available on the web and then, as you become experienced, you may want to invest in better recording equipment or more storage for your podcasts. For a comprehensive list of podcasting software and services, go to www.podcastingnews.com.

Recording your voice

1 Plug in and set up your microphone (see page 230). Load the Audacity recording program. Click on the down arrow above the main window to open the drop-down list of input options; select either **Microphone** or **Analog Mix**. Click the red **Record** button and start speaking. As you do, a blue squiggly line appears that represents the sound of your voice.

● Watch what you say

Although the internet promotes free speech, there are laws that apply to both what you can say and what you can broadcast. You shouldn't need to check with a lawyer, just use your common sense about what you say. Make sure you don't use material without the permission of the copyright holder and that you don't use your new-found podcast fame to defame anybody else.

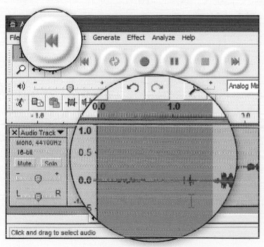

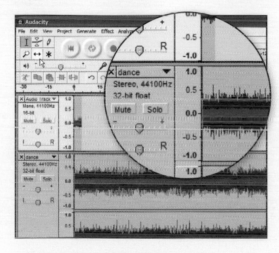

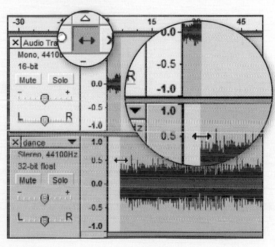

Remove awkward silences

2 Click the yellow **Stop** button to finish recording. Then click the purple **Skip to start** button to rewind, and click **Play** to hear your recording. To rerecord choose **Undo** from the **Edit** menu. If you have a silence at the beginning before you spoke, move the cursor to where the squiggles begin and, holding down the mouse button, drag left. Let go then press **Delete** on your keyboard.

Add a prerecorded clip

3 If you want to add some music to your recording, go to the **Project** menu and choose **Import Audio**. Navigate to where the music file is stored, click on it then click **Open**. Audacity adds it as a new stereo track underneath the one you've already recorded. First reduce the volume of the audio track then click **Play** to hear your voice and the music playing together.

Arrange the order of play

4 Now the spoken intro you recorded and the imported song start playing at the same time. To fix this so the intro starts first, select the **Time Shift** tool (the double-headed arrow button towards the top left of the screen). Click and drag the bottom sound file to the right so that it doesn't start to play until the top one finishes. Click **Play** again then readjust the clip's position if you need to.

Tune in to podcasts

Listening to what other people have created is inspirational and informative. Before you create your own podcast, use a free program like Apple's iTunes to listen to others. Load iTunes (see page 238) and click **Podcasts** in the left-hand column. From here you can listen to any podcast in the directory by clicking on it, or click the **Subscribe** button, bottom right, to receive the current show and all future episodes automatically.

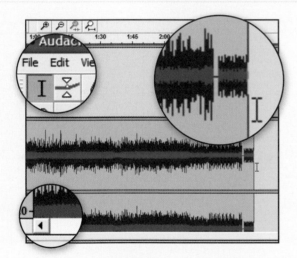

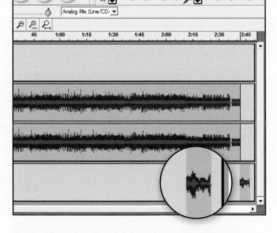

Some more talking

5 Before adding another voice track you need to indicate to Audacity at which point the new recording should begin. Use the horizontal scroll bar at the bottom of the screen to scroll the tracks along to the left so that you can see the end of the piece of music you imported. Switch back to the standard (I-shaped) cursor at the top left of the screen and click once at the end of the music track.

See your recordings

6 Record your voice again as in step 1. Audacity creates a new track, but it's probably not visible on screen. To see everything you've recorded, go to the **View** menu and choose **Fit in Window**. Then from the **View** menu choose **Fit Vertically** and you'll see your new recording in the bottom track. Carry on adding voiceovers and importing audio files until you've finished.

Identity tags

7 Go to the **File** menu and choose **Export as MP3**. Audacity opens a box telling you that your recordings will be mixed into a single stereo recording. Click **OK**. In the dialogue box that appears, navigate to where you want to store the podcast then type in a name for it. Click **Save**, then fill in the form shown above. These 'tags' will help to identify your podcast later on.

● Promote your show in iTunes

Since iTunes is so popular, it makes sense to get your show included in its listings. Create your podcast as shown in this project, then go to www.podomatic.com (see below) and click **Podcast**. When you reach your show page, click the **Personalize my podcast** link. When the new screen appears, click the **iTunes** tab and then click the **Apple's website** link. Follow the instructions to add your podcast to iTunes' directory. You will need iTunes installed on your PC (see page 238) and have set up an account at the iTunes Music Store, but promoting your podcast is free.

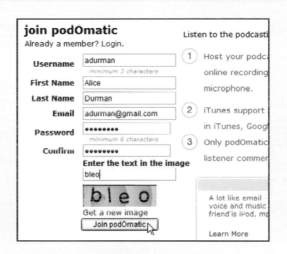

Prepare to broadcast

8 Now you've created your show, you need to find somewhere on the internet to store and broadcast it. Go to www.podcastingnews.com, scroll down the page and find the **Resource Pages** on the left. Click **Podcast Hosts** and it displays a selection of sites that you can podcast from. To follow this example, go to www.podomatic.com and click on the **Register** link at the top of the page.

Set up a podOmatic account

9 Invent a user name for yourself and type it into the box indicated. Now type in your real name and email address. Next, think of a password – it must be six or more characters long – type it into the **Password** box, and then again in the **Confirm** box. Finally, type in the characters that appear in the image at the bottom. Finish by clicking the **Join podOmatic** button.

Describe your show

10 You're now asked to fill in some details about your 'station', including its title, a 'tagline' and some keywords that describe the station's content. You can also add a picture of yourself or of a logo for the show that you've created using an image-editing program. Click **Browse**, navigate to where the picture is stored on your PC and then click **Open**.

Ex-directory podcasts

Here's how to subscribe to a podcast that isn't listed in iTunes. Use Google to search for podcasts and then go to one of the directories listed, such as www.podcastalley.com. Find a show you're interested in, select it and then click **Subscribe**. Copy the podcast address and switch back to iTunes. In iTunes, click the **Advanced** menu and choose **Subscribe to Podcast**. Paste the address into the box and click **OK**.

Do it in style

11 From the next screen, select any categories that you think describe your podcast. Hold down the **Ctrl** key as you click the mouse if you need to choose more than one. Choose a visual style for your page from the choice of four at the bottom. In this example, the **Candy** theme is being selected. Click the **Save all preferences** button and your podcast page is finished.

Attract listeners

12 Click on the **Click Here** link on the show page and fill in the boxes on the screen that appears. These describe the type of show that you've recorded together with keyword tags and information on its content. The more detail you can include here the better the chance you have of attracting listeners. When you've finished adding details, click the **Import** button.

Upload your show

13 After a moment, your web browser will open a new window. When it appears, click the **Browse** button. You'll see a standard Windows file box. Navigate to where you stored your podcast on the hard disk, click it once to select it and then click **Open**. Back at the web browser window, click the **Use File** button. After a moment, your podcast will start to upload.

Using Audacity's effects

This project describes Audacity's most basic recording features, but the program lets you do much more. This includes adding special effects to your podcast such as reverb and echo, as well as introducing smooth fades so that one sound clip blends smoothly into the next. Although more sophisticated audio editors exist, Audacity has all the features you need to get started in podcasting and, best of all, it's free.

Sounds across the universe

You can hear what it's like out in the far reaches of the universe via podcasts produced by NASA's Jet Propulsion Laboratory (JPL) in Pasadena, California. The lab has sent robotic spacecraft to every planet in the Solar System except Pluto. JPL missions also study the universe beyond, searching for Earth-like planets around far-flung stars.

The podcasts include sounds made from radio emissions during a lightning storm on Saturn, which is much like the crackling noise on a radio during a thunderstorm on Earth. There are also interviews with NASA scientists. For the podcast news feed go to www.jpl.nasa.gov/multimedia/podcast.

Send email invitations

14 Click the **Publish** button. If you use Yahoo!, Gmail or Hotmail, podOmatic can import email addresses from your address book. If not, you can type them into the boxes provided. Once you've added addresses, scroll down and you'll see that podOmatic has automatically written an email inviting people to listen to your podcast. Click on the **To send** link to dispatch the mails.

Play your broadcast

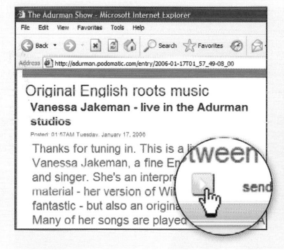

15 At the next screen, click the **Back** link and podOmatic will take you to your podcast radio station screen, where you'll see the entry for your first podcast. You'll see the title for your show, the description underneath and also a green **Play** button at the bottom. As you add further shows, they'll be listed on this screen. For now, click on the green button to play the podcast.

Listen up

16 After a moment, podOmatic opens a window and displays the Windows Media Player controls, the picture you uploaded in one of the previous steps, plus links on the left that allow listeners to recommend your podcast to their friends, leave comments for you and so on. Click the **X** at the top right to close the window and stop the podcast when you want to stop listening.

Just the job

Impress employers by posting your CV online

A great-looking CV helps people know what you have to offer. Putting it online means employers can view your past experience, qualifications and interests with just one click. Either place the page on your own website, send it to one of the many specialist job-seeking sites on the internet, or email it directly to recruiters. Add links and you can show off your experience far more than it's possible to on paper. All you need is Microsoft Word to start building your web pages.

PROJECT TOOLS: Microsoft Word
SEE ALSO: Your home page, page 256

• What makes a good CV?

Keep your CV relevant. If you're applying to a number of companies, don't send them all the same CV – highlight details, experience and qualities that are applicable to a specific job. Ensure that the key facts such as qualifications, availability and your contact details are on the top of the first page, so that people see them at first glance. Keep it brief – prospective employers won't want to wade through pages of information. Add a small photo that shows you looking alert and interested. Lastly, always check the spelling and the layout carefully for errors.

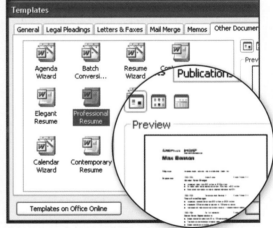

Write your CV in Word

1 Start by creating an ordinary CV using Word. Use the built-in **Resumé** templates and wizards in the **Other Documents** tab of **Templates** (**File** menu, **New**, then **On my computer**) if you wish. They're more American than European in style, so you may prefer to create your CV from scratch. Begin by working out all the key details of your career, such as the dates of your different jobs.

● Look for a job online

There are hundreds of recruitment sites online, such as Guardian Jobs, http://jobs.guardian.co.uk (right), Manpower, www.manpower.com, and Monster.com, www.monster.com. Newspapers and magazines often advertise jobs on their websites, and may also provide advice and information about the companies, industry issues and technology. Some sites will alert you to job adverts by email before they appear in the newspaper.

● CVs on CD

Make a splash by sending your CV on a CD. Include examples of your work on the CD that people can see simply by clicking a link. The easiest way to do so is to copy all the files for your website onto the CD. For the sake of clarity you may wish to change the name of the first page from index.html to your name, for example Fred Smith CV.html.

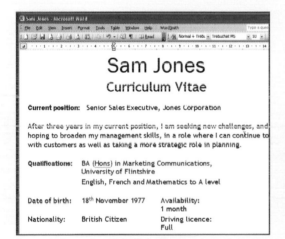

Lay out the information

2 Type your details into Word, with the most important information at the top of the page – the job you're doing now, your key qualifications and basic personal information. If you need to hold a driving licence for your job, include that; if a job involves travel or working abroad, state your nationality. This section should show off your qualifications and suitability for the kind of job you're seeking.

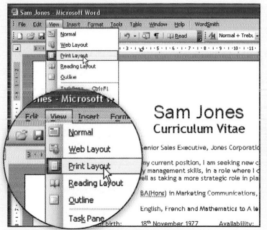

Check the printed appearance

3 Choose **Print Layout** from the **View** menu in Word to see how your CV will appear when it's printed out. Ensure that everything is lined up neatly and that the most important information will fit on the first page, and try to keep to a maximum of two to three pages. Busy prospective employers won't read most CVs in full, so attract their attention with the information at the top of the first page.

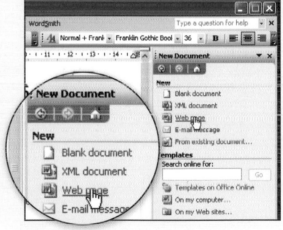

Create a new web page

4 Choose **New** from Word's **File** menu and, in the **New Document** panel, choose **Web page**. You can simply save your paper CV as a web page, but it's better to create something more eye-catching, with pictures and other information tailored to look good on a computer screen. As with a printed CV, the first page has to grab attention and encourage people to find out more about you.

● Email your CV

It's quick and convenient to send your CV by email. Many email programs will let you copy and paste the information directly from your web page to create something that looks similar to your Microsoft Word version. But bear in mind that some email programs will reformat your CV so it looks different when it arrives. The best way to preserve the CV's formatting is to send it as a PDF (see 'See it clearly with Acrobat', page 295).

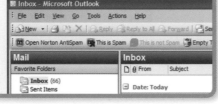

● Covering letters

If a job advertisement asks for a handwritten letter with your CV, don't type it on your computer. Use the letter to highlight parts of your CV that are most relevant to the job advertised and explain why you're interested in the post or company. Don't use a standard letter for each job application, rather tailor your letter to sound enthusiastic about a specific company and what it does, and explain how you'd be the perfect person for the job.

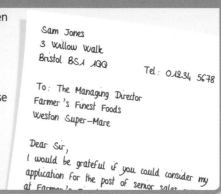

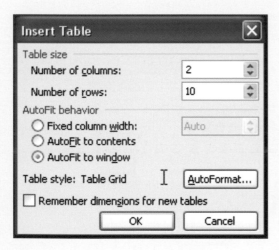

Use a table for layout

5 From the **Table** menu, choose **Insert** then **Table**, and build a table with 2 columns and 10 rows. For the first page of your CV, copy only the most important information from your original Word document, paste it into the table and format it to look attractive and easy to read. Add rows if needed by choosing **Table**, **Insert** then **Rows below**. Delete any unwanted rows using **Table**, **Delete** then **Rows**.

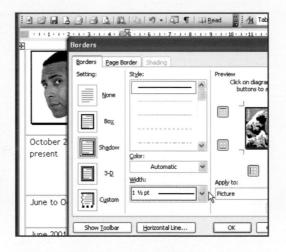

Add a picture of yourself

6 Click inside the top left cell of the table. In the **Insert** menu choose **Picture** then **From file**. Find a picture of yourself and add it to the page. Right-click on it and, in the pop-up menu, choose **Borders and Shading**. Select **Shadow**, and try different settings in the **Width** box to achieve the effect you want. Click **OK** then preview the page in your browser by selecting **Web Page Preview** from the **File** menu.

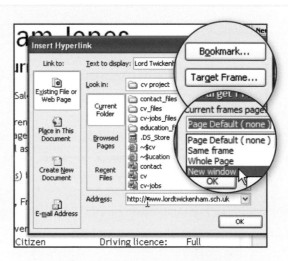

Add links to companies or colleges

7 Add links within your CV to places where you've studied, or products that you've worked with, so employers can find out more about your skills. Right-click on the page and choose **Hyperlink** from the pop-up menu. Type the web address in the **Address** box then click the **Target Frame** button. Click the small arrow next to the **Current frames page** box and choose **New Window**. Click **OK**. Click **OK** again.

Write it online

Many websites let you post a CV online, by uploading your existing one to sites such as www.cvposter.com, or by filling in a form with questions and answers. Your information will be stored and automatically searched by companies with jobs to offer to see if you fit their requirements.

See it clearly with Acrobat

Many documents intended for downloading and distribution on the web are converted into a format known as PDF (Portable Document Format), which was developed by Adobe. Save your CV as a PDF document, and you can be sure that people will be able to view it on their computer as you created it, even if they don't have the same program. While they can print it, they can't change it by mistake. You need either Adobe's Acrobat software, www.adobe.com, or an alternative, such as the free PDF Creator, http://sourceforge.net/projects/pdfcreator, both of which can export any printable document as a PDF file.

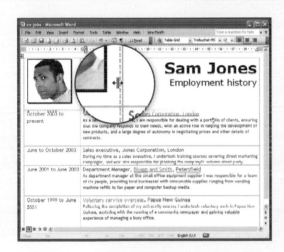

Split your CV into pages

8 The height of each row adjusts automatically as you add text. To adjust the column widths, click and drag the vertical lines between the table cells. Create a page for each section of your CV, such as education, employment and interests. Keep each page concise, with the most current information at the top, and your photo on the first page. Try to keep each page to a single screen of information.

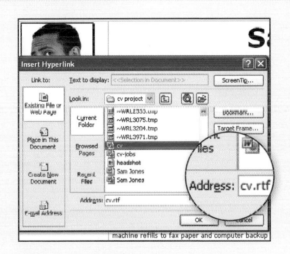

Add your printable CV

9 Employers may want to make a copy of your CV, but web pages printed out won't look very good. Open your original CV in Word and choose **Save As** from the **File** menu. Select **Rich Text Format** as the document type since such files will open with any word-processing program. Save the file in the same folder as your web page and create a link to it from the main CV page (as in step 7).

Organise your website

10 Create a folder on your website called CV and copy all the CV files – web pages and images – into it. If your CV will be the only item on your website, rename the main CV web page index.html. This enables people to see your CV by typing /cv/ at the end of your usual web address. Don't put anything on your site that you wouldn't want employers to see.

Face to face

Hear and see your friends online using video chat

Thanks to the internet, it's easier than ever to keep in touch with friends and family. Using the latest video chat software and a broadband net connection, you can even see them and talk face to face, whether they're in the next town or halfway around the world. And it doesn't cost a fortune – just buy a cheap 'webcam' (see page 16) and use free software such as MSN Messenger.

PROJECT TOOLS: Webcam ● MSN Messenger, http://messenger.msn.com
SEE ALSO: Getting started with the internet and email, page 14

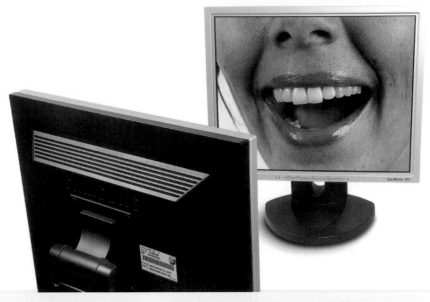

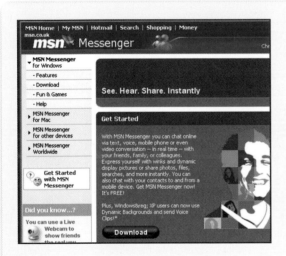

Start MSN Messenger

1 To get the latest version of Messenger, type http://messenger.msn.com into your internet browser, follow the links to download it, then run the setup program. During the setup procedure, choose to use your email address to create a .NET Passport (see page 16), which is the ID people will use to chat with you. You can create a new Hotmail ID (Microsoft's free email service) and use that instead if you prefer.

Sign in automatically

2 Start the MSN Messenger program. If you've used Messenger before, then your email address will appear automatically in the box on this screen. If it doesn't, type in the address you used in step 1. Tick the box beneath if you want Windows to sign you in automatically in future, so your friends can chat with you whenever you turn on your PC. Type your password then click **OK**.

Find a friend

3 To chat with people, you need to add them to your contact list. Click **Add a Contact** at the bottom of the Messenger window. Click **Create a new contact from an e-mail address**, then click **Next** and enter a friend's address. On the next screen, you'll be able to send an automatic email, asking your friend to install Messenger, too. Click **Finish** and you'll be returned to the main Messenger screen.

● Smooth running

To make sure you have the best possible connection, close programs you're not using when you want to have a video chat. Avoid downloading email and large files too, since they can cause video display problems. Most video chat programs have an option to automatically detect your network and connection settings for best results. Make sure the room you are sitting in is well lit and remember that any movement behind you, such as traffic, will affect the picture.

● Online chat software

MSN Messenger is easy to use but it's not the only way to chat online. The two other most popular chat programs are AOL Instant Messenger, www.aol.co.uk/aim (below), and Yahoo! Messenger, http://messenger.yahoo.com, both of which are free and allow you to chat face to face using webcams. Sign up with all three, so you can chat with people whichever one they use. You can run all three programs at the same time.

● Protect yourself

Windows XP comes with a built-in 'firewall' – an essential program that prevents intruders accessing your PC over the internet while you are online. When you run MSN Messenger, the firewall may pop up a dialogue box asking whether you wish to 'Accept connections' or 'Become a server'. Click **Yes** to accept. If your PC is connected to the internet through a wireless network, the network modem may include its own firewall. Check the modem's user manual on how to configure it for MSN Messenger.

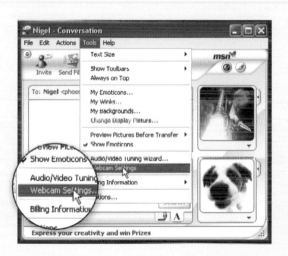

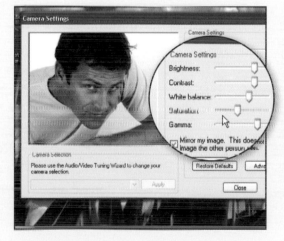

Get ready to talk

4 To begin a conversation with someone on your contact list, double-click on the person's name. Start typing to send a message. Talking to someone you can see is easier. So, click the **Tools** menu at the top of the chat window and click **Webcam Settings** to bring up the **Camera Settings** screen. Make sure that your webcam is plugged into the PC, and that its software is installed.

Are you sitting comfortably?

5 You need to ensure the picture from your webcam is clear and bright. Alter the brightness and colour if necessary. Click **Close** after you've set up your camera. Make sure that you're sitting in a good position and that your face can be seen clearly. To check that the sound is set up correctly for your video chat choose the **Audio/Video Tuning Wizard** from the **Tools** menu.

Smile, you're on camera

6 Click the **Webcam** button at the top of the chat window and click **Start a video conversation** to start the video chat. When your friend accepts, this is what you'll see: the big picture shows your friend and the smaller one is you. You can carry on typing too, if you want, or just sit back and chat. To switch to full-screen chat mode click the diagonal arrow to the right of your friend's picture.

Essentials

A quick reference guide to the tools and techniques, and the photo, music and home-office software, you'll need to get the most from the projects in this book

The creative talents of Excel

Use your spreadsheets for more than just tables and calculation

A spreadsheet is great for manipulating numbers or any other type of information that can be laid out in a table format. It will compute totals and statistics, and update its answers automatically if you change any of the figures. The best-known spreadsheet program is Excel, part of MS Office.

When you start a new spreadsheet you're presented with the usual Windows toolbars and menus, and a grid of feint lines. On closer inspection, you'll see that each row in the grid is identified by a number and each column by a letter. The grid is larger than can be displayed on screen (all you see is its top left-hand corner) and extends to 256 columns and many thousands of rows. The leftmost column is A, and the rest are labelled alphabetically. Wherever columns and rows intersect, they create cells. Think of a cell as a box identified by its column letter and row number.

Once you've mastered a few simple techniques, you'll find a spreadsheet is as useful as a word processor and much better at handling lists and

tables. But spreadsheets are highly adaptable too. And even the most experienced spreadsheet user is likely to use only a small percentage of the features and formulae on offer.

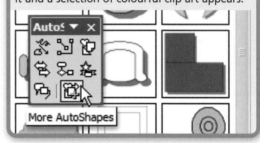

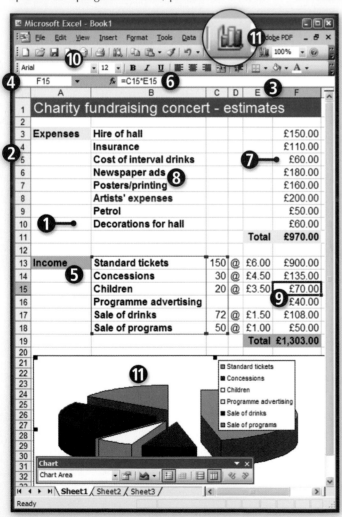

1 Cells are boxes containing values, labels or formulae. This one is empty.

2 Rows are numbered 1, 2, 3 and so on.

3 Vertical columns run from A to Z, then AA, AB, AC and so on. Together rows and columns provide a reference to every cell in the sheet.

4 The active cell number shows you in which cell you can make entries or amendments, in this case the active cell is F15 (column F, line 15).

5 Shading cells with different colours makes a sheet easier to understand.

6 Excel's editing bar shows the contents of the active cell, which for F15 is the formula =C15*E15 (the asterisk means multiply).

7 Values are simply numbers. This cell contains the number 60, formatted as currency.

8 Labels are usually alphabetical, or a mixture of letters and numbers. They make it clear what the figures in the spreadsheet represent.

9 Cells containing formulae perform calculations. The editing bar (point **6**) shows any formula applied to the active cell.

10 Standard formatting buttons just like those in Word can be found on the Excel spreadsheet toolbar.

11 You can create a chart representing any highlighted cells by clicking the Chart wizard, then choosing from a selection styles.

An area that's often overlooked is graphics. It's a simple task to represent a table of figures in the form of a graph or chart. And you can borrow it to enliven Word documents and PowerPoint presentations, add it to a DTP layout or incorporate it in any Windows document.

You can also create graphic documents without trying Excel's number crunching side at all. Select **Insert** then **Diagram** to create and edit pyramid or Venn diagrams, say, or use **Insert**, **Picture** then **Organization Chart** to start drawing charts.

● Save as a web page

You've built a great spreadsheet, and you want to share it with others. But what if they don't have Excel? One solution is to save the spreadsheet as a web page and email it, or just upload the page to your own website, where anyone can view it using their web browser. Click **File**, **Save As Web Page** and then enter a filename. Tick the **Add Interactivity** box if you want to allow people to enter their own data into your spreadsheet. Then click **Save**.

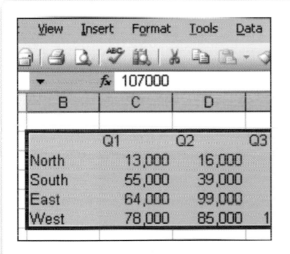

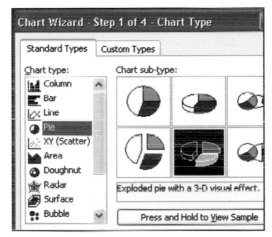

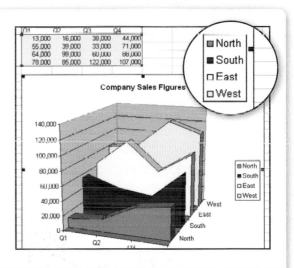

From figures to chart in 60 seconds

1 Anyone can produce tables of figures in Excel but they're a little dull. So why not bring them to life by producing a chart, complete with fancy 3D graphics? It's so easy you'll have a stylish chart produced in under a minute. Start by dragging the mouse cursor over your chart values, including the headers, click **Insert** and then **Chart** to launch the Excel **Chart wizard**.

Pick the best chart style

2 Excel offers 14 different standard chart styles, and each one comes in several sub-types. So a pie chart comes in regular, exploded and 3D versions, for instance. Select one that fits your data, then click and hold **Press and Hold to View Sample** to see a live preview. Click **Next** when you're happy, ensure Excel is using the right range of cells to represent your data and click **Next** again.

Add a few finishing touches

3 Now you can optionally enter a chart title, and captions for the graph axes X and Y – and Z, if it has one. To include your original table of figures on the graph base, select the **Data Table** tab, then tick the box marked **Show data table**. Click **Next** and then **Finish** to see the completed chart. Wish you'd fine tuned it a little more? Right-click the chart for a range of editing options.

Show it off with PowerPoint

Create stunning presentations with graphics, sound and animation

Although originally intended as a business program, Microsoft PowerPoint has many other uses, thanks to its ability to incorporate pictures, animations, sound and video clips into a screen-based slideshow. This makes it ideal for documenting a holiday, producing a school project, creating an interactive bedtime story for children, or even a multimedia quiz with sound and pictures. PowerPoint comes with ready-made templates that include attractive colour schemes and backgrounds, and placeholders for your own text, pictures, animations and other elements. This makes it easy to create an original slideshow that, courtesy of the free PowerPoint Viewer available from www.microsoft.com/downloads, runs on any PC.

● Say it with sound

You can use sounds to add atmosphere, drama or even comic effect to your slideshows. Almost any kind of digital sound may be added to a slide – for example, background music or a sound effect – and you can choose the point at which it plays back, perhaps when the slide first appears, after a set period of time or when you click the mouse button.

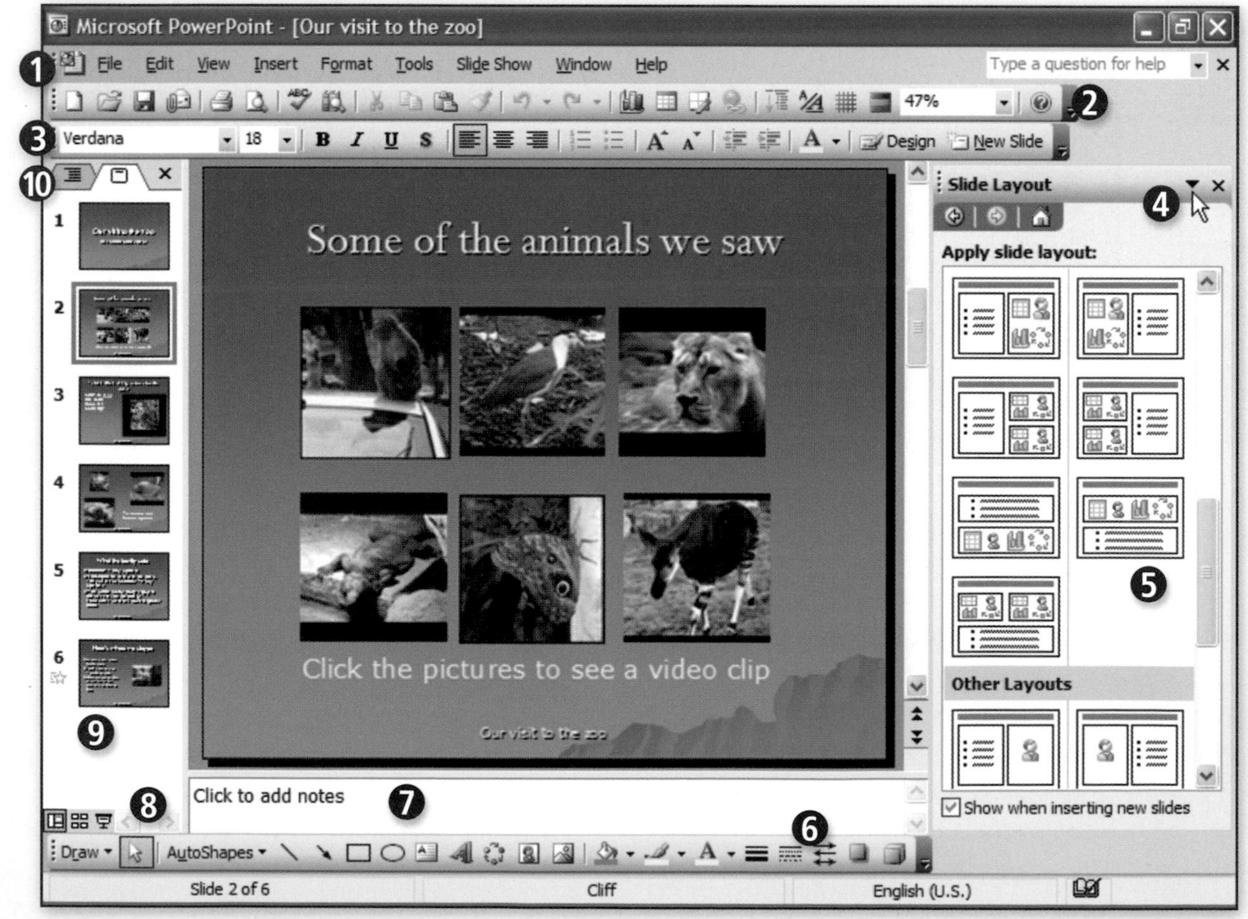

---

1 PowerPoint's main menus.

2 Use these buttons to open and save files, print out your presentation, and cut, copy and paste items.

3 Click the buttons on the text formatting toolbar to change the way text appears on a slide.

4 This arrow opens the task pane menu, where you can find help, load clip art, and select preformatted designs and colour schemes for your slideshow.

5 Predefined designs are available whenever you create a new slide.

6 The drawing toolbar contains tools to add graphics such as boxes, lines and arrows to a slide.

7 Here you can type notes to yourself about any particular slide.

8 These buttons let you display your presentation as shown here or as a screen full of small slides (thumbnails); the right-hand button starts the slideshow from the current slide.

9 Your slideshow in miniature. Click on one of the slide thumbnails and it will appear in the centre of the screen.

10 Click the outline tab to see your slideshow represented down the left of the screen as a series of text headings, sub-headings and bullet points.

ESSENTIALS

● Fades, wipes and other effects

A PowerPoint slideshow is tied together using video-style fades or special effects that create a smooth transition from one slide to the next. If you use them judiciously, these transitions can add impact to your slideshows. PowerPoint includes nearly 60 fancy visual effects that are ready for you to use. Click the **Transition** button in the toolbar to see what's available, then select the slide you want the effect to start from and choose a transition from the list. Settings include the option to run each transition automatically or on the click of a mouse. You can also adjust the transition speed, and play a sound of your choice at the same time.

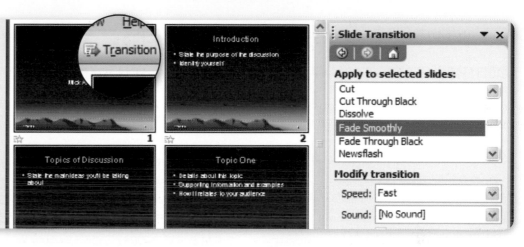

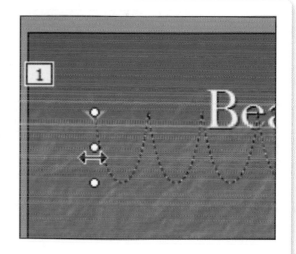

Add effects to your presentation

1 Here is a typical slide. Normally, the heading appears at the same time as the rest of the slide, but you can animate its entrance to add interest. Click on the heading with the right mouse button and choose **Custom Animation** from the pop-up menu. Click the **Add Effect** button; choose **Motion Paths** and then **More Motion Paths** from the sub-menus. This opens the animation gallery.

Choose an animation

2 Scroll down the list of animations and when you see one that you like, click on it and watch the heading come to life. When you've chosen the right animation, click **OK** to close the box. Look carefully on the slide and you'll see the path of the animation, represented by a line. In this example, it's a squiggly line. Click once on the animation path to select it.

Adjust the path

3 You'll notice the perimeter is marked by small white circles, called 'handles', that you can click on with the mouse and, still holding down the mouse button, drag in or out to change the path your animation will follow. Here the path is being extended to the left so the heading glides up and down across the length of the slide, rather than bouncing up and down in the middle.

Become a digital sharp shooter
Your guide to taking photos and video like a professional

Understanding camera controls

The size of the hole through which light comes into the camera is the 'aperture', the length of time the hole is open is the 'shutter speed', and these add up to the 'exposure'. Your camera automatically works out the right exposure for each picture so it doesn't come out too bright (overexposed) or dark (underexposed).

The larger the aperture, the smaller the 'depth of field'. That means only objects at a certain distance will be in focus, while those nearer to the camera and those further away from the camera appear blurred. Most cameras have an 'aperture priority programme', labelled Av. You can fix a large or small aperture, and shutter speed adjusts accordingly. Alternatively, 'shutter priority' (Tv) lets you set a fast speed, so a moving object will appear sharp and still, or slow, allowing 'motion blur' to give an impression of movement.

By selecting your camera's shutter priority programme, you can shoot fast to freeze motion such as falling water, or slow to let it flow.

Why scour the internet looking for photos for projects, when you can take your own? And today's compact cameras are quick and simple to use. Whether you choose a traditional film camera or digital, there's no need to do anything more than point and shoot. But that doesn't mean you should take pictures without any thought. Paying attention to a few basic principles will improve the quality of your pictures, giving you a good basis for your PC

image-editing projects. The better the quality of the original photo, the better the result of the editing process, whether you're giving your picture a final polish or trying something more creative. On these pages you'll find out some of the reasons why photos come out badly and how to avoid them. You'll also learn how your camera's manual controls can help you achieve great results in tricky or unusual circumstances.

One good piece of advice that applies especially to digital cameras is simply to take more pictures. Shoot the same subject at least three times, varying your camera settings and position so there's a good chance of getting one shot that you're happy with.

Keep your subject sharp

Your camera focuses automatically on whatever is in the centre of the frame. So if you compose a picture with the subject to one side, the camera may focus on the background and the subject won't be sharp. To avoid this, point the camera directly at the subject and press the shutter button halfway down. A beep or an indicator light will confirm you've fixed the focus. Keeping the button held halfway, move the camera to compose the shot then fully press the button.

Get closer with macro

To take close-up shots, simply select your camera's macro mode, usually indicated by a small icon of a flower. This will let you focus as close as 2 to 20cm depending on your camera. Normally a flash is overpowering, so it's been switched it off here.

Near and far in focus

A large depth of field ensures everything is in focus, both close and distant – keeping the lilies in the foreground and the trees in the background sharp. To achieve this, set your camera to aperture priority (Av) or manual mode and select the biggest 'f' number, usually f8 or f11.

Expose your subject correctly

It's tricky to get a good photo of someone if there's a strong source of light in the background, such as a window. The rear light will cast the person's face into shadow, and the camera's auto exposure will be confused by the high contrast between dark and light areas. Most cameras have a 'backlight compensation' mode that you can select when taking such shots. You can also try the half-press trick, as with focusing, to lock on the area you want correctly exposed.

Shake and blur

Wobbling the camera will spoil a photo because everything becomes blurred. But here blur is used to heighten the dramatic effect of the horses speeding past. This is 'motion blur'. A faster shutter speed (see 'Understanding camera controls', page 304) will reduce the effect.

Avoid photo pitfalls

Some of the most common mistakes in photography are the most obvious. Ensure you're holding the camera steady, and preferably braced using a tripod or at least a solid support of some kind – tables, walls and benches are all useful – so that you don't blur the picture. Check the viewfinder or, even better, the LCD screen and make sure that everything you want in your picture is within the frame, without being too small. If there is little light, find a way to get more, either by opening curtains or shutters, turning on electric lights or using flash.

Remember, flash only works well at a distance of 2 to 5 metres from the camera; any less will 'white out' your subject,

while the flash won't illuminate anything further away. Finally, remember the worst photo is the one you didn't take at all: keep your camera handy.

Digital film

With a traditional camera, your pictures are stored on a roll of film. A digital camera stores images on electronic memory cards. These come in a range of shapes, sizes and storage capacities, depending on the make and model of camera. The type most commonly used in compact cameras is Secure Digital (SD), while professional cameras use the slightly larger Compact Flash cards. Sony products use a proprietary type of card called Memory Stick. And mobile phones that have cameras built in often use postage-stamp sized cards known as Mini-SD. It makes little difference what format your camera uses, but you can only insert the correct type of card.

All these cards are based on a technology called 'flash memory' that keeps what's stored even when the camera is turned off. So, having filled up the card, you can take it out and leave it to one side while you shoot on another, then transfer the pictures to your PC when you're ready.

You could keep all your photos stored on cards indefinitely, but it's an expensive way to preserve them. It's best to copy them to your PC then back them up onto recordable CDs or DVDs. You can then reuse your memory card or cards to take more pictures.

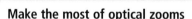

Make the most of optical zooms

Zoom is an important feature to look for when buying a camera. It's useful both practically, to get more detailed shots of distant subjects, and creatively. Using zoom changes the relationship between foreground and background. Nearer objects don't look so huge, and there's more difference in focus at different distances, so you can make your subject stand out sharply against a blurred background.

All of this is only true of 'optical zoom' (see the picture top right), which works by moving lenses within the camera. 'Digital zoom' doesn't affect the picture captured by the camera, but magnifies the centre of it to fill the whole frame. The resulting image (as seen in the picture middle right) is far less clear and the pixels are clearly visible.

Up close and personal

Portrait shots don't have to include the whole head and shoulders. Experiment with unusual angles and get in close, but don't waste too much time composing the shot – if you're slow off the mark you will miss the moment. Try to maintain eye contact with your subject.

When darkness falls

Night shots require exposures between 1 and 4 seconds, but also try experimenting in shutter priority or manual modes (see 'Understanding camera controls', page 304). To keep your camera steady, use a tripod or balance it on top of a wall; the self timer will eliminate the chance of wobbles. Unless you have a friend in the foreground, switch off the flash.

Sparkling action shots

Capturing sparklers requires a combination of a flash for the person and a long exposure for the sparkler. Set your camera's shutter speed to around 2 seconds (see 'Understanding camera controls', page 304) and force the flash to fire – some cameras call this a 'slow synchro' mode.

Exaggerate depth of field using macro

Macro mode isn't only for shooting small objects (see page 304). You can also get a dramatic depth of field effect by positioning the camera very close to an object and using macro to focus on it. More distant objects will be progressively blurred.

Relief for red-eye

When you photograph a person using the flash, light reflected from the back of the eyes glows red, known as 'red-eye'. In low light – when you'd be using flash – the eyes' pupils are wide, increasing the effect. Red-eye reduction, an option on most cameras, fires off several mini flashes to make the pupils contract. Thankfully, red-eye is quickly remedied in most image-editing programs.

Shooting better video

There are different considerations to bear in mind when you film with a camcorder. As with a camera, try to keep it still, preferably by using a tripod. This is harder when using zoom, which magnifies smaller movements. For this reason, don't use zoom when filming a headshot, as you would for a portrait photo, because the person's head will waggle in and out of frame. Instead, get closer. Since background objects will be in focus, watch out for gaffes such as trees sticking out of people's heads.

Use the zoom function to set up shots, not to zoom in and out while filming, as this looks poor in the finished video. On occasion, a very slow zoom in or out can be effective. Frame your subject carefully as you won't get the chance to crop later.

As with still photography, avoid digital zoom. Always try to record for at least 10 seconds before stopping to film something else, or you may not have enough footage to work with when you come to edit your video.

Image makers

Learn how to transform your photos with the help of Photoshop Elements

With an image-editing program, you can make almost any imaginable alteration to a photo or scanned-in picture. First, you need to have the picture as a digital file. It could come from your digital camera, or it may have been taken on film – you can have photos put on CD when you have your film processed, or use a scanner to copy prints onto your PC (see page 322).

Image-editing programs have 'photo', 'paint' or 'image' in the name. Examples include Microsoft Digital Image Suite, Corel Paint Shop Pro, and Adobe Photoshop. Photoshop is the most powerful image editor and has a popular lower-cost version called Photoshop Elements, which is the program used in this book (see pages 12 to 13). Image editors are distinct from

other kinds of graphics programs such as drawing software, which creates pictures from geometric shapes and isn't suitable for editing photos.

Having opened an image file in your program, you can alter it in a variety of ways. At the simplest, you can turn it around, straighten it up or 'crop' it, which means that only a chosen rectangle is kept while the rest of the picture is

1 Most image-editing programs have a similar set of tools arranged in a toolbox such as this. Some tools are unique to each program.

2 Tools are used with the mouse and affect the picture only where you click. The menus offer adjustments that affect the whole image.

3 Each tool has settings to adjust how it works. You set these in the Options toolbar.

4 A photo browser lets you look through small 'thumbnail' views of all the pictures on your PC, a CD or DVD to find the one you want.

5 Use the various selection tools to draw around an area of a picture so that you can alter that area without affecting the rest of the image.

6 You can place several pictures on top of each other in transparent layers. An ordinary picture file has one layer, called Background.

7 Ready-made styles can be applied to layers. To turn a plain circle into a translucent 3D button click one of these styles.

8 Photoshop Elements' Photo Bin shows all the pictures you've opened. You can quickly switch between them or copy from one to another.

9 Click these swatches to change the colours that will be applied when you use tools such as brushes.

● Finding ready-made images

With the help of Google's Image Search facility at www.google.com/images, you can find thousands of free photos online – type in the subject you want and click **Search**. But without permission from their owners you may use them only in private projects. For 'royalty free' pictures, which come with the legal rights to use them as you wish, subscribe to a service such as www.clipart.com or pay a small fee per picture from www.istockphoto.com. Also good value are clip-art discs such as Greenstreet's *10,000 Photos*, www.greenstreetsoftware.co.uk.

discarded. Using colour correction and adjustment commands, you can change the overall appearance of a picture, for example if it's too light, too dark or the wrong colour. Specialised tools will correct common problems such as 'red-eye' (see page 307), where flash photography causes people's eyes to appear red.

There are special effects for more creative projects, too. Many tools work directly on areas of a picture using the mouse as it it were a brush. You can paint colour onto an image, even make a painting from a blank canvas and apply effects freehand. For example, you can lighten, sharpen or smooth the area you paint over. You can also use a 'clone' tool to paint one part of a picture over another – for example, painting grass and sky over a telegraph pole to remove it from a landscape.

Functions can be applied to the whole of an image or just to selected areas – options help you mark out exactly the parts you want (see page 320). You can also split the image into separate layers, arranged like transparent sheets stacked one on another (see page 314).

Image-editing techniques

There are various effects you can apply to your images, ranging from traditional photographic tricks, such as turning an image into a negative, to imitations of artistic styles such as oil painting or mosaic tiles. It pays to experiment, but always keep a backup copy of your original photo.

In the first example, above, a picture of a flower has been turned into a neon sign using an effect called **Glowing Edges**. Not only the colours but even the shape of a picture can be changed radically.

Photoshop Elements offers many ways to distort all or part of an image. In the second example, right, a distortion effect called **Polar Coordinates** is used to make the flower appear as if it's inside a glass ball.

If you want to alter only part of an image, you can make a 'selection'. There are several ways to do this, as you can see on pages 320 to 321. Once you've made a

selection, it's shown by a flashing dotted outline, and any adjustment or effect will work only inside this. In the example below, the flower has been selected (as seen in the screen on the opposite page) and made brighter and sharper, while the background has been made darker and more blurred. This makes the flower stand out more.

Or you can even use a photo as the basis for abstract art, or to create a background texture. In the final example, below, a 'craquelure' effect has been applied, giving the impression of a cracked painted surface.

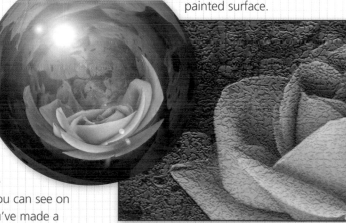

Pixel perfect
Get to grips with the principles of colour and image resolution

A digital image such as a photo is made up of a grid of 'pixels' (the word is derived from 'picture cells'). The number of pixels is its 'resolution'. Think of it as a huge mosaic, with millions of square tiles of different colours forming the picture. From a distance, the tiles in a mosaic are small enough that you don't notice them; you just see the picture. In the same way, as long as enough pixels are packed in, a digital picture appears sharp and clear.

For this you need about 300 pixels across and 300 pixels down every square inch of a printed page. A PC monitor has about 100 pixels per inch. So, for best results, you can only print out a picture about a third as large as it appears on screen when displayed at 100% or 'actual size'. In practice, though, 150 pixels per inch will often produce acceptable results.

Colour in the digital world

Your monitor generates colours on screen by varying the amounts of red, green and blue (the three colour 'channels') in each pixel. The number of different colours that can be displayed is determined by an image's (or monitor's) colour

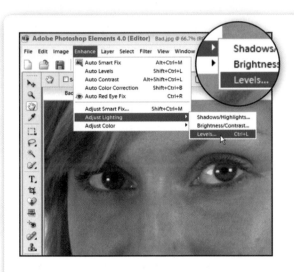

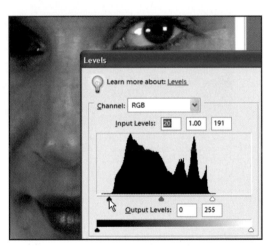

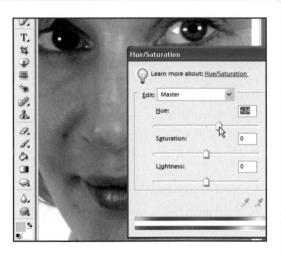

Correct a problem photo

1 This photo, opened in Photoshop Elements, has obvious colour problems. There's little contrast and the colours look odd. When judging colour, it helps to get an overall impression of any 'colour cast'. Look at the picture alongside another one that you know you're happy with. You can also judge from familiar picture elements, such as the skin tone, as here, or the whites of the eyes.

Adjust tone levels

2 To improve the tone and colour of your photo, check the **Enhance** menu and select **Auto Levels** or **Auto Color Correction**. One of these may provide an instant fix. For more control use **Levels** (press **Ctrl+L**). A graph displays the distribution of colour values in the image. To increase contrast, drag the black slider on the left and the white slider on the right inwards to the edges of the graph.

Tweak the colour

3 Now there's more contrast, but the colours are still wrong. Choose **Adjust Hue/Saturation** from **Adjust Color** on the **Enhance** menu (or press **Ctrl+U**). The problem here is hue: that is, what colour things are, rather than how bright (saturation). Move the **Hue** slider. In this case, a move to the right makes the skin look more natural. The lips and eyes look better too.

depth, expressed as a binary number (zeroes and ones). Most equipment uses a colour depth of 8 'bits' – the binary digits that store digital information – for each of these channels, giving the equivalent of the decimal numbers 0-255. For example, bright red is R=255, G=0, B=0 (full red, no green, no blue). Three channels of 8 bits gives a total of 24-bit colour, called 'true colour' because it's enough to represent all the colours that the human eye can distinguish.

Your digital camera or scanner records the colour value of each pixel. Your PC manipulates those values when you edit images, and your monitor and printer then display the colours for you to see. 'Colour management' is needed to make sure they all interpret colour values the same way. This is done automatically by Windows and software such as Adobe Photoshop Elements. Always turn on colour management where it's offered, and tick the option to save a 'colour profile' with each picture so that other hardware and software will know how to handle it.

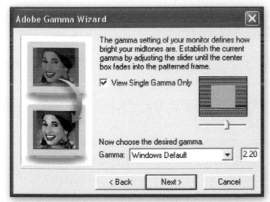

*Run the Adobe Gamma program, found in **Control Panel** on the **Start** menu, to perform a simple calibration that will help make sure your monitor is displaying images correctly.*

Size matters

The resolution of an image is usually given in 'dots per inch' (dpi). The term '300dpi' means 300 dots across and down each inch. 'Dots' here means pixels. Don't confuse these with the dpi ratings of printers, which refer to ink dots, of which dozens are needed to print each pixel. Digital cameras are rated in megapixels, referring to the total number of pixels (in millions). For a photo to print at 8x6in and a resolution of 300dpi, you need 8x300x6x300 = 4,320,000 pixels, just over 4 megapixels.

An image stored at high resolution.
The same image stored at lower resolution.

*Elements' **Resize** option illustrates how the number of pixels in your image divided by the resolution equals the printed size.*

Storing a 'true colour' digital picture requires 24 bits multiplied by the number of pixels, which soon adds up to a lot of megabytes to fit on a memory card or on your PC's hard disk. One way to save space is to reduce the number of pixels, for example by setting your digital camera to a lower resolution. Another is to use data compression, such as that used in JPEG (pronounced 'jay-peg') image files. When you store a picture in JPEG format, colour information that the eye won't really notice is discarded. In your digital camera or image editing software, you set the level of compression to balance quality against size. Remember that once data is lost, you can't get it back.

Image stored with heavy JPEG compression.

Paper, inks, printers – action!

How to get the best printouts from your pictures and layouts

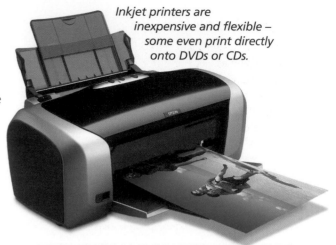

Inkjet printers are inexpensive and flexible – some even print directly onto DVDs or CDs.

Your creative projects may begin on your PC screen, but often the result will come out of your printer. One of the joys of using Windows is that with a little practice you can get perfect printed results every time, even with an inexpensive printer. In fact, a run-of-the-mill colour inkjet printer – probably cheaper than a meal for two in a restaurant – will churn out professional-looking documents for as long as it's got ink in its cartridges.

Inkjets are by far the most popular kind of printer and most can handle any paper size, from a 6x4in photo to an A4 page. Print quality depends not only on the printer but also on the paper you choose: with glossy photo paper, results can be indistinguishable from a traditional colour photo, while printing won't look as rich or crisp on plain paper.

Why inkjet printers are so cheap is an open secret. Printer manufacturers don't make much of their profits on the actual printer, but on

what goes inside it: the refills. If you check the prices in your local stores or on the internet, you'll see that, relative to the purchase price of the printer, ink refills are expensive. That means you should think before you print; especially with large colour photos.

Printer settings

Windows programs work on the 'what you see is what you get' (WYSIWYG) principle, meaning that your printed work appears as it does on screen. But translating an image into dots of ink is a complicated process, so your printer comes with 'driver' software to control it. When you choose the **Print** command in any program, the box that appears will include a **Properties** or **Options** button to take you to settings provided by the printer driver. For example, you select what kind of paper you're using and adjust colour settings according to the type of document you're printing. Such settings provide the best quality for each print job.

Print quality is limited by the resolution of your original image, too. This doesn't apply to text in a word processor, which will print smoothly at any size. But when you print a digital photo, the largest size at which it will look sharp in print depends on the number of pixels it contains (see page 311). If you create a new document in an image-editing program, remember to set its width and height to the size you want to print it and its resolution to 300 pixels (or dots) per inch.

Letting the experts do it

You don't have to print out your artwork yourself. There are lots of companies that offer photo printing services, including high street shops such as Boots and Jessops. You can take your digital camera's memory card into a shop and pick up the prints later. Or you can upload pictures from your computer over the internet and get quality prints on proper photographic paper sent to you in the post. You can sometimes even arrange for enlargements, or special items such as mugs or T-shirts.

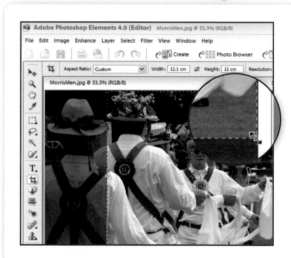

Print your own CD box artwork

1 Run Elements and select **Edit and Enhance Photos**. Choose **Open** from the File menu to load a suitable image file for your CD cover. Press **C** for the **Crop** tool. In the **Options** bar at the top, set **Width** to **12.1cm** (4.75 inches) and **Height** to **12cm** (4.725in). Set the **Resolution** to **300 pixels per inch**, for high-quality printing. Click on your picture; hold the mouse button and drag to make a rectangle.

ESSENTIALS

Printing to PDF

Instead of giving someone a printed document you can email it as a Portable Document Format (PDF) file. Anyone can view and print PDFs using Adobe Reader, a free download from www.adobe.com. To make PDFs, you use a PDF 'printer driver': when you go to **Print**, it lets you save as PDF instead. Free PDF printer drivers include PrimoPDF from www.primopdf.com and Pdf995 from www.pdf995.com.

Installing a PDF printer driver enables you to 'print' any document to a PDF file from any program. Pages appear on screen just as if they were printed.

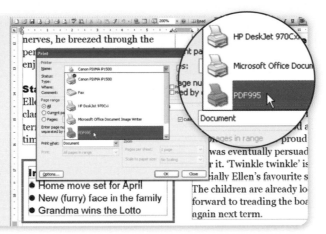

Ink refills

Save money by refilling the plastic cartridges that hold the ink for your printer instead of discarding them when empty. You can take your used cartridges to a high street refilling service or buy your own kit. Kits can be bought from computer stores, stationers and most big supermarkets. Printer makers don't recommend using non-original replacement cartridges or refills on the grounds that the inks are inferior.

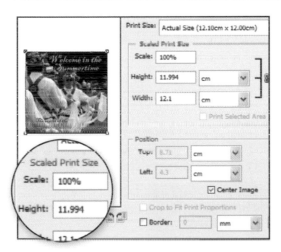

Add a title

2 Adjust the rectangle to enclose the area you want to use, holding the spacebar to reposition it. Double-click, or click the tick symbol at the bottom right of the rectangle, to crop and size the picture. To add some words, press **T** for the **Text** tool. Click on the picture and type your CD's title. Click and drag over the text to highlight it, and then use the **Options** bar to choose the font, size and colour of your text.

Edit the text

3 Click the tick symbol at the far right of the **Options** bar to finish editing your text. If necessary, press **V** for the **Move** tool and reposition your title, then press **T** to return to the **Text** tool. Click elsewhere on the picture to add more text in the same way. When your design is finished, choose **Print** from the **File** menu. You're shown a mini preview of the printout. Make sure **Scaled Print Size** is set at **100%**.

Choose the paper, and print

4 To confirm the size of paper you're using, click **Page Setup**. Click **Print** to show a box where you can confirm which printer you want to use. Click the **Properties** button to go to the settings provided by the printer driver. Finally, click **OK** to print your CD insert. You could print a label for the CD, too: sticky labels are available in kits, while some inkjets can print onto printable CDs.

Editing multi-layered images

Take your creativity further by combining images in layers

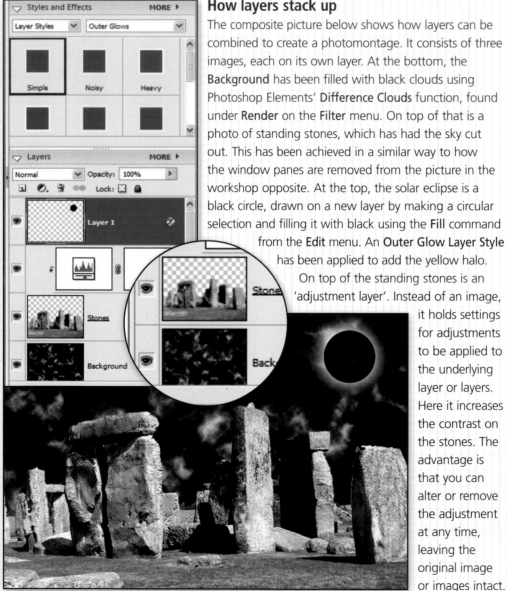

How layers stack up

The composite picture below shows how layers can be combined to create a photomontage. It consists of three images, each on its own layer. At the bottom, the **Background** has been filled with black clouds using Photoshop Elements' **Difference Clouds** function, found under **Render** on the **Filter** menu. On top of that is a photo of standing stones, which has had the sky cut out. This has been achieved in a similar way to how the window panes are removed from the picture in the workshop opposite. At the top, the solar eclipse is a black circle, drawn on a new layer by making a circular selection and filling it with black using the **Fill** command from the **Edit** menu. An **Outer Glow Layer Style** has been applied to add the yellow halo.

On top of the standing stones is an 'adjustment layer'. Instead of an image, it holds settings for adjustments to be applied to the underlying layer or layers. Here it increases the contrast on the stones. The advantage is that you can alter or remove the adjustment at any time, leaving the original image or images intact.

Blending layers

Each layer has an **Opacity** control, which sets how transparent it is, from **100%** (solid) to **0%** (invisible). It also has a blending mode. **Normal** blending means the image in the layer covers what's underneath. There are many alternative blending modes. With **Multiply**, colour in the layer is added to underlying colour, darkening the image. In **Screen** mode, only lighter areas of the layer are seen. Experiment and you'll soon get the idea.

An important aspect of image editing is the ability to combine pictures. For example, you can take a photo of yourself and superimpose it on a picture of a famous location. You can also assemble a collage of items collected on your holiday, or overlay a complete image on top of another, to create the effect of a double exposure.

To achieve such images you use 'layers'. Think of layers as transparent sheets with pictures printed on them. Wherever part of a layer is empty, the picture below shows through. You can make the pictures themselves more or less transparent, too. Any number of layers can be stored in one image file. The **Layers** box lists them in order, from top to bottom, and you can make each temporarily visible or invisible. Where there's no visible content on any layer, you'll see a checkerboard pattern.

The current combination of visible layers is what you see in the main editing window and it's also what's stored if you save your work as an ordinary image file such as a JPEG (see page 311). When you save in your software's own format, such as Adobe Photoshop Elements' .PSD, all the layers are kept so you can edit them independently again at a later point.

Layer styles

A layer will often contain a 'cutout' shape surrounded by empty space (transparency). Use selection tools to cut out objects from photos or make shapes with drawing tools. You can then choose from a range of **Layer Styles** to add effects. A soft shadow effect will make the object appear as if it's floating above the underlying picture. **Layer Styles** can also be more complex, such as this 3D button, produced from a plain circle.

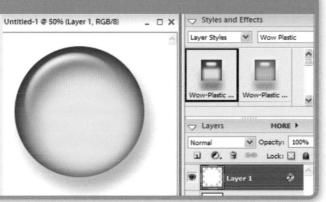

Flattening your layers

Image files containing multiple layers can only be stored in certain formats. Always save your work in Photoshop's native format (.PSD) so that everything will be present and editable when you load it back in. But to send the final image to anyone else, put it up on a website or add it to a Word document, you'll need to save it in a standard format such as JPEG (see page 311). The resulting file will look identical to the image you're saving, but cannot be broken down into separate layers.

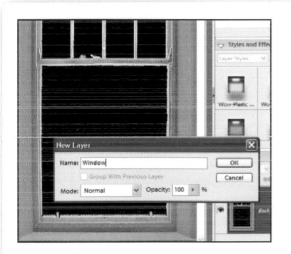

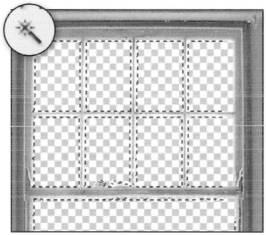

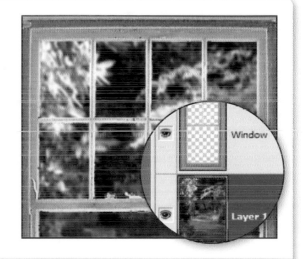

Build a simple photomontage

1 Run Photoshop Elements and select **Edit and Enhance Images**. Using **Open** from the **File** menu, open a picture of a window taken at night. The panes appear black. To cut out parts of this picture, you first need to put it in a layer. Go to the **Layer** menu and choose **New**, then **Layer From Background**. In the box that appears, give your layer a name such as Window and then click **OK**.

Create transparent sections

2 Press **W** for the **Magic Wand** tool. In the Options bar, set **Tolerance 8**, tick **Anti-aliased** and untick **Contiguous**. With this tool, click on any pane of the window to select all the black areas. (Find out more about how this works on pages 320 to 321.) Press **Delete** to erase the selected areas. A checkerboard pattern indicates that they're transparent. Press **D** to deselect.

Assemble the pictures

3 Open a picture of an outdoor scene. Press **V** for the **Move** tool. Click on the outdoor photo and drag it onto the window, then position exactly. In the **Arrange** menu, choose **Send Backward**. The outdoor scene's layer moves behind the window layer, and the scene shows through the transparent panes. If necessary, click and drag the scene to reposition it independently within the window.

Liquify your photos

You can distort images in endless different ways with Photoshop Elements' **Liquify** feature, found under **Distort** on

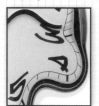

the **Filter** menu. The idea is that your picture acts as if it's printed onto a sheet of soft modelling clay. By clicking and dragging on the picture with the various tools, you push, smear or twist the image. Use this for subtle adjustments, or to alter shapes radically – think of the Salvador Dalí paintings where solid objects become fluid – or, probably most fun of all, to tweak faces into caricatures.

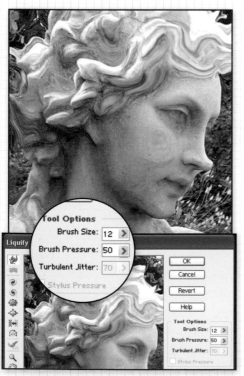

Special effects showcase
Discover the amazing possibilities of image-editing filters and effects

Adobe Photoshop Elements comes with a huge range of special effects, often described as 'filters'. They work in a similar way to the basic colour and tone adjustments that you can see on pages 310 and 311, but filters let you make more dramatic and complex changes to your pictures.

An important aspect of filters is their ability to distort images. With simple colour or tone adjustment, the resulting image may appear different to the original but it would still match up if you laid one on top of the other. Only the colours are changed, not the composition of the picture or the shapes of objects within it. With many special effects this limitation is removed. The picture could be inflated to resemble a balloon. You can alter the image so that ripples radiate out from the centre as happens when a stone is thrown into a pond. Below and opposite you can see some examples of Photoshop Elements' filters, all found on the various sub-menus of the **Filters** menu.

While sharpening gives the impression of greater detail, some filters work by removing detail. **Cutout**, found under **Artistic**, divides a picture into areas of flat colour. You can choose how many colours are used and how faithful the result is to the original image.

Most photos will benefit from a little sharpening. The best filter to use is **Unsharp Mask**, found under **Sharpen**. The less sharp the picture, the higher you set the **Radius**, usually 1 to 4 pixels. Increase the **Threshold** to avoid sharpening fine detail, which can look grainy.

Diffuse Glow, found under **Distort**, gives any photo a romantic atmosphere. The edges of lighter areas are blurred so that they appear to glow. Simultaneously, the picture becomes grainier by adding random dots of darker and lighter colour.

The **Pinch** filter smoothly distorts the whole picture to expand or contract the centre. With a positive setting, as seen here, the centre gets smaller: notice how the size of the face is reduced compared to the hair. A negative setting would give an inflated appearance.

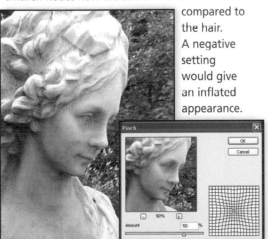

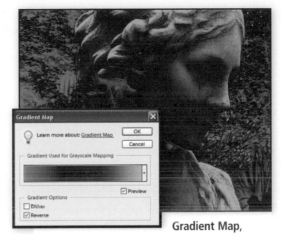

Gradient Map, found under **Adjustments**, allows you to make radical colour changes. Imagine you told a decorator to paint your house, and gave him the numbers of colours on a paint maker's chart. But he used the wrong chart and all the colours were different. **Gradient Map** has this effect on your picture.

The **Sketch** sub-menu provides a range of black and white effects. **Photocopy** simulates the output of a poor-quality photocopier, breaking up the picture into blobs of black on a white background. You can adjust the level of detail to make the copy fairly good or almost unrecognisable.

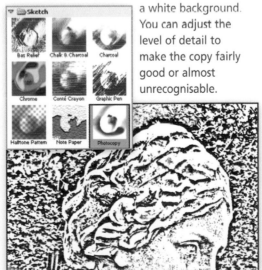

The Lighting Effects filter

Photoshop Elements' **Lighting Effects** is a clever filter that can be used in two different ways. First, it can shine lights

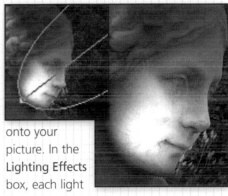

onto your picture. In the **Lighting Effects** box, each light is shown as an oval, and you can adjust its size and shape to control where the light falls. Secondly, the filter can combine the lights with a texture to create a 3D effect. The texture comes from a special kind of image called a 'channel'. As described on page 310, every picture consists of red, green and blue channels. Choosing one of these as the texture channel creates an unusual effect, turning detail in the picture into 3D bumps.

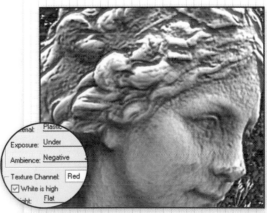

Brush up on your options

To use the **Brush** tool, click its icon in Elements' toolbox, or press **B**. Of the four icons in the **Options** bar at

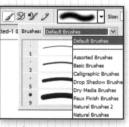

the top, you need the first, **Brush**. Just click on it or press **B** again until it's highlighted. To the right, click the black triangle by the brush sample to show

other brushes. Use the pop-up menu to switch between sets of brushes and then pick a brush from the list of samples. Adjust its size using the option to the right. Move the pointer onto your picture to see the current brush's size and shape.

Finally, the blending **Mode** determines how the paint will interact with the existing image. Choosing **Normal** covers up whatever you paint over. By switching to **Multiply**, for example, and reducing the **Opacity**, you can build up colour gradually as you might with watercolour paints.

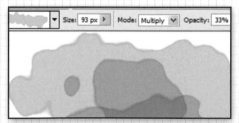

The tools of the trade

Explore Adobe Photoshop Elements' painting and drawing tools

Image-editing software has always had a tool called a 'brush', which has never behaved much like a real brush. Today, the **Brush** tool in programs such as Adobe Photoshop Elements still falls short of providing an exact simulation of real painting, but it has a wide range of other uses too, many of them nothing to do with brushes. Whether you want to draw your own picture from scratch or add scribbled, painted, chalked or splashed elements to a photo, the **Brush** tool has the answer.

Getting the result you want begins with browsing the sets of brushes supplied with the

program. You can also tweak any brush extensively or even make your own custom brush (see page 319, opposite). When you're ready to paint, set the colour that you're going to apply by clicking the **Foreground Color** swatch at the bottom of the main toolbox and choosing from the **Color Picker**. Click on your canvas and, holding down the mouse button, drag to paint. Remember you can always use **Undo** (press **Ctrl+Z**) and try your brushstroke again.

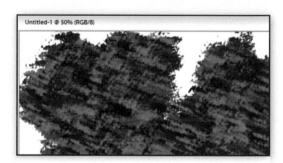

Among the many types of brush available, the **Calligraphic Brushes** are relatively simple, consisting of a plain hard-edged line or oval tipped at an angle. They can be used to mimic a traditional pen nib for line drawings or lettering. You can achieve the best results using a graphics tablet (see the box opposite).

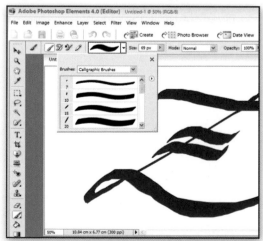

Some of Elements' brushes are complex. The brush shown here is **Heavy Smear Wax Crayon**, from the **Dry Media Brushes** set, with **Hue Jitter** turned on so that the colour of the stroke varies continuously between the currently selected **Foreground** and **Background** colours.

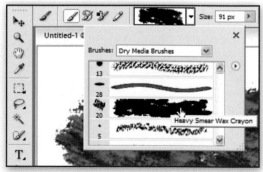

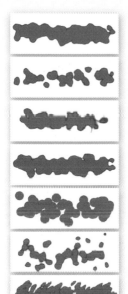

The **More Options** pop-up in the **Options** bar lets you customise a brush's properties. The samples, left, all result from drawing a rough horizontal line with the same basic brush (top). Each property has been altered in turn: **Spacing**, **Fade**, **Hue Jitter** (colour variance), **Hardness**, **Scatter** and **Roundness**.

◯ Graphics tablets

A 'graphics tablet' allows you to draw and paint in a more natural way than with a mouse. This is a plastic-coated pad that plugs into your PC and comes with a separate pen. The pen doesn't make any marks, but as you move it around the pad its position is reflected by the pointer on the PC screen. Your image-editing software will also respond to you pressing down with the pen, for example when applying a wider stroke or a stronger colour.

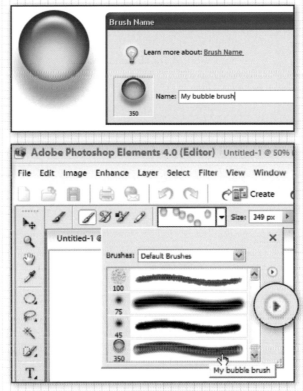

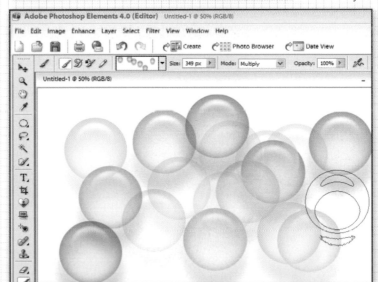

Create your own brush

You can create a custom brush in Photoshop Elements from any kind of image. One method is to make a selection around an interesting texture or object within a photo. Then go to the **Edit** menu and choose **Define Brush From Selection**.

Here's an example of a slightly different approach using a graphic created by a **Layer Style**, as described on page 315. Having applied a style to a shape within a layer, go to the **Define Brush** command on the **Edit** menu, which brings up a box where you can give your brush a name (see left, top). This is added to whichever set of brushes is currently selected in the **Options** bar.

Painting with your brush

Scroll to the bottom of the list and click on your brush. This is a good time to click the blue triangle symbol to the right and choose **Save Brush** from the pop-up menu so it's available the next time you run Elements. Now click and drag to paint. You'll probably need to use **More Options**, at the far right of the **Options** bar, to make adjustments to your brush. For example, if it just seems to make a solid line when you paint, increase **Spacing** and/or **Scatter**.

Photo surgery

Transform your photos with cutouts and cloning

Making selections

In Photoshop Elements and other image editors, you'll find the same basic selection tools in the toolbox. Simplest are the **Rectangular** and **Elliptical Marquee** tools: click and drag over your picture to select a rectangular or oval area (below).

The **Lasso** lets you draw around an irregular area of your image with the mouse. With the **Polygonal Lasso** option (below), you can draw a series of straight lines, which doesn't demand such a steady hand.

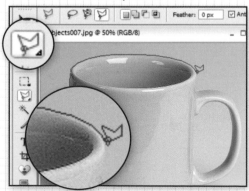

If an area you want to select is even in colour, click anywhere within it with the **Magic Wand** tool to select it all. A **Tolerance** setting controls how much is selected. The **Magic Wand** is usually set to **Contiguous**,

meaning it selects a single area. Untick this option to select all areas of similar colour: one click separated the pale seed head below from its dark background.

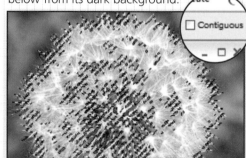

Using any of these tools makes a new selection, forgetting what was selected before. But holding down a key adds the new area to the existing selection (**Shift** in Photoshop Elements) or subtracts it (**Alt**).

When you edit photos on your PC, you don't have to limit yourself to adjusting colour and lighting. You can move people around within a scene, erase objects or even combine several images to depict a fantasy scene.

The keys to this are the selection and cloning tools. When you make a selection, you outline an area of a picture, like cutting around it with scissors. You select a particular person or object, copy the selection and paste it onto another photo using the **Copy** and **Paste** commands on the **Edit** menu. There are several ways to make selections, and to help you get what you want you can add areas to a selection or subtract from it, and so build it up bit by bit.

While a selection is active, any changes you make to the picture affect only that area. If you adjust the lighting or apply a special effect, everything outside the selection stays as it was. To edit the whole image again, you deselect. In Adobe Photoshop Elements you do this from

In your image-editing program the currently selected area is shown as a flashing dotted outline. In this example, the background has been selected using the **Magic Wand** tool. To add together areas of different tone or colour, click several times holding the **Shift** key.

the **Select** menu. You can also invert a selection, so everything that wasn't selected now is, and vice versa (also done from the **Select** menu).

Selections aren't so good for removing objects, as deleting a selection leaves a hole in your photo. But by using cloning you can paint one part of an image over another, for example to cover an unwanted building with extra sky or add a missing button on a coat.

Once an area is selected, you can change it without affecting the rest of the picture. Here, the background has been replaced with a photo of a car using the **Paste Into Selection** command from Photoshop Elements' **Edit** menu.

The **Clone** tool copies one area of an image over another. Click once on where you want to start copying from and then paint the copy where you wish. Here, the selection is left active, protecting the original baby, while extra copies of it are cloned into the background.

Using the Clone tool

Imagine a paintbrush that picks up bits of an image from one part of your canvas to paint with elsewhere, either on the same layer or on a separate layer. The 'source' point, where the paint is picked up, and your brush remain in unison as you move around the screen.

You start by holding down a modifier key – in Photoshop Elements it's **Alt** – while you click on your picture to set the 'source point'. Releasing the key, click within the image where you want the cloned copy of the source point. As you continue to paint, by clicking and dragging, the area around the source point appears wherever you paint.

This palace (above) has been altered by cloning the left-hand section over the tower. The source point is set at the top of the first

arch. Painting begins at the same point on the last arch and continues to the right.

You can also use blending modes (see page 314) with the **Clone** tool. Below, the middle flower has been cloned using **Lighten**, so it replaces only the dark background.

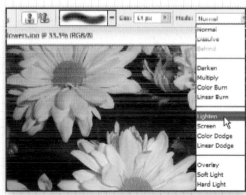

Scanning without frontiers

Put your flatbed scanner to more creative use

You can take a picture of almost anything with a digital camera, but it's less useful when you want to capture a document such as a page of a book or a craft collage. You may also have albums of photos you'd like to store and edit on your PC alongside your digital snaps. You can perform all these tasks with a flatbed scanner.

You can buy a scanner by itself or as part of a 'multi function' device that includes a printer. Each scanner comes with its own program to make scans, which can integrate closely with other Windows programs. That means a menu command for your scanner will be added to your image-editing software, such as Adobe Photoshop Elements. Programs may also be included with your scanner for other purposes, such as optical character recognition (OCR), which converts a scan of a printed page into text that you can edit in a word processor.

A flatbed scanner works in a similar way to a photocopier. You place the item you want to scan on a glass plate, and cover it with a hinged lid. When you start the scan, the 'scanning head', under the glass, moves from one end to the other. This builds up a picture that is sent to your PC. An image digitised in this way can be treated in exactly the same way as a photo taken with a digital camera.

Most flatbeds also allow 'transparency scanning', meaning that you can work from negatives or slides rather than prints. An extra lamp inside the lid shines light through the transparency. Standard 35mm film is very small, so your scanner has to work at much higher resolution than with a print, and you may not get such sharp results. Film scanners, which only take 35mm negatives and slides, provide even more detail than you'd get from a print but they're expensive.

Don't limit yourself to obviously scannable things. Think of your scanner as a general-purpose close-up camera and you'll get more value out of it. You can scan three-dimensional objects, as described in the workshop on the right, even your hands. But don't bother trying your face, as the bright light would hurt your eyes, even if you could stay still long enough.

Keep it clean

Everything on the scanner glass will be clearly reproduced in your scan – including hairs and fingerprints. Clean the glass regularly with an optical cleaning cloth, and try not to touch it when placing items to be scanned. Don't forget the same goes for the objects you're scanning. When scanning sharp objects position them on the glass with care. If you notice unwanted marks in a scan you've already done, all is not lost: a command such as **Dust & Scratches** in Photoshop Elements will help get rid of them.

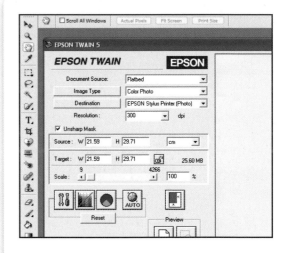

Scan solid objects

1 Run Elements and choose **Edit and Enhance Photos**. Next, go to the **File** menu and click **Import**. The devices listed should include your scanner. Select it to open the scanner's software. You'll see a range of settings, and the scanner will warm up and start an automatic preview. If you haven't placed anything on the glass, the preview window will show the plain surface of the scanner lid.

ESSENTIALS

● Choose the right resolution

The best resolution for printing is 300 dots per inch (dpi). So if you intend to print your scanned image the same size as the original, scan it at 300dpi. But remember, if you want to print it larger, you need higher resolution: for example, 600dpi for twice the size. If you don't want to work out the scanning resolution yourself, most software lets you choose an output resolution, such as 300dpi for print, and then set the scaling factor or print size that you want.

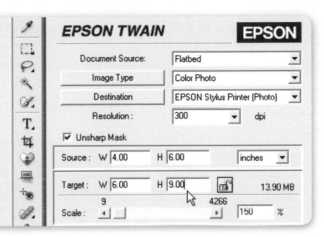

● Scanning modes

Scanner settings (see the workshop below) should suit the material that you're scanning. For example, use the highest-quality colour setting for colour photos or objects, or greyscale for black and white documents such as text pages. Switch to **Transmissive** mode if you're scanning transparencies or film negatives. Colour and tone controls can normally be left on **Auto**. An **Unsharp Mask** option will make images appear sharper but may also reveal more dust, so leave sharpening to Photoshop Elements.

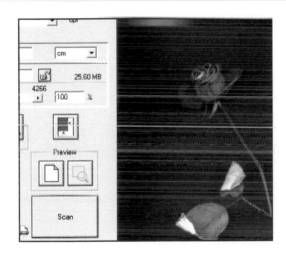

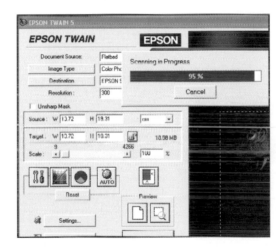

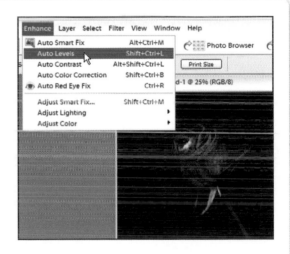

Arrange your object on the glass

2 Place your object carefully on the glass, face down. In this example it's a rose. Avoid stone or metal objects with sharp edges that could scratch the glass. You won't be able to close the lid, but you can place something over the object as a background. Here it's a black sheet of paper. Press the **Preview** button in the scanner software to see how your object looks and rearrange it if necessary.

Adjust scanning settings

3 Make sure all the settings are correct for your scan (see the boxes at the top of this page for tips). Check that you're scanning in colour – a setting for colour photos is fine – and at the appropriate resolution. In the preview window, click and drag to draw a box around the area to scan. When everything's set up, click **Scan** and wait for the scan to complete.

Edit and save the scanned image

4 The scanned image is displayed in Elements. Close the scanning window if it's still visible. Now use the image-editing functions to correct the image if necessary. For example, **Auto Levels**, from the **Enhance** menu, improves a dull scan. Go to **Save** on the **File** menu to save your scan. Choose the JPEG file format and use a high-quality setting to keep the detail you've captured.

A photo library in a flash

Organise your snapshots with Google's free Picasa photo manager

Quick fixes

Picasa includes a number of useful built-in effects and adjustments that you can apply to your photographs to make them more

interesting. Here's a photo of some cider bottles in a basket. Click the **Effects** tab in the left-hand window and then apply any of the effects by clicking on them once.

For more subtle changes, load a photograph into the main screen and then click the **Tuning** tab. Drag any of the four sliders left or right with the mouse to decrease or increase the effect.

Some photos are spoiled by poor composition. By clicking on the **Crop** button under the **Basic Fixes** tab you can 'draw' round the part of the image you wish to keep. The faded area around the shed will be removed when you click the **Apply** button.

You can add drama to a photograph in many different ways. The photo below was let down by a washed-out sky yet by clicking the **Effects** tab, choosing **Graduated Tint** and then selecting a new colour for the sky, the original has been improved dramatically.

Thanks to digital cameras, PCs are filling up with photo files. But digital cameras routinely assign them incomprehensible names such as DSC01557.JPG, so the more pictures you store, the harder it is to find the one you want.

Picasa, which you can download free from http://picasa.google.co.uk, organises all the photos and movies on your PC's hard disk in a flash, sorting them by date. It makes it easy to preview photos singly, or as part of a slideshow. You can move and copy photos between folders, set up labels (virtual albums that group together photos from many different folders), rate your photos using a star system, print them out, email them – Picasa resizes them

● Alternative image viewers

Adobe's Photoshop Album Starter edition, www.adobe.com/products/photoshopalbum/starter.html, offers many similar features to Picasa, and is also free. If space is tight, then IrfanView, free from www.irfanview.com, is a good choice; while FxFoto, from www.fxfoto.com, also offers features for fixing poor photos automatically. Even Windows Explorer – the file manager built into Windows – does a reasonable job if you don't have too many photos, displaying a browser (below) when you double-click an image file.

automatically so that they won't take so long to send – and create a photo web page with them. Picasa turns photos into wallpaper for your desktop, and lets you create collages out of multiple photos, contact sheets for printing, even posters and slideshow CDs.

It also includes powerful features for renaming entire groups of photos and has a fast, easy to use search feature. New photos are added to Picasa's catalogue automatically and, once the program is set up, you don't have to do anything. It's not as versatile as Adobe Photoshop, but Picasa offers excellent photo-fixing features. So, for example, you can crop photos, straighten them out, alter their colours and add special effects such as sepia, graduated tint and soft focus. There's even a special button called I'm Feeling Lucky that, when you click it, analyses the photo and applies those changes that Picasa thinks will improve the image.

Exporting from Picasa

Once you've edited a photo, you'll need to export it in order to make the changes permanent. Click on the thumbnail in the browser window that represents the picture and then click the **Export** button. Click the **Browse** button and choose where to copy the picture, drag the image size and quality sliders left or right with the mouse and then click **OK**.

1 Click the headings to open Picasa's standard Windows-style menus

2 These large buttons control four key program features. Import loads pictures directly from a digital camera; Slideshow displays the photos in the current folder full size, one by one; Timeline displays a calendar-based carousel of your photos; while Gift CD is a quick way of copying pictures to a blank CD to share with friends.

3 Find photos by typing their filename, title or caption keyword into the Search box.

4 Click the Starred button to display only those photos that you've given a star rating. If you click the Movies button, then Picasa will display movies but not pictures.

5 Drag this slider to display pictures based on the date you added them to the library.

6 Double-click a thumbnail to open it for editing.

7 Zoom in and out of pictures and thumbnails by dragging the slider left or right.

8 These buttons let you print and email pictures, create a collage, send pictures to friends via the Hello service, add pictures to your blog, order prints via the internet or export pictures.

9 The star button lets you tag your favourite photos, while the other two rotate pictures left or right by 90 degrees.

10 The Picture Tray displays any pictures you've currently selected, to export for example. Drag thumbnails here from the main browser window.

11 Hold allows you to add pictures from different folders to the Picture Tray, Clear removes them and Label lets you add a caption.

12 A list of folders on your PC that contain pictures. You can set Picasa to update the list manually, or automatically as images are added.

Font families

Typefaces (sometimes shortened to 'faces') often come in families. A standard family consists of four versions. The normal font is known as 'roman'. A slanted version with slightly different letter shapes, used for emphasis, is 'italic'. 'Bold' has thicker strokes, making it look heavier; this is commonly used to draw attention to headings. Finally, 'bold italic' allows for emphasis within bold text.

A family may contain many more variations. 'Light' will have thinner strokes than roman, 'heavy' thicker than bold. Following the same idea, the different fonts within a family are known as 'weights'.

Windows fonts are defined by a series of points, lines and curves (see illustration top of page 327), which means they can be scaled to any size and printed without any jagged edges appearing. Font size is measured in 'points' (an old typesetting measure). Body text is usually between 9 and 12 points; headlines 30pt or larger.

Times Roman
Times Italic
Times Bold
Gill Sans Light
Gill Sans Regular
Gill Sans Ultra Bold

Times and Gill Sans are examples of widely used serif and sans serif font families.

Character development
Understand what fonts are for and how they work in Windows

The letters of the alphabet are the same in every book, magazine and advertising hoarding, but their appearance can vary considerably. A set of characters (letters, numbers and symbols) designed in a particular way is called a font. Originally, this referred to a box of metal letters, and now to a file installed on your PC that enables it to display those characters. The design itself is called a 'typeface'. Popular typefaces have familiar names such as Times and Arial.

Typefaces are classified in various ways. The first distinction is between 'serif' and 'sans serif'. Serifs are small flourishes on the ends of the lines, or 'strokes', that make up a character. Sans serif means they're absent ('sans' is French for 'without'). The text you're reading now is a sans serif font; most books and newspapers use serif faces, which are thought to be easier to read in large quantities.

There's also a loose division between text and display faces. Text faces are clear and unfussy, good for books or newspapers. A display face will be better suited to posters, packaging, signs and anywhere a small number of letters or words needs to make a big impression. Also useful are symbol fonts such as Microsoft's Wingdings and Webdings, where letters of the alphabet are replaced by miniature clip-art images.

⦿ Where to find fonts

Tens of thousands of fonts exist, from reworkings of centuries-old designs to innovative new typefaces. The best, available from suppliers such as FontShop at www.yellowblack.com, can be expensive. But you can get cheap fonts, many of good quality, in large collections such as Greenstreet's *1000 Professional Fonts* by visiting www.greenstreetsoftware.co.uk. To download free fonts, try visiting www.1001freefonts.com and www.acidfonts.com. Watch out, though, for missing characters such as the Euro symbol.

How to install and remove fonts

1 Any Windows application that deals with text will let you choose between fonts. The fonts available are those for which font files have been installed on your PC. Quite a few fonts are included with Windows, and others may be added when you install programs. These files are normally kept in the **Fonts** folder. To see this, go to **Control Panel** on the Windows **Start** menu and double-click the **Fonts** icon.

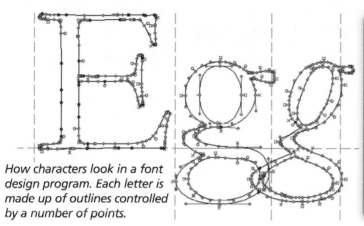

How characters look in a font design program. Each letter is made up of outlines controlled by a number of points.

Design your own typeface

Typeface design is a highly skilled discipline but it can be fun to have a go yourself. FontLab, www.fontlab.com, offers two simple font design products – TypeTool and SigMaker. With TypeTool 2 you can edit characters, copy them between fonts, and even draw fonts from scratch. SigMaker lets you scan your signature and add it to a font. At www.fontifier.com, you can go further and make a complete font, for a low price, out of a scanned example of your handwriting.

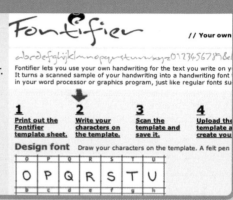

// **Your own**

Fontifier lets you use your own handwriting for the text you write on your It turns a scanned sample of your handwriting into a handwriting font in your word processor or graphics program, just like regular fonts su

1 Print out the Fontifier template sheet.
2 Write your characters on the template.
3 Scan the template and save it.
4 Upload the template a create you

Design font Draw your characters on the template. A felt pen

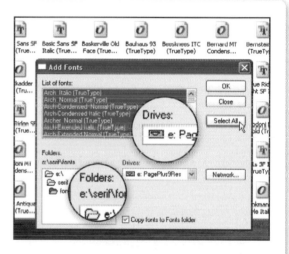

Display a font preview

2 Each font file shows the full name of the font that it contains. Notice that each member of a font family has its own separate file. To see what any font looks like, double-click it. A box appears showing all the details of the font along with a sample using the traditional typesetter's test, 'The quick brown fox jumps over the lazy dog' – a sentence containing all the letters of the alphabet.

Install and uninstall fonts

3 If there are any fonts you no longer want, delete their files by clicking the filename and then pressing the **Delete** key. To disable a font temporarily, simply move its file out of the **Fonts** folder into another folder, such as **My Documents**. You can move it back later. To add new fonts, go to the **File** menu in the **Fonts** window and choose **Install New Font**. The **Add Fonts** box appears.

Import new fonts

4 Under **Drives**, choose the disk that contains the fonts you want to add, perhaps a font collection CD or your hard disk. Under **Folders**, find the folder on the disk that contains the fonts. As soon as you select a folder containing fonts, they're listed in the window above. Highlight a font you want by clicking it – hold the **Ctrl** key to select more than one or click **Select All** for all of them – then click **OK**.

Hold the front page!

Master the fundamentals of desktop publishing with Microsoft Word

Typography and layout

A page usually contains several different kinds of text. To make the main 'story' or body text easier to read, you divide it into paragraphs. It's also common to add a 'crosshead' after every few paragraphs; this is a subheading that summarises what's coming up. Crossheads are often the same size as the body text but in a heavier typeface. If you're mixing text and graphics – in a newsletter, for example – you'll also need a style for captions. It's important that your captions stand out from the body text. For that reason, italic fonts are often used.

At the beginning of each new story you'll want a headline in a larger size. For the sake of readability you should avoid using serif fonts (see page 326) or anything that's too fancy. Headlines consisting of all capitals should also be avoided in most cases as they

can be hard to read. You can often increase impact by choosing a colour other than black.

With larger text, you may need to alter spacing. In Word, highlight the text to adjust and choose **Font** from the **Format** menu, click the **Character Spacing** tab in the **Font** box, set **Spacing** to **Condensed** and increase the **By** setting to reduce the space between characters even further. The spacing of individual characters is adjusted by 'kerning', for example to even up the space around an apostrophe (') – see screens below.

To kern headlines automatically, tick the **Kerning** option and, in the **Points and above** box, choose a point size (see page 326) slightly larger than that of your body text. You'll still sometimes need to adjust the spacing of awkward letter combinations such as 'W A' or 'tt' in certain fonts and sizes.

Producing a newsletter or brochure used to require specialist equipment. Today, it's something that anyone can tackle using a home PC. Desktop publishing (DTP) is the term for using a computer to prepare page layouts for printing. There are various programs designed specifically for this purpose (see below) but you can also use Microsoft Word or other word processors to achieve great-looking results.

DTP is all about combining words and pictures, whether into a single-page poster that you print once or a magazine that you send to a print shop for multiple copies. You start by deciding the widths of the margins and the number of columns on each page. These will normally apply to all the pages, making your publication's design look consistent, but you can vary them wherever necessary.

On each page, you'll put text in the columns, and add headlines, pictures and other items. Each element is held in a box that you can move around and resize. The box itself may have a tint or outline, or can just be an invisible container for the text or picture.

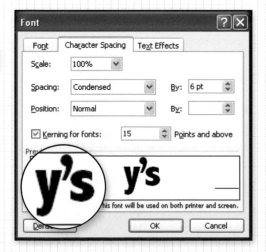

● Dedicated software

DTP programs give you more control over your layouts. Microsoft Publisher, included with some editions of Microsoft Office, has good basic features and integrates closely with other Office programs. Serif PagePlus, www.serif.com, is simple to use and can save files in the standard form that a print shop would ask for if you wanted your publication professionally printed. A cheaper option is Greenstreet's Publisher, www.greenstreetsoftware.com.

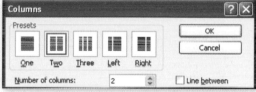

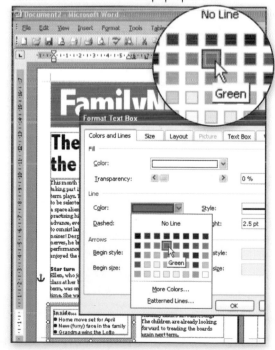

8 The Columns box, available from the Format menu, lets you choose how many text columns to fit on each page, and set their width and how much gap to leave between them. You don't have to keep the same arrangement of columns all the way through. For example, you can type your main heading across the page, press Return to finish it, go to Columns, set up a number of columns and choose This Point Forward to continue your text in columns.

9 This panel appears when you choose New from the File menu. Use the options under Templates to find ready-made DTP-style documents.

10 To change the appearance of a box, click it with the right mouse button and choose the Format command from the pop-up menu.

1 Word's main display shows your pages with dotted outlines around the boxes containing the various items that make up your layout.

2 Use the Print Preview command from the File menu to see the page without these outlines, exactly as it will appear when printed.

3 For DTP projects, change Word's View setting to Print Layout. This shows everything in its correct position on the page.

4 You can use the commands on the Insert menu to add items such as pictures and text boxes to your layout.

5 To create a headline, type the words you want at the beginning of your story, highlight them and go to Insert, Text Box.

6 Having highlighted some text by clicking and dragging with the mouse, use the options in this toolbar to change its font and size.

7 Use the commands on the Format menu for more control over text. For example, choose Paragraph to open a box where you can change settings such as the amount of space between lines. Choose Font to change the colour or spacing of text.

Media Player sights and sounds
Be entertained by Windows' all singing, all dancing media jukebox

Thanks to CD-quality sound and a sharp, colourful screen, your PC does a great job of delivering music and video right to your desktop.

To join in the fun and enjoy movie trailers, internet-only promotional video clips, digital music and radio, you'll need a 'media player', a program to help you find, store, organise and play back sound and video. In a perfect world, one media player would be able to handle all of the most popular sound and video file formats, but because there are many competing 'standards' you'll probably use a couple of different ones.

Start with the program that's included with Windows XP, Windows Media Player, because it's powerful, versatile and free. With Media Player you can make digital copies of your CDs

and transfer the tracks to a portable digital music player such as an iPod, or to a pocket PC or mobile phone. You can use it to find and buy music via the internet (either entire albums or individual tracks) and to create a library of all your music that's easy to search and quick to access, complete with cover artwork, album name, artist and year of recording.

Media Player can handle almost any kind of audio and video file. But if you come across something that it can't play, you can usually download from the internet a small, free add-in, called a 'codec', that helps it understand the format and play the music or video file. In most cases Media Player even offers to download and install the update automatically if it can't play a file. There are exceptions, such as Apple's proprietary QuickTime format – popular with all Mac users and on websites that have movie trailers to download or watch online. Another is a media-file format developed by a company

called Real that's widely used for listening to live or recorded internet radio and watching online TV. Notably, all the BBC's radio stations, TV news broadcasts and the BBC 'Listen again' service are available in Real format. For that you'll need to download the free RealPlayer (see the box above).

Media Player's Now Playing view includes swirling electronic lightshows called 'visualisations'. There's a selection built in, and you can download hundreds more, free, from the internet at sites such as www.wmplugins.com and www.microsoft.com/windows/windowsmedia/mp10/getmore/visualizations.aspx.

Download new free 'skins' that will completely change the look of Windows Media Player from www.microsoft.com/windows/windowsmedia/mp10/getmore/skins.aspx.

Buy music

The easiest way to buy music via the internet is to make sure you're online then start Media Player. Click the **MSN Music** button at the top and you'll find thousands of individual songs and whole albums to download.

composer. You can make your own compilations by creating a playlist, giving it a name and then dragging tracks into the list using your mouse.

11 Once you've plugged in a portable music player, clicking the Start Sync button transfers songs slected from your PC playlists to your player. Click the Sync tab (**1**) to choose what to sync.

1 Clicking any of the tabs – Now Playing, Library, Rip, Burn, Sync and Guide – changes the contents of Media Player's main window. Here, you can see the Library with the playlist window on the right, the album/playlist window in the middle and the category window on the left.

2 Using the transport controls you can play, stop or pause, and jump to the next or previous track.

3 Drag the volume slider left or right with the mouse to decrease or increase playback volume.

4 The Now Playing List displays tracks on the album being played or current playlist selection.

5 Click here to visit the MSN website, where you can listen to and buy individual tracks or entire CDs.

6 You can search your library for music tracks, albums and artists by typing a name into the empty box then clicking Search.

7 The album/playlist window shows the names of the individual tracks, the artist and the album they come from.

8 Media Player can display a list of internet radio stations that you can listen to over the internet.

9 When you click the Start Burn button, Media Player will burn all the songs in the current playlist onto a blank CD. This feature requires a PC with a CD/DVD writer.

10 Media Player automatically sorts your music collection into categories, for example by genre or

Types of PC sound

Sound in the PC world can be divided into two main types: digital audio and MIDI (Musical Instrument Digital Interface). Digital audio is created whenever you record a voice or an instrument that makes a noise. Simple PC recordings are known as 'WAV files' (short for wave files), which take up a lot of space: one minute of CD-quality sound will take up 10Mb. MP3 and WMA (Windows Media Audio) files are also digital audio, but compressed to save space – a four-minute MP3 song will take up around 4Mb. The relatively small file size is perfectly suited to portable players such as the iPod and even mobile phones. Media Player lets you choose how much compression to use when copying tracks from a CD. There's a trade-off between file size and audio quality, but it is possible to make MP3 recordings that, to most ears, are indistinguishable from CDs.

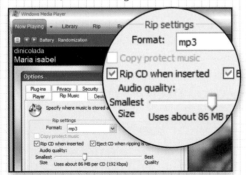

MIDI files aren't digital recordings at all. Rather, they contain instructions that tell MIDI instruments such as synthesisers or your PC's soundcard which notes to play, for how long, and what sounds to use. As a result, MIDI files are tiny by comparison.

PC performer
Turn your computer into a powerful digital recording studio

When it comes to sound, a typical home PC can do much more than play CDs and DVDs. You can use it to record and play back anything you wish, from your voice to complete songs that sound as if they are being played by a band.

For simple recordings – a voice, a piano or guitar – plug a microphone into the appropriate

connector on your PC's soundcard (look for the 'mic' symbol). Open Windows Sound Recorder by clicking **Start**, choosing **All Programs** and then **Accessories**, **Entertainment** then **Sound Recorder**. Finally, click the **Record** button (red dot).

Orchestra in a box

Your PC doesn't just record music from the world outside. At its heart is a soundcard that can reproduce the performance of almost any musical instrument, from pianos to timpani (see box, page 333). There are freeware programs available with which you can compose MIDI music (see left), such as Quartz AudioMaster, **www.digitalsoundplanet.com/SoftwareHouse**. Or you

can buy complete music-production programs such as Cubasis (see below), **www.steinberg.net**, that allow you to mix live instruments and synthesised sounds (generated by your soundcard or by an external music keyboard), overdubbing instruments one at a time to create an ensemble performance. You can edit your recordings to correct mistakes, add professional-style effects such as reverb and echo and then mix the results onto an audio CD.

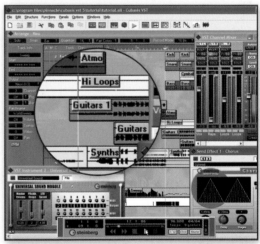

Downloading sounds

Start by visiting www.samplenet.co.uk where you'll find hundreds of sounds, including drums, guitars, orchestras and vocals. For special effects and humorous sound clips, go to www.Ilovewavs.com. Try www.looperman.com for general audio sounds. You'll find complete songs programmed as MIDI files to download too at sites such as www.musicrobot.com.

What soundcards do

Every sound that your computer makes is generated by its soundcard – from the simple beeps and dings in Windows to complete CD-quality music tracks recorded digitally on CD, DVD or your hard disk. A soundcard also has its own internal synthesiser capable of emulating all the sounds of an orchestra. Budget soundcards are integrated into the PC's main circuit board. More sophisticated systems involve separate plug-in boards and even external boxes with sockets for connecting microphones, external audio equipment and surround-sound speakers.

Software choices

If you want a good free program to edit sounds you record yourself, try Audacity at http://audacity.sourceforge.net. If you prefer to create music using professionally prerecorded sounds, sometimes called 'samples' or 'loops', go to www.sonymediasoftware.com/download/freestuff.asp to download a free copy of ACID Xpress. For a moderately priced program that records both audio and MIDI files try Cakewalk's Sonar Home Studio, which is available at www.cakewalk.com/homemusicians.asp.

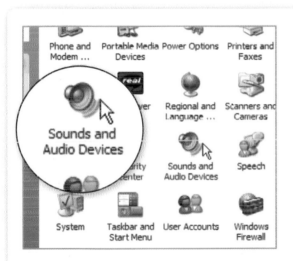

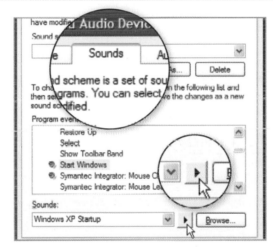

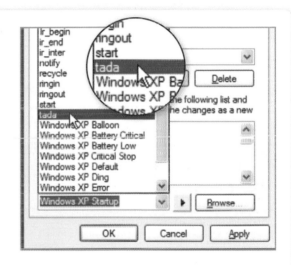

Change Windows' start-up sound

1 You can change most of the sounds Windows makes – the sound it makes when it starts up, for example. Click on the **Start** button; choose **Control Panel** from the menu and a window will open. If your screen doesn't look like the one shown here, click the **Switch to Classic View** command on the left of the window. Find the **Sounds and Audio Devices** icon and double-click on it.

Display the list of Windows actions

2 When the **Sounds and Audio Devices Properties** box appears, click the **Sounds** tab. You'll see a list of Windows actions. A small speaker icon indicates those with sounds associated. Scroll down and click on **Start Windows**. 'Windows XP Startup' is displayed in the **Sounds** box. Click the **Play** button (a small triangle) to the left of the **Browse** button to hear the familiar start-up sound.

Select a replacement sound

3 You can choose any WAV file (see page 332) as a Windows sound by clicking **Browse**, navigating to a file on your hard disk, then clicking **OK**. Or you can choose one of Windows' built-in sounds by selecting one from the **Sounds** drop-down list. Click the **Play** button to hear the new Windows start-up sound. If you're happy with it, click **OK**. Otherwise you can choose again or click **Cancel**.

Useful terms and technologies

A quick reference guide to help you cut through the computer jargon

While all attempts are made to avoid jargon, there are times when only the technical term will do. This glossary explains common terms that you'll come across while working through the projects in this book. You'll also find it a useful reference to computer technology in general. To help you get more from the definitions, some technical words are highlighted, in blue, to indicate that the term is defined more fully elsewhere in the glossary. Menu items, on-screen buttons and keyboard keys are highlighted in **bold type**. Web addresses are in red.

A

ActiveX A feature of some web pages that adds interactive elements such as controlling playback of a movie, or installing files onto your PC. As a safety measure, Internet Explorer asks you, before running an ActiveX feature on a web page, whether you want to allow it to run.

ADSL Asymmetric Digital Subscriber Line. Type of broadband internet supplied through your existing phone line. A plug-in splitter box allows you to use your phone for voice calls while your PC is connected to the internet.

analogue A device or a signal that moves or varies continuously rather than in the discrete steps of a digital equivalent. An old-fashioned thermometer, for example, using an expanding and contracting column of mercury, is analogue, while a thermometer with an LED display is digital. Two other familiar analogue devices with digital equivalents are clocks and radio tuners. Computers work digitally, by converting words, music and pictures into numbers, so that they are infinitely reproducible with no loss of quality.

animated GIF A single graphics file containing a sequence of images that play as a simple animation. GIF animations are easy to make and are often small in size, which is ideal for use on web pages and emails.

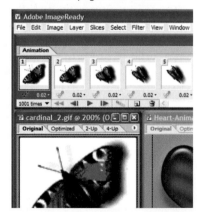

anti-aliasing A technique that reduces the jagged or 'stepped' appearance of objects on screen – particularly noticeable when text or graphics are magnified. Windows uses a form of anti-aliasing called ClearType to aid readability of text.

anti-virus software Software designed to detect and remove malicious programs from your PC and incoming emails. Regularly updates itself to combat new threats as they appear.

aspect ratio The relationship between the width of the image on a PC monitor and its height. A standard PC monitor has a 4:3 aspect ratio, meaning that its height is three-quarters that of its width. This is true both of its physical dimensions (in centimetres or inches) and its screen resolution (for example, 1024x768 pixels). Wide-screen PC monitors and TVs have an aspect ratio of 16:9 (so the height is nine-sixteenths that of the width).

audio file Any sound that's designed to be stored and played back on a PC. Popular formats include WAV, WMA and MP3 files.

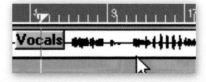

AutoCorrect A feature found in programs such as Microsoft Word and Excel that corrects or replaces commonly mistyped words automatically as you type.

AutoFill Allows spreadsheet programs such as Excel to complete sets of headings automatically. For example, type Monday into a spreadsheet cell, grab the corner handle of the cell and drag it across or down over the six adjacent cells, and they are filled with the days Tuesday to Sunday.

AutoFit Method used by programs to adjust elements on the screen (for example, tables in Word or columns in Excel) to use the available space most effectively.

AutoShapes Ready-made graphic elements such as rectangles, circles and stars that you can add instantly to a word-processing, design or page-layout document.

AutoText Frequently used blocks of text and graphics – for example, a letterhead, scanned signature or standard greeting – that you can insert instantly into a document by simply typing a keyword or selecting from a list of AutoText items.

B

banding A printer malfunction that produces visible horizontal bands across a page instead of a smooth gradation between different colours.

bandwidth The amount of data that you can send or receive over a network, usually your internet connection, in a fixed period of time. Expressed as bits per second (bps). The higher the bandwidth, the faster the connection.

Bézier curve A curve defined by a series of anchor points along its arc; moving the points with the mouse changes the shape of the curve.

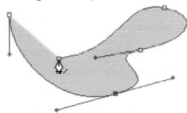

bit The smallest unit of computer memory, a contraction of 'binary digit'. A value of a single bit can be only either 1 or 0 – like counting on one finger. A byte is a sequence of bits – 8 bits make 1 byte; 1024 bytes make one kilobyte (Kb); 1024 kilobytes make 1 megabyte (Mb); and 1024 megabytes make 1 gigabyte (Gb).

bitmap An image made up of tiny dots or pixels. If you zoom in close, you'll see the dots grow in size, and if you keep enlarging a bitmap it leads to a blocky appearance. (See dots per inch.) To produce large bitmaps without loss of quality you must ensure you have used as many dots as possible to create the image, which is why most good-quality digital cameras offer resolutions of more than 5 million pixels (5 megapixels). There are many types of bitmap files, but the most common are identified by the file extensions .BMP, .GIF, .JPG and .TIF.

blending A technique used by image-editing programs to combine or 'blend' two images. This is done by placing one image on top of the other and then controlling the relative transparency and other settings of each to produce a new image.

blog A diary or log that you store on a website and update regularly. Blogs can include photos as well as links to other blogs and websites, and are usually free to set up.

BMP Type of bitmap picture file that can be used by most Windows

programs. For example, desktop wallpaper on a PC is a BMP image.

broadband Short for broad bandwidth. An internet connection that's much faster than a dial-up modem. It transmits large amounts of data at high speed over phone lines or cable, making it possible to watch TV or videos, or listen to CD-quality music over the internet.

browser A program such as Internet Explorer used to view web pages and surf the internet. Sometimes applied also to programs such as Picasa that enable you to browse the pictures stored on your PC.

brush An image-editing tool that lets you draw freehand within an image on screen in chosen colours or textures. Most image editors let you choose from a vast range of brush shapes, sizes, styles and settings.

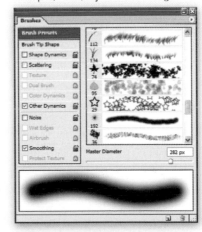

burn The process of writing data such as photos, documents, music or videos onto a blank CD or DVD.

C

capture To transfer video footage from your camcorder, via a cable, onto your PC, prior to editing in software such as Windows Movie Maker. You can capture still images from your PC screen to memory by pressing the **PrtScn** keyboard button.

CD-ROM Stands for compact disc read-only memory. This is the data equivalent of the audio CD – the disc used is identical, but the way it's recorded is different. Data on a CD-ROM cannot be changed, added to or erased, unlike blank CD-R discs, which you can add your own data to, and CD-RW (rewritable) discs, which can be recorded over again and again.

CD writer A CD drive included with most home PCs that can burn data, such as music and video, onto recordable CD discs.

clip Short section of video or sound.

clip art Ready-made pictures and photos that you can use in your documents and web pages. Sold in collections on CD-ROMs and downloadable from the internet.

cloning A method of painting freehand with colours and texture copied from one part of an image onto a different part of the image. Cloning is used to tidy up blemishes, remove unwanted objects from photos or create special effects.

CMYK Cyan, Magenta, Yellow and Black (K is used for black, rather than B to avoid confusion with the colour blue). These are the primary colours used in commercial printing processes to print magazines, packaging and posters. Combining them in different percentages produces a wide range of colours and tones.

c:100%	c:100% m:100%	c:50% m:100%
m:100%	m:100% y:100%	m:50% y:100%
y:100%	c:100% y:100%	c:100% y:50%
k:100%	k:50%	k:25%

codec Acronym for coder/decoder. Most video and sound stored on a PC or downloaded from the internet is compressed to save space. Codecs are programs that then decompress the video or sound so that it will play.

colour depth Relates to the number of colours that can be displayed in an image, and is expressed as a binary number. An 8-bit image can have up to 256 different colours, whereas a 24-bit image can include up to 16 million colours. A 1-bit image can use only black or white.

colour palette Although your PC may be able to display millions of colours, not every picture needs or uses that many. The actual colours used in any image make up its colour palette.

compression A way of making a file smaller by rearranging or removing non-critical information. Compressed files are quicker to download or send as attachments.

cookies Small text files that are copied to your PC after you visit a website. Typically, they contain any preferences you set, such as your user name and key interests, so that the site remembers you on your next visit.

crop To select the part of an image that interests you and trim off the rest. In an image editor such as Photoshop Elements, the **Crop** tool is used to highlight the part you want to keep then delete the rest. It's also possible to crop an image in Microsoft Word, but the cropped edges are just hidden, not deleted.

cutout Part of a picture that's been selected or highlighted then cut out for use elsewhere in the same image or in a different image. Photoshop Elements and other image editors can keep cutouts on separate transparent layers so they can be repositioned or resized at any time.

D

depth of field The range between objects in a photograph that are at different distances from the camera but remain in focus. The lens aperture (like the iris of the eye) governs the depth of field. A small aperture increases depth of field. This is why daylight shots (where there is plenty of light and the aperture contracts to compensate) tend to be sharper overall than poorly lit interiors (where the aperture dilates to let as much light as possible into the camera).

dialogue box A small window that appears in connection with a program running in Windows to display messages and information, and to show configuring options and settings. When a dialogue box contains a large number of options it may be separated into sections using tabbed dividers, like an old-fashioned card index.

digital Refers to data – sounds, images, video – stored as a series of distinct numbers rather than as a

continuously variable (analogue) signal. Sound is converted from analogue waves into digital data simply by measuring its amplitude at extremely tiny intervals. Graphical information is stored digitally by dividing a picture into a grid of tiny points and then storing the colour of each point as a set of three numbers representing the amount of red, green and blue at that location. Once data has been converted into its digital format (digitised), it's easy for the computer to handle because the digital information can be translated into the zeroes and ones of the binary system in which computers do their processing.

digital camera A still camera that captures images when light is focused through the lens onto an electronic sensor. The camera records the colour of each of the millions of pixels that make up a digital picture. Images are stored digitally on small memory cards, rather than on film. You can transfer images to a PC for editing, then erase them from the camera to make space for new pictures.

digital video Video recorded using a digital camcorder or converted into a digital format. Unlike older analogue video systems, such as VHS, digital video can be transferred to a PC, copied and edited again and again without any loss of quality.

digital watermark An electronic tag attached to content, for example a piece of music or a picture, which identifies the owner, copyright holder and authorised users.

digital zoom A feature found on cheaper cameras and camera phones that simulates the effect of a real (optical) zoom lens by digitally enlarging the centre of an image. The effect is the same as resizing part of a photo using image-editing software.

digitise To convert analogue images, sound or video (such as old records or VHS tapes), transfer them to a PC and store in digital form.

dissolve A visual effect used in video-editing and presentation programs to move smoothly between scenes or slides, fading one scene out while the next fades in.

domain name A unique text name used to distinguish one website from another. For example, bbc.co.uk and radiotimes.com are domain names.

dots per inch (dpi) The number of dots that a printer can print on each linear inch of paper, or the number

of dots used to make up a linear inch of a digital image. The greater the number of dots per inch, the smaller each dot and the clearer the picture. Many inkjet printers can print at more than 1440dpi, but most computer monitors display at around 92dpi.

drag and drop Clicking and holding the left mouse button on an object, then moving the mouse to drag it elsewhere on screen, and releasing the button to drop the object.

drawing tablet An electronic pen and pad connected to a PC. Used by designers and artists, who find it a more natural and precise way of drawing than using a mouse.

driver Software that translates instructions from Windows into a form that can be understood by a hardware device such as a printer or a graphics card.

drop cap Large, decorative upper-case letter at the start of a paragraph that drops into the lines below it.

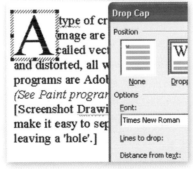

DVD Digital Versatile Disc. A CD-like disc that can store roughly six times as much data as a CD-ROM.

DVD writer A device included with many home PCs used to burn data, music or movies onto a blank recordable DVD disc.

E

email Messages sent electronically over the internet. You can send messages to anyone who is also connected to the internet, provided you know the recipient's unique email address. This always takes the form of user@somewhere, where the part before the @ sign identifies the individual and the part after identifies where the email account is held. To send and receive emails you need a program like Microsoft Outlook Express, which is included with Windows. Alternatively, you can open a web-based email account with Hotmail (http://hotmail.co.uk) or any similar email provider, and handle your emails using a web browser.

encode To convert a file from one digital format into another, often to compress it or make it smaller.

equaliser An expanded set of tone settings found on audio programs and media players that allows fine volume control over different parts of the sound spectrum.

export To save a document or file created in one program in a format that can be opened in another. If you've saved a photo in Photoshop Elements but want to send it to someone who doesn't use Elements, you could export the file in JPEG format, which can be opened in any web browser or graphics program.

exposure The amount of light that falls on the electronic image sensor in a digital camera while you're taking a photograph.

F

favourites A menu item on the Internet Explorer web browser where you can store the names of those sites you visit frequently.

fill Tool used by graphics programs to paint an enclosed area on an image by filling it with a colour or pattern. Also called **Paint Bucket**.

filter A visual effect, such as mosaic, watercolour or impressionist, applied to an image to enhance or transform it. Photoshop Elements includes dozens of filters, each with its own settings to customise the way the effect will be applied.

firewall Software or hardware that protects a computer or network from attack or hijack by an unauthorised third party over the internet.

FireWire A fast data connector found on many PCs; particularly suitable for transferring digital video from a camera. Also referred to as an IEEE 1394 connector.

Flash Multimedia design software used on many web pages to create elements such as menus and animations.

flat-panel display Computer display screen that achieves its thin profile by using LCD (liquid crystal display) technology rather than a cathode-ray tube (CRT). Flat panels save space, produce fewer emissions and don't distort the picture at the edges as older TV-style monitors can.

focal length An indication of the angle of view, or zoom factor, of a camera lens. The shorter the focal length, the wider the angle of view. In digital photography the focal length of a lens is measured as the distance from its optical mid-point

to the surface of the image sensor. Because there's a wide variance in sensor shapes and sizes, the focal length of digital camera lenses is often expressed by its 35mm (film camera) equivalence. A 24mm lens is considered wide angle, 50mm roughly equivalent to the human eye, and greater than 135mm is classed as a close-up or telephoto lens.

font A particular style of type, such as Helvetica or Arial. Most fonts can be displayed and printed in different sizes. They can also be styled in bold or italic, or with other effects.

FTP File-transfer protocol. A popular way to upload and download files to and from a website. Some FTP programs, such as SmartFTP, www.smartftp.com, are free for personal use.

G

Gb Gigabyte. A measure of storage equivalent to 1024 megabytes (Mb), although it's convenient to regard a gigabyte as 1000 megabytes.

GIF file Graphics Interchange Format. Image format particularly useful for web graphics thanks to its small file sizes and features such as transparent backgrounds and animation (see animated GIF).

graphics card A circuit board in your PC that contains the electronics and connections required to display images on your computer's screen.

graphics program Software that can display, edit and manipulate images, whether paintings, photos or line drawings. Adobe Photoshop Elements and Microsoft Paint are examples of graphics programs.

greyscale An image made up of a range of tones between black and white. The quality of a greyscale image depends on the number of different shades of grey that are used (just as a colour image's quality depends on the number of shades of red, green and blue).

grid Most design programs let you display a grid as a background to drawings and page layouts, making it easier to line up different elements. If you switch on the **Snap-to-grid** feature, objects you position with the mouse will snap into place to the nearest grid line.

groups See newsgroups.

H

halftone A method for representing an image using only black dots, where darker areas are made up of

larger dots and lighter ones consist of smaller dots. This is similar to the process used to print black and white photographs in newspapers.

handle The 'grab handles' at the corners of a picture or graphical object that's being resized or repositioned in Word or in an image editor. Click the left mouse button and drag a handle to change the size or proportions of the object.

hanging indent Used in documents where the first line of a paragraph starts flush with the margin but subsequent lines are indented at a fixed distance from the left. Each entry in this glossary is an example of a paragraph with a hanging indent.

header/footer Text that appears at the top or bottom of each page in a document – for example, the document name, its author, the date it was last edited and the page number. In Microsoft Word there are areas at the top and the bottom of page 1 that are dedicated to headers and footers. Whatever you type in these areas will appear on subsequent pages.

History Web browsers such as Internet Explorer remember where you surf on the internet and keep a record of all the websites in a 'History' list. To return to a site you visited recently, you can choose it from the list.

home page Refers either to a personal web page you create yourself, or to the website you always visit first when you connect to the internet. The latter is also often known as your start page.

hotspot A public place where you can connect to the internet wirelessly using your portable PC or pocket computer. Some hotspots

are free to use; for some others you'll be asked to pay a small fee.

HTML Hypertext Markup Language. A set of layout commands and tags designed for electronic publishing. All web pages are built using HTML. Web-page design programs, such as Microsoft FrontPage, allow you to position items on the screen and format them visually, but when you save the page it's stored as a text file containing HTML commands.

hue The main characteristic of a colour that distinguishes it from other colours in the spectrum. In image editing it's represented by a number between 0 and 359 and usually picked off a colour wheel displayed on the screen.

hyperlink Text or graphic on a web page that you can click with the mouse to jump to another part of the page, a different page on the same site or a page on a different site. Text hyperlinks are typically underlined in blue to distinguish them from plain text. You can also create hyperlinks in many Microsoft programs, including Word, PowerPoint and Excel.

I

image editing Using a graphics program such as Adobe Photoshop Elements to alter the composition, colours and other characteristics of an electronic painting, drawing or photo.

import Method used by one Windows program to open a file created by a different Windows program. Importing a file in this way may not preserve all of the original formatting but usually keeps the data intact.

instant messaging Text chat in real time over the internet between two or more people using a program such as Windows Messenger. Instant messages can also include photos, animations and even videos.

internet A global collection of interconnected computers and networks. It's used by millions of people and organisations to host their websites as well as for sending and receiving email.

internet service provider Usually abbreviated to ISP. A company that offers access to the internet so you can browse the web and send emails. There's usually a sign-up fee, followed by a monthly charge.

internet telephony Also known as VOIP (Voice Over Internet Protocol), this technology allows you to use the internet to make telephone calls. Both parties need PCs equipped with a microphone and speakers, or headphones, and special software, such as Skype, www.skype.com, to make the calls. Generally, the software and the calls are free.

IP address Every computer, while connected to the internet, has a unique Internet Protocol (IP) address expressed as four numbers, each separated by a dot. For example, Google's IP address is 216.239.39.99.

iTunes A media player created by Apple, closely associated with iPod personal music players. iTunes has many of the same features as Windows Media Player, including playlists, a video player, visual effects and the ability to burn CDs.

J

jaggies Ugly, stair-like steps that appear at the edges of shapes where there should be a smooth, straight line or graceful curve. This is caused when an image is displayed at too low a resolution.

JPEG file Also known as JPG, and pronounced 'jaypeg'. A compressed graphics file format widely used on the internet for storing and displaying photographs. JPEG photos take up little space and download fast. The compression quality can be specified (in the **JPEG Options** dialogue box) when saving an image as a JPEG file. The more compressed the file, the smaller the file size, although compressing an image can degrade its quality.

jukebox A computer program for copying, compressing, playing and managing music tracks. One of the best-known examples is Musicmatch Jukebox, available in both free and paid-for versions. Once music has been captured and compressed, usually in the form of MP3 files, the jukebox software provides ways of searching for music and organising it into playlists for specific purposes.

K

kern When you type onto your PC, the individual characters that make up the words are evenly spaced. Sometimes, it's necessary to adjust, or kern, the space between one or more of the letters – an excessively wide gap between certain letters, for example, or where two letters touch. Headings that use large characters often create problems with gaps that require kerning.

L

landscape Turn an ordinary A4 page on its side, so the longer edge runs horizontally, and you're looking at a landscape page. See also portrait.

layers Graphics programs such as Photoshop Elements use layers to help organise complex images. For example, you could use one layer for the main image, a second for text and a third for a frame or colour effect. Think of layers as drawings on transparent sheets. Each can be edited independently, making it possible to change one part of a picture without affecting the others.

layout The arrangement of text, images and other graphical elements on a page when creating documents such as newsletters, posters, presentations or web pages.

leading The measurement of the space between lines of text in a document. In a typical paragraph of text, line spacing is constant, but it's possible to alter it line by line – for example, when adjusting lines of large text to use as headings.

legend In spreadsheet charts, the key explaining what the patterns or colours attached to each data series or category of data represent.

levels The amount of brightness, contrast and colour in the shadows, midtones and highlights of a photo. In Photoshop Elements you can adjust levels manually or optimise them automatically with **Auto Levels**.

line art A term for pictures that are made up of black and white only, without any shades of grey.

loop A short section of digital sound recorded in such a way that it can be copied many times then arranged end to end in sequence to form a continuous passage of music.

lossy Any compression method that throws away unimportant data to reduce the size of a file, such as JPEG image files or MP3 sound files. The compressed version will contain less detail, but the difference is often not noticeable to eye or ear.

M

Magic Wand An image-editing tool that selects automatically all pixels within a specified colour range. Useful for making quick cutouts.

mailing list A list of addresses stored in a spreadsheet or database that can be merged into a standard letter to save typing each address.

marquee The dotted line outlining a selection in a graphics program. This might be a neat rectangular area or an irregular shape created with a freehand tool or magic wand.

mastering In music production, the creation of a final set of fully mixed audio files complete with effects that are ready to be duplicated onto recordable CDs.

Mb Abbreviation for megabyte, which is a measure of the data capacity of a storage device. One megabyte is 1,048,576 bytes, but it's easier to think of a megabyte as a million bytes. Main memory (RAM) is measured in megabytes.

Media Player Microsoft program included with Windows XP that plays back music, video and internet radio. You can also use it to buy music albums online, burn your own CDs, create playlists of music you already own and copy tracks to a personal digital music player or Windows mobile phone.

megapixel One million pixels. Used by digital camera makers to describe the resolution of their products. The more megapixels, the better the quality of the image you'll get.

MIDI Musical Instrument Digital Interface. PCs, synthesisers and soundcards equipped with MIDI connectors can send and receive instructions that tell them which notes to play, which instruments to use and which effects to apply. MIDI files are much smaller than digital audio files such as WAVs or MP3s.

mixer A device used in music that adjusts and mixes together sounds from separate sources or balances separate parts of a multi-track song.

Music programs such as Cubasis include a software mixer that you operate by moving the sliders up and down using your mouse.

modem A device that converts digital electronic signals from a PC into analogue sound signals that can be transmitted over a phone line. It gets its name from the term MODulator/DEModulator. With the growing popularity of broadband computer connections using digital lines, the term 'modem' has been borrowed to refer to any electronic

device that connects a PC or a computing device to the internet.

Movie Maker A Microsoft program supplied as part of Windows XP that allows you to edit video clips and add special effects and titles to create your own movies.

MP3 A way of storing music digitally that compresses the sound data, making the finished file smaller so it downloads quickly and takes up less storage space. An MP3 file may also include embedded information about the artist, album and track name, year of release, and even album cover art.

MPEG A method of compressing and storing digital video. MPEG-2 is used for DVD movies, while MPEG-4 squeezes files to make them suitable for transmitting over the internet.

N

netiquette An unofficial set of rules describing good behaviour on the internet. For example, TYPING EMAIL MESSAGES IN CAPITALS is considered rude because it looks as if you're shouting.

newsgroups Internet-based discussion groups centred on a particular topic or interest. After subscribing to the group, you can read messages from other members and use an email program such as Outlook Express to write and post messages of your own.

O

OCR Optical Character Recognition. The conversion of a scanned page of text into a form that can be opened and edited in a word processor. Most OCR programs can read text at a wide range of sizes, fonts and styles, and even convert a complex page layout into an editable form.

OpenType A type of scalable font that works on both Windows PCs and Apple Macintosh computers. It's called 'scalable' because it can be displayed and printed at any size without losing clarity. OpenType is an extension of the Windows TrueType font standard.

optical zoom A camera feature that enlarges the image to be captured by changing the focal length of the camera lens. Unlike a digital zoom, the subject is magnified without any loss of resolution.

P

page break The point at which one page ends and the other begins. In Microsoft Word, you can manually insert a page break in your document by holding down the **Ctrl** key on your keyboard and pressing **Enter**.

Page Setup In any program that produces printed output, including Word and Excel, this command – under the **File** menu – allows you to establish options and settings for page elements such as margins, headers and footers, gutter position and page orientation.

PDF Portable Document Format. A document type that can display any page layout exactly as it was designed, regardless of the computer on which you are viewing it. The electronic manuals included with commercial software are often PDF documents. To read a PDF document (identified by a .pdf suffix on its file name) you need the free Adobe Reader program from www.adobe.com.

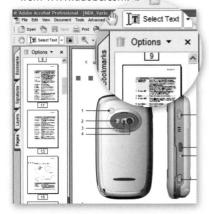

pixel An individual dot on a computer screen or on a printed image. The number of pixels horizontally and vertically determines the detail and quality of image that can be displayed. See also resolution.

playlist A customised list of music or videos you wish to play. Playlists are used in programs such as Windows Media Player and Apple iTunes, and in personal digital music players such as the iPod. You can create a playlist yourself by selecting individual tracks or let Media Player build one for you automatically using criteria you've set.

plug-in A small software program that works in conjunction with a larger application to add extra features to it. For example, Photoshop Elements includes plug-ins that perform special effects on images. Many are supplied already installed with the program, and you can buy or download extra plug-ins to perform new special effects.

podcast A sound recording – a kind of personal radio show – uploaded to a website. Visitors download the podcast file for listening to on a PC or a personal digital player such as Apple's iPod (hence the name).

POP3 Post Office Protocol 3. This is a standard for sending and receiving messages over the internet. The use of POP3 is a kind of agreement between your PC and the computer sending your mail on how that mail should be packaged and delivered. Microsoft Outlook Express, for instance, conforms to this method of handling email so is known as a POP3 email client.

portrait Orientation of a document or picture in which the short edges are horizontal and the longer edges vertical (the opposite of landscape).

preview Displays how a document will appear when it's printed. By previewing the finished document on the screen before committing it to paper you can make last-minute corrections to the formatting and save on printer ink.

primitives The basic geometrical shapes included in the toolbox of any graphics program. Rectangles, polygons, ellipses and lines are the 'building blocks' with which more complex images are created.

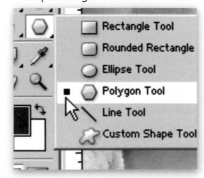

R

RAM Randon Access Memory. Usually refers to the main memory inside your PC, used to store and manipulate data while the computer is switched on. Unlike data on a hard disk, the RAM's contents are lost when you switch off the PC.

RealAudio A compressed sound-file format that's designed for streaming over the internet while it's being listened to. RealAudio is popular with radio stations that 'broadcast' over the internet, such as the BBC's Audio On Demand service at www.bbc.co.uk/radio/aod. If you want to listen to RealAudio, you need the RealPlayer program, which can be downloaded from http://uk.real.com.

Refresh button When a web page takes too long to load into Internet Explorer, you can use the **Refresh** button to make sure you're trying to load the latest version of the page.

refresh rate The number of times per second that an image on the screen is redrawn. The more often redrawing takes place, the less flickering you'll see in the image.

resolution The number of pixels in a digital image, computer monitor, camera or scanner, expressed as either separate horizontal and vertical resolution (for example 1280 x 1024) or multiplied together as a single figure. The higher the resolution, the finer the detail that can be reproduced.

RGB Abbreviation for red, green and blue, the colours used on a PC monitor. By combining these colours in various strengths (expressed either as a percentage or in numbers from 0 to 255) it's possible to create all the colours of the spectrum.

rip To copy tracks from a music CD onto your PC's hard disk using a program such as Windows Media Player. You can then play back songs ripped in this way through your PC's speakers or copy them onto a portable digital music player.

ROM Read Only Memory. Any data storage device that can be read but not written over or re-used – such as CD-ROM and DVD-ROM discs.

runaround Feature that allows text to wrap round pictures automatically without you having to alter each

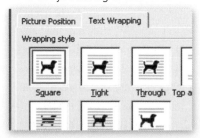

line individually. Programs such as Microsoft Word include several types of automatic runaround.

S

saturation The percentage concentration of a specific colour. The more saturated a colour, the more vivid it appears. Turn down the saturation in an image and it becomes more pastel or muted.

scanner A device that converts drawings, photos, documents, slides or films into data that can be used and manipulated on PCs. The most common type of scanner is a flatbed scanner – a device with a glass top covered by a lid (similar to the top part of a photocopier). The original printed document, typically up to A4 size, is placed face down on the glass plate. A photo-electric sensor measures the light reflected from it and records it as a digital image.

screensaver A picture or animation displayed on your screen when the PC has been idle for a set period of time. Some screensavers require you

to enter a password before you can start using the PC again.

selection Anything highlighted with the mouse, whether it's an item on a menu, a paragraph of text, part of an image selected with a marquee, or an entire picture.

sequencer A program used for composing and arranging music. Some programs, like ACID Xpress and eJay, are designed to arrange prerecorded clips of music; others can also incorporate MIDI-equipped instruments such as synthesisers. All produce CD-quality compositions.

skin Many programs, including Windows Media Player, can be given a complete facelift with the help of replacement graphics, buttons and menus, collectively known as a skin. Thousands of skins are available for free download from the web.

slide master A PowerPoint slide on which you can include information and formatting that you want to appear on every slide in a

presentation – for example, a title, the date, a link to a particular website and company logo.

SMTP Simple Mail Transfer Protocol. One of the methods by which email is sent on the internet. In a mail program such as Outlook Express, SMTP handles outgoing messages and POP3 delivers incoming mail.

soundcard A device that plugs inside a PC and generates sound signals for games, speech and music. Soundcards can also record analogue audio from many different sources and convert it into a digital format ready for editing on your PC.

spam Any email that appears in your inbox unsolicited, usually trying to sell you something. Most promote get-rich-quick schemes, dubious pharmaceutical products, diplomas or degrees, and other junk. Never reply to a spam email because doing so confirms your email address is active and you'll receive more spam.

stitch A feature in photo-editing programs that joins together a series of separate photographs to create a panorama. Many digital cameras include a stitch mode, allowing you to take a sequence of aligned photos for subsequent stitching.

storyboard In film-making, a way to plan filming by drawing simple comic strips that represent each scene and camera angle. The term is also used in Windows Movie Maker for video clips represented as a strip of stills that you can rearrange by dragging and dropping within the storyboard.

streaming Instead of downloading a sound file to your PC and playing it from your hard disk, some websites use streaming, where the audio file stays on their servers and is played over your internet connection.

styles A word processor such as Microsoft Word includes a number of built-in styles that you can apply to documents to give them a specific appearance. You can also create your own. Style components include the font you want to use, its size, emphasis (for example, whether the text is bold, italic or underlined), colour, paragraph alignment and tab positions.

T

template In word processing and desktop publishing, a template is a predesigned file containing formatting, graphics, text and place holders (dummy text) to help create standard document types such as memos, newsletters and calendars. You type over the place-holding text to replace it with your own. In a spreadsheet program a template contains formulae and labels ready for the user's own data.

theme This feature changes the visual appearance of Windows without altering the way it works – similar to a skin but with more elements. Themes can replace Windows' fonts, colour schemes, window width, desktop background, sounds and screensaver.

thumbnail A miniature version of a picture within a graphics program, on a website or in Windows Explorer. Thumbnails load quickly and enable you to decide whether you want to open the full-size versions.

TIF file Also expressed as TIFF. A graphics file type used by many programs on Windows PCs and Apple Macintoshes. It's preferred by professional graphic artists and designers but can produce large files. TIF files may be compressed to reduce file size but, unlike JPEG files, there's no loss of quality.

timeline Similar to a storyboard, a timeline – found in video-editing programs – displays all the elements associated with a digital movie, split into separate tracks below the editing window. For example, there could be a track for thumbnails of video clips, another for music, one for transitions and effects, and one for titles.

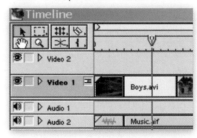

title overlay Text that you can place on top of a video clip or still image, usually in a video-editing program such as Windows Movie Maker or a presentation program such as Microsoft PowerPoint.

toolbox A collection of editing tools, in a self-contained box, within a graphics program. Similar toolboxes also exist in office programs such as Word and Excel.

transition A visual effect used in movie making and presentation programs when one scene or slide changes to the next. Typical transitions include cross fades (one image fades out as the other fades in), wipes (one image sweeps into view over the other) and dissolves (one image disintegrates, revealing the new image beneath).

transparency A quality, also called opacity, assigned to layers in an image-editing program that allows shapes and colours on background layers to show through.

TrueType A font standard invented by Microsoft and Apple that allows you to display and print text to large sizes without losing quality. See also OpenType.

TV tuner Hardware that allows you to receive and display analogue or digital TV on your PC. TV tuners are available as expansion boards that fit inside desktop PCs or as credit-card-sized cards for laptop PCs. Most have software that lets you record programmes on the hard disk.

TWAIN A means by which scanners and other hardware devices, mainly cameras, communicate with graphics programs. The TWAIN driver is installed on the PC and handles the transfer of data from the device to the graphics program. Popular belief is that TWAIN stands for 'Technology Without an Interesting Name'.

U

updates Most software develops all the time, so occasionally you need to download updates from the internet that improve reliability, add new features or fix security problems. You can set up Windows XP to update automatically.

URL Uniform Resource Locator. The unique address of a web page on the internet, as distinct from its domain name. For example, microsoft.com is a domain name, while http://office.microsoft.com/en-us/officeupdate/default.aspx is a URL that points to a specific page for Office updates on the Microsoft site.

USB Universal Serial Bus. USB connectors are included on every home PC and allow you to connect peripherals such as printers, scanners and digital cameras.

V

vector graphics A system of drawing objects using curves and lines, as opposed to pixel by pixel as in bitmap images. Vector images can be resized with no loss of detail.

video compression Most video stored and played back on a PC has been compressed to make it smaller. If you edit video using a program such as Windows Movie Maker, the final movie is compressed before it's saved to disk. You can choose the type of file it's saved as and the degree to which it's compressed, depending on whether you intend to watch it on your PC, make a DVD video or stream it from a web page.

virus A malicious code designed to replicate itself, often by secretly infecting your emails. There are many kinds of virus, from those that steal sensitive information or erase files to others that just display mischievous messages. Some, called Trojans, lay dormant for months until triggered on a specific date.

visualisations Often-stunning light-show-style add-ins for programs such as Windows Media Player that play back in time with the music and respond to the beats and tones with pulsating patterns.

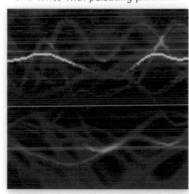

W

watermark Text or an image that can be printed behind the content of a word-processed document. It's often used to denote a draft or confidential document.

WAV file Waveform Audio Format file. A type of digital sound file commonly used by Windows. The sound you hear when Windows starts is a WAV file, and music programs such as ACID Xpress use WAV files to create songs.

webcam Small, inexpensive video camera whose output is viewable on a web page. Some digital snapshot cameras can also be used as webcams. The images from the camera are periodically updated on the web page. A webcam may also be used for video chat but only on a broadband connection.

Web mail A way of sending and retrieving your emails by logging in to a web page. An alternative to email programs such as Microsoft Outlook Express, web mail has the added convenience of letting you check your mail from any computer. Examples include Hotmail, Yahoo! Mail and Google's Gmail.

website hosting If you want to set up your own website – for example, www.yourname.com – you have to rent space on an internet server, where you can store it. Hosting companies provide the space and tools with which you can then manage your site.

Wi-Fi Wireless Fidelity. A way to connect PCs wirelessly to the internet (through a wireless modem or Wi-Fi hotspot) or to a home network. Wi-Fi capabilities are built into many handheld and portable computers, and can be easily added to a desktop PC by plugging a Wi-Fi network card into a USB port.

wireframe Used by graphics programs to create a 3D image using only a wire-like frame. It's usually the stage before adding a texture map or rendering the object completely in 3D.

wireless network A way to connect computers and computing devices without using wires. For example, two PCs can share a wireless internet connection, a printer or the same music collection. If you're out and about, you can also connect to the internet using a wireless hotspot. See also Wi-Fi.

WMA Windows Media Audio. A file format created by Microsoft to compete with MP3 and which produces smaller files with the same sound quality. The Windows Media Video (WMV) file format does the same task for video.

Index

Page numbers displayed in **bold** type indicate main entries.

INDEX